Jacques Lacan
and the
Philosophy of Psychoanalysis

Ellie Ragland-Sullivan

JACQUES LACAN AND THE PHILOSOPHY OF PSYCHOANALYSIS

UNIVERSITY OF ILLINOIS PRESS Urbana and Chicago

© 1986 by the Board of Trustees of the University of Illinois Press
Manufactured in the United States of America
C   5   4   3   2   1

This book is printed on acid-free paper.

Library of Congress Cataloging in Publication Data

Ragland-Sullivan, Ellie, 1941–
    Jacques Lacan and the philosophy of psychoanalysis.

    Bibliography: p.
    Includes index.
        1. Lacan, Jacques, 1901–1981. 2. Psychoanalysts—
    France—Biography. 3. Psychoanalysis—Philosophy.
    I. Title.
    BF173.LI5R34   1986   150.19'5'0924   84-16125
    ISBN 0-252-01184-8 (alk. paper)

Dedicated

to

Henry and Caroline Sullivan

and

Lucile Stowe and Terry Porter Ragland

for

their support and inspiration

CONTENTS

PREFACE AND
ACKNOWLEDGMENTS

Jacques Marie Émile Lacan (1901–81) may well be the most important thinker in France since René Descartes and the most innovative and far-ranging thinker in Europe since Friedrich Nietzsche and Sigmund Freud. Lacan's formation was that of a psychoanalyst in the Freudian school. His reappraisal of Freud's theories, however, and particularly his scrutiny of Freud's earlier observations on symbols and language gradually led him to a rereading of the founder's texts so comprehensive and so radical that it virtually constituted a new vision of man. Lacan's teachings ended an era when it was still possible to talk about the human psyche without reference to the ethos of language that structures it and that hence conditions all conscious and unconscious perception. In this sense Lacan's revolutionary theories in psychoanalysis have immediate and indisputable relevance for philosophy, linguistics, literary theory, and the wider disciplines in the human sciences. Traditional philosophical dilemmas regarding the nature of the perceiving subject and its relation to objects; the status of human knowledge; the meaning of discourse and culture; the mystery of sexual—not to say human—identity; the meaning of freedom: all are problematized and illuminated in startling fashion by Lacan's psychoanalytic thought.

The purpose of this book is to lay out the complex and elusive ideas of Jacques Lacan for the interested English-speaking reader as clearly and comprehensively as possible. This is no small task. We do not have public access to the bulk of Lacan's still unedited and unpublished Seminars, which were held from 1953 to the late 1970s. Many commentators on Lacan, therefore, work from and on the *Ecrits* (1966), made up of thirty-three essays. In the preface of Anika Lemaire's book *Jacques Lacan* (1970), Lacan described the *Ecrits* as "unsuitable for a thesis, particularly an academic thesis: they are antithetical by nature: one either takes what they formulate or one leaves them. Each of them is apparently no more than a memorial to the refusal of my discourse by the audience it included: an audience restricted to psychoanalysts" (p. vii, 1977 English translation). I have taken this admonition seriously and have used the Seminars to illuminate the *Ecrits*, and not the reverse.

In keeping with Lacan's own widening of the boundaries of disciplines in his Seminars, the audience to whom my book is addressed would include psychoanalysts, psychiatrists, psychologists, literary theorists and critics, anthropologists, philosophers, sociologists, linguists, and feminists, among others. Building on those books that already grapple with Lacanian epistemology and clinical method, as well as Lacan's own texts, I have tried to show why "understanding Lacan" (Eugen Bär) is partially an exercise in rethinking familiar words and concepts that Lacan redefined. By doing this Lacan kept the value implicit in a term or thought, but amplified it, often with explosive force, thus showing us that to invent special jargon was to sidestep descriptive insights that language has already pinpointed. Anglophone readers, nonetheless, express the hope that someone will explain Lacan to them in their own terms. This is simply impossible. To do so would permit an interlocutor to retain assumed meanings, providing the comfort of resolution, but only the *illusion* of understanding. Lacan intended to bring about a reconceptualization of the conventionally assumed and unquestioned words by which Western people have come to describe themselves. Lacan's teachings, therefore, can only be approached in light of his own use of language. To call this language "jargon" infers that there is a classical language—a metalanguage—under which all other epistemologies can be subsumed.

Let us beware, then, of grappling with Lacan's ideas by minimizing or oversimplifying them. Many of Lacan's former pupils, as well as commentators from various disciplines, do exactly this. They latch onto a single idea; this, then, is erroneously taken to be the sum of Lacan's contributions to psychoanalysis, literary theory, or whatever. It is interesting to note that such minimizing tendencies vindicate Lacan's claim that individuals make the world of their thought equal to their own conscious understanding of it. The situation is not helped by the casual mistranslations, which also keep Anglophones from "hearing" Lacan (e.g., the *moi* has been rendered as the id). The challenge for any interested reader, then, is how to approach this dense thought and unfamiliar use of language and to ascertain precisely what Lacan meant.

My effort to shed light on the complexity of Lacan's teachings is fourfold. First, each chapter of my book attempts to elaborate one major concept, along with subsidiary and related ideas. In each succeeding chapter I bring into play the material under scrutiny in the previous chapter. In this way I have tried to break down some of the confusion that arises from reading Lacan himself, where all his concepts are perpetually in play as well as in formation. Second, I have used empirical studies and data from other disciplines in an effort to support Lacan's hypotheses. In this way I hope to forestall a pragmatically oriented reader who would reject out of hand Lacan's theoretical-philosophical methods of inquiry for lack of the familiar inductive "proof." I have, therefore, found it useful to adduce Anglo-American studies, particularly in the fields of psychology and neurolinguistics, to provide incidental corroboration. Citing experimental evidence in this way goes quite against the grain of Lacan's habits of mind, but, since this book is intended for those of the English-speaking tradition, I have hoped to gain thereby in clarity while vindicating, not betraying, the force and originality of Lacan's insights.

Third, I have quoted Lacan at length so he may be read for his own sake, whether any one or other of my exegetical interpretations be correct or not. To this latter end I have adhered to Lacan's statement that his own words will stand against "texts faithful in pillaging me, but never deigning to pay me back. Their interest will be that they transmit what I have said literally; like the amber which holds the fly so as to know nothing of its flight" (Lemaire, 1977, p. xv). Fourth and last, I have aimed for a greater readability by using a narrative-expository style, as against Lacan's hermetic style; in contrast to Lemaire's epigrammatic style; John P. Muller and William J. Richardson's outline format; Anthony Wilden's neopositivistic documentation, and so on. Finally, I hope my approach will help in the ongoing quest to make sense of Lacan. But my book will not be the clear and "complete summary of the basic ideas which constitute" Lacanism to which Lemaire overoptimistically aspired. Such a summary would be a contradiction in terms.

The hope has been expressed that a chronological ordering of Lacan's teachings by historical periods will provide final clarity and insight. This is, indeed, a seductive approach, and one which has been applied to Freud's texts. But such a tactic implies a linear progression in insight. Lacan taught us that such a manner of reading Freud has led us to undervalue the majesty of Freud's scattered and elusive discoveries. Although one can trace clear periods of focus and development in Lacan's teachings, any periodization also follows Lacan's flight from institution to institution. This attests to the dangerous (political) nature of Lacan's words. But what is truly gripping and unsettling is that Lacan often waits years to answer a question posed twenty years before. His pronouncements constantly double back on themselves and consequently defy chronology. I have respected chronology in the sense that I have provided dates for specific ideas. To elucidate a single concept, however, I have not scrupled to juxtapose material as far apart as the 1930s and 1970s where necessary.

Finally, I should add that I have followed the recommendation of Professor Jacques-Alain Miller that the term Other (*Autre* in French) not come into English in such a way as to make it seem a fixed concept. Throughout my text I have written Other(A), unless it was typographically awkward (as in Otherness or Other's and so on). Lacan designated the capital A of *Autre* as a mathematical symbol— something that does not mean anything in itself—that attracts and sustains multiple meanings. Miller has written (in the *Encyclopaedia Universalis* 18[1980]:111) that this *Autre* is less a concept than a letter A. It intervenes in Lacan's theory on several levels, but all of which distinguish themselves by a dimension of exteriority and a determining function in relation to the human subject.

I record here my gratitude to the National Endowment for the Humanities for a generous Research Fellowship, which allowed me to complete the writing of this book, as well as to the University of Illinois at Chicago for granting me the period of leave to take advantage of it. I am also grateful to my colleagues, Professors David O'Connell, Marie-Odile Sweetser, Ruth El-Saffar (all of the University of Illinois), and Professor Emil Karrafiol of the University of Chicago for a critical reading of my original proposal, and to Vice-Chancellor Richard Johnson (University of Illinois), Professor Félix Martínez-Bonatti (Columbia University), and Professor Floyd Gray (University of Michigan) for writing on my behalf to the National Endowment Foundation. I am particularly grateful to Floyd Gray for his unflagging belief in my work over a period of years. I also owe a debt to Professor Mona Thelander for introducing me to Lacan's *Ecrits* in 1971, and to the following esteemed conversation partners for their invaluable insights and suggestions: the Lacanian psychoanalyst Dr. Stuart Schneiderman (New York City); Professor Art Efron (Department of English, SUNY-Buffalo); and the clinical psychologist James E. Glogowski (SUNY-Buffalo). I also thank Professor Frederick Wyatt (Freiburg University) for offering useful comments and criticisms on my project in its early stages, and Professor Norman Holland (University of Florida–Gainesville) for providing pertinent bibliographical material and encouragement. I thank Professor Michel Grimaud (Wellesley College) for the helpful essays he sent while I was composing the book, and Professor Nigel Dennis (University of Ottawa) for continually supplying current references to Lacan in England and Spain, and Drs. Kurt and Roswitha Reichenberger (Kassel University) for articles on Lacan in German. I also thank Professor Franco Ricci (University of Ottawa) for keeping me abreast of the work done on Lacan in Italy. I thank the faculty of the Center for the Psychological Study of the Arts (SUNY-Buffalo) for their invitations to speak and their penetrating questions that pushed me to forge ever clearer links between Anglo-American thought and Lacanian teachings. I also thank Professor Ghyslain Charron of the Philosophy Department (University of Ottawa) and Dr. Hector Warnes (Head of Psychiatry at the Ottawa University Hospital) for reading sections of my manuscript. The other people who provided useful articles, books, ideas, and correctives are too numerous to name, but I thank them all. Finally, I should like to thank my husband, Professor Henry W. Sullivan, for his constant encouragement, practical guidance with the manuscript, and his role in helping me to see the scope of the task I had undertaken.

I have used standard translations of Lacan's works when available (principally Sheridan's). All other renderings into English of Lacan's untranslated texts, and of untranslated French texts by other authors, are my own.

INTRODUCTION

The word philosophy in the title of this book may seem provocative and require explanation. It is intended to be both paradoxical and controversial. Any reader of Jacques Lacan (or this book, for that matter) will quickly realize that Lacan was steeped in philosophical knowledge and influences while always critical of the claims philosophy had made throughout the centuries. Lacan praised the wisdom of the Stoics, Plato, Aristotle, and of recent philosophers from René Descartes on. But although he gave philosophy its just due for pinpointing specific problems, he indicted it for never having discovered that the intentionality of discourse and the source of knowledge lay in networks of unconscious meaning.

Philosophy and psychoanalysis converge on certain topics, such as the analysis of love, desire, death, affect, the body, and so on. Psychoanalysis is generally thought, however, to be the antithesis of philosophy. Not only is psychoanalysis concerned with the Real of sex, the implications of being masculine or feminine, and the pain of symptoms, but it also uses "clinical" methods of analysis in contrast to the "intellectual" ones of philosophy. Lacan was the first psychoanalyst to blur the distinction between a picture of psychoanalysis as the province of emotions and philosophy as that of mind. He revealed substantive and functional "inmixing" of thought and affect. Both derive from representations and objects, their "energy" supplied by a dynamically repressed bank of unconscious "thought." But essentially Lacan was able to join philosophy to psychoanalysis because he viewed language and its effects as the agents by which an unconscious is formed. He also saw language as the conscious means by which individuals learn to master the early trauma of separation through the process of naming, thereby representing themselves as totalizable (that is, nameable).

By making language a factor in the earliest experiences of mentality and sensory response as well, Lacan could postulate coexisting and intermingled "logics" of affect (the patheme) and language. Lacan's teachings would, in this sense, place logic before ontology, epistemology, or ethics. But the logic at issue is that of unconscious structure (or order), which precedes the conscious logic of true-false propositions. Lacan, therefore, belongs to a long line of thinkers who have puzzled over the origins and interplay of causes and effects; the relations between corporeal and incorporeal events; the structure of psyche in its links to soma. Unlike any predecessor, however, Lacan postulated that a phonemic chain was taken in from the outside world at the start of life through physical hearing—or lip and sign symbols for the hearing impaired. Mingled with visual and identificatory perceptions these early phonemes will serve as one elemental basis on which secondary representations will be built. Such phonemes are also the basis for eventually attributing meaning to mental representations. In a more global sense the gaze (a visual image) and the voice (an aural image) are introjected by a newborn baby. In tandem with other images they create a primordial lining to perception that makes it impossible for human beings to distinguish later between inner and outer perceptual effects.

In 1975 Lacan asked: "Who doubts—in point of fact everything called philosophy has to this day hung by this slender thread—that there is an order other than that along which the body thinks it moves."[1] Lacan's teachings fault traditional philosophy for never having fully understood that meaning only exists at all because it can refer to perceptions already structured (ordered) in a realm of repressed (unconscious) representations (references). Grammatical language becomes merely an adorning, not of the unconscious phoneme, but of the human "subject determined by being, that is to say, by desire" (Mitchell and Rose, *Feminine Sexuality*, pp. 165–66).

When an infant begins to speak coherently, it retains a sense of the primordial Otherness that first infused its natural being, this latter becoming a part of unconscious meaning. The point at issue here is that language enters into perception and cognition long before it stabilizes into a formal grammar. A kind of "thinking," which one might call "desiring," exists prior to the condition for thought. But unconscious language is altogether different from the same language used for conscious discourse. Unconscious "meaning" may be assonantal, homophonic, or may combine an image, object, or person by some elusive identificatory association. But insofar as the Lacanian unconscious always contains sounds and words, Sigmund Freud's need to postulate a hierarchized verbal preconscious is obviated. Freud's gradation from a visual unconscious to preconscious and then conscious life would merely intuit the visual, verbal combinations that Lacan was able to place side by side.

Through his sweeping innovations Lacan claimed to have uprooted both philosophy and the empirical sciences from their methodological grounding in deceptively transparent givens and circular hypotheses. As early as 1946 Lacan said: "You will perhaps be surprised that I venture beyond that philosophical taboo which thumps away on the notion of the true in scientific epistemology, since the time that speculative theses permeated the latter from the so-called Pragmatist School."[2] In other words, most contemporary philosophy remains allied with scientific method and both shun unconscious knowledge in favor of unexamined postulates that answer the question before it is asked. By the same token, Lacan redirected psychoanalysis away from its rejection of the intellect. Psychoanalysis prior to Lacan, and even today, restricts its attention to emotions, personality, fantasies, and the "self," disconnecting all of these from the question of "mind." Such psychoanalysis puts no premium on the opaquely rich language of believed self-descriptions that the analysand "mindfully" employs. But if the unconscious possesses knowledge—indeed shows the obverse of conscious knowledge in psychosis—then Lacan's rereading of Freud promotes a theory of mentality (inseparable from sexuality) at the point where Freud leapt into the impersonal idea that body (sexuality) ruled mind, thus marooning "mind" elsewhere.

We might depict Lacan's relation to Freud as was Voltaire's to Descartes. Descartes put God in brackets and Voltaire removed them, thus canceling the concept of God as a person. Freud put mind in brackets, which Lacan removed, thus revealing the source of mentality as alien, fixed, and permanently subjective. After Lacan, reality, rationality, and objectivity appear as comforting illusions—*points de capiton*—amid the truths of plurality, ambiguity, and uncertainty. When I speak of a philosophy of psychoanalysis, then, it is in the sense that "mind" is circumscribed by narcissistic drives, by unconscious Desires, and by repressed verbal myths that govern a seemingly "free" intentionality, and only apparently natural sexuality.

When I speak of a philosophy of psychoanalysis, I also refer to the numerous concepts that Lacan elaborated from his clinical experience and that can be isolated by his readers and discussed as such. Now if the ordinary philosophical discourse is an analysis of consciousness, Lacan's discourse analyzes the unconscious. But since any theoretical analysis must take place in the conscious realm, it follows that any discussion of the unconscious must in some degree become formalized. In this sense Lacan was a perverse philosopher, but a philosopher all the same. His map of the unconscious is structural. It shows us how unconscious structures are formed, how they work, and how they reveal themselves in four different orders in conscious life: the Symbolic, the Imaginary, the Real, and the Symptom. Lacan's structural map may not, however, deliver any message unless one grasps that the structures are themselves "messages."

Perhaps Lacan's provocative relationship to philosophy can be clarified a shade further by examining Antoine Vergote's interpretation of Lacan as reported by William Kerrigan in his introduction to *Interpreting Lacan* (1983): "In his lopsided dedication to the signifier, Lacan mounts a theory that is impotent before the great issues of meaning and reference; he leaves us not in the world, but in a closed circuit of signifiers."[3] But this is very far from the case. As Jacques-Alain Miller said in 1980: "Wherever Lacan's influence has been felt, his teaching has been used to exalt the play of signifiers. But this is not what Lacan is about, not at all."[4] The confusion here lies partly in the human drive toward rapid closure (termed "suture" by Miller), easy understanding, and meanings to be had pat. On Vergote's reading Lacan would have returned to Freud's unconscious, to its sepulchral majesty and power, only to have its scope whittled down as ego psychology has done, this time to signifiers "transparent" to consciousness. Lacan taught that although the same kind of laws operate both unconscious signifiers (*perceptum*) and conscious ones, the signifiers of the two realms are not linked in a one to one way. Furthermore, grammatical language and unconscious representations function according to different kinds of logic.

Lacan's most revolutionary insights concern precisely how meaning is produced. To what do references ultimately allude? How is intentionality structured? What is the role of an Imaginary chain of narcissistic closure in protecting individuals from unconscious knowledge? Lacan has exploded the self-imposed confines of psychoanalysis and progressively denied traditional philosophers their consciousness-bound terrain. He revealed words as a *connaissance*, the means by which individuals seek to handle unconscious knowledge. Since the unconscious is opaque, conscious knowledge of it is actually a *méconnaissance*, a misrecognition. Unconscious knowledge (or *savoir*) arises from an alien Desire, which renders a human subject an object of Otherness; from the arbitrary assignment of sexual "identity"; from the beliefs that knit together *moi* repetitions to screen out the more elemental and fragmented messages in the Other(A). Lacanian psychoanalysis subverts philosophical traditions, then. "Meaning" is not in itself full, but indicates the direction in which words fail, the "beyond" to which they point. Lacan (after Freud) showed us how negation is itself "truth-functional." The speaking subject (*je*) denies any knowledge of a source of meaning beyond its own utterances, and the subject of being (*moi*) misrecognizes its identificatory reflections in the Other(A). A Lacanian psychoanalysis thus reveals the contradictory nature of meaning and reference that has been foreclosed from analyses of thought, beginning with Plato's "justified true belief" concept (*Theaetetus*). Plato's distinction of a "knowing-that" from other kinds of knowledge is known today as "propositional knowledge" and serves as the source of the "logician's logic" based on true/false propositions (Wittgenstein).[5] By making contradictions implicit in knowledge, Lacan renewed the search for the foundations of logic and language beyond propositional logic, demonstrating how an unconscious dialectic overdetermines conscious meaning in its allusion to a repressed discourse. Here Lacan went beyond Jacques Derrida, who stopped at metaphor and was content to show the substitutive interchangeability of binary opposites. Lacan also went beyond Paul Ricoeur, who admits to a binary metaphorical functioning of representational symbols, but implies that their source is innate, while energy itself is biological.

Lacan connected "energy" to narcissism (the metaphorical *moi*) and Desire (the metonymy of the Other) to mental representations, showing the causative role of each in the "drive" that conditions meaning and reference. In his effort to dramatize the multilinear movements behind any act of consciousness, Lacan redefined signifier, signified, *parole*, metaphor, metonymy, discourse, knots, and so on. In our conceptions of perception and behavior he moved us out of a static nineteenth-century universe into the kinesthetic, dynamic century to come. He taught us that consciousness is not consciousness *of* something, but is a mode of perception that negotiates unconscious Desire and repression by substitutions (object *a*): one substitution being language itself, and another being meaning. Lacan showed that conscious meaning negotiates Other(A) knowledge, which lies outside the closures of grammar (*je*) or individuality (*moi*). But the Other(A) can be studied, in reference to the other and to the object *a* (Mitchell and Rose, *Feminine Sexuality*, p. 164).

Such study amounts to a philosophy, whether we like it or not. But the Lacanian "philosopher" is not, as Jacques-Alain Miller has pointed out, the philosopher "as characterised by Heinrich Heine in a sentence quoted by Freud, 'with his nightcaps and the tatters of his dressing-gown, patching up the gaps in the structure of the universe.'"[6] In Kerrigan's introduction to *Interpreting Lacan* he characterizes Wilfried ver Eecke's views on Lacan's relationship to philosophy as follows: Lacan's philosophical ideas served him as metaphors and indicators, ways of pointing toward his insights rather than constituting them (p. xviii). William J. Richardson goes in the opposite direction, trying to open out the philosophical and theological horizons that, according to Richardson, Lacan (following Freud) tried to shut down (p. xix).

I propose a third possibility. If psychoanalysis concerns the Truth of meaning and the Truth of being, and in its search subverts the "truth" of philosophy textbooks, then Lacan's references to philosophy are a part of his effort to close the discipline down, but only to reopen it under new management. Philosophical ideas do not serve him as metaphors at all, but as genuine insights about Real human life. Lacan said that Plato had to invent the Ideal when "lack" forced itself on him in the form of metaphysical impasses in thinking the world and the Real.[7] Lacan called Plato's Ideal the Other(A) and explained its dynamic movement in contrast to the static essences by which Plato had defined it. G. W. F. Hegel had to postulate successive syntheses when he could not admit that the dialectic was finally an irresolvable and contradictory motion. Martin Heidegger grasped the dynamic and anticipatory nature of Being, but failed to see that the limitations of Being-as-becoming stemmed from retroactivity: the determinism of the unconscious. Descartes could not really find certainty in doubt, but in fact attested to the human *passion* for certainty (closure), despite the reality of doubt.

The aging Lacan looked to logic to graph the truths that he had earlier described in words. But his logic was not that of traditional philosophy. It concerned, rather, what Miller has termed "the logic of the origin of logic—which is to say, that it does not follow its laws, but that, prescribing their jurisdiction, itself falls outside that jurisdiction" ("Suture," p. 25). Having grappled with Lacan's texts for over ten years, I have come to view his latter efforts as attempts to arrive at demonstrable proof, falling on the side of physics and mathematics. Miller has commented on Lacan's graphs, warning that there is an inadequation between the graphic representation and its object (the *object* of psychoanalysis), that *object* being a study of the unconscious. Therefore, Lacan's schemata are to be taken as didactic. Their relation with structure is one of analogy that is itself inadequate. That is, the graphs neither ground reality nor retain anything measurable. They are reduced, like the real, to representatives of a given fantasy of which a point or cut provides the structure itself.[8] Lacan himself, when first presenting his now celebrated Schéma L in 1955, said it would not be a schéma or even a model if it presented a solution. The schemata are, Lacan said, a way by which to fix ideas that call forth a weakness in our discursive abilities.[9]

Lacan's mathemes, knots, and graphs, nonetheless, represent his refusal to be reduced to the interpretive subjectivity of every interlocutor, as well as his concern to leave behind formalizable laws for those who could and would follow him. François Roustang's caricature of Lacan's last period—a man flailing and lost, who turned to logic in a desperate effort to achieve a discourse of mastery—is the opposite of the Lacan whom I have found, a Lacan whose destiny was to be master of a discourse so complex and profound that few could heed it. He lived with the unusual burden of seeing further than his fellow beings. I would go so far as to predict that subsequent study of Lacan's picture of psychic apparatus will infer an ordering into traditional philosophy itself. Logic—structure or order—is primary and primordial, followed by ethics (mirror-stage Desire and Oedipal Law creating an unconscious that moralizes). Less primordial than an Other(A) source of ethics would be the place of ontology: the narcissistic *moi* joined to Desire. Epistemology would follow suit, describing the world through *je* ("mind") codes. Metaphysics would testify to an awareness of the multiform and contradictory planes on Lacan's psychic map. Finally, theology would mark a return to the Other, to a place where ultimate questions are posed within the confines of fading and ineffability.

Finally, it is not my intention to offer a detailed analysis of Lacan's relationship to the many disciplines that influenced him, such as linguistics, anthropology, and philosophy, nor even of the Freudian concepts that Lacan interpreted anew. Neither have I described Lacan the practicing clinician, the Lacan who is best understood by those he taught in Paris and by the analysands whose analyst he was. Nor have I discussed Lacan's unique style. This style is of a piece with his concept of the unconscious and is illustrative of the natural proximity of the unconscious to dreams and to literature. Instead, I have sought to synthesize the major concepts by which Lacan built a bridge between psychoanalysis and philosophy. In this way I hope to shed further light on the Lacan who dwells somewhere between his oral teaching and the textual renderings of those presentations. This same Lacan offered theories that explained the links between the late and early Freud. Since no word exists to describe such an endeavor I have called it a "philosophy of psychoanalysis" in keeping with Lacan's description of the psychoanalyst ("Discours de Rome," 1953) as "a mediator between the man of care and the subject of absolute knowledge" (Sheridan, *Ecrits*, p. 105). Thus, my title is meant to be a question as well as a statement. Lacan often said he had neither a "worldview" nor a philosophy claiming to give the key to the universe. His particular aim was to elaborate the notion of the human subject. His novelty was to bring the subject back to its dependency on meaning. How does one know? From what place? By what means? Although Lacan did not give us a philosophical grid with which to interpret the unconscious, he did give us points to join between conscious and unconscious realms: a praxis, a theory, and some methods for revealing the presence of the unconscious. I speak of a philosophy of psychoanalysis, then, because Lacan portrayed "mind" and the human subject as arising indistinguishably in our early formation, so that affect and ratiocination are ultimately inseparable. Finally, Lacan's true domain was that of *philosophia* (Greek, the love of truth), whose locus lies in the Real of the unconscious.

JACQUES LACAN
AND THE
PHILOSOPHY OF PSYCHOANALYSIS

1

WHAT IS "I"?

LACAN'S THEORY

OF THE HUMAN SUBJECT

THE PURPOSE of this chapter is to establish and explain Lacan's fundamental contention that the human psyche is composed of two different "subjects": an objectlike narcissistic subject of *being*, and a *speaking* subject. In a brief preamble I outline the main points of contact and—more importantly—of difference between Lacan and Freud on the topology of the psyche. The first of the seven remaining sections attempts to reconstruct and problematize the evolution of the "I" as the pivot of Western consciousness from the fourteenth to the twentieth centuries. Second, in place of the less complete accounts offered by other researchers on the genesis of the human subject, I outline in detail Lacan's hypotheses concerning early infant perception: the celebrated premirror and mirror stages (from o to approximately eighteen months of age). The way is then clear for a scrutiny of the crucial role played by narcissism and identification in the formation of the *moi* (section three). In the fourth section I try to define the *moi* and show its various functions. Fifth, I describe the *moi* in its field of relations to narcissism, aggressiveness, and the "truth" of being as manifested throughout adult life. The penultimate discussion deals with Lacan's original reinterpretation of the Freudian superego. The chapter closes with a seventh section showing how the first of the Lacanian subjects (the *moi*) gives rise to and remains perpetually entwined with the second (the *je*) for the duration of all conscious life.

Jacques Lacan's picture of the human subject—what we commonly call the ego or self—is admittedly enigmatic. It stands in contradiction to the post-Cartesian, empirical, and pragmatic basis of most current Western thought that considers the ego to be a fixed, whole

entity that is innate or instinctual, and—if not divinely—then genetically, neurophysiologically, chemically, or developmentally determined. For this reason, the terms "ego" or "self" are misleading
in understanding Lacan's concept of the subject, since they imply a
wholeness or totality that he refuted by his literal reformulation of
the Freudian idea of an *Ichspaltung* or a splitting of the subject.
While the Lacanian ego (or narcissistic *moi*) is intrinsically unified,
the human subject is split into conscious and unconscious parts. In
developing this theory Lacan gave far greater attention to the problem of subjectivity than to any ego function.[1]

Between 1936 and 1949 Lacan came to define the ego in terms of
narcissism, as an infant's own image encountered in a mirror. During this same period he introduced the concept of a subject distinct
from the ego, which he defined as whoever is speaking.[2] In 1946 and
again in 1948 Lacan described the ego as the conscious data individuals have about themselves (the origins of which are in the passions
of desire, narcissism, and aggressiveness).[3] The ego is developed in a
primordial discordance between natural being and identification
with the forms of the outer world. In other words, *alien* images—i.e.,
not innate—first constitute the ego as an *object* of its own identificatory mergers. Later, in conscious life, the *moi* does not seek to
question or analyze the nature of its own structuration. A primordial
repression of the fact that the roots of being are reflective of an
infant's immediate milieu leads to a fundamental misrecognition
of the "truth" regarding what constitutes the ego. In 1955 Lacan
defined the ego as that which is reflected of one's form (an Imaginary object) in one's objects (individuals engaged in relationship). In
a continual effort to describe the paradoxical complexity of the
subject/object planes on which the human subject coexists, Lacan
elaborated his celebrated Schéma L in *Séminaire* II in May 1955.
This "little schéma," he said, illustrates the problems raised by the
moi and the other, by language and the "word" (p. 284).

Lacan placed the schéma that outlines contradictory movements
that motivate individual and interpersonal psychic life in a privileged place when he later published the *Ecrits* (in 1966). It was located in the first essay, "The Seminar on *The Purloined Letter*."[4]

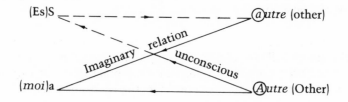

The question of what causes human existence is posed from the place of the Other(A). *Moi* is both an alienated subject and object of the Other(A). S denotes the subject of speech, the *je* that directs its discourse toward others who in turn catalyze the impact of the Other(A) upon the *moi*. Akin to the Saussurean bar which Lacan borrowed to depict a separation between conscious and unconscious discourse—reshaping the notation for the linguistic sign as S/s—one finds the same effect in the Schéma L, where Lacan used solid lines to depict the unconscious relationship between *Autre* and *moi*, and between *autre* and *moi*. The broken lines that Lacan sketched in from the point where the Imaginary and unconscious intersect infer the unconscious acting indirectly upon speech, writing, and human interrelations.

In large part, the ensuing pages of this book will examine the discrete differences among the four parts that constitute a human subject. Lacan described the subject as stretched over all four corners of the Schéma L. By piecing together Lacan's *dires* one can, I hope, assess his contributions to a clearer understanding of subjectivity, perception, memory, meaning, representations, "identity," and so on, as they derive from the structuration of the quadrature of the human subject. The Lacanian conscious "subject" is composed of two seemingly unified and "intelligent," but different, modes of formation and function: the *moi* and the *je*. The Lacanian psychoanalyst Stuart Schneiderman has spoken of the larger split between conscious and unconscious meaning: "To the extent that what is spoken rarely coincides with what the ego intends to communicate, there is a splitting between ego and subject. Ultimately the subject is the subject [*supposé*] of the unconscious, and it speaks most truthfully, as Freud stated, in slips of the tongue and other errors showing that the ego's censorship is suspended (Schneiderman, *Returning*, p. 3). This "psychopathology" of everyday life finds its source in the Other(A). Lacan went further than Freud here, teaching that the unconscious leaves no human action outside its domain because the unconscious is fundamentally discordant with being. The unconscious governs behavior (action), discourse, and "personality" in reference to a *savoir* that, paradoxically, determines and transcends the human subject as being. We shall see that being (*être*) is in large part an attribute of the *moi*.

The Lacanian ego (*moi* or o[1]) is not the subject of the unconscious, then. Nonetheless, this ego occupies a "subjectlike" space in consciousness and refers indeed to those unconscious aspects of being that delineate a sense of "self." Put yet another way, the *moi* is an ideal ego whose elemental form is irretrievable in conscious life, but it is reflected in its chosen identificatory objects (alter egos or ego ideals). The subject of speech (S or *je*) is distinct from the subject of identifications (ego or *moi*), but they interact all the same. The conscious subject, thus viewed, is made up of "inmixed" symbolic chains including unconscious relations and associations. Together these actually compose what we call mind and direct cognitive development. Fittingly, Lacan described thought as a complex of relations, not as consciousness of something. Functioning as a unit, then, the two subjects generally appear as one, except in what Lacan called a "strange contingency of the subject." In certain contexts the subject unravels, revealing a disintegration of its apparent unity: in dreams, jokes, slips of the tongue and pen, neurosis, psychosis, unexpected affects, obsessively repeated identity themes, love, anxiety, and so on.[5] Although they are not quantifiable, such unravelings point to formalizable intersections among the different perceptual orders. Lacan explained this in *Séminaire* XX (1972–73) by referring to the "knots" in being created by the effects of the mirror stage and Oedipal dramas in the genesis of the human subject.[6] This difficult concept will be discussed later.

Lacan has said that his theories are not meant to cover the whole field of experience, that he has no *Weltanschauung*, only an ontology (as does everyone—whether naive or elaborated). He stressed that the purpose of *his* ontology was to reinterpret Freud's texts, and nothing more. This reinterpretation evolved over a fifty-year period.[7] In his First Seminar in 1953 Lacan explained his approach to the Freudian corpus in this manner: "In order to permit you to orient yourselves through the ambiguities which renew themselves at each step in the analytic literature . . . to arise to the point where the empirical effort of researchers meets with a difficulty in managing already existing theory. It is what creates the interest of proceeding along the path of commentary on texts."[8] If one is to understand Lacan's effort, it is crucial to recognize his claim that his interpretation is not a revision of Freud's thought, but a return to the true spirit of Freud's text—a neo-Renaissance exegesis. Viewed thus, one can share Lacan's idea that part of Freud's genius and legacy lay in his documentation of even that which he failed to comprehend. Although Lacan accepts the fundamental insights contained in Freud's oeuvre, he insists that Freud's thought remains open, both as a whole and in several of its articulations. Freud's work bears the living mark of the different stages of its elaboration. By stressing that Freud's many contradictory concepts should be rethought, Lacan maintained that Freud's genuine discoveries can only become clear—not through historical exegesis or empirical testing—but in light of recent finds in contemporary anthropology, in relation to the latest problems in philosophy, and by establishing their equivalence to the functional laws of language and to various models of mathematical thinking.

Considering himself a Freudian fundamentalist, Lacan always disagreed with what he considered to be the false and deceptive directions taken by the Anglo-American psychoanalytic and psychological establishments. In this spirit he criticized the psychologizing of Freud by neo-Freudians, as well as by Freudian innovators and reconstructionists. He indicted them for reducing Freud to one or another aspect of his thought and then proceeding to substantivize this as a single explanation for human behavior. Ernest Jones picked up on symbolism, for example, and Sandor Ferenczi on the biologism in Freud; more recently, Heinz Kohut has investigated narcissism, and so on.[9] Lacan viewed Freud's oeuvre as a gold mine of multiple galleries—some pursued, others abandoned—but all recorded as attempts to understand the complexity of the human psyche in its relationship to the world.

Generally speaking, Lacan felt that there has been a tendency toward a "dynamic" repression of Freud's topographical or structural unconscious system, and a reification of ego theory based either on new data, or on an effort to purge Freud's writings of elements that are accused of having no empirical basis. Lacan alleged that in this way psychoanalysis has been reduced to a study of behavior; to a quasi-biological theory of instincts; or to a medical therapy that conceives an analysand's psychic life as symptoms to be diagnosed as a disease, and so forth. By pursuing Freud's nineteenth-century metaphors in their own terms, instead of updating them in relation to the evolution of modern thought in other areas, many modern-day psychoanalysts and psychologists have followed in the line of Heinz Hartmann's New York School and objectified an ego psychology that erroneously depicts the ego as an agent of adaptability, synthesis, and integration—an agency of the total person—thereby giving ever greater sway to the role of consciousness in determining being.[10]

Sherry Turkle suggested in *Psychoanalytic Politics* that Lacan's first major disagreement with the orthodox psychoanalytic establishment occurred in 1949, when he presented his theory of the mirror stage as formative of the human subject to the sixteenth International Psychoanalytic Association in Zurich. At that time most analysts followed Anna Freud in her emphasis on the ego's powers to marshal mechanisms of defense and adaptation; Lacan maintained that the ego did not exist at all as a unified entity.[11] Lacan accused such analysts of putting so much faith in an autonomous part of the ego that they had come to correlate it with an absolute and objective reality. By imputing a strong, healthy, and "realistic" ego to themselves, partisan analysts or psychologists equated their own concept of reality with truth. Lacan, on the other hand, rejected the neo-Freudian juxtaposition of a reality ego and a neurotic one, calling this a clean-cut split, an obsessive fantasy.[12] By the same token he rejected the widely accepted view that there can be a definitive split between fantasy and reality, a view that would equate the concepts of fantasy, falsity, subjectivity, irrationality, and—conversely—reality, truth, objectivity, and rationality.

Lacan's rereading of Freud is thus a protest against the notion of the conscious ego as a unified perceiver (*percipiens*) or "organ" of adaptation and synthesis. While this operational or functional idea has grown into a hard and fast analytic doctrine, Lacan claims that the Freudian unconscious has become insignificant, almost transparent, and impotent.[13] In contradiction to the standard picture of the Freudian ego, portrayed in static terms of unity, continuity, and genetic, developmental gradualism, Lacan unveils the dynamic and dialectical Freud he has uncovered. The reinterpreted Freudian ego has become a split subject, governed by the subjectivity of intention in its necessary link to Desire, narcissism, and aggressiveness. Our fond hopes for an objective ego are, from this perspective, an illusion. Therefore, Lacanian epistemology is not only a critique of psychoanalysis, but also of philosophy as well, or of any theory whose primary adhesion is to the idea of an objective, conscious ego of perception. Lacan, moreover, reversed the standard notion that Freud's insights were chronologically progressive. The early developments in Anglo-American psychoanalysis emphasized the later direction of Freud's view of ego formation as an adaptive mechanism. Although the ego was seen as the surface of the id—a pleasure principle—the two were differentiated by contact with the outside world, which engendered the ego as a kind of reality principle. Lacan has reached back to Freud's early theory of narcissistic identification and made *that* the cornerstone of his evolving picture of the human subject (Laplanche, *Life and Death*, p. 81).

By taking up Freud's project in reverse—that is, by transferring the privileged subject of perception from the realm of consciousness to that of unconsciousness—Lacan has gone against Freud's insistence that no such complex unity as an ego could exist from early in life. Freud, he maintains, could not pursue the implications of his discoveries because there were no adequate metaphorical tools to support the conceptualizations nascent in his thought. In Freud's earlier writings—"To Introduce Narcissism" (1914) and "Mourning and Melancholia" (1916)—as well as in his later distinction between ego ideal and ideal ego ("Group Psychology and the Analysis of the Ego" [1921]), Lacan finds backing for his own theory that the elemental subject of perception and intentionality is formed by primary identifications between the time of birth and eighteen months of age.[14] In his doctoral dissertation (1932) Lacan claimed that since Freud did not see the concrete tendencies of the ego, he failed to understand its concrete genesis.[15]

Survey of the "I"

Some remarks on the evolution of subjectivity in the Western tradition from the medieval period to the present—with examples selected from French literature—will set the stage for my fuller presentation of Lacan's view of the subject. We shall see that Lacan's subject of the unconscious is neither innate nor substantive, but, as a mirror of its own structuration, it interacts with its environment to change its own reflection. It then resurfaces through the speaking subject and in relationship dynamics. The kaleidoscopic shifts in social conceptions of the "self" as revealed by history will bear out Lacan's claim that the subject is a network of identificatory and linguistic relations formed by the effects of the external world as they correspond to survival needs and demands for recognition.

In contrast to the Occidental subject of scientific civilization, the medieval spiritual subject was largely anonymous and hardly differentiated in consciousness from the hierarchical locus it occupied in a feudal and theocentric world order. Communal religious feeling provided the cement of social awareness, while outward, objective concentration on meeting the ritual obligations of this life (as a mere foreshadowing of the life to come) precluded any sense of interiority.[16] François Villon's formula "Ce suis-je?" with its inverted order of identity—requiring a preposed object to complete it—captures this feeling well (Sheridan, *Ecrits*, p. 70). A series of upheavals—political, natural, demographic, and economic—hastened the end of the medieval ecclesiastical system toward the close of the fifteenth century. But spiritual and intellectual factors (for example, Dante's questioning of first causes, the Great Schisms, the diminished prestige of the papacy under the degenerate Borgias and Medicis, and Erasmus's exegetical scrutiny of biblical translations) awakened the beginnings of a personal and individual "I," sensible of a divinity withdrawing its transcendent presence from human affairs.

As maritime exploration extended Europe's literal horizons and Renaissance canvases depicted man more hugely against the newly discovered perspective of painted horizons, humanist scholars, feeling a new jubilation at their own subjective existence, placed a heightened value on the here and now. The Reformation viewed human life and the soul's salvation as resting precisely on the autonomous behavior of the individual. Even Protestantism, apparently backward-looking in the predestinarian pessimism of a Martin Luther, represented a crossing of medieval transcendence and Renaissance immanence, attended by a greater confidence in salvation and correspondingly lesser anguish of soul. François Rabelais caught the new spirit and the mind's boundless appetite when he had an abbey built, unlike any other, with the motto over its gate: "Do what you will."[17]

But within the logical economy of a developing individualism, the ecstasy based on the hope of gigantic possibilities was short-lived. Once the human subject had undertaken tasks of personal judgment and perception, it increasingly doubted and questioned the rule of traditional authority, breeding the unhappiness born of frustrated certainty. Finding little that was immutable on which to rely in the external world (as the spiritual foundations of Europe were shaken by religious wars), the Renaissance subject withdrew from a critique of issues themselves to an examination of the criteria by which issues could be discussed at all. Questioning its own perceptions, and thus casting doubt on the evidence of the senses—a state of mind often characterized as baroque—the predicament of the "I" was most succinctly summed up in Montaigne's pregnant and unanswered question to himself: "Que sçais-je?" (What do I know?)[18] Lacan has praised Montaigne as the one who centered himself, not in skepticism, but around the living moment of the fading (Greek, àphanisis) of the subject's conscious understanding or certainty. And in that Lacan calls him a fecund and eternal guide (Séminaire XI, p. 203).

But the actual birth of the human subject, seen as a distinctive presence with specific attributes, occurred in the seventeenth century. Just as the medieval subject centered its perceptions confidently in God or a feudal overlord, the Renaissance and baroque subject still clung to the autonomy of its own perceptions, however illusory these might seem. In Lacan's view, this stance—clinging to an autonomous self-view in the presence of fading illusions—intimated an "unconscious" aspect of being which later centuries would try to explain. But though philosophic and religious skepticism had set the human subject on an unnerving quest (after all, if it questioned church and Scripture, king and divine right, nature, and its own memory or sense perceptions, what could it know for sure?), an answer was supplied by Descartes. Resting his certainty on doubt, Descartes introduced the subject to the world as indistinct from its own psychic function and thus, Lacan says, founded modern science (*Séminaire* XI, p. 47). By assuring himself that while doubting everything and anything, this act of doubting as an act of thought could at least assure the certainty of the subject's own being (*Cogito ergo sum*), Descartes set thinkers on the path of reifying this thinking subject: in the final analysis it was all they had left on which to rely (*Séminaire* XI, p. 37). At almost the same historical moment in which the subject of thought was enthroned by Descartes, Lacan finds a testimonial to the split between the subject of speech and that of being in Molière's *Le Misanthrope* (1666), where Alceste is unaware that he is as inauthentic as those hypocrites whom he criticizes (*Séminaire* XI, p. 203).[19]

But, in general, Molière was atypical of the seventeenth-century subject of classicism. The latter reacted against sixteenth-century skepticism by placing its trust in "good sense" via the faculty of reason—which was held to be able to distinguish between true and false—a faculty shared by everyone. The result was a concept of universal and cosmopolitan man. Thus, the idea of a centered universe that was so dear to the seventeenth century had its parallel in Descartes's *Cogito*, which centered being in reason and thought.[20] In the Enlightenment era, however, uncertainties resurfaced and even God finally fell to the doubts already conjured by the subject. This suggested to late eighteenth-century thinkers that the reasoning agent of classicism was no more effective in solving the riddles of ontology and metaphysics than were any of its earlier manifestations. Man was merely a compilation of sensory data, said Etienne Bonnot de Condillac, Julien Offray de la Mettrie, and others: *l'homme machine*.

The advent of Romanticism, however, brought with it the third elevation of the human subject since (1) it had been intuited in the Renaissance and (2) it had received its Cartesian grounding in scientific thought. For the Romantics, the "I" was the seat of emotion, creativity, intuition, imagination, mystical unity with the Absolute—the source of all that was Good and True—and so able to transcend reason and understanding. Unfortunately, all too often ending in suicide, madness, or isolated lyricism, the Romantic subject was not generally sufficient to societal demands. In the mid-nineteenth century the excessive subjectivity of the Romantic "I" was dethroned, first by the "I" of Realism, seen as representative of surrounding social and economic forces, victor or victim depending on the circumstances. And external objects were portrayed as more important than the subject in controlling human existence. Honoré de Balzac, for example, wrote about people whose lives were epitomized by money. Naturalism logically followed Realism. Moving even beyond the controlling power of economic and social forces, Naturalists depicted the determinism of genetic and biological forces and natural selection. The "I" had become the product of biomechanistic determination.

From the fourteenth to the nineteenth centuries, then, the "I" is clearly not a stable structure. With the advent of Freud in the late nineteenth century, the conscious mind was no longer thought to be in control of itself. Looking away from the deterministic explanations that characterized his milieu, Freud proposed that hysteria and madness, as well as other phenomena, had their roots in memories repressed in an unconscious mind. With Freud, the subject could no longer sustain the equation: mastery, lucidity, and self-transparency = consciousness. Although orthodox Freudian theory counts few strict adherents today, Freud's thought pervades our ethos. A plethora of twentieth-century thinkers have relativized the human subject not only in terms of language and socioeconomic forces but also in light of Freud's theories on sexuality, narcissism, and so forth. But, despite an awareness that unseen forces affect behavior, the twentieth-century Occidental subject is still a mixture of the medieval "I" believe; the Cartesian "I" think; the Romantic "I" feel; as well as the existential "I" choose; the Freudian "I" dream, and so forth. Even more basically, Lacan considers the twentieth-century subject to be that of empirical science. By finding its proofs in a kind of nineteenth-century materialistic positivism, the empirical subject believes in the transparency and objectivity of its own perceptions and has faith in a continuity between the perceiver and the perceived and between consciousness and reality. Ultimately, the empirical "I" seeks methods by which to attain objective verification of its hypotheses. Linking its powers of observation to its Cartesian privilege of reason, the empirical subject has, not surprisingly, deified science and technology.

Lacan has denounced this abuse of the *Cogito*—the philosophy of the supremacy of mind and consciousness over the whole of the phenomena of human experience. What he finds significant in Descartes

is not that doubt validates the powers of reason, but that doubt impugns any verification at all adduced by the subject. This fact should
lead individuals to question the agent of their certainty: the perceiving subject of consciousness. In Descartes's own words Lacan finds a
passion for certainty (which is far from the same thing as certainty
itself): "I have an extreme desire to learn to distinguish the true
from the false—in order to see clearly in my actions, and walk with
assurance in this life" (*Séminaire* XI, p. 202). Although Descartes
started out with the idea of possessing knowledge as the first principle of his *Discourse on Method*—"Ne rien accepter pour vraie que
je ne la connûsse évidemment être telle" (To accept nothing as true
which I did not clearly recognize to be so)—Lacan asserts that it is
via Descartes that philosophy relinquished certainty forever. According to Lacan, the human subject is not the living substratum of
subjective phenomenon nor any kind of substance nor any being of
knowledge in a primary or secondary *pathie* nor any *logos* that
would incarnate itself somewhere. Instead, Descartes's subject appeared at the moment when doubt recognized itself as certainty
(*Séminaire* XI, p. 116). In one paradoxical motion Descartes both
affirmed and denied an unconscious space in being. Now, centuries
later, thought and certainty continue to chase each other and proliferate to infinity, but never reduce themselves to each other in an even
equation. In this way the limitations of the *Cogito* are revealed. Instead of basing his trust in reason and empirical testing, Lacan studied the phenomena of plurality and ambiguity in their own right. He
concluded that humankind is characterized by implicit subjectivity,
ambivalences, and miscommunication. The question of "rightness"
is not to be answered in the domain of empirical testing, therefore,
and certainly not before one has recognized the tester's unconscious
foundations in Desire and power, and in relation to narcissistic experiences (and expectations) of otherness.

At the point where Descartes finds the certainty of his being in
doubt ("I am assured, in that I doubt, of thinking"), Lacan maintains
his thought intersects or converges with that of Freud, who found
his proof of an unconscious in the place where he also doubted—
in dreams (*Séminaire* XI, p. 36). What counted most for Freud in
the dream communication was his "certainty" (*Gewissheit*) at the
tangled and obscure point in the dream where he no longer saw
clearly (*Séminaire* XI, p. 36). In describing the unconscious mind
Freud emphasized his certainty that in the dream's navel—that place
of ambiguity and resistance—lay the sign of some truth: something

to preserve. Lacan interprets Freud to mean that he staked his confidence in the existence of an unconscious on a dreaming subject,
which experienced itself on awakening as fading, elusive, and doubtful (*Séminaire* XI, p. 45). The implied subject that Freud found *chez
soi* in the dream is, in Lacan's estimation, the *Es* of *Wo Es war, soll
Ich werden*. Freud's German phrase, taken from his 1932 *Introductory Lectures*, has been translated into English by Ernest Jones as
"Where the id was, there the ego shall be." The psychoanalyst Marie
Bonaparte translated the phrase into French as "Le moi doit déloger
le ça." In "The Freudian thing, or the meaning of the return to Freud
to psychoanalysis," Lacan objected to both translations. He pointed
out that Freud always used the nouns *das Es* (the it) and *das Ich* (the
I) when speaking of his post–1920 topology. *Das Es* meant the id,
and *das Ich* meant the ego. But in 1932 Freud, surprisingly, dropped
the articles and used the simple pronouns *Es* (it) and *Ich* (I) in his celebrated formula *Wo Es war, soll Ich werden*. Lacan glossed Freud's
phrase anew to mean: "Where the unconscious subject (*Es war/
c'etait*) was in a locus of being, from there I (*Ich*) must come to
light." Not only should the phrase be rewritten, Lacan said, it should
produce a new verb: *s'être*. In other words, Freud's formula means
that it is one's duty to emerge from a place of unconscious being to
recognize the truth, that one's being derives from having been an object of unconscious and alien principles. Only in the movement of
seeing oneself emerge from the unconscious can knowledge become
truth. What Freud did not clarify, however, was that the *Es* is not an
impersonal, unstructured, and instinctual id, but an unconscious,
perceiving entity that inhabits a locus of being. The *Es* is a constellation of signifying relations, a talking subject. Thus, in opposition to the *Cogito*, Lacan offers the *Ça parle*—"It speaks"—that is,
the unconscious subject (*Séminaire* XI, p. 45). Lacan's rephrasing
would indicate the absolute subjectivity governing the human subject. Any recognition of unconscious meaning would yield truth.
This is the opposite of the ego perceptible in conscious pleasures, or
of the *moi* in the labors of alienating identification (Sheridan, *Ecrits*,
pp. 128–29).

The philosopher and Lacanian commentator Elisabeth Roudinesco
believes so many thinkers have erred in their interpretation of Freud's
famous description of the dream as "the royal road to the unconscious" because they have made it an object of secondary-process
(i.e., conscious) thought. Thus Carl Jung, Gaston Bachelard, Ernest
Jones, and others have mistakenly turned Freud's discovery of the unconscious on its head by thinking of it as myth and symbol.[21] Lacan,

on the other hand, takes the dream quite literally as a "discourse" spoken by an unconscious subject and, what is more, in the language of everyday discourse. This dream discourse becomes a rebus or enigma, however, because it is formed and reorganized by the primary-process laws of condensation and displacement and, thus, is distorted by the time it surfaces to the conscious level.

One of Lacan's most original contributions to psychoanalysis lies in his postulation that the laws of the psyche, known as condensation and displacement, act analogously to the laws of everyday language. Roman Jakobson has shown that linguistic displacements, combinations, substitutions, referential differentiations, and so forth can all be subsumed under the rhetorical categories of metaphor and metonymy.[22] Now Lacan did not suppose that linguistic metaphor and metonymy create the laws of the psyche, nor did he suggest that psychic laws are innate. To my understanding, primary-process laws evolve as identificatory processes that function by means of mimesis and perceptual fantasies (*fantasmes*). Introjection and projection are the means by which infants acquire a sense of identity in reference to the objects, symbols, and effects of the outside world. The Lacanian explanation of how individuals acquire and use the system of internal representations—by which they later encode reality—stresses that the primary process (in dreams, for instance) functions by the same laws as secondary-process thought, although the "logic" works differently at each level. The unconscious wields imagistic material—including many images that are phonetic—while conscious life works with linguistic material. Gilles Deleuze and Félix Guattari miss the point when they claim that the unconscious cannot really be composed of rhetorical figures (i.e., representations) since these would be "abstract."[23] The "abstract" or enigmatic manifestations of the unconscious will always be decoded in conscious life to reveal fragments and details from the concrete realm of language and event that constitute mentality by the "law of the subject."

Insofar as the perceiving subject takes in *perceptum* from the outside world that makes up unconscious networks of "meaning," Lacan postulated that there is no innate "self" that evolves logically in terms of genetic, developmental, archetypal, narcissistic, or cognitive material. Man develops as a "symbolic," desiring animal in response to cognition and mastery needs. These, in turn, derive from a prematuration in motor skills during the first eighteen months of life and from the neonate's lack of any innate means by which to understand its own perceptions. The ensuing chapters of this book develop the Lacanian idea that cognitive capacity, perception, and memory will mature in an individual, throughout life, by mediation of human relationships and within language.[24]

As Freud's career evolved, he veered ever further away from his pre–1920 topology and its interest in the unconscious.[25] Lacan saw Freud's difficulty at that point as twofold: how to avoid repressing the insights implied by his discovery of the unconscious; and how to characterize systematically the unconscious which, by definition, lies beyond system and thought. Freud repressed his own discovery, and his followers have likewise ignored Freud's *early* insights by substantifying the unconscious in light of Freud's post–1920 thought. Lacan, insistent upon the idea that the unconscious is essentially structural and linguistic, used Descartes to radicalize Freud. According to Lacan, Descartes did not really prove that the human subject finds its certainty in its capacity to doubt. Instead, he prefigured Freud's theory that an unconscious is proved by an obscure part of the dream. Although they did not realize it, both thinkers proved that the human perceiving subject is itself disunified. By pushing Descartes two steps backward, Lacan interprets the *Cogito*—which he describes as puny and a homunculus—to claim that man only imagines himself man, from the fact that he imagines himself (*Séminaire* XI, pp. 129–30). That one represents oneself in speech, the latter already a step removed from experience and thus an alienation from the natural, becomes proof to Lacan of the phenomenon of a division of the subject (*Ichspaltung*). In this way, Lacan has reinterpreted Freud's concept of the "splitting" (*Spaltung*) of the subject into conscious and unconscious parts, in order to make the split itself a participant in the subject's conscious discourse, as well as a manifestation of the most profound level of the unconscious.[26] Whether he looks at Descartes's daylight conscious realizations of uncertainty, or at Freud's nighttime unconscious experiences of the dream (which fades upon awakening), Lacan finds proof that the human subject is itself discontinuous, contingent, and fundamentally unreliable. Thus, the idea of a static and substantive inner reality waiting to be found or that of a deep structure waiting to be uncovered—whether one refers to philosophical truth, linguistic presupposition, or psychological experience—is merely an example of a comforting myth of wholeness and ontological resolution.

When Freud proposed his second topology in 1920, the ego came to be the subject of consciousness and played a central role. Although Freud retained the concept of the unconscious as a subterranean force that conditions and interferes in conscious thought and behavior (making the ego an encumbered master in its own house),

the ego was basically seen as a conscious agent of mediation between the instinctual id and the social superego. Although Freud's
chronological evolution in thought away from the unconscious and
toward the id-ego-superego model has generally been accepted as a
progressive growth in insight, Lacan has quite literally accepted
Freud's original estimate of *The Interpretation of Dreams* (1900) as
his most significant work. Freud came closest to describing the unconscious itself here, in *Wit and Its Relation to the Unconscious*
and in *The Psychopathology of Everyday Life.* He was mistaken
about the unconscious when he later tried to explain it in terms of
the biological metaphor of his day.[27] In 1915 Freud said: "All the acts
and manifestations which I notice in myself and do not know how
to link up with the rest of my mental life must be judged as if
they belonged to someone else; they are to be explained by a mental
life ascribed to this other period."[28] In Lacan's innovative linking of
Freudian thought to structural linguistics, this "other scene" or
stage in a theater (*ein anderer Schauplatz*) becomes the radical Otherness of the unconscious: the inscribing of an alien discourse in an
individual. By looking at Freud's texts as enigmas to be solved in the
light of recent discoveries in other disciplines, and by linking such
contemporary concepts as relation, structure, and network to the
amorphous realm of subjectivity, Lacan has tried to demonstrate
that Freud lacked the intellectual tools to proceed further in his discovery of a structural (topographical) unconscious. Such profound
theoretical disagreements with orthodox neo-Freudianism played a
role in Lacan's resignation from the Paris Psychoanalytic Society in
1952 and in the refusal of the International Psychoanalytic Association to grant him the status of training and teaching analyst in 1962.

Lacan viewed language and the unconscious as distinct, closed
systems that work by different kinds of logic. That they are, nonetheless, dynamically intermingled offered Lacan a solution to Freud's unresolved problem: How can the unconscious think? The answer is
via the elusive subject of an unconscious network of signifying representations. Lacan designated this subject by the letter "S" barred
thus: $\rlap{/}{S}$. In other words, the conscious subject cannot speak or think
of its unconscious aspects in a unified fashion. The speaking subject, therefore, has its roots in subjectivity and undertakes all its
quests (sexual, intellectual, or material) in relation to its Otherness
to itself. But by the Other(A) Lacan alternatively meant different
things. In keeping with his picture of the subject as dialectical,
multileveled, fluid, and dynamic, Lacan's Other(A) refers to the various external forces that structure a primary and secondary uncon-

scious. The Other(A) then, is more than the Real other or mother of early infant nurture. In contradistinction to object-relations theory, Lacan's special attention to the relationship between infant and mother during the mirror stage does not mean that the unconscious is created in a static one-to-one equation or with the force of a biological bond. Any constant nurturer could fulfill the function of mother. The formulation (m)Other is meant to express the idea that the human subject first becomes aware of itself by identification with a person (object), usually the mother.

Later the Other(A) refers to the Symbolic other, or to the real father, i.e., the secondary unconscious created by subjugation to the social order of symbols, rules, and language. In a broader sense the Other(A) infers familial prehistory, as well as the social order of language, myths, and conventions. Schneiderman has written: "The Other can be considered to be the space of the community, a space which man will make over, organize, and impress his stamp upon, to make himself the cause of his unnatural existence."[29] Elsewhere he has observed: "Otherness is always and irreducibly outside the subject; it is fundamentally alien to him. Insofar as the discourse of the Other agitates a singular subject, it forms the Freudian unconscious" (Returning, p. 3). Essentially, then, the Other(A) is a concept of continuity between consciousness and unconsciousness, between identifications and language. In the light of his view of unconscious, or Other(A) "discourse" as opaque and elusive, floating somewhere between inside and outside, Lacan glossed the Cogito anew to read: "I am not wherever I am the plaything of my thought; I think of what I am wherever I do not think I am thinking."[30] The unconscious subject emerges from the Other's discourse as an object of Other(A) Desire, but generally does not "hear" (i.e., know) itself in conscious discourse.

The Pre–Mirror- and Mirror-Stage Theory

Some critics have called the concept of the mirror stage Lacan's myth (just as the instinct was Freud's, or the collective unconscious was Carl Jung's).[31] Other commentators have described the mirror stage as Lacan's only piece of "empirical" data. Lacan himself evolved the concept in an attempt to fill in the gaps left by Freud's varied and contradictory notions of the ego, which changed shape according to the psychic system in which it participated. In Freud's first topology, the ego was less important than Freud's elaboration of conscious, unconscious, or preconscious systems schematized variously as the functional, the descriptive, the topographical or structural, the dynamic, the systematic, or the economic. Within the dynamic system, for example, where the unconscious was equated with the repressed, the ego represented the pole of personality that defended itself against repressed material and was therefore motivated by anxiety and neurotic conflict. Freud's economic system concentrated on the principle of constancy expressed in the opposition of pleasure and displeasure. Here the ego was a factor in the liaison of the psychic processes. But in the second topology of id-ego-superego, the ego's defensive operations had become largely unconscious, i.e., linked to the id. In 1955 Lacan described the contemporary neo-Freudian view of the ego as one taken from Freud's article "The Id and the Ego" (1923), according to which the ego is the differentiated—i.e., conscious—part, organized by the mass of the id. In this context the ego has been equated with the perception-consciousness system.[32]

In his essay "The mirror stage as formative of the function of the I as revealed in psychoanalytic experience," Lacan presented his mirror-stage theory to the sixteenth International Congress of Psychoanalysis at Zürich in 1949. He had first presented this hypothesis in 1936 and published its main ideas in the encyclopedia article "La Famille" in 1938.[33] He had absorbed the influences of Henri Wallon's work on imprinting behavior and on social relativity in the constitution of the human emotions; the research of Konrad Lorenz and Nikko Tinbergen on animal imprinting; the phenomenon of transitivism by which children around eighteen months of age impute their own actions to each other; and studies of children about eight months of age, who mirror each other's gestures, as observed by Charlotte Bühler, Elsa Köhler, and the Chicago School of the 1930s. In the 1940s Lacan described mirror-stage identification of an infant with another between six and eighteen months of age as a dialectical instance in development, which permanently situated the human subject in a line of fiction and alienation.[34] Although Richard Wollheim is typical of those who claim that Lacan has adduced no evidence for the significance of the mirror stage, the psychoanalytic critic Arthur Efron has pointed out, in a long and thoughtful study, that the fusion state between mother and infant is a fact, "one not the property of psychoanalysis."[35] This "fact" has been given various interpretations by students of human behavior. Dr. Robert Weiss, for example, believes there is a "need" for attachment that is biologically built in to all human beings, an evolutionary legacy. There is no psychopathology in attachment needs, in his view, but a common response to the social context.[36] Lacan makes this "fact" the hypothesis of his

epistemology, the major proofs of which are (1) its own internal coherence, (2) the new illumination it sheds on Freud's work, and (3) its
unexpected power to make sense of humble details of daily life
otherwise ignored, unexplored, or thought to be eternal mysteries.
Later I shall show that a multitude of "empirical" studies (Anglo-
American, German, and others), which are not attached to any over-
arching theory, paradoxically lend support to Lacan's theories on
neonate perception and mirror-stage identification.

Lacan has called the first six months of human life the pre-mirror
stage and describes it as a period in which an infant experiences its
body as fragmented parts and images. During this time the infant has
no sense of being a totality or an individual unit, because a prematuration at birth (by comparison with other animals)—a phenomenon termed fetalization by embryologists—marks human babies as
uncoordinated and physically helpless. In the human's natural (or
biological) reality, Lacan says, there is an organic insufficiency, inasmuch as any meaning can be given to the word "nature" (Sheridan,
Ecrits, p. 4). Lacan has described this organic insufficiency as a
"lack of coordination of his own motility . . . intra-organic and relational discordance during the first six months" (Sheridan, Ecrits,
pp. 18–19). In a mathematical effort to explain his concept, Lacan
has symbolized the newborn as a zero, or blank, insofar as the infant
lacks both individuality and subjectivity. Nonetheless, the infant
perceives the world around it from the start of life. Other psychoanalytic observers have noted the same phenomenon. René Spitz observed in 1965 that some infants, immediately upon birth, are able
to perceive shape, size, and three-dimensionality. And in 1959 Ernest
Schachtel in Metamorphosis: On the Development of Affect, Perception, Attention and Memory reported that F. Stirnimann's work
with over fifty infants demonstrated they had remarkable perceptual
capacities and even sensorimotor coordination.[37] Nevertheless, the
human infant cannot walk, talk, or obtain food on its own, but spends
much time just gazing and hearing. Lacan has therefore stressed that
earliest perception is inseparable from the effects of the outside
world, both linguistic and visual. He thinks, furthermore, that since
the primordial subject of unconsciousness is formed by identification with its first images and sensory experiences, it will thereafter
reflect the essence of these images and objects in identity. The radical idea that the infant actually becomes the image or object in primordial fantasy is an experience Lacan calls primary identification,
while pointing out that the nature of symbolic incorporation is generally misunderstood.[38]

In 1948 Lacan listed specific images as the archaic *imago* of the fragmented body, which constitute what used to be termed the "instincts." These are images—i.e., mental representations—of castration, mutilation, dismemberment, dislocation, evisceration, devouring, bursting open of the body, and so forth and have a formative function in composing the human subject of identity and perception (Sheridan, *Ecrits*, p. 11). If we look at this Lacanian idea in the light of Efron's discussion of the differences between psychoanalytic concepts of infant rage (is it innate or environmentally induced?), some possible clarifications suggest themselves. According to Lacan, perception and bodily experience are mutual correlatives in the first six months of life. Given the abundant cultural instances of what can only be construed as bodily mistreatment of newborns, a future question to answer is whether the roots of aggression lie in the very first corporal experience?[39]

More important at present, however, is the pursuit of Lacan's challenge to the received idea that human identity evolves from biological and developmental first causes. Put simply, Lacan points out that images and language are *nolens volens* already present before birth, before any of the developmental stages are embarked upon, and before any genetic potential is unfolded. In consequence, the effects of images and language condition each biological and developmental stage as it occurs. But this primacy of the outside world in structuring identity is inseparable from the infant's lack of survival sufficiency. The infant compensates for its physiological prematuration by a necessary assimilation or integration of the world around it. Hence, *any* human identity (o^1) will later be highly personalized, since the conjuncture of images, effects, and objects that fundamentally compose it is variable and infinitely combinable.

Lacan's theory here casts doubt on any neopositivistic picture of the ego as a product of impersonal, evolutionary forces. It also casts doubt on the static aspect of object-relations theory (of Melanie Klein, Donald Winnicott, W. Ronald D. Fairbairn, among others), which depicts the infant as fused with the mother and, consequently, the "same" as she is. "Similar to" or "associated with" does not mean "the same as." Insofar as perceptual fusion with discrete objects underlies mirror-stage fusion with others (at six to eighteen months), the pre–mirror-stage infant has already become the objects it sees and the experiences it has in its fundamental fantasies. Lacan praised Klein for having intuited this period of pre-mirror reality, and he equated such elemental fantasies with the first layer of reality, thus making reality essentially synonymous with individual perception. In this way he rendered the concept of *reality* irretrievably subjective and symbolic. This is so even before incorporation of the mother as a totality has begun.

J. Laplanche and J.-B. Pontalis have called the idea that the mother is interiorized in the first six months a genetic or corporal perspective. The beginnings of an identity are thereby organized as the progressively differentiated surface of the psychical organism.[40] In other words, perception begins with the linking of the corporal being that *is* the infant to the signifying or meaningful material outside it: i.e., images and language (part-objects) in tandem with their effects on sensory-perceptual being. The result, as Michèle Montrelay (a practicing psychoanalyst in Paris) points out, is that the Real of the infant, the maternal body and objects, signals confusion for the infant. As she puts it: "Confusion and coincidences: hearing is very close to the eye, which is seen by the child as an eye-ear, an open hole."[41] The visual-verbal impact may cause confusion, but it also forms what Lacan has called "letters" (abstract signifiers) of the body in the pre-mirror stage. These are the effects of touch, sound, the gaze, images, and so forth as they intermingle with sensory response. In this way, the human body becomes eroticized in relation to its earliest experiences of the outside world.

By "letters" Lacan often meant the effect of language, which creates and informs the unconscious: "letters" defined as localized signifiers. By "letters" of the body he meant the impact of difference or otherness on being.[42] In Lacan's opinion, the erotogenic zones that Freud named—mouth, anus, phallus, genitals—become so because they are singled out from adjoining, connecting zones by the primacy of their function in early infancy. Because they are distinguished as "different" or meaningful, they later play a key role in drive and sexual desire (*Séminaire* XI, p. 172). From such a perspective, sexual pleasure is not inherent in body parts or in hormones per se. Lacan found no sexual "natural language," therefore, with certain rules and messages written into it as did Claude Lévi-Strauss—a notion which Noam Chomsky has pertinently criticized—but he does find effects, impressions, and hallucinatory images attached to corporal and perceptual experience from the pre-mirror stage on. By reading backward from the adult to the infant, Lacan hypothesized adult sexual pleasure as first inscribed at the instant of lived pleasure, at the edges (*bords*) which originally demarcated each erotogenic zone of "difference." In the light of this theory, the voice and eye—as part objects of Desire—would also be seen as "erotic" organs. Serge Leclaire has described the subsequent dilemma of understanding human nature as a "disintrication" of the body and words, always to be taken up again.[43]

Lacan postulated an irreducible symbolization of the body in the first six months of life, followed by a mirror stage that anchors body identification to the human *Gestalt*. This theory indirectly answers Efron's query: "If the infant has a complete body and has a sense of that body, then the whole theory of object-relations, based as it is on painfully coordinating what had previously been part-objects into some whole object—undergoes drastic deflation" (Efron, "Psychoanalytic Theory," p. 38). Lacan argued that even though body image or ego is experienced as permanently incomplete, both are composed of a series of discrete unities. But because an infant first perceived (or judged) its body to be a collection of discrete part-objects, adults can never perceive their bodies in a complete fashion in later life (*Séminaire* I, p. 200). Pre–mirror-stage identificatory fusions have been described by Leclaire as primary unities (or primary pleasure), which serve as reference points for secondary unity (pleasure or constancy) in mirror-stage identification (*Psychanalyser*, p. 132). Identity, thus viewed, is excentrically layered, first by a passive perceptual fusion with transient images or objects whose matrices are the part-objects of Desire, and second, by the occurrence of a species-specific active identification with body form. After the mirror stage, sights, sounds, words, dicta, and familial and cultural myths add up to the narcissistic (*moi*) fixations that sustain the sense of having an identity during adulthood, even though they were put in place in childhood.

But what actually permits an infant to pass from a passive pre-mirror to an active mirror stage, and then to a post-mirror stage? Why *are* part-objects woven into whole ones? All child development research points to six months as a crucial stage. That the six-month-old infant—having already achieved such milestones as raising its head or grasping objects—can gradually move from a period in which it had little power to effect major alterations of its own body to one in which it can initiate rolling over and sitting up without assistance means that the infant has passed from a state of relative helplessness to one where it can change its own spatial relationship to its environment. This potential must surely usher in major perceptual changes. As the infant gradually assimilates its new relation to the world of objects, its previously blank smiles become crows of joy when a familiar shape appears (re-cognition): itself in the mirror, its mother, others, and "substitute" objects as well. In my estimation, motor control—the biological capability to propel itself or maintain itself in an upright position—would condition the perceptual advance in development. But biological evolution does not itself *cause* psychic development. Rather, mastery of physiological prematuration—what Lacan called an "original misery"—by identificatory processes would enable the mirror-stage infant to celebrate its new spatial relationship to the world. Perhaps a severely deprived infant would be retarded in the elemental biological advances. Although mirror-stage perception is later irretrievable to consciousness, it can be logically inferred as a structure, i.e., transformation of the subject from feeling itself a series of imagistic unities to experiencing itself as a unified body.

But before a sense of identity begins to confer the unified shape of the *moi* during the mirror stage, the elemental structure of the subject has been diacritically woven in terms of heterogeneity. Underlying the mirror-stage drive toward fusion and homogeneity, we find the earliest experience of "self" in parts, fragments, and differences. The primordial objects of Desire, which fill in the gap between perception and the infant's incoherent effort to process information from the outside world, are: the breast, excrement, the phallus (as Imaginary object), and the urinary flow. "An unthinkable list if one adds as I do," Lacan said, "the phoneme, the gaze, the voice—the nothing." In Jean-Claude Milner's formula $\mathscr{S} \Diamond a$, the $\mathscr{S}$ represents the speaking subject as unaware of the nature of its formation and the source of its Desire (its "truth"). The letter a stands for the objects of Desire, themselves split off ($\Diamond$) from any transparent meaning. This formula emphasizes the heterogeneity of the object of Desire, its Real character of Otherness that predates a sense of the Imaginary mother in the mirror stage.[44] These original objects were introjected prior to any awareness of difference (i.e., representability). Although they inscribe themselves as residue or "traces," they are not *perceptum*, for they offer no specular image or alterity. Lacan located the roots of identity in such archaic images. But he did not mean (as did Klein) that these original spatially situated images were introjected directly. Lacan asks how an object can *be* introjected? He answered that image, sound, effect, and sensory response combine to form individuality as an identificatory composite—or representational entity—somewhere between inside and outside. Wilden has pointed out that "representation" means performance (of a play), as well as translating both the Hegelian and Freudian word for representation: *Vorstellung* (Wilden, *Language of Self*, p. 104). This "somewhere" corresponds to Lacan's ego (o^1) and subject (S), primordially linked by a "join" both unfathomable and unfixable. In the Schéma L, one may see the origin of this join in the primordial Other. In consequence, some Lacanian commentators have referred to the specular *je* or the presubjective *moi*.

The literary critic Michel Grimaud has pointed out that, although the noted psychoanalyst Heinz Hartmann has conceded that perception, memory, and cognitive processes are anterior to analytic structures, Hartmann persists in presenting the human as a closed, neo-Freudian system in which the reduction of instinctual tensions is capital. Grimaud continues: "Hartmann stresses instincts although we know now that the baby is an apprentice from birth, and not instinctually."[45] Other empirical researches in Anglo-American psychology, which actually vindicate Lacan's theories, have shown that newborns have sophisticated perceptual and physical capabilities. In 1977 Andrew Meltzoff and M. Keith Moore conducted a series of tests on neonates and discovered a talent for precise sequential imitation—a talent Piaget assigned to children between eight and twelve months of age. Meltzoff and Moore found in repeated and varied tests that the newborns imitated the following actions: pursing the lips, sticking out the tongue, opening the mouth wide, and closing the hand. They have concluded that this imitative ability may be "innate." If so, they say, we must revise our current conceptions of infancy, which hold that such a capacity is the product of many months of postnatal development.[46]

In 1948 Lacan had already pointed out that a ten-day-old infant is fascinated by the human face (Sheridan, *Ecrits*, p. 18). Efron has compiled abundant empirical information pointing to the perceptual capabilities of the neonate. Spitz, for example, found that during the third month the infant could follow the adult's face with his eyes.[47] Other studies verify that a baby can distinguish its mother from other people at about seven days, by means of a finely developed sense of smell.[48] Experiments in the 1960s found that infants a few weeks old could learn to distinguish between a full nipple and an empty one held against opposite cheeks.[49] Efron believes this indicates infants have a functioning memory, ordinarily considered an ego function absent in the neonate for a substantial time.[50] At twelve weeks, infants who were shown their mothers' face in combination with someone else's voice indicated that they knew something had been radically changed.[51] And in another experiment, Michael Lewis of Princeton established that six-month-old babies are less frightened when approached by young children than by adults, but that babies were surprised—not frightened—when approached by midgets: in other words, by the wrong face on the wrong body.[52] Efron's compilation of data demonstrates brilliantly that a revolution has been going on since the 1960s in the United States in the study of young infants. This revolution constitutes a shift from considering the infant "a passive organism who was the object of forces which determined development" to mapping out the capabilities, as well as the limits, that infants do have.[53]

Despite all this, in current Anglo-American psychological and psychoanalytic *theory*, perception is usually equated with consciousness; memory, cognition, and ego development are seen as "late" occurrences; and the unconscious remains largely synonymous with the instinctual. While Klein believed that the infant cannot distinguish between fantasy and non-fantasy and while Spitz concludes that the newborn had no faculty of perception, representation, or volition, Lacan has indirectly related the actively busy and mimicking infant of American empirical studies to perception and cognition theories. He has made identificatory fantasies, interactions with others, and the effects of language causative in mental development and reality conception.[54] The neonate's first response to the world is to record representations of that world in a series of fantasmatic images that build bridges between its "helplessness" or boundarylessness and the outside world in order to ensure its survival.[55] From this perspective, an infant's capabilities are not innate manifestations of intelligence (a static concept), but evidence of biostructural deficiency—a lack of self-sufficiency—and of the infant's consequent dependence on objects in its gradual mastery over inadequacies in motor skill and identity. It is senseless, therefore, to accuse Lacan of ignoring the outside environment, as did Melanie Klein, for he makes initial dependence on that environment a permanent and enveloping dynamic in perception and intentionality.

After the transition to the mirror stage, the infant more obviously identifies and interacts with the primary caretaker, whose *imago* is introjected as a perceptual totum. During the six- to eighteen-month period, the child also learns to recognize an image of itself in a mirror, often in jubilation (Sheridan, *Ecrits*, p. 18). The identification with a *Gestalt* of his own body is paralleled in the infant's relating to the mother's *imago* as if it were his own. The mother is introjected as *objet a* (a desired object), which, in this context, Lacan terms a representation of one's own *Gestalt*. In Schneiderman's words: "He takes it upon himself. He puts the image on, or as Lacan would say, he assumes it as his own" (*Returning*, p. 4). In 1949 Lacan described "the function of the mirror stage as a particular case of the function of the imago . . . [its purpose] to establish a relation between the organism and its reality . . . between the *Innenwelt* and the *Umwelt*." The early identification with a *Gestalt* is a biological (natural) phenomenon. But this early identification also constitutes the first alienation for an infant, a split between outer form (big and symmetrical) and an inner sense of incoherence and dissymmetry. Lacan places this split at the heart of human knowledge (Sheridan, *Ecrits*, p. 5). Human beings will forever after anticipate their own images in the images of others, a phenomenon Lacan refers to as a sense of "thrownness" (akin to Heidegger's theory of the human subject).

In linking pre–mirror- and mirror-stage identifications to the development of cognition, Lacan stresses that pre-mirror experience submerges the infant unawares into its surroundings. Mirror-stage identifications entail the *discovery* of difference, and the concomitant experience of awareness or delimiting alienation. I have adapted Lacan's use of Gottlob Frege's philosophical mathematical logic to symbolize the transition to the mirror stage by designating the infant as having passed cognitively from 0 to 1. The jubilation of the infant discovering itself in the mirror—which comes from the assumption of a kind of mastery over the preceding lack of coordination—occurs because its mirror image is fixed like a statue, the symmetry of which apparently reverses the baby's form by contrast with the turbulent movements that animate it (Sheridan, *Ecrits*, pp. 2, 18). The first subjective human knowledge, therefore, comes from a fascination with the human form, which an infant perceives to be an ideal unity. Mirror-stage identification with an external image of the human form both symbolizes the acquisition of a mental permanence and also marks the subject's destined alienation away from the naturalness of spontaneous fusion and toward a cultural dependency.[56] Society and language further widen a gap for which means must then be devised to paper it over.

As stated above, the idea that infant and mother seem fused during the early months of life is far from new. The psychoanalyst Margaret Mahler, among others, has commented at length on dependency and separation.[57] More recently, the child development researcher Burton L. White has said: "By the time a child is two years of age, and often much earlier, he will have established a very elaborate and detailed social contract with his primary caretaker. I personally believe that contract is relatively hard to subsequently alter or modify against its established direction. I think that what children acquire in that first two years is the first set of social skills and attitudes they will begin to use with all people" (*First Three Years*, p. 128). White here comes close to describing the mirror stage, but without really understanding it. The originality of the fusion theory belongs to Klein, who created it, and to Winnicott and others, who—in Efron's words— "tamed it into a psychoanalytic description of what happens in infancy" (Efron, "Psychoanalytic Theory," p. 10). The theory of fusion with the mother is, in fact, object-relations theory. But Lacan can never be accused of simply appropriating a theory of "two body psychology," which he considers as erroneous as a "two ego psychoanalysis." The infant takes the mother to be its own anchor or center (Frege's 1), but this fusion is not static. Lacan considers it an ongoing source of intrasubjective, existential conflict in the here and now. This conflict is played out around issues of presence/absence and recognition dynamics. There is never a period of prefusion or defusion from the (m)Other, therefore, since she is psychically represented at first (zero to six months) in relation to fragmented images or objects of Desire, and then—as a whole object—becomes the source of one's own body image. At the end of the mirror stage, she is repressed as the primordial pivot of Desire in one's unconscious. In this connection she acts as the mediator of Law in reference to the Father's Name.

In *The Mermaid and the Minotaur* (1976) Dorothy Dinnerstein described an interdependence of mother and child according to which the infant's first self is actually the mother's self. She views individuality as breaking away from the mother and neurosis as falling back into her purview.[58] Lacan added the step of making the effects of this first invasion the source of a primordial unconscious. Later the mother's Desires and words are transformed by the substitutive, displacing nature of primary-process laws, and *eo ipso* are not directly available to consciousness. Lacan, thus, subverted the apparent symmetry of the self's double in the mirror. For underlying any sense of mirror-stage symmetry through identification with the human totum there flows a piecemeal system, a network of fragments and part-objects, which first served to symbolize a void during the pre-mirror stage. To sum up so far then: infants lack physical coordination in the first six months of life despite well-developed visual capacities. Lacan located this pre-mirror experience as the source of the common fantasy or dream of a fragmented body. A compensatory identification with whole forms follows in the subsequent mirror stage (six to eighteen months), and this establishes a feeling of unity. Such unity is, nevertheless, imposed from without and consequently is asymmetrical, fictional, and artificial. Lacan explodes the supposed "unity" of the neo-Freudian ego as a tenuous illusion. His mirror stage must, therefore, be understood as a metaphor for the vision of harmony of a subject essentially in discord.

It follows that the drama of the mirror stage moves from a sense of insufficiency to one of anticipation, but not ultimately to one of unity. The mirror-stage structure will disrupt the seeming autonomy and control of the speaking subject later in life. Lacan theorized that adults will always be caught up in the spatial lures of identification with their *semblables*. They will perceive reality in terms of successive pre–mirror- and mirror-stage fantasies, which extend from the fragmented body image (recuperable in dreams, paintings, drug experiences, or psychosis) to a *Gestalt* of the whole body, and finally to the assumption of a subjective armor—the alienated identity whose rigid structure will mark a subject's entire mental development (Sheridan, *Ecrits*, p. 4).[59] But though the mirror-stage experience of localization of the body signals the beginning of a sense of identity, this unity has been found *outside* and, accordingly, the destiny of humans is to (re-)experience themselves only in relationship to others.

In 1936 Lacan gave a paper entitled "The Mirror Stage" at the fourteenth International Psychoanalytic Congress in Marienbad, Czechoslovakia. Taking this alleged bibliographical ghost as her starting point, psychoanalytic critic Jane Gallop has written an essay "Lacan's 'Mirror Stage': Where to Begin?" (see note 33, above). Indeed one might well "begin" with Lacan's 1932 dissertation and its study of feminine paranoia and narcissism, and then proceed to the obvious influence of object-relations theory on Lacan's thought. One might even imagine this "unseen" paper describing the fusion between infant and mother as a "looking-glass phase" of development.[60] From a bibliographical point of view, however, Lacan's first paper on the mirror stage is thought to pose a problem. In Sheridan's translation of Lacan's *Ecrits* one reads in a bibliographical note that an English translation of the 1936 mirror-stage paper appeared in the *International Journal of Psychoanalysis* 18 (January 1937), under the title "The Looking-glass Phase" (Sheridan, *Ecrits*, p. xiii). Upon looking in the journal in question, Gallop found under the title "The Looking-glass Phase" simply the words "J. Lacan (Paris), The Looking-glass Phase." "There is no version, not even a summary of the paper," says Gallop, "although the other papers from the Congress are summarized" (Gallop, "Lacan's 'Mirror Stage,'" p. 119).

Carrying her researches further, Gallop discovered in Lacan's 1966 edition of the *Ecrits* a footnote in the introductory essay to part II

("De nos antécédents"), where Lacan says that he did not deliver the mirror-stage text for the report of the 1936 Congress (p. 67n). Gallop concludes that there is no published version of the original article on the mirror stage and follows this deduction with an analogy to the difficulties of beginning to work on Lacan's teachings. "Now my point is not really or not simply to be fastidious about chronological order, but rather to point to some difficulty around the question of where to begin, some slight confusion about the 'beginning' of the *Ecrits*, some trouble about where (and how) to begin reading Lacan" (Gallop, "Lacan's 'Mirror Stage,'" p. 119). The answer is to be found, however, in the same passage (*Ecrits*, 1966, p. 67n).

The note on page 67 of the *Ecrits* refers the reader to pages 184–85 of the same edition.[61] In 1946 Lacan opened a conference on "psychogenesis," recounting his psychiatric days at the hospital Bonneval. In the report entitled "Propos sur la causalité psychique" he spoke of his mirror stage, saying it would be better to call it the "mirror phase." He then recounts a story of having given a paper on this topic to the 1936 Congress in Marienbad, at least up to the point coinciding with the beginning of the tenth minute of his presentation when Ernest Jones, presiding, interrupted him. The implication is that Lacan was not permitted to continue, or chose not to go on. He does say, however, that some Viennese colleagues gave his ideas a warm welcome. Later, in his 1966 introduction to part II of the *Ecrits*, Lacan referred to the Marienbad experience as having taken him, and those accompanying him, to the heart of a technical and theoretical resistance within international psychoanalysis. The invention of the mirror stage constituted a problem that would become more and more evident (*Ecrits*, 1966, p. 67). Earlier, in 1946, Lacan had told those attending the conference on psychogenesis that the essence of his mirror-stage paper (that he had not given to the Marienbad Congress for publication) was to be found in some lines of his article on the family, which had appeared in 1938 in the *Encyclopédie française*. Henri Wallon, whose own work on the family had helped Lacan shape his mirror-stage ideas, was the director of the volume in which Lacan's article appeared (*Ecrits*, 1966, pp. 184–85). This probably explains why Lacan chose to unveil his mirror-stage theory in this particular publication, instead of with the Marienbad collection. It also explains a bibliographical riddle that has stymied successive commentators.

By 1949 Lacan's ideas on the mirror stage were fully recorded in the essay "The mirror stage as formative of the function of the I as revealed in psychoanalytic experience" (Sheridan, *Ecrits*, pp. 1–7).

In other words, the mirror stage plays a major role in forming the basis of mentality. When a child stops trying to possess or be the object in the mirror at around eighteen months of age, the specular subject of identification has turned into a social one. Or, to quote Schneiderman, the mirror stage ends when the child can recognize that its parents are not entirely responsive to inarticulate demands (*Returning*, pp. 4–5). I would suggest an additional reason that eighteen months marks an epiphanic developmental moment. Having mastered motor coordination, infants are no longer preoccupied with spatial location of the body. It seems logical that their psychic energy could better be placed in coping with the next sequential task required by their surroundings: that of mastering the "foreign" language that has pervaded their ethos for eighteen months, but in whose social "communications" they do not truly participate. In Chapter 5 we shall consider Lacan's hypothesis that the mirror stage comes to a close with the entry of the Oedipal conflict and gradually gives rise to the coherent use of language. Instead of treating images as if they were real, the post-mirror child begins to represent them in words and so passes from a state of "nature" to one of culture and language (Sheridan, *Ecrits*, p. 98). Symbolic (i.e., differential) elements—the ability to name things—replace Imaginary ones (i.e., images) in an identificatory reshaping of the subject. The imagistic and fantasmatic subject of identifications continues, nonetheless, to coexist (in a double inscription) with the subject of language and cultural codes throughout life.

Lacan's mirror stage has been misconstrued by literalist attempts to render it inseparable from the experience thereby implied: an infant's recognition of its own shape in the apparatus of a mirror.[62] Lacan never intended to link the appearance of a human ego to a looking glass, nor even to the fact that—like Narcissus—an infant could see its reflection on the surface of a body of water. The scenario of the infant at the mirror is the index of something that has always occurred, with or without that apparatus: The mirror serves as a metaphor and a structural concept at the same time that it points to a crucial experience in psychic development. The Lacanian commentator Anika Lemaire says that by viewing the process of humanization in mirror-metaphor terms Lacan eschews the problem of ethnological and historical relativity in favor of a formalizable mathematics of the subject.[63] Our identity evolves in a paradoxical context, then, out of a feeling of Oneness, which is really made up of two beings (*le trait unaire*).[64] Nevertheless, Lacan said that this "little reality" (*ce peu de réalité*), the spatial captivation or fixation by the mother's *imago*, determines humans as already alienated from other beings in all later endeavors (Sheridan, *Ecrits*, pp. 3–4).

A feature that distinguishes the end of the mirror-stage drama is that "Cain and Abel" jealousy by which the infant identified with its mother is envious to the death of *anyone or anything* that threatens the union (Sheridan, *Ecrits*, p. 5). Many commentators including St. Augustine have provided support for Lacan's description of primordial jealousy. In the French analyst's view, when the infant symbiotically bound to its mother wishes away the threat to this symbiosis (Frege's 1) and yet angrily blames the intruder, the confusion of the two moments gives rise to the paranoiac structure of the ego. Henceforth, aggressiveness is basic to the makeup of the ego and reappears as resentment, feelings of inferiority, and in other manifestations. Ernest Becker has described the exhibition of jealousy in sibling rivalry as "all-absorbing, relentless, a critical problem which reflects the basic human condition."[65] His observation that sibling rivalry extends beyond childhood is not new, nor are Lacan's theories on interdependency. Lacan's originality lies in his claim that the dynamic of mirror-relation identification is the intrasubjective route not only to personal conflict and misunderstandings but also to an organized, unconscious mode of perception, to adult fixations, Desire, a reality discourse, and human bonding. Lacan need not seek prototypes for human behavior in turn-of-the-century myths such as mechanistic energy, an instinctual id, collective archetypes, presymbolic sensorimotor sequences (Jean Piaget), or the "selfish" gene. As stated above, any infant bears traits of its biological and genetic inheritance, but these characteristics are activated and developed in a preexisting context of images and language—in already elaborated social situations—and in this sense they can only be called secondary. The subject formed by pre–mirror- and mirror-stage identification is so individual and personal, indeed, that Lacan has called it the *moi* (the o¹ in Schéma L).

Narcissism and Identification

The history of psychoanalysis has been, at least in part, the history of efforts to uncover ever more primitive sources of psychic development.[66] In his attempts to clarify Freud's views on narcissism and identification, Lacan has found the sources of psychic being in earlier stages and in more concrete places than did Freud. Havelock Ellis first attached a psychological sense to the word narcissism in 1898 in reference to autoeroticism or any other form of sexual expression excited in the absence of another person. Freud first used the term in 1910 with reference to the Greek myth to mean psychic energy directed toward one's own ego. In an effort to explain the object choice (sexual libido) of male homosexuals, he said that they indirectly and narcissistically loved themselves as the mother had loved them (Laplanche and Pontalis, *Vocabulaire*, p. 261). This explanation presented more problems than solutions. What is there that is sick or lethal in self-love? Why, in fact, did Narcissus die?

In the Daniel-Paul Schreber case (1911) and in *Totem and Taboo* (1913), Freud viewed narcissism as an intermediary stage between autoeroticism and object love. According to this scheme, there were three love stages in sexual evolution: autoeroticism, homosexuality, and heterosexual or object love. In 1914 he published "On Narcissism: An Introduction," in which he described the role of libidinal investments—love for self and other—in the ensemble of psychoanalytic theory.[67] By adumbrating a principle of conservation of libidinal energy, Freud established the idea of a balance between an ego libido (self-love or narcissism) and object libido (love for other or sexual choice) through which the one enriched itself at the expense of the other (Laplanche and Pontalis, *Vocabulaire*, p. 261). But the investment balance of narcissism's libidinal energy might shift. He saw the ego in psychosis, for example, as disinvesting the other (object) and consuming the whole charge.[68] After "Mourning and Melancholia" (1916)—in which he broadened the concept of narcissism to include identification with the lost object—Freud was to evolve a distinction in his 1920 topology between primary and secondary narcissism. Indifferentiation of ego and id and a total absence of object relations were said to characterize primary narcissism. This was found in newborns, psychotics, or those in mourning or depressed. But in secondary narcissism, the ego was actively differentiating itself from the id by its adaptive function, and through identification with others (Laplanche and Pontalis, *Vocabulaire*, p. 262). In "Group Psychology and the Analysis of the Ego" (1921), he referred to the narcissistic investment in self as an "ideal ego," and the objects toward whom ego libido flows as "ego ideals."

Having looked at love in terms of identification with the chosen sexual partner(s) in "Three Essays on the Theory of Sexuality" (1905), Freud had reduced it to two types: (1) narcissistic love based on self-identification with a person one would like to be or to resemble, and (2) anaclitic or attachment love based on an object choice or a person one would like to have. Freud saw the narcissistic type as immature or regressive, because these individuals love someone who is either what they once were; what they would like to be; or someone once a part of themselves. The mature or anaclitic type is said to be genitally differentiated: a man of this type loves the woman who feeds him, while an anaclitic woman loves the man who protects her (parental substitutes). Freud further hypothesized that—insofar as women have ill-defined ego boundaries—they are more prone to narcissistic love than men (see Chapter 5). When, in "Mourning and Melancholia," Freud added the idea that narcissism is a factor in depression (i.e., identification with the deceased beloved could impoverish the ego), he had established the Freudian principle that has become the basis for a contemporary psychoanalytic theory of internalized object relations.

During the period of profound modification of his system around 1920, Freud did not abandon his 1914 notion of a narcissism contemporaneous with the formation of the ego through identification with others. He stressed, instead, the primary and secondary differences. One of the difficulties that Lacan has found with Freud's idea of primary narcissism—a state which would find its prototype in intrauterine life and be reproduced later in sleep—is that this standpoint implies a newborn has *no* perceptive opening on the exterior world. The logical impasse is obvious: How does one bring a monad enclosed in and upon itself to the progressive recognition of others? Laplanche and Pontalis have also pointed out the problem of using the term narcissism to discuss a state of nondifferentiation between ego and id, since no specular or identificatory relationship exists (*Vocabulaire*, p. 264).

Freud's terms describing identification are not any more constant than those depicting narcissism. The psychoanalytic critic Jim Swan has expressed the opinion that the development of all Freud's theories records his struggle with the contradictions in the concept of identification (see p. 7). One may find at least three types of identification in Freud's texts. In primary identification, the original, pre-Oedipal link to the mother is connected to the oral stage. Later Freud designated the Oedipus complex as a secondary identification, made by introjecting the *imago* of the same sex parent. In his 1914 article Freud's focus on identification in sexual object choice found its primacy in the relationship to the mother. In 1921 he advanced the idea in "Group Psychology and the Analysis of the Ego" that there is a presexual identification with the father, which is the prototype of later group ideals and identification with a leader (*SE*, vol. 18). In this article he says: "Identification is known to psychoanalysis as the earliest expression of an emotional tie with another person. It plays a part in the early history of the Oedipus complex. A little boy will exhibit a special interest in his father: he would like to grow like him and be like him, and take his place everywhere" (*SE*, 18:105). But, third, in "The Ego and the Id" (1923), the pre-Oedipal infant does not distinguish sexually between mother and father: The first identification here occurs with both parents, not just the father.[69] Again, in the *New Introductory Lectures* (1933), Freud compared identification with the oral-cannibalistic incorporation of another person—reaffirming the oral pre-Oedipal link to the mother in primary identification.[70] In this way he retained the idea that mature or secondary identification is masculine (active and independent) as opposed to feminine (passive and dependent). The picture is confusing, then, because we see identification functioning at pre-Oedipal and Oedipal stages, and alternatively as an active, passive, or reciprocal process.

New interpretations of the roles of narcissism and identification in human behavior have for some time created a forum for theory and debate. Object-relations theorists (Klein, Winnicott, Michaël Balint, Edith Jacobson, and others) have stressed the processes of identification and differentiation in self-other relations. Here the child-mother relationship is central to a developing sense of identity. The psychologist Erik Erikson sees identity as a complex series of developmental interactions between a person and the environment.[71] The literary critic Norman Holland bases his arguments for making meaning in reading dynamics on an "identity theme."[72] The term is borrowed from Heinz Lichtenstein's 1961 article, in which an identity principle was suggested as a replacement for Freud's death instinct.

Currently, object-relations narcissism is at the center of a psychoanalytic debate between the American-based analysts Heinz Kohut (d. October 1981) and Otto Kernberg. Both men have sought to ascertain the origins of narcissism and how to treat the "disorder." While Kohut saw primary narcissism as an arrest occurring in normal developments—a confused, shifting sense of self—Kernberg views it as a defense against dependency, rage, and envy, and has elaborated the concept of the "borderline personality."[73] Although both men treat narcissism as potentially pathological, Kohut has striven to humanize narcissism, whereas Kernberg retains a more conservative Freudian picture of narcissistic disorders as inseparable from Oedipal problems. A summary of Kohut's influence has declared: "Narcis-ʋism has long been viewed as a negative, self-serving emotion which alienates others and keeps the self from fulfillment. In current psychological theory, narcissism is being perceived as a natural consequence of early neglect, and an empathic attempt to experience other objects as extensions of the self in order to reintegrate them with the nuclear self."[74] Kohut defined the primary narcissistic self as grandiose and exhibitionistic and proposed that it subsists as an archaic *imago* underlying the secondary narcissism through which an infant identifies with its parents. The self thus portrayed is an imaginary structure in the mind, and the ego is the agency of reality. If the original mothering (primary narcissistic process of mirroring) was extremely bad, the adult may later manifest fragmentation of both body and self-image. If there was early insufficiency in parent idealization or secondary narcissism—identification with positive self-objects—the adult may display "object hunger"—the unfulfilled search for satisfaction in relationships. Kohut's goal as analyst was to respond warmly and empathically to an analysand, in an effort to help him or her unite the nonintegrated or repressed (isolated, split-off, disavowed) aspects of the grandiose self into the adult personality or "reality ego."[75] In this way he hoped to transform archaic narcissism into realistic goals and self-esteem (Kohut, *Analysis*, p. 192).

In one sense Lacan was more conservative than either Kernberg or Kohut, who both linked narcissism to identification. Like Freud, Lacan saw the narcissistic "investment" of objects and identification (object libido) as different phenomena, although not in a seesaw libidinal balance (as Freud wrote in 1914). Unlike Kohut or Kernberg, Lacan did not consider narcissism as pathological per se. Instead, he presented narcissism as the irreducible and atemporal (spatial) feature of human identity. Rather than attribute the persistence of narcissistic wounds in an adult to "bad" mirroring or insufficient parental idealization, Lacan located narcissistic difficulties in a lack of psychic separation from the (m)Other and the resultant incapacity to submit to the metaphorical reality principle: the Law of the Name-of-the-Father, or the Oedipal structure. The key to his theory goes back to the idea of prematuration at birth. Because there is an inherent "lack" in being, narcissism is the necessary assumption of an *alien* ego, taken on in the erotic captivation of the infant by the image of the other. During the mirror stage the infant wants to possess the mother because she provides an object of constancy and continuity that do not reside within. Hence, *identification* with a particular object provides the narcissistic kernel of any identity that will contain a mixture of "bad" and "good" objects or effects. But this identification is secondary; the drive toward object orientation as a means of compensation is primary. Still, just as the earliest form of the narcissistic ego subsequently reflects the paradise of a child's first loves, any *moi* will be elaborated throughout life by added layers of love objects who serve as ego ideals and are chosen in the image of early relinquished objects, even those one might consider "bad."

By rejecting Freud's idea of autoeroticism (primary narcissism) and extending the scope of his concept of secondary narcissism, Lacan made identification the means by which an ego (o^1) is formed and narcissism its foundation. In "The Ego and the Id" (1923) Freud described the character of the ego as "a precipitate of abandoned object-cathexes and [which] contains the history of those object choices" (*SE*, 19:29). But, Freud maintains, a healthy ego, ideally, will fend off those influences. According to Lacan, because Freud lacked our current knowledge about ethnology and the role of mimesis in animal behavior, he abandoned his insights about the importance of narcissistic identification in ego development. The pre-mirror, fantasmatic merging with images is what Lacan has called primary identification; his secondary identification is the mirror-stage fusion with others as objects (Freud's secondary narcissism). Lacan therefore views Freud's secondary narcissism, with its attributes of permanence as manifest in ego ideals (others), as the basic process of humanization, as well as the cornerstone of human interrelations. It lies at the heart of all social exchange—well in advance of that marriage exchange out of which Lévi-Strauss would construct society.

The critic Anthony Wilden has pointed out that by reinterpreting Freud's concept of ego ideals as the alter ego of the *moi* Lacan was led to make "more and more explicit statements derived from the Kleinian observations of children" (*LS*, p. 267). Lacan thought that by pushing back the limits within which we can see the subjective function of identification operate, Klein showed us the primacy and centrality of the body as the real and fantasmatic origin of identification and symbolization (Sheridan, *Ecrits*, pp. 20–21). But the pre-specular body to which Lacan refers has no sense of its boundaries. Here the "objects of Desire" (sucking, excrement, the voice, the gaze) loom as the primary imagistic and sensual matrices that will help the neonate orient its body in the world. Lacan's dynamic picture replaces Klein's static one with the fluidity or flux of perceptual experience and stresses again the link between object incorporation (or fusion) and man's specific prematuration. By postulating a phase of structuring prior to Klein's conception of internalized good and bad, of whole- and part-objects, Lacan emphasized the crucial importance of the ambiguity of inside/outside, boundary/non-boundary distinctions which underlies the process of introjection and projection itself.[76]

But, according to Laplanche and Pontalis, Lacan's subject of pre-mirror primary identification has its prototype, even before Klein's stress on objects, in the ego of Freud's "The Id and the Ego," where the ego is first and foremost a body ego or projection of a surface, as well as a surface entity (*Vocabulaire*, p. 81). Indeed, in refutation of those critics who consider that Lacan ignores biology and sexuality, one must heed Lacan's repeated insistence that *being* is above all body (*Séminaire* XX, p. 127). By this, however, Lacan does not mean instinctual stages, impersonal drive, or witness of a parental sexual scene. In moving primary narcissism away from Freud's solipsistic notion of it, Lacan redefined this as the corporal image that the subject evolves of itself. It follows, therefore, that every person has already been libidinized from the start of life.

A coefficient of this primary eroticization of the body is aggressiveness. While many students of human behavior consider aggressiveness innate, Lacan finds it to be one more proof of a pre-mirror building up of identity from the outside. Aggressive intentions are linked to the earliest *imagos* of body disintegration, well in advance of mirror-stage identification with a totum. "There is a specific relation here between man and his own body that is manifested in a series of social practices—from rites involving tattooing, incision, and circumcision in primitive societies to what, in advanced societies, might be called the Procrustean arbitrariness of fashion" (Sheridan, *Ecrits*, p. 11).[77] Lacan has located the reappearance of prespecular fragmentary images—such as bursting, dismemberment, and so forth—in the play of children between two and five years of age, and later in dreams, fantasies, painting, and poetry, as well as in sadistic crimes and perversions. In his review of Lacan's thought, Wollheim has described Lacan's theory of aggressiveness as "the infant's reaction to early mirror-derived images of its body. . . . Aggression is the infant's response to the tensions, threats, and, above all, confusions attendant upon primary identification" ("The Cabinet," p. 39). Wollheim is confusing primary identification and the mirror stage here. In the first six months of life the infant is unaware of a specular relationship to the world. Only with the secondary identification of the mirror stage are archaic images and effects of primary identification linked to mirror recognition dynamics. From the start of mirror-stage awareness, aggressiveness or "infant rage" seems to me to be a response to loss of constancy or continuity (i.e., psychic potency). Later in life aggressiveness will become a reaction to the loss of self-esteem or prestige.

After the mirror stage, aggressiveness is more specifically related to separation/recognition dynamics and is at the base of the paranoiac structure of the human subject. Herein Lacan has made a leap from his early work on the phenomenology of experience to what he calls a formula of equivalence: the equivalence of aggressiveness as a part of the libido and paranoid states. Aggressiveness can harken back to primary, corporal narcissism, then, or can be a coefficient of secondary narcissism that functions by secondary identification with others (ego ideals). Secondary narcissism permits a person to form a libidinal relationship to the world in general (*Séminaire* I, p. 144). It also serves to appease aggressiveness through narcissistic identification: self-love displaced onto an-other.

This picture may become somewhat clearer after a brief look at Lacan's four patterns of psychoanalytic narcissistic transference, which Martha N. Evans has described in an article in the *Psychoanalytic Quarterly* (1979). First, an analysand identifies with the analyst in terms of his or her own identity. The emphasis is on likeness and the analyst is perceived as a counterpart (like Kohut's twinship transference). Second, the analytic confrontation aims to reactivate the mirror-stage splitting, that is, to break down the ideal unity or mirror *imago* that Lacan equates with secondary identification and that was initially counterposed between six and eighteen months to the boundaryless, disconnected sense of body and experience of the pre-mirror stage. In this phase of transference, the analyst is cast as an ideal by the analysand and identified with the Other(A) which, as Schneiderman points out, Lacan has described as the "supposed *subject* of knowing" (*Returning*, p. vii). Evans compares this second stage to Kohut's idealizing transference. In the third stage the ideal image of the analyst should be seen as an illusion, the realization of which parallels a disintegration of the analysand's supposition of "knowing." This, Lacan metaphorically terms "death," for the unified *moi*—the subject of narcissism or the ideal ego—gives a person a sense of "self" cohesion. Any unraveling of the strands that went into weaving that identity as a conviction of "being" causes a de-being of being: a sense of fragmenting.

The primordial *moi* is the scaffolding of individuality that was formed through primary identifications with images, objects, and others as a strategy of defense: to block the apprehension (splitting sensation) which comes from the difficulty of situating the infant body in the world. Secondary—i.e., mirror-stage—identification brings an intimation of unity and continuity via the human *Gestalt*. When the other (analyst) reflects an ideal unity—supports one's *moi* identifications—the narcissistic slope of the *moi* is gratified. When the ideal is shattered, the avatar of aggressiveness arises and shows itself in projected blame, disenchantment, intimations of fragmentation, and so forth. The goal of aggressiveness here is to protect the *moi* from perceiving the tenuous fragility of its own formation. Lacan has frequently drawn attention to the danger implicit in any disintegration of the *moi* by reason of its close relationship to death; the *moi* is a point of *recoupement* between the common discourse of everyday speech (in which a subject is caught and "alienated") and his or her psychological reality (*Séminaire* II, pp. 245–46). The insistence of the *moi* on retaining its (fictional) unity of individual perception constitutes what psychoanalysts call resistance. From another perspective, however, one might call this stubbornness a survival insistence (the repetition which Lacan has placed "beyond the pleasure principle").

The fourth stage entails recognition of the *moi*'s source in the Other(A). The French psychoanalyst Moustapha Safouan has said the nicest definition one can give the end of analysis is "death's death," for it is a matter of an invitation to live beyond that which fixed one in the identical (Schneiderman, *Returning*, pp. 166–67). "Knowledge" or recognition of the unconscious is the path to relative cure or symptom relief. The transference is not really, then, to the analyst, who only serves as a guide to the learning of the signifiers in the Other's discourse: the analysand must learn the alienness of the Other(A). The speaking subject (*je*) conveys the identity drama of the *moi* (Who am I? How do others see me?). But inasmuch as "saying" and "being" are not the same things, ineffability dwells at the level of consciousness. Clarity and "truth" reside in the unconscious Other(A), where the discrete articulations of one's identity exist as "pure signifiers" concerning birth, love, procreation, and death. The unconscious meanings attached to these signifiers appear at the surface as hieroglyphics. Even though an analysand may, therefore, at one stage take the analyst to be her or his alter ego (specular ego ideal), the other in the mirror can never be a relationship of identity, but merely a dialectical experience of resemblance and hence a replay of mirror-stage discordance. In this context, narcissism and identification emerge as clearly different functions (actually at war) for, as Wilden points out: "It is always a question of each trying to take the other's place" (*LS*, p. 168). Others give identificatory shape to a *moi* that, paradoxically, seeks the meaning of its own alienation through others' (ego ideals) and in language. If an analysis is to succeed, then, aggressiveness (that is, negative transference) *must* occur, since it is the initial "knot" of the analytic drama (Sheridan, *Ecrits*, p. 14).

Tension, anxiety, conflict, ambiguity, and oscillation characterize all human behavior. They have their explanation in the nonpeaceful coexistence of the specular *moi* of narcissism, aware of but divided from the Other(A) from which it was formed, and forced to verify itself through others, despite the Real flux and instability of human response amid changing patterns of identifications and events. This quest is undertaken, moreover, through the indirect and yet further alienating path of language. Lacan's *moi* is most appropriately a narcissistic structure, then, since Narcissus died of his failure to embark on the quest for alterity (i.e., Echo).[78] "I have succeeded there where paranoia fails," Freud said, a statement which Lacan interprets to mean that when the subject's roots in the Other(A) become apparent, an opening can be made through the speaking *je* by which one can interrogate the paranoid—i.e., dialectical—instance of knowledge which inhabits us. Narcissism therefore holds the personality together, but its negative effects of alienation, rivalry, grandiosity, and aggressiveness can only be perceptually mediated in the realm of Real event. At such times, the social subject of consciousness may glimpse the movements of the narcissistic subject of identity, briefly rendering it an object of awareness. It is fitting, then, that Lacan should describe his analytic praxis as a space in which to induce a controlled paranoia: "What I have called paranoiac knowledge is shown . . . to correspond in its more or less archaic forms to certain critical moments that mark the history of man's mental genesis, each representing a stage in objectifying identification" (Sheridan, *Ecrits*, p. 17).

Lacan views secondary identification with others as a replay of primary identification with the mother. The former is, in consequence, an intentional mechanism for objectifying the narcissistic *moi* both in its primary and secondary characteristics. As stated at the outset, Lacan's picture of narcissism is more comprehensive than those theories which make it only a pathology. We have also seen that it provides a conceptual link between fragmentation and unity, between relationships and language. And this makes any use of language dialectically charged and dependent on an out-of-sight meaning system. In this way, Lacan's theory obviates the contradictory contentions of Freud that (1) narcissistic love is felt toward someone who represents what the lover once was, and (2) mature love is felt toward parental substitutes. These views would make all relational love rigidly role bound and necessarily out of step with current thought in the human sciences. Even Kohut's picture of primary narcissism as reflected in "object hunger," isolation, dependency, or low self-esteem—in opposition to realistic self-esteem—is less descriptive of a "character disorder" than typical of any human person's propensities under certain kinds of stress. Lacan, of course, has a theory of neurosis that we shall duly consider (Chapter 5) and here narcissism does play a role, insofar as neurosis entails an imbalance between the subject and the Other(A). But in Lacan's epistemology one can never be "rid" of the narcissistic *moi*, or integrate it into a whole "self," since this would be tantamount to being rid of the source of identity. It would also be tantamount to being rid of any active unconscious in the sense that the *moi* points "beyond" to its own formative (and informative) origins. One can, however, become intermittently aware of one's own *moi* and its role in recognition dynamics and thus gain a measure of freedom in psychic distance from the Other(A). One can rarely *not* depend on others, however, to validate one's narcissism and point the way to the "truth" in the Other(A).

Answering Freud's quandary about the source of energy at the service of the reality principle, Lacan replaced Freud's biological concept with "narcissistic passion" (Sheridan, *Ecrits*, p. 21). The goal of this energy is the interaction with others, which is intended to assure the *moi* of its value. In *Séminaire* XI (p. 219), Lacan described the object of love (its aim or goal) as identification with the object (person) of love. To be desired is the object of love, more basic than the desire to be "made love to" (Sheridan, *Ecrits*, p. 19).

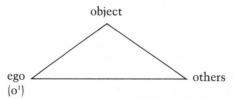

But because the *moi* does not reflect upon itself, it does not know that its goal is recognition: in other words, that to be desired is the libidinal object, not a person per se (*Séminaire* XI, p. 220). Elsewhere Lacan points out that a child does not depend so much on its mother, as on her love (Sheridan, *Ecrits*, p. 198). In such a context Desire derived from lack (*manque-à-être* or want-of-being) elicits Desire as exchange. Consequently, others function as screens onto which the identity drama is projected ("I am . . .") via the "play" (*jeu*) of prestige, bearing, shame, rivalry, and so on—the supposedly insignificant stuff of everyday life (Sheridan, *Ecrits*, p. 307). But though Lacan sees natural maturation as dependent on a cultural mediation (via the pacifying function of ego ideals), others alone cannot terminate or resolve the identity quest (Sheridan, *Ecrits*, pp. 5–6). The identity question is endlessly repeated as a circular message from the Other (A) discourse ("I am. . . . Am I not?") to the Other(A), via the other. This process is constantly "in play" in the order of the Real. From such a perspective, any psychoanalytic theory that hypothesizes ideal "ego mastery" through genital (object) love or integrative "wholeness" is simply a self-deluding myth, a compensatory fiction of ontological wholeness (*Séminaire* XI, p. 216). The "I" can achieve a certain balance and harmony through love. But in the Lacanian intrasubjective dynamic between the *moi* and the Other's Desire and their refraction through the distortion of language and via the intersubjectivity of relationship, this balance will be like the eternal ebb and flow of the sea.[79]

The philosopher Paul Ricoeur has stressed that Freud's concept of narcissism points to the drive that exists in place of reflection (the *Cogito*). Generally speaking, Lacan developed this theory, calling narcissistic knowledge and endeavor a false or aborted *Cogito* (Wilden, *LS*, p. 527). In other words, "truth" does not lie along the paths of introspection or reflection. By viewing narcissism as the force behind human drive, but by locating its fuel in the Desire to be desired or for *recognition*, Lacan taught that *cognition* (as a philosophical dilemma of mind) is governed by narcissism and Desire. Thus, given the scope of Lacan's theory, it would be an error to equate thoughtlessly his narcissistic *moi* with Kohut's grandiose, archaic self, since the two psychoanalysts conceptualize the human subject quite differently. There is no whole "self" in Lacan's epistemology. Kohut depicted the "self" as an image or structure in the mind, whereas for Lacan the *moi* is one of the constituents of mind (Kohut, *Analysis*, p. xv). Although it is also the source of grandiosity and infantile identity fixations, Lacan's *moi* is far more than an infantile, archaic form. As the kernel of identity and subjectivity, Lacan's *moi* builds a bridge to others, plays a role in governing intentionality, and is the purveyor of one's view of reality within one's conscious life, as well as the agent of drive (*Trieb*) (see Chapter 2). Moreover, while Lacan does not abandon drive theory—although he reinterprets it—Kohut does. Lacan's *moi* is, therefore, dynamically engaged, but Kohut's archaic "self" is a static entity buried in a remote past. Kohut never succeeds in defining this archaic "self," nor does he link it to effects other than parenting (mirroring). Whereas Kohut equates the mother with the archaic mirror image, and the father with the later idealized self, Lacan refused to view the psyche's formation in terms of a simplistic, A gives rise to B causality, explaining it instead in terms of mathematics and symbols. The early mother is internalized as the source of one's own narcissism, prior to the acquisition of individual boundaries, while the father's subsequent, symbolic role is that of teaching these boundaries—he is a limit-setter. As a result, the father is later both feared and emulated, since his presence has taught the infant about laws and taboos. Structurally speaking, woman becomes identified with sameness, and man with difference. It is to a more exhaustive discussion of the Lacanian *moi* that we must now turn.

The *Moi*

As the unconscious subject of identifications and narcissism, the *moi* assumes a place of privilege over the speaking subject, rendering the latter opaque and discontinuous. Lacan has said that his own return to the unconscious ego as center and common measure is *not* implied in Freud's discourse. On the contrary, the further the reader advances in the third stage of Freud's oeuvre (after 1932), the more the conscious ego is portrayed as a mirage or a sum of identifications (*Séminaire* II, p. 244). By emending this Freudian line of thought and by rendering the identificatory ego unconscious—i.e., unaware of itself—Lacan went beyond the notion of a synthesizing ego function and beyond the proverbial pleasure principle to what actually is "beyond": the common discourse where the *moi* (a composite of ego) shows up as repetitive themes (*Séminaire* II, p. 244). In his 1957–58 Seminar Lacan elaborated this theory. It has been published as the essay "The Subversion of the subject and the dialectic of desire in the Freudian unconscious" (Sheridan, *Ecrits*, pp. 292–325). But Lacan's picture of the *moi* is not easy to grasp, in part because he makes no behavioral separation between conscious and unconscious surfaces, although the conscious and unconscious are fundamentally separate and belong to different orders. One cannot therefore simply dismiss the *moi* as the unconscious and the *je* as consciousness, because both participate in both systems.

Some commentators have tried to clarify these ambiguities by a chronological presentation of Lacan's evolution or by a source study of thinkers who have influenced him.[80] But to "understand" Lacan, one would actually do better to immerse oneself in the hermetic, baroque style which he has purposely created as a metaphor of his thought. The subject of reality reconstruction or subjective perception—the *moi*—is elusive, kaleidoscopic, and evanescent, whereas the subject of meaning and speech—the *je*—seeks to "translate" the *moi* while adhering to cultural stipulations. To convey this idea of two modes of meaning fighting to occupy the same space, Lacan frustrates his interlocutors by stylistically holding meaning in suspension, instead of appeasing their human propensity for unity, resolution, and easy answers.[81] When *Cogito*-style definitions are just out of reach, Lacan finds his intended effect in a kind of pointillism in which intellect, affect, knowledge, and so forth are simply means for coping with a split in the subject and the resultant insatiable Desire (*manque-à-être*), which destines humans to be questing, lacking creatures.

As the nonverbal agent of specularity and identifications, the *moi* leads the game of human interaction. But it is essentially in an unstable posture. Subjects reconstitute themselves for each other, Lacan says, by exchanging ego (*moi*) through language (*je*) as symbols. Paradoxical though it may sound, Lacan's *moi* is therefore structured and not chaotic, dependent and not independent, human and not biological, intentional and not aimless. But it is inherently paranoid because, given the specular logic peculiar to it, the *moi* can only experience itself in relation to external images and to the gaze of others. It follows, therefore, that the *moi* cannot be reduced to its first lived experience. It began as a dialectical structure and, throughout life, each metamorphosis and successive identification with others again challenge its delimitations (Sheridan, *Ecrits*, pp. 19–20). It is possible therefore to say—another paradox—that the subject's identity is both fixed and continually *en jeu*. Put another way, the two major aspects of the *moi* are (1) the formal stagnation or fixation of feelings and images, which constitute the subject and its objects (others) with attributes of permanence, identity, and substantiality; and (2) the inherent gaps, ambiguities, and scars in the *moi*, which surface in the speaking subject and throw its apparent, although illusory and contradictory unity into question (Sheridan, *Ecrits*, p. 17). It is comprehensible from this perspective that adult maturation will not depend on innate (i.e., genetic or neurological) and instinctual (i.e., oral, anal, genital) developmental sequences, but on the cultural mediation of others (Sheridan, *Ecrits*, pp. 5–6). Whether a person clings rigidly to early identity fixations or gains enough intellectual or mental distance to observe and modify them will determine the history of that person's life.

The structuring of the elemental *moi* in the pre-mirror and mirror stages has already been discussed. The precise manner of this structuring can be subsumed under two general principles: the gaze (*regard*) and what Lacan calls "scripting" (*l'écriture*). Scripting is the effect of language, made up of voice, sounds, and the phonemic chain. It leaves traces, tropes, and figures—perceptual residue—the impact of which combines with visual matter and identifications to fix an unconscious text that transcends *moi* fixations and delimitations. Although both the gaze and the voice are intangible and abstract, they are palpably material in their effects (the fifth dimension now discovered by mathematicians) and in the associations they catalyze in the infant. Lacan's originality lies in his proposition that the gaze and voice are assimilated as part-objects (*objet a* or mental representations) even before they are connected to the mirror-stage experience of identification (where the voice and gaze are attached to particular persons). Woven into a primordial representational layer, the gaze or voice can later return in dreams, art, or psychosis—or in other experiences in which the *moi*'s unity is unraveled—as disembodied fragments. In such situations the gaze is disconnected from the eye as seeing and the voice from hearing. They become, in other words, silent witnesses to a solipsistic discourse: the pre–mirror-stage infant gazes, stares, explores with its eyes—and the gaze itself is among the objects or images that it takes in. "In our relationship to things," Lacan says, "as constituted by the path of vision and ordered in the figures of representation, something glides, passes, transmits itself from stage to stage, in order always to be in some degree eluded there—It is that which is called the *regard*" (*Séminaire* XI, p. 70). Existentialist philosophers demonstrated that the *regard* is always "out there." Lacan connects it to dreams and shows that it is also always "in here": the gaze of the Other(A).

In his First Seminar (1953–54) Lacan described the dream as a way of remembering one's relationship to objects; a sign of exhaustion of regressions, and thus a threshold to the Real; a sign, therefore, of restructuring one's relationship to objects. To know the *moi* (the exceedingly difficult task of seeing one's subjectivity as an object), one must be taught to read backward in a topological (spatial) sense, but in the immediacy of present time. In this Seminar Lacan seemed mostly preoccupied with an idea of the dream as a manifestation of the reconstruction of a subject's story *in the present*, a temporal rewriting of history (p. 20). In the dream the rewriting refers to the gaze, which Lacan finds in the place of the unconscious code: the Other(A). We should recall that the human subject was prefigured in primordial forms, even before its physical objectification in the dialectic of mirror-stage identification with the mother, and before language conferred on it its communicative function as a speaking subject in the wide world. The purest testimonial to this is in dreams where objects appear in an enigmatic text. In the dream the "I" shows its component parts, shows that it has always already been somebody. In putting forth this theory, Lacan answers Maurice Merleau-Ponty and other phenomenologists who claim that we have no right to "guess at" the subjective—which we cannot quantify and on which we cannot reflect. Distinguishing between the visible and the invisible, Merleau-Ponty wonders how we can comprehend that alter ego, the "other than me who is the reflected I reflected on, for myself who reflects."[82] Lacan's answer is that one can only grasp elusive fragments and that the "strange contingency" (his phrase) is not between the visible and invisible, but in a disintegration of unity in the subject.

In the dream a person is no longer subjected to the *regard* of the conscious world, which can offer comfort, judgment, seduction, and so on. Instead, the gaze of the Other(A) both sees and shows, ensuring that the subject does not grasp itself as it does in conscious thought. Awake, one is such-and-such for others; asleep, one is such-and-such for no one. Lacan interprets this to mean that the primitiveness of the *regard* is marked in the dream, where the roots of identity and essence are linked to seeing as gaze rather than seeing as eye, and therefore show themselves as prior to intersubjective (mirror-stage) imperatives (*Séminaire* XI, p. 72). When Tchoang-tseu dreams that he is a butterfly, for example, he seizes some root of his own identity: what he *was*, what he is in his essence, and that through which he is Tchoang-tseu. Awake, he is Tchoang-tseu for others; asleep, a butterfly for no one. Asleep he does not wonder if, when he is Tchoang-tseu awake, he is not a butterfly in the process of dreaming. Viewed in this way, dreams are the home of the primordial source of being in terms of anteriority and narcissism (*Séminaire* XI, pp. 72–73). But dreams are not the unconscious; they are distortions of a Real unconscious (Other) part of being as it regresses to the level of perception.

But how can one really believe that a *moi* exists? Wilden has cited Leclaire's description of the *moi*'s function as formation, information, deformation (*LS*, p. 171). Lacan teaches his interlocutors that the *moi reveals* itself in the present speaking through the *je* (the S of Schéma L) by which it is not recognized (*Séminaire* XX, p. 108). It is more enlightening, then, to ask *toward whom?* a discourse is directed, since characteristic intersubjective modes of the *moi* in adult relations are identificatory. These latter are spontaneous fusions or aversions that cause the *moi* to slide frantically (*glissement*) in its rejection or acceptance of the other, or sometimes in an ambivalent alternation. In its intrasubjective relationship to the Other(A), *moi* discourse is that dimension in experience which is reflected in Desire, boredom, confinement, revolt, prayer, sleeplessness, and panic. "It" or this Other-thing "thinks rather badly, but it does think. For it is in these terms that it announces the unconscious to us: thoughts which, if their laws are not quite the same as those of our everyday thoughts, however noble or vulgar they may be, are perfectly articulated" (Sheridan, *Ecrits*, pp. 192–93). Elsewhere Lacan says: "One can see to what the language of the ego [*moi*] is reduced: intuitive illumination, recollective command, the retorsive aggressivity of the verbal echo. Let us add what comes back to it from the automatic detritus of common discourse: the educative cramming and delusional *ritornello*, modes of communication that perfectly reproduce objects scarcely more complicated than this desk, a feed-back construction for the first, for the second a gramophone record, preferably scratched in the right place" (Sheridan, *Ecrits*, p. 139).

The *Moi* in Its Field of Relations

We have said that narcissism and aggressiveness are correlatives in Lacanian thought.[83] They first make up the formal structure of the mirror-stage *moi* in a presubjective period (Sheridan, *Ecrits*, pp. 19–20). Prior to speech and the birth of subjectivity the *moi* has become characterized by conflict and tension because it depends on specular recognition from another for its own existence and perpetuation. In consequence, the primordial coalescence of the *moi* occurs in a state of aggressive rivalry, which may be formalized as follows (from Wilden, *LS*, p. 173).

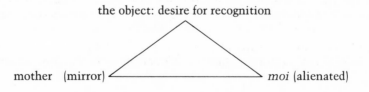

the object: desire for recognition

mother (mirror) ← → *moi* (alienated)

Given this state of aggressive conflict, it is hardly surprising that Lacan found Hegel's so-called master/slave dialectic useful in describing his *moi*. The truth Lacan found in this dialectic was a radical description of the human subject's aggressiveness. Lacan's Schéma L sets out the intra- and intersubjective dialectic of narcissism and aggressiveness in terms of identificatory interaction between (1) the *moi* and the Other(A), and (2) the *moi* and others. In Hegel's master/slave conflict the struggle revolved around pure prestige: the slave's goal was to become the master by cancelling him out; the master only remained such in reference to a slave who must by definition be interminably defeated (Wilden, *LS*, p. 79). The French analyst equated Hegel's master with the Lacanian Other(A)—the locus from which the subject speaks and desires throughout life, but in a distorted translation of Other(A) data (Sheridan, *Ecrits*, p. 198). Viewed in this way, the *je* is an object of the Other's discourse

$$(S \diagdown \diagup O).$$

Coextensive with language, yet desiring from within, the *je* mistakenly thinks it can represent its own totality by designating itself in a statement (Sheridan, *Ecrits*, p. 315). This is the pertinence of the master/slave model: the speaking subject is oppressed from within by Other(A) messages as well as by identity fixations of the *moi*. The latter is paradoxically fashioned in reference to—and in rivalry with—its own Other(A), but obliged to wait for recognition and judgment from others in the world outside. Man is, therefore, inclined to a whole range of aggressive behavior: from envy and jealousy, persecution mania, identification with an aggressor, and truly aggressive acts, to mortal negation of self or other (Lemaire, *Lacan*, p. 181).

Freud described conflict as arising from the libidinal push for pleasure/gratification up against the demands of reality. But Lacan placed an intrinsically conflictual, frustrated, and potentially paranoid subject at the surface of language. "This ego," Lacan says, "whose strength our theorists now define by its capacity to bear frustration, is frustration in its essence. Not frustration of a Desire of the subject, but frustration by an object in which his Desire is alienated and which the more it is elaborated, the more profound the alienation from his *jouissance* becomes for the subject" (Sheridan, *Ecrits*, p. 42). By "this ego" I interpret Lacan to mean *moi*, which as an object of the Other—not a subject of speech—is limited to a few nar-

cissistic fixations and aggressive coordinates. Lacan's *moi* was originally constituted by an identification with another as whole (body)
object in the mirror stage. Gradually acquiring an "identity," the
moi is a narcissistic subject that is perpetually threatened by its own
Otherness to itself. Rather than the agent of strength it assumes itself to be, the subject is victim of the illusion of strength. Logically
enough, Lacan saw Hegel's struggle to the death between master and
slave as the ultimate theory of aggressiveness in human ontology:
the admission that death is included in the narcissistic *Bildung*. But
because the speaking *je* is weighed down by "messages" from the
Other(A) and limited by *moi* objectifications, it is too involved in
acting out this drama at the level of relationship to be aware of its
own subjugation. In any specular interaction between persons, instead of finding mastery—a neo-Freudian, synthesizing function of
the ego—we see that any *moi* (o') constitutes others, its objects (o),
by a law of imaginary reduplication and—sadly enough—in a relation of hostile exclusion that structures the dual relation of o' to o'
(i.e., between the *moi* of person A and person B). Lacan says that this
apportionment never constitutes even a kinetic harmony, but is established on the permanent "you or me" of a war (Sheridan, *Ecrits*,
p. 138).

In strict contradiction to Anglo-American trends in the study of
ego psychology, which proclaim the ego to be infinitely pliable,
adaptable, or capable of synthesis and integration, Lacan depicts the
moi as a formal, limited, and irreducible structure. Seen in this light,
the *moi* conforms with the register of any person's experience. It *can*
for this reason be fixed in a formalism based on recognition needs
and their resultant narcissistic and aggressive intentionality (Sheridan, *Ecrits*, p. 21). Made like an onion, the *moi* is geometrical and
spatial. It is constituted by layers of successive identifications or fusions, by which it then constitutes reality and its objects (*Séminaire*
I, p. 194). In conscious life the *moi* appears as persona, role, or appearance rather than as consciousness or even subjectivity. While adhering to language, the *moi* makes implicit demands for response
and recognition, in which statements of opinion and manifestations of knowledge are inverted questions of identity posed to the
Other(A) via the other ("Who am I really? What am I to/of you?").
The dialectic nature of all dialogue parallels this evocative aspect of
language use. In Lacan's epistemology, the *moi* ensures that there is
always more in language (an insistence or intentional pressure) than
what is being said. The *moi* makes any form of discourse as overdetermined as does the dream or neurotic symptom.

The passionate organization of the *moi* is in direct proportion to its function of providing cement to being and of assigning value to words and experiences. In this sense it is roughly equivalent to what we normally call emotions and hence the source of dogmatism, pretension, grandiosity, and so on. One may, therefore, look at Lacan's *moi* as a nexus of unifying and moralizing tendencies. The Lacanian psychoanalyst Octave Mannoni has written an essay on the *moi* as source of belief and mystification. Hypothesizing its reflection in the commonplace phrase "I know . . . but all the same" (*Je sais . . . mais quand-même*), he points out that the issue of belief raises the problem of the *moi*'s paradoxical connections to truth.[84] The adult subject of meaning and speech (*je*) "knows" there is no Santa Claus or Easter Bunny, but most people want their children to believe in them "all the same." Why? The fantasies and myths of childhood make up *moi* identificatory truth, but they can only be justified—i.e., retained and reintegrated—through one's children. The original source or *raison d'être* of these fantastic myths would be explicable by societal efforts to understand the mysteries of being, as well as the genesis of humankind. By this criterion Lacanian *savoir* is the sum of prejudices which composes a person's knowledge.[85] But "knowledge" here refers to the Other's discourse—the Real *subject* of knowing—or *le savoir supposé sujet*—which forms the foundation of any conscious knowledge. Everything emanates from the Other(A) in the sense that this discourse feeds into *je* language as a kind of eternally active subterranean emitting station, which sends out to others, in inverted form, the messages about individuality that it wishes to receive. The reflection of one's own *moi* from others is a virtual reflection and, in this sense, the human subject is a circular body that remains always equal to itself (*Séminaire* II, p. 282).

According to Lacan, ego psychologists err by taking the *moi* (what they call the ego) to be a reality or something integrative that holds the planet (i.e., person) together. Instead, he says, it is others in Real situations who enable the *moi* to reconstitute itself continually. These others, therefore, hold the human subject together by their recognition and reflection. We cannot make the error of reducing Lacan's *moi* to some whole or unified culmination of the preverbal stage, then. The French critic Julia Kristéva has drawn attention to the *moi* as an amalgam that surfaces in adult life to sow difference, fragmentation, and discontinuity in a language-unified field. Lacan himself has stressed that the *moi* exists on two different planes: that of the mirror (o), and the one which he calls the "wall of language" (*je*) (*Séminaire* II, p. 255). Because of the "wall of language," there is no transparent image of identity or reflexivity in oneself but instead a relationship of profound Otherness (*Séminaire* II, p. 276). Beyond the "wall of language" a person is captive of mental images that also block vision of "who" one is. Beyond the mirror—others—and beyond language, Lacan located the void (or emptiness) beyond the image.[86]

The relationship between *moi* and *je* calls into question the issue of "truth," much as their source in the Other(A) has led Lacan to a critique of the source and function of knowledge (*savoir*). In Lacan's thought "truth" is not to be found in the place of traditional knowledge—facts, theories, history—for these merely contain so many ever changing doxa, socioconventional codes, and interpretations of events. "Truth" is to be found, in part, in the *je*'s recognition of the fictional structuration of the *moi*. The *moi* inserts itself as the affective dimension in language and relationship, becoming recognizable as an object, principally in terms of repeated identity themes. When the *je* is thrust into suspension or vacillation (that is, when unified meaning is moved aside), the *je* can de-objectify itself by objectifying its own *moi* (*Séminaire* XI, p. 223). The dialectical symbolism by which Lacan characterizes this dynamic construes the *je* in reference to a two-object topology: (1) its own *moi* as object, and (2) the other of relationship as an alter ego which leads back to the Other (with whom a subject unconsciously "communicates").

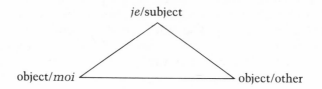

Paradoxically, as soon as the *je* disengages itself from the *moi* and sees its alien source in the Other(A), the *moi* assumes the status of a mirage and gradually becomes no more than one element in the object relations of a subject (*Séminaire* I, pp. 218, 229). The key to relative psychic health and self-knowledge lies in the direction of *je* de-objectification from *moi* fixations. Such distance can bring symptom relief and some degree of "truth." In the ideal analysis, or in the ideal analyst, the *moi* would be absent. But this ideal remains virtual, says Lacan, for there is no subject without a *moi* (*Séminaire* II, p. 287).

Lacan has modified phenomenological and psychoanalytic concepts of object relations by differentiating and restating the three modes of human relationships: subject/object; object/object; subject/subject (Wilden, *LS*, p. 175). By dividing the subject into two meaning systems—that of relationships (objects) and that of language—Lacan can speak of the being of language (*je*) as the nonbeing of objects (*moi*). The *moi* reflects the objectifications in personality and also objectifies others, i.e., perceives others in terms of its own mnemic representations and creates them in its own image. It follows, then, that Lacan will portray the speaking *je* as outside the object (*Séminaire* I, p. 218). The *je* may, nonetheless, apprehend its own *moi* in fragments and in objects, in nonsense, dreams, witticisms, and so forth (*Séminaire* XI, p. 192). In this way, the *je* can learn, can differentiate, can restructure its *moi* (which is merely a relation in a system), and can gain a measure of freedom.

Lacan therefore refuses existentialist or phenomenological (metaphysical) conceptions of subjectivity, with their implicit departure from the postulate of a human nature. There is no human nature, Lacan says, neither collective nor innate. But there is structure and process; and these are universal and formalizable. The French philosopher Jean-Marie Benoist concludes, after Lacan, that "the image of the individual conceived as an independent subject, a source of meaning, finds itself relativized, the term of a relation, an element interdependent on others, in the web of a network. At the heart of each structure, some behaviors of alliance and relationship find themselves determined or rather conditioned by a code and its underlying rules—which signifies that the subject does not choose them, even within the framework of a fundamental or original choice that the existentialists called the 'project'" (Benoist, *Révolution*, p. 117). The speaking, conscious *je* of existentialist choice and phenomenological perception is, by Lacanian standards, delimited by unconscious Desires and *moi* narcissism and, therefore, a fettered subject that only possesses the illusion of autonomy and of infinite access to choice and comprehension.

Freud's celebrated formula—translated into English as "Where id was, there shall ego be" (*Wo Es war, soll Ich werden*)—is usually interpreted to mean that psychic health and integration consist in replacing the pleasure principle (id) by the reality principle (ego). Lacan has recast this formula to read: "Where the *moi* was, there shall *je* place itself" (*Là où c'était, peut-on dire, là où s'était, voudrions-nous faire qu'on entendît, c'est mon devoir que je vienne à être*) (Sheridan, *Ecrits*, pp. 128–29). In other words, *je* (S) has become aware of its broader dimensions. As stated earlier (p. 12),

Lacan says the *Ich* must be where the *Es* was (*Séminaire* II, p. 288). Consequently, if one were to reduce Lacan's *moi* to Freud's id and assume that psychoanalytic cure lay in eradicating the subject of identity in favor of that of speech, one would miss Lacan's basic point. It is true that the *je's* ultimate and total refusal to recognize the alien and fictional nature of the *moi* (which it represents) can result in lack of individuation, psychic pain, and—at the limit—lead to mental illness or suicide.[87] But such truth is difficult to reach, since the *je*, even when in doubt, believes itself to be one and the same as the persona or role that actually betrays the presence of a *moi*.

Throughout his text, Lacan denounces the common illusion that identifies the conscious self with the knowledge conveyed from the unconscious Other(A), and then attributes to the conscious subject a reality in the order of being (Lemaire, *Lacan*, p. 180). For the "true" subject—albeit fictional—is not centered in the perception/consciousness system nor organized by the reality principle. Instead, what the conscious subject takes as its own autonomous perceptions is a function of denial and misrecognition (Sheridan, *Ecrits*, p. 6). Lacan located "being" in language, and nonbeing on the side of objects. Beyond the (neo-Freudian) ego is an unconscious subject of "truth" which speaks, unknown to the speaking *je*, and to the alienated, objectified *moi*. This subject is the Other(A), which Freud recognized in the death instinct. Lacan joined the Other(A) and the death instinct by his concept of the phallic injunction to separation (and ensuing loss) (*Séminaire* II, p. 204). Lacan once described the locus of a tendency toward suicide as residing in the Imaginary knot that constitutes the *moi*, thus relocating Freud's death drive within the heart of narcissism itself (Lacan, *Ecrits*, p. 186). Thus separation, being, and repetition all play their role in Lacan's dynamic reformulation of Freud's concepts of ego, the death drive, and a literal splitting of the subject (*Ichspaltung*).

The Superego

Before concluding our remarks on the *moi*, we must consider Lacan's interpretation of the Freudian supergo. What was to become the supergo started out as the censor in Freud's *Interpretation of Dreams* (1900). Its mission was to deceive the ego by cutting off forbidden parts from consciousness (*Séminaire* I, p. 220). In his post-1920 topology Freud claimed that the more the instincts (id) were repressed, the more moral, severe, and demanding the superego would become. But psychoanalytic clinical experience as reported in the United

States has not validated Freud's notion of the superego. As we saw, Lacan has recast Freud's second topology—id, ego, superego—to make narcissistic passion one source of human drive. But, having collapsed the Freudian id and ego into the *moi*, and extended the id into the realm of unconscious Desire, what does Lacan do with the superego? He makes it the structural mechanism by which the identificatory *moi* is repressed as an ideal ego and the social *je* formed, and thus a part of both subjects. Klein postulated a superego functioning in an infant as early as three or six months. Because Klein saw the infant as fused with the mother (experienced as a collection of good or bad part-objects), any threat of separation from her supposedly provoked sadistic fantasies of vengefully destroying her. In Klein's view a tendency toward alternating guilt and reparation provided the kernel of a superego at this early stage.[88] In my understanding of Lacan, there is no infant sadism per se, but only the experience of building into a "self" via identification with objects, first through passive fusion, and then through active identification. Perception and identification make the human subject a representational composite from its genesis. By reinterpreting introjection and projection, Lacan explained how part-objects constitute a primordial unifying lining to perception, but paradoxically reveal the inherent disunity of the ego's construction. Lacan also replaced Klein's theory of sadistic fantasies with a theory regarding infant efforts to master incompetence and helplessness via identification with objects. It would not make sense from his perspective to place "intentional" guilt and reparation in the earliest infant experience. Instead, the kernel of a superego is formed concomitantly with psychic separation from the mother at the end of the mirror stage (eighteen months of age).

Freud first portrayed the formation of the superego as correlative of the decline of the Oedipus complex. Renouncing the satisfaction of Oedipal desires, and startled by the forbidden, a child transforms his or her libidinal investment in the parents to an identification with them and interiorizes the incest interdiction. The result is the formation of a superego, which judges or censors in relation to the ego (Laplanche and Pontalis, *Vocabulaire*, pp. 471–72).

In the framework of his second theory of psychic apparatus (after 1920), Freud used the term *Ich Ideal* (ego ideal or *idéal du moi*) to reflect the aspect of the personality resulting from the convergence of narcissism (idealization of the ego) and identifications: first to the parents, later to their substitutive replacements, and finally to collective ideals. Earlier, in his 1914 article "On Narcissism," Freud had made a connection between the ego ideal and censorship, in which the ego ideal was an intrapsychic formation that projected the ideal as a substitute for the narcissism lost in childhood. But in the 1921 article "Group Psychology and the Analysis of the Ego," Freud distinguished the ego ideal from an ideal ego (*Ideal Ich* or *moi idéal*). He described the ideal ego as being forged on the model of infantile narcissistic omnipotence. Freud did not, however, pursue this distinction, or even make it clear. In the *New Introductory Lectures* (1932), he attributed three functions to the superego: self-observation, moral conscience, and a function of the ideal (Laplanche and Pontalis, *Vocabulaire*, pp. 184–85).

By capitalizing on Freud's nascent distinction in 1921 between an ego ideal and an ideal ego, Lacan explains why he thinks Freud had difficulty in linking the ideal ego to the superego. Instead of being superego functions, both functions of the "ideal" are identificatory manifestations of the *moi*. Hence, Freud's nascent concept of ideal ego would refer to primordial narcissistic fixations (primary identifications), while the ego ideal that Freud had described so extensively would correspond to secondary identifications with others. Placed in the secondary realm of language and exchange, the function of the ego ideal (one's own alter ego as reflected in others) is to command the play of relationships (*Séminaire* I, p. 161). Within a Lacanian purview, the ideal ego is linked to a primordial sense of self as it enters into the projection of one's being in requests or demands, while the ego ideal is the reflection of one's idealized *moi* identity in the secondary narcissism of relationships (*Séminaire* I, pp. 140–41). In 1957–58 in his Seminar on the formations of the unconscious, Lacan described narcissism in the formula i(a), where the ideal and its objects *seem* to converge: i = ideal; (a) = *autres*/objects. But he stressed the essential difference between the object/other defined as narcissistic (ego ideals) and the function of the *objet a* defined by Schneiderman as "an object which causes someone to desire" (see ch. 2, n. 17). Recorded as traces from pre–mirror- and mirror-stage identifications, the first "objects of Desire" or ideal signifiers predate a person's relationship to others. Because Freud did not conceive of a primordial mentality, Lacan believed Freud made a mistake. By seeing a convergence between ego (Lacan's *moi*) and ego ideals (Lacan's others) in dreams and hypnosis, Freud confused both as objects of Desire, representing wish fulfillment. Lacan's efforts have gone in the opposite direction; he tries to maintain a distance between the ideal ego and ego ideals (alter ego) and to separate both of these from the mechanism of desiring. In this way the subject can survey itself in its fundamental fantasies and displacements, instead of disappearing into the identificatory exclusion and closure of "apparent same-ness," which occurs in the relating of ideal ego to ego ideals in rela-tionships (*Séminaire* XI, pp. 241, 245).

At around eighteen months of age, the identificatory representa-tions that compose an infant's incipient *moi* undergo a transition from perceptual "presence" to repression. The *moi* had its origins as a break in "natural" consciousness, a mirror-stage, secondary struc-ture built into a gap in being. In a structurally similar way, the phal-lic signifier (which gives rise to the Law of the Name-of-the-Father) imposes a scission in the *moi* (*Séminaire* I, p. 220). Mathematically speaking, some third term (usually the father, but possibly the moth-er's brother or someone else) appears to the infant as an obstacle to symbiotic unity with the mother. It therefore requires three persons to teach the infant that the mother and itself are not one but two beings. This intervention initiates the true passage from nature to culture in ternary or Oedipal terms (see Chapter 5). The infant pain-fully begins to learn its own behavioral limitations and psychic boundaries: in a word, to become individuated. At approximately the same time that the infant begins to use words coherently—that is, to symbolize or represent experience—the presence of the father is per-ceived as an implicit "no" (*non*) to total identification with the mother. Since the mother actually served as a unifying focus for the infant, separation from her is so traumatic that Lacan metaphori-cally terms it Castration. When he talks of Castration, therefore, he means the psychic impact of loss, difference, and individuation, and not biological emasculation in any literal or natural sense.

By "phallic signifier" or Phallus, Lacan means the symbolic or rep-resentational agent of separation, and not the male sex organ per se. There is only an equivalence when gender identification is confused in language with the Oedipal drama. Language then attempts to de-scribe the indescribable in reductionist terms of biology, archteypal myth, and the like. The father has no innate magic or intrinsic bio-logical supremacy. It is, instead, the symbolic effect of his dividing presence to which Lacan points. Lacan refers, therefore, to the Law of the *Name*-of-the-Father, a play on the identical pronunciation of French *non* and *nom*. Viewed thus, law ("no"), Desire, and language become indissolubly linked in conscious associations whose rela-tional links reside in the unconscious Other(A). The Lacanian super-ego starts out as a metaphor for the structural impact of intervention in the infant/mother dyad. The verbal capacity to symbolize absence by words such as "here" or "there" (*Fort! Da!*) becomes an inten-tional mechanism for surviving the pain of awareness and individuation. All in all, insecurity, anxiety, and fear are engendered in the first eighteen months of life: first from a primordial sense of fragmentation; then from mirror-stage dependency; and finally from the trauma of separation.

Lacan was certainly not the first to observe these phenomena. His originality lies in the epistemological use he makes of Freud's text to explain the mysteries of the human drama. American psychoanalyst Margaret Mahler noted years ago what child psychiatrists and child-development researchers have now confirmed: that the dread of loss of the mother is the universal and first profound trauma of human life (see note 57). Mahler appears not to know Lacan's work, but has described the separation trauma between fifteen and eighteen months of age as having its prelude in the six- to eight-month-old infant's growing wariness of strangers and attachment to its primary care-taker. At eighteen months, Lacan presumed an originary splitting into an unconscious object (whose primary source of identification is the mother) and a conscious subject (who is progressively alienated throughout life into linguistic and cultural dicta). The agent of this split—the phallic signifier—is associated with the trauma itself and, moreover, harks back to the earlier mirror-stage anxiety, which was played out around the Desire for recognition.

By eighteen months of age, the human subject has been twice divided. After the second (phallic) division, the *moi* gradually becomes its own alter ego—its reflection found via others—and thus opposes itself in language and in reference to the Law of the Name-of-the-Father to the elemental truth or primary introjections of its own constitution. In other words, language is such a distortion and deferral of experience that presubjective perception is repressed, albeit dynamically. The *moi* (which was initially mother-oriented) gradually comes to identify with the father as a secondary introjection identified with cultural ideals.[89] While the (m)Other remains as the unconscious source of primary identity with objects of Desire, the father comes to represent conscious (i.e., public or social) ideals: a dual perspective coexists in the interior of the *moi*. In consequence, the human subject grows ever more profoundly characterized by alienation, denial, and misrecognition of its own identificatory roots. Perhaps our Western cultural bias in favor of the "rational" or logical begins with a mistrust of image/object in favor of the word.

When an infant begins to learn its place in the world, to submit to the laws that structure its particular social network and to internalize them, it has acquired a superego. Lacan has described the superego as the ballast or limit of the *moi*: the sociocultural refusal of supremacy to the omnipotent "miraculous infant" (ideal ego) of the prediscursive period. One could describe animals as having a specular *moi*—that is, identifying with a *Gestalt* of their species and with certain objects. But animals do not develop an unconscious. The Lacanian unconscious is the combined result of spoken language, a prematuration at birth, and mimetic identification. A relative helplessness during the first eighteen months of life makes of man a strange creature of symbolic contingency and self-alienation. To illustrate this, Lacan has remodeled Freud's second topology as follows.

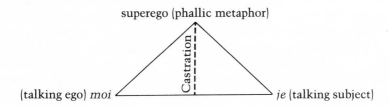

By pushing infants to learn differences and accept compromise, the phallic superego is the paradoxical agent of psychic health and social adaptation as well as the harbinger of repression and censorship.[90] The Oedipal structure, therefore, dramatizes the tragedy of natural man: the choice given to an infant is between inadequate individuation (the consequence of which is neurosis—dancing to another's tune—and at worst psychosis) or adequate "self" boundaries learned through undergoing the pain of Castration.

The phallic superego, then, introduces the eighteen-month-old child to a world of differences and to the value of exchange. Furthermore, inasmuch as the Lacanian superego is an equivalent of language, the link among law, language, society, and "communication" is elemental. Of course there can be "system" and "order" (as in the natural order of the planets) and "communication"—including what semioticians call the natural language of animal societies—without spoken language. But Lacan portrays the unconscious as that memory space created by human language in compensation for separation from the mother and reinforced at the behest of the father. Language provides a plurivalent meaning system that stabilizes identificatory narcissistic and aggressive *moi* inclinations, as well as a means to divert or sublimate the latter through distance, difference, and mediation. But by comparison with the power of *moi* forces, the handmaidens of language systems—reason, logic, or philosophy—seem but secondary. They testify to man's heroic efforts to survive in harmony, fairness, wisdom, intelligence, and peace, to opt for "communication" despite the obvious realities of miscommunication, the indeterminacy of language, and plurality of interpretations.

Whereas Kohut stressed the superego function of internalizing parental images as a way to make culture man's expressed wholeness, Lacan sees its primary role as the initiator of culture via the injunction to differentiation and later to substitutive exchange. For both, social systems derive from the structure of the superego rather than the other way around. Such views run counter to Freud's notion of society as the sublimated and symptomatic outcome of man's repression of his bodily being and sexual nature, the result of inhibiting the pleasure principle in the service of the reality principle.[91] Nonetheless, criminals, psychotics, children, hysterics, and others attest to the *moi*'s absolute drive to subvert, deny, and deconstruct law's artificial and oppressive manifestations. In Schneiderman's words: "The function of the Name-of-the-Father is its subversion" (letter of Aug. 13, 1981, p. 1). So Lacan presents us with another paradox. The *moi*'s will to omnipotence is not merely a matter of selfish vanity but one of self-survival, since the first Desire of any human is the absolute one for recognition (the Desire to be desired), itself linked to the Desire to *be* a unity. But equally important, both to personal and social well-being, is the diminution of the *moi*'s narcissistic drive for power and recognition at the expense of the other. Deleuze and Guattari and other writers who propose that one can escape the abuses of patriarchy and capitalism by flowing with the desiring flux based in the Other(A) misread Lacan. Lacan once called the *moi* a *chancre* or canker sore: a superimposition of an intrinsic unity on biological being (Schneiderman letter, p. 2). And that canker reflects the human propensity for grandiosity, narcissism, and aggressiveness. In this sense, the phallic superego saves the individual from psychosis, and society from genocide, while also imposing tyranny and alienation on being.

From the *Moi* to the *Je*

The topic of Lacan's Second Seminar (1954–55) was the *moi*. Some of the questions to which he evolved answers during that year provide an appropriation to a fuller consideration of the *je*. Lacan's response to the main question—What is the nature of the principle which rules the human subject?—was the *moi*. The principal function of the *moi* is to transform everything into secondary energy or libido and pull each of us along (*traîner*). It is not the master who drives the horse, Lacan said, but the horse itself. In other words, the *moi* is itself a primary libido (or energy) that gives life and focus to the speaking subject. The latter would otherwise be a neutral automaton, mouthing the cliches and conventions of a given culture. In his First Seminar Lacan had already described the *moi* as an organized being that can be considered an object. He pointed out that people consider their individuality to arise from the fact of being an organism (with genetic, biological, and neurological aspects), instead of from an organized *being*, out-of-view. This misconception gives them the idea that they are subjects (willing and controlling their lives) rather than objects of alien fictions and Desires (*Séminaire* I, p. 218). The critic Jonathan Culler has noted a rethinking of this misconception in France: "There is a central axiom which modern research [the 'human sciences' in France] has established: that the individual cannot function as a principle of explanation, for it is itself a highly complex cultural construct—a result rather than a cause."[92] Seen in this light, "consciousness is a ruse of the ego (*moi*) imposed on the subject."[93]

As the subject of linguistic distinctions and differences, the *je* stabilizes the *moi* by anchoring its sliding identifications and spontaneous fusions through naming and labeling these responses. In this way, the speaking *je* provides a sense of unity to the opaque yet potent force. Although the narcissistic and aggressive structure of the *moi* pushes it to obliterate differences and perpetuate identificatory sameness, the subject of language and meaning tempers these intentions by rules and cultural conventions (*Séminaire* I, p. 218). It is increasingly evident, therefore, how crucial is the role of the *je*. Even though intrinsically unified, the *moi* has no guarantees that its question of identity will be answered by others' reinforcement, which renders its existential condition unstable. It is not hard to observe people talking, reading, or writing in an ongoing effort to validate this elusive *moi* story of identity. It was fixed early, in terms of a few themes and limited to certain identifications and to someone else's Desire and discourse. The *moi*, in Lacan's words, is deceptive, alien, and decomposable (*Séminaire* II, p. 74). This explains his paradox that the *moi* is both unified and fixed (in the Imaginary) and floating (in the Real). In looking at its fixed aspect (ideal ego), Lacan has warned his interlocutors not to jump to the incorrect conclusion that the *moi* is transparent. He states that there is no whole ego: no little man in the big man. Indeed, the opposite is true. The *moi* depends on others to validate it in the Real, and on the *je* to "translate" it—to give it shape and form—in the Symbolic, even though the *je* performs this function unawares.

But this brings us a provocative enigma in Lacan's thought: if the *moi* cannot, by definition, be transparent, how can it be knowable? A few of the ancillary engimas generated by this paradox are: Is it assimilable? Reducible? Symbolizable? Is it something? Or can it *not* be named or grasped, but only structured? (*Séminaire* II, p. 82). Is it real or imaginary? (*Séminaire* II, p. 284). The *moi* is, unfortunately, not susceptible of any one definition; it is prismatic, like Lacan's other concepts. The *moi*, for example, is an object of the unconscious, but it is *not* the unconscious. The *moi* is not conscious of itself as an object (its alien "self"), and yet it occupies a space in consciousness. Again, because it is limited to a few fixations and therefore finite, the *moi* is the enemy of Desire; Desire, on the other hand, is insatiable and infinite.[94] But, since the *moi*—an Imaginary function—can only reconstitute itself as an alter ego in the Real realm of experience and verbal interchange, its ideal ego form is both inscrutable and irreducible. Akin to the Heisenberg principle in physics or the "Compton effect" in electron microscopy (an object modifies when under scrutiny), the *moi* is a dialectical project of becoming, a suspension, a set of signifying potentials, which never ceases to displace Desire along an endless chain in the incomplete story of identity.

All this notwithstanding, however (and despite its incapacity to reflect on its own primordial origins), the *moi* can be intermittently grasped as repeated identity themes (signifieds). The individuality of an individual is not a general principle of explanation (as Culler has rightly stated), but one of ontological unawareness. Put another way, at the same time that the *moi* occupies a space in consciousness, it serves as a principle of "resistance." But this does not mean (as Culler has implied in his indictment of Norman Holland) that Other(A) meaning is consequently inaccessible (Culler, "Prolegomena," p. 55). Through the mediation of another; by reading backward; by decoding language and relationships in terms of substitutions and displacements (metaphor and metonymy) for the *objet a* of Desire; by paying heed to repetitions; by reading dream texts as messages to and from the Other(A), an individual may become conscious of some of the components that went into forming the *moi*. Fragments and details can be grasped.

Unlike Freud's impersonal and instinctual id, Lacan's *moi* encompasses gender, genetics, the cyclical rhythms of biology, even its own identificatory formation (its "materiality"). A set of images, traces, effects, and desiderata imposed on biological nature formed the kernel of a *moi* at that point where concrete experience of the outer world was molded by the physical needs of prematuration. Earlier than Karl Marx's cog in a social wheel, more elemental than Bishop George Berkeley's solipsistic Idealism, the moi's raison d'être is to fill up a Real lack in the human organism. So, in answer to the questions posed by Lacan in the Second Seminar the moi can never be assimilated in any final, conscious integration (as Freud claimed for the id, or Kohut for the grandiose self). On the other hand, an awareness of repetitious identity themes can be assimilated into consciousness. Again, the moi is not reducible or symbolizable, because it is itself an organized mode of being and perception made out of images and signifiers, but formed as an effect of the Real. It is both something—individuality—and nothing. The Greek ὄντις ("nobody") fairly describes the moi as "nothing" innate, although it is a patchwork conglomerate of the organism's surrounding sphere; the Greek ἐγω (ego) also describes the moi.[95] It can, moreover, be fathomed as a structure of disruption in the je's unified discourse, as it positions itself in relation to authority (the phallic signifier) and recognition requisites.

In Anglo-American tradition (where ego and consciousness are often equated and assumed to be transparent functions), Lacan's splitting and elliptical decentering of the subject may seem perverse. But Lacan did not find the roots of being or mind in static concepts such as reason, meaning, essence, or ideology, or in organic and neurological characteristics. He looked instead to dialectical processes that link cognition and perception to an unconscious knowledge via the effects of language and identificatory mergers. Although the speaking je appears to represent the totality of the subject, Lacan points to the confusion between moi and je ("me" and "I") as the source of the ambiguity around the pronoun "I"—a linguistic shifter—whose function is to represent itself, but which masks itself instead. Spoken language reinforces this ambiguity by conferring an objective status on the "I" (Fages, Comprendre Lacan, p. 65).

The moi and the je essentially inhabit different realms and are not, therefore, responsible for the same functions. The proportional role division in an adult is about half and half. As a specular subject, the moi (whose Imaginary function has to do with images and forms) does not confuse itself with the je. The latter distinguishes itself from the moi because it can equivocate (Séminaire I, p. 218; Séminaire XX, p. 108). Elsewhere, Lacan refers to the je as the "dummy" in bridge, who unknowingly poses the question of one's (stupid) existence. Hence the je remains outside the fixations that objectify the moi, although it refers to the moi in using the verb "to be." Statements of the "I am . . ." or "I will be . . ." or "I am/you're not . . ."

variety reflect the narcissistic interplay between ideal ego and ego ideal. Leclaire has called the *moi* the third person pronoun of the dream, as opposed to the first person *je* and second person *tu* of the order of language (Leclaire, "On tue," p. 87).

When the *je* presents itself as an autonomous unity, its certainties and assertions convey an effort to insulate itself from the scandal of primary-process (Other) knowledge. By this Lacan did not mean incest wishes. He meant the knowledge that someone else's fictions and Desire are living through one, as well as the fear of separation and loss of center or of control. His view would confirm Aristotle's claim that "society was not constructed for the sake of life, but from defect, from death and the flight from death, from fear of separation and fear of individuality."[96] From this it follows that Lacan will view the characteristic *je* modes in dialogue as opposition, negation, denial, ostentation, and lying. Since the *je* is deceived by its Otherness to itself and capable of mendacity, there can be several *je*s or signifying representations in language. But there is only one *moi*, although it shows itself differently under varying sets of signifiers (*Séminaire XI*, p. 189). The *moi* attaches itself to the *je* as an intentional pressure bent on finding the conclusion to its own partially written story. People, things, words, or ideas become stage props (*objet a*) in the *moi*'s dramatic quest for narcissistic fulfillment. The two subjects are, therefore, connected as in a Möbius strip, different but of one piece.

To forestall any untoward confusion between Lacan's split in the human subject and the "divided self" of R. D. Laing, it must be stated that their topologies are antithetically opposed.[97] A symmetrical or binary division cannot be made between the *moi* and the *je* in any case, since both participate in consciousness, in the unconscious, and in an alternating balance of influence. Laing (following Winnicott) makes a Rousseauesque division between true and false images of self ("true" belonging to the natural and good inner self and "false" to the distorting, repressive effects of the social realm). The true (authentic) self can be driven mad by false (inauthentic) situations and experiences. Lacan's subject, on the other hand, is a paradox of true and false and unique in its linking of primary and secondary process via transformational laws. No final separation exists, therefore, between the inside and outside realms. While Laing reflects his existential bias by making madness a phenomenon of the Real and, by extension, a sociopolitical event, Lacan's picture is apolitical because he renders all perception symbolic and subjective.

Lacan has, however, been concerned with sociopolitical realities in a structural sense. He has deplored the current era of Western historical development during which social evolution has strengthened and paralleled the very alienation and narcissism in terms of which the *moi* was first structured. Moreover, as Turkle documents in *Psychoanalytic Politics*, Lacan was extremely preoccupied with bringing psychoanalytic awareness into the universities and with democratizing institutions by subverting their phallic tendencies to hierarchy. Early in his career, Lacan pointed out that modern man has done two particularly perilous things to his social life. By progressively divorcing himself from those ego ideals and cultural gods which permit positive identificatory merging and concomitant escape from the solipsism of the *moi*, (1) he had overprivileged the conscious subject of science, reason and philosophy—whose characteristic mode is based on denial of unconscious truth, and (2) he had thereby identified himself with his own illusions. Lacan thought that the human subject's principal function should be a continual effort to overcome its own internal, libidinal alienation, following on from what he calls the paranoiac principle of human knowledge. Instead, Western man has proudly capitulated to that alienation and then enshrined it as a social ideal. But, even though we know the *moi* constructs itself by, from, and for the Other (with all the accompanying problems described above), it is privileged in relation to things by comparison with the speaking *je*. The *je*—sure of itself even in its doubt—Lacan finds to be inane and fooled by the false recurrence to infinity of the reflections that constitute the mirage of consciousness and its handmaiden "objectivity." Nonetheless, those who work on thought are "mystified" to the point that they actually claim to see some progress in interiority (Sheridan, *Ecrits*, p. 134). The *moi*—the seat, not the pulpit, of perception—looks elsewhere than the *je* (and calls its perceptions intuition or love).

While Freud's ego is generally seen as an agency that can speak truth when its defense mechanisms have been pinpointed and analyzed, Lacan's conscious speaking subject is the enemy of truth. By its structural formation, it is a mechanism of defense, first against the pain of separation and, later, against any knowing of its own tenuous roots. The task of learning who one is begins by mastering separation from the mother through those preverbal games that play around the presence or absence of both material and human objects. The attachment of words to objects—as in Peekaboo! or the child's game with the bobbin reel (*Fort! Da!*) that Freud described—marks the beginning of "self"-awareness (Sheridan, *Ecrits*, p. 104).[98] The game with the reel prefigures the special role language will play in the continuing human effort to supplement the "want-in-being" created by the separation drama. Language and the phallic signifier split the child in two directions: (1) repression of mirror-stage identifications, which make up the primary unconscious Other(A), and (2) alienation into the words, which gradually cease so transparently to symbolize objects and become autonomous symbols themselves.

The British psychoanalyst of object-relations theory, Donald Winnicott, viewed the neonate as fused with the mother and, consequently, omnipotent in its own sense of being. He has likewise postulated that infants become aware of external reality through games and play. Like the Dutchman Johan Huizinga, Winnicott finds "play" at the heart of nearly all human activity. While Huizinga found no biological origin for play, however, Winnicott talks of the "play instinct" and suggests problematically that it originates in the genes.[99] Lacan's attention to human prematuration at birth, linked to his theory that man consequently locates himself in the world in relation to objects, yields a more logically consequential argument than Winnicott's hypothetical "play gene." The joy associated with infant play (Lacanian mirror-stage *jouissance*) is attendant upon unity-conferring recognition from, and mastery over, the outside world. This joy is also related to the infant's growing sense of unity, felt as a mastery over body movements. While Winnicott located "transitional objects" somewhere between inside and outside, Lacan made language itself a transitional object, a "material" entity in terms of the substitutive and representational mechanisms which compose it (*Séminaire* XI, p. 216). Language slowly cuts the subject off from its pre-speech fusions and naturalness (*jouissance*) and imprints the cultural myths which adults later assume they have consciously deduced or understood through a process of education. What the *je* does *not* understand is that it is only a cultural signifier, controlled both from within and without.

As stated, Lacan's *je* is coextensive with speech or enunciation, but takes on its fuller sense in relationship to what it represents itself as speaking for, i.e., the subject (*Séminaire* XI, pp. 78–79). Descartes first recast the role of the speaking subject and identified it with reason. Freud dethroned reason when he discovered the disunity of the mind. In a reinterpretation of Ferdinand de Saussure's term, Lacan has put forward the Other's *parole* as rendering language use itself (as well as relationship dynamics) overdetermined and evocative. By referring to others in an implicit request for response and recognition, language anchors reason in Desire. Lacan consequently viewed linguistics as closed and static and advanced in its stead his own *linguisterie*. This hypothesizes language as a discontinuous system, because language contains both conscious and unconscious meaning systems in a double inscription (*Niederschrift*). Caught up in the dialectical significance of *moi* and other, humans forever seek to know (possess), yet free themselves from the Other(A) that inhabits them and that has been gradually built up through life as an alienation from within: a *je te trompe*. Determined retroactively, the *je*'s enunciation comes from a "lie"—the subjectivity of myths and Desires—enunciated in the Other: s(A) (*Séminaire* XI, p. 128).

Object-relations theory's picture of interpersonal relations as reflective of an internal relation to objects seems imprecise and hazy when compared with Lacan's formulations. Lacan problematized psychoanalysis by taking the differences between "I" and "me" seriously. By opposing the subject of opacification to the psychological subject, and by showing the subject of certainty as divided, he showed that there are no clear-cut polarities between subject and objects, inside and outside, self and other, conscious and unconscious. He also complicated philosophy by making others—human interdependence—the sole proving ground in human causality, and unconscious intentionality the motive force. The objectifiable "I" of scientific empiricism and the philosophical *Cogito* fail to embrace the complexity of being because they see interaction as occurring between autonomous minds. In this view each person is simply subject or object for the other, and truth is to be found in thought and meaning. If there were no unconscious Real, such a view of the subject would be correct, and we would be left with an Idealist universe of representations to infinity. But, Lacan says, Freud showed us that something Real in the psyche speaks—in dreams—in the full sense of the word "to speak" and lies outside consciousness (*Séminaire* I, p. 218).

In Seminar Eleven (1964) Lacan was preoccupied with the dream as the revelation of the most profound division of the subject. This split is revealed or felt upon awakening, when the subject has not quite returned to the Real world. But the subject is conscious that it (the unconscious subject) was present in a dream (*Séminaire* XI, pp. 67–68). The experience of a sense of fading or disappearance of the dream designates this split in which the dreamer knows he produced a kind of meaning, but loses himself beyond it (*Séminaire* XI, p. 191). The split in being presents itself to Lacan, not between the visible and invisible as Merleau-Ponty notes, but in the form of that "strange contingency," a disintegration of unity in the human subject.

Lacan's *je* has variously been described as a matter of alternating commutations (Leclaire); a metonymy of its own meaning; the emergence of the being of non-being (Sheridan, *Ecrits*, pp. 300, 307); and the subject of a split (*fente*), which is defined in terms of its own radical insufficiency (*Séminaire* XI, p. 67). In his First Seminar (1953) Lacan announced that he would discuss the concept of a split subject. He argued that the phenomena of everyday life gave proof not only of arbitrariness of meaning but also of fear and anxiety as well (*Séminaire* I, pp. 281, 240). Characterized by permanent discontinuity, this Lacanian subject could find no resting place for mediation. The aim of classical philosophy towards a *savoir absolu* never leads to anything that could illustrate the Hegelian vision of successive syntheses, no *Dimanche de la vie* (There are no Sundays off in life), Lacan said, where there is no more opening in the subject's heart (p. 201). Psychologists, philosophers, or scientists who look for truth in "resolution" are therefore destined to be disenchanted, since the very impulse toward harmony is an attempt to deny the inherent "want-in-being" and its intimations of fragmentation and death. Psychologists such as Erich Fromm, W. Reich, Laing, Kohut, *Gestalt* therapists, and others have erred in the direction of trying to substantify and totalize psychic reality (*Séminaire* XI, p. 69). In fact, no being can ever seize the fundamental and radical articulation which it is. Even the Other's Desire, which makes up the unconscious discourse, is not a *Dasein* (being or existence), for it can only ever be partially captured, and even that indirectly, intersubjectively, and transindividually. The problem at issue in Lacan, then, is not merely a redefinition of the human subject, but a redefinition of all related concepts: truth, knowledge, meaning, for a start. Wilden has phrased the problem this way: "It is precisely in their relationship to Knowledge that the Freudian and the Hegelian subject differ. For Hegel, one can say that Truth is immanent in the progress of the dialectic toward Knowledge; for Freud, however, Truth is the unanswerable question of the 'Who (or what) am I?'" (*LS*, p. 308). Lacan has offered the place of the Other and the specular *moi* in answer.

In answer to our opening question "What is 'I'?" we may conclude by saying that in conscious life two subjects appear: the subject of individuality and the subject of speech (which has the capacity to lie, deny, and misrepresent) (*Séminaire* I, p. 218). But the Real subject is that of the unconscious, and it is beyond both *moi* and *je*. There will never, then, be only one subject, e.g., the savant who looks at the ensemble and hopes one day to reduce everything to a game determined by symbols enveloping all the interactions between objects (*Séminaire* I, p. 218). Nor is the subject of identifications and objectifications—the *moi*—an ego or identity in the psychological sense. The subject is, instead, an unbridgeable gap between a person's perceptions and alienation in relation to an external *Gestalt*, an internal discourse, and Desire. Any "I" will mirror the history of its own structuration in the Other(A). The intermingling of two apparently unified modes of meaning—the *moi* and *je*—each already contingent and relative, establishes perception and its "translation" in terms of tension, fading, discontinuity, and incompletion, instead of as the developmental, objective, and linear process we assume it to be. Rimbaud once said, "Je est un autre" (I is an other). Lacan explained the poet's intuition.

2

LACAN'S
FOUR FUNDAMENTAL
CONCEPTS OF PSYCHOANALYSIS

In his Seminar Eleven (1964) Lacan interpreted what he described as Freud's four fundamental concepts of psychoanalysis. (1) *Drive* (*Trieb*) appears as a composite of need, Desire, and demand (*demande*). (2) The *unconscious* has become the discourse and Desire of the Other(A). (3) *Repetition* is equated with identity. (4) *Transference* triggers the unconscious into action via specular relations. Lacan's reformulation of these Freudian concepts is not intended as a reconstruction of Freud's thought, however, but as a recuperation of the meanings of Freud's monumental discovery. At the same time Lacan is concerned to answer the question: Is psychoanalysis a science? In Seminar Eleven he responds that psychoanalysis is a science because it has an object of study—the unconscious—which can be formalized.[1] By insisting that "science" should be defined by its theory, however, and not by praxis or technique, Lacan aimed to separate clinical practice (praxis)—which is characterized by talking (*l'acte de la parole*)—from psychoanalytic theory. In his efforts to formalize theory, Lacan used new concepts, graphs, mathematical formulas (mathemes, knots, circular configurations), and reformulations of standard concepts in other disciplines to clarify some unequivocal truths about psychoanalysis, as well as to depict impasses in thought.

The purpose of this chapter is to do justice to Lacan's salient emphasis on psychoanalytic theory and show how he arrived at his conclusions. I shall deal with each of his four fundamental concepts in the order outlined above. I will distinguish between those original insights of Freud that Lacan preserved and those that he nursed from their nonelaborated Freudian embryo. The chapter is addressed primarily to the reader interested in psychoanalysis and is not conceived as a polemic. Since it provides the key to so much Lacanian theory, however, it is also essential to any overall understanding of Lacan's importance for cognitive theories, literary theory, sociology, philosophy, theology, feminism, and any other discipline that seeks to understand or "apply" his thought.

Freud's Drive or Instinct Replaced by Need, Desire, and Demand

Freud adhered to dualisms and binary distinctions (Eros versus Thanatos, for example) which often left him wondering what to do with what did not fit. Lacan obliterated these dualisms, offering instead a three-tiered explanation of the drive which motivates human beings.[2] To achieve this, Lacan gave new meaning to the familiar terms "need" and "desire"; his third term—*demande*—is not a traditional psychoanalytic concept. Its usual translations—request or appeal—*can* be found, however, in law. Briefly put, Lacanian "need" is purely physical and aims at survival. "Desire" is rooted in the unconscious as a referential "content" for Desire-as-libidinal function, which is displaced into conscious life. "Request"—taken psychoanalytically to mean a "demand" for love or an "appeal" to the Other(A)—reveals the presence of unconscious Desire and narcissism in conscious life as an intentional pressure within language.

Any comprehension of Lacan's theory of drive requires an exploration of his distinction between need, Desire, and demand. Freud was born in 1856, three years before the publication of Charles Darwin's *The Origin of Species*. In much the same way that Darwinians saw nature, Freud viewed the dynamics of the human mind in light of the competitive struggle for existence that prevailed in nineteenth-century industrial Europe. It is, therefore, not surprising that Freud's classic psychoanalytic theory is first and foremost a biological psychology of innate forces.[3] Freud originally thought that "drives" were composed of bodily energy—ambivalent, impersonal, meta-biological entities—forcing their way in a specific direction.[4] Constantly preparing the ground for internal warfare between aggressive and erotic tendencies, these *Triebe* were construed as the source of innate aggression. It is easy to see how such energy could be viewed as instinctual.

In his "Three Essays on the Theory of Sexuality" (1905) Freud postulated the source of *Trieb* as a quantifiable state of corporal excitement or state of tension, whose "object" was variable and contingent, intercalated somewhere between psyche and soma, and conveyed by representations of ego instincts (preservation of the individual) and sexual instincts (continuity of the species).[5] In 1915 Freud added the concept of a libido whose function was to unify the different phases of sexuality: oral, anal, and genital (*Séminaire* I, p. 139). In *Beyond the Pleasure Principle* (1920) he subsumed the ideas of ego versus sexual "drives" or "impulses" in a new cosmic dualism: Eros (life) versus Thanatos (death). In Freud's last works "drive" came to include the notion of individual drives as well as that of cosmic ones. He fittingly redefined *Triebe* as "somatic demands upon mental life," thus reflecting his gradual move from "drive" theory to ego theory (Rieff, *Freud*, p. 31).

But before we can proceed to Lacan's interpretation of the biological Freud, and to his presentation of Freud's unconscious as primarily symbolic and relational, we must rethink the standard biological picture, which deters many readers from paying heed to Lacan's rereadings. By James Strachey's own admission in his notes to the *Standard Edition*, his choice of the English word "instinct" to translate Freud's *Trieb* is problematic: "the only slight complication is that in some half-dozen instances Freud himself uses the German *Instinkt*, always, perhaps, in the sense of instinct in animals."[6] Like the New York psychoanalyst Heinz Hartmann, Lacan has respected Freud's distinction between *Instinkt* and *Trieb*.[7] Freud used *Instinkt* to describe animal behavior, fixed by heredity and characteristic of a species, and so having to do only with phylogenesis. But to mark the energy which motivates human beings, he used the word *Trieb* (German *treiben*, to drive or push). While Hartmann has made the distinction only to reaffirm the idea that drive comes from innate instincts, Lacan has taken Freud's own contradictory ideas on drive theory as indicative of a problematic area. Lacan's reconceptualization of *Trieb* eliminates much confusion surrounding Freud's sometimes arbitrary interchange of the terms drive, libido, and energy. Lacan effected this by separating the terms entirely from *Instinkt*, which is a narrow biological term having nothing to do with human motivation.

We come now to the Lacanian distinction between need, Desire, and *demande*. The Freudian commentator Richard Wollheim wrote that he failed to find a coherent account of the distinction between *demande* ("appeal") and Desire in any commentaries on Lacan's thought. Motivated to correct this lacuna in the secondary literature, Wollheim attempts his own interpretation—an erroneous one, as we shall see.[8] Wollheim perhaps fails to make the necessary leap from the biological Freud to Lacan's structural Freud because he, too, belongs to the generation of thinkers who are used to considering "drive" theory in terms of instincts. In his perfunctory and supercilious article on Lacan ("The Cabinet of Dr. Lacan," p. 36), Wollheim wrote: "The newly born [Lacanian] infant, victim of the prematurity of birth peculiar to man, is at the mercy of unbounded and unmediated instinct." Wollheim's misunderstanding here arises, first, from his misinterpretation of need and Desire, as well as of Lacan's rejection of the term "instinct." Lacan does not, however, retain a strict French equivalent for *Trieb*, which he translates as *pulsion*, thereby not entirely abandoning the German meaning of "push" (*treiben*). Indeed, he gives a meaning to "drive" that is actually closer to "energy" than to "push" (*la poussée*) (*Séminaire* XI, p. 148). Recently, the Chicago analyst Bruno Bettelheim has admirably proposed that the English word "impulse" lies closer to the meaning Freud gave to *Trieb*, as well as being similar etymologically to the felicitous French rendering *pulsion* ("Freud and the Soul," p. 89).

Lacan opposed the Freudian idea that psyche and soma are always joined representationally in some fashion. *Pulsion* or "energy" localizes itself in the human organism prior to any sense of psychic representation or affective charge. In the prespecular period *pulsion* is pure expansion, pure corporality, but never "instinct" (*Instinkt*). Although Lacan does retain the four terms by which Freud qualified *Trieb*—*Drang* = pressure; *Quelle* = source; *Objekt* = object; *Ziel* = goal—he locates the source of "drive" in Freud's concepts of Eros and Thanatos. In *Beyond the Pleasure Principle* Freud suggested that the death drive (*Todestriebe*) controls both individual libido and aggression. The goal of Thanatos was not, however, death-seeking, but a drive to return to an anterior, tensionless state in order to preserve the self (*Modern Concepts*, p. 55). Eros also kept the meaning of "self"-preservation insofar as Freud sometimes described it as a principle of constancy. Today most neo-Freudian psychoanalysts view the death drive as a mythology. In the opposite direction French psychoanalysts in Lacan's wake have rekindled the fire under drive theory, particularly the death drive, whose manifestations are described as abounding in aggressive hostility, depression and sadomasochism.

Following Lacan's distinction between structure and "substance," J.-B. Pontalis in an essay tries to explain Lacan's concept of "death work." Pontalis postulates the death drive as a more elemental process in being than the unconscious representations that show up in "dream work" as fragments of the *moi* and that are intimately related to body reality (primary narcissism). The primary energy which aims at constancy per se is nothing more than the identificatory mergers that provide a sense of mastery and continuity to the neonate (whose experience is one of Real incomprehension). The concept of a secondary energy is contiguous with the *moi* and is what Lacan links to the identity mechanism of repetition. Any deconstruction of the *moi* partakes of "death work." Pontalis writes: "It is in its fundamental process of unbinding [of the ego], of fragmentation, of breaking up, of separation, of bursting, but also of enclosing—[a] process that has no aim but its own accomplishment and whose repetitive nature brands it as instinctual—it is here that the death instinct operates. This is a process that no longer has anything to do with conscious death anxiety, but that mimics death in the very kernel of being."[9] Lacan's paradoxical statement—that the death instinct is merely a concept, but the only place where man can approach the register of life (*Séminaire* II, p. 113)—means that, although "death work" is created by an unraveling of the *moi*, "cure," symptom relief, or freedom can only be reached by deconstructing the *moi* text to articulate the messages in the Other(A) that control a person's destiny.

By combining conceptual elements from Thanatos and Eros, Lacan offered his innovative concept of *pulsion* as a primary energy whose aim is to suppress all tension to keep the organism constant (*Séminaire* XX, pp. 100–101). "Drive" energy, therefore, has nothing to do with kinetic energy, controlled movement, or the rhythms of biology (*Séminaire* XI, p. 150). In the pre-mirror stage primary energy aims only at the constancy of satisfying physical need. In the mirror-stage *pulsion* becomes connected to the infant's pleasure in object constancy—*jouissance*—in relation to a primordial Other and at that time is linked to a growing psychic awareness. Lacan has named this phenomenon Desire or secondary energy, which finds its limit and sustains itself as such by crossing the threshold of constancy (homeostasis) imposed by Freud's pleasure principle (*Séminaire* XI, p. 32).

Since the primary energy which aims toward the satisfaction of constancy can never become an "object" of consciousness, the "object" of analysis must focus on secondary energy (or Desire). To clarify this idea Lacan made a distinction between primary and secondary representational energy. Because perceptive faculties exist well in advance of motor control, the prespecular infant introjects—i.e., represents mentally—images and objects, but does so unaware by a kind of incorporative fantasmatic merger that one could interpret by Frege's mathematical concept of o. Actual *recognition* of images and objects—awareness of differentiation or otherness—characterizes the mirror-stage infant (Frege's concept of 1). The tragedy of the human condition is implicit in Lacan's theory that both the object and goal of the drive toward constancy converge in the Desire to be desired: in other words, to be recognized by the mother so that the infant feels one with her. This early dependency on an external and, therefore, *inconstant* source of "self" determines human drive to be always greater than the sum of its parts. In adult life no symmetry is possible between the structural drive toward a mirror-stage psychic illusion of unity and the Real objects meant to satisfy the "drive."

Lacan described need very simply as an organic drive toward organic satisfaction. It is limited to the consumption that characterizes a newborn's appetite and is aimed at the mother. Need—synonymous with primary energy—is therefore satisfied in the domain of Real experience and event (*Séminaire* I, p. 59). Although Lacan's conception of need resembles Freud's 1905 theory of ego instincts, which aimed at survival (food) and culminated in the oral and maternal character of primary identification, he sheds a different light on the Freudian theory.[10] Lacan, too, emphasizes the maternal and corporal nature of primary identification in its link to food, but he stresses the effects of the experience and its representational residue, as opposed to Freud's emphasis on the Real biological event. For example, the breast as a primordial cause of Desire either yields something or nothing. Orality later attaches itself to objects—food, drink, sexual acts, and so on—or to nothingness as in anorexia. One can read backward to the earliest structuring of perception in relation to incorporation, and to the formation of an ideal ego. Later the ideal ego will be the most primitive source of demand, reflecting something beyond an object requested.

In the first six months of life a few images are constituted for the "instincts" themselves, Lacan said, for example, sucking/the breast; excrement; the voice; the gaze; the nothing; the urinary flow (Sheridan, *Ecrits*, p. 11). In Seminar Eleven Lacan reduced the prespecular *pulsions* to four and linked them to corporal images or part-objects—oral (breast), anal (the buttocks), scopic (the gaze), *invocante* (the voice)—and said *they* support human Desire or "drive." All other "drives" may be seen as partial, even the idea of "genital drive," which does not exist in the unconscious (*Séminaire* XI, p. 49). These prototypical images make up the perceptual matrices to which other images attach themselves and form "hallucinatory" meaning networks. But need is intransitive: the prespecular infant is invaded by these archaic images commensurate with corporal experience and sensation. In the mirror stage need matures into Desire via recognition from the other. Desire is commensurate with "drive" energy.[11]

Desire arises as a transitive state, then, as well as a psychocognitive, perceptual pivot. Lacan's noninstinctual drive theory thus valorizes aspects of being usually thought mysterious or beyond consideration because unquantifiable. Going with the flux and "electricity" of human interdependence, Lacan leads away, not only from those who explain mind by body, but also from static "self" theories. Lacanian Desire is correlated with a *symbolic* "instinctual" chain from the start, although none of the primordial representations will ever be retrievable to conscious memory. Lacan, nonetheless, makes sense of the Kleinian theory of early introjection of part-objects. But he goes beyond Melanie Klein to depict these objects as signifying data that are gradually *organized* into perceptual networks of meanings and relations, and on which all later constructions of reality are built. The French critic Julia Kristéva has referred to the prespecular moment of sensory representability as a presemiotic *pulsion* or a corpora and has hypothesized a rhythmic and tonal link between it and the origins of poetry. I would also link the magnetic pull of music to this early formative period.

Lacan's conception of Desire is markedly different from Freud's need or sex/pleasure view of it. Freud imagined that the psychic apparatus was set in motion by a wish (*Wunsch*) or a desire (*Begierde*) and oriented toward distinguishing the agreeable (pleasure principle) from the disagreeable (reality principle). Many conceptual problems have arisen from Freud's fantasy/pleasure and reality/displeasure split. Why do adults, for instance, find pleasure in reality? Conversely, why is fantasy often disagreeable? More important, who decides where to draw the line between fantasy and reality?

All this notwithstanding, Lacan continually reformulated his concept of Desire. In 1936, under Hegel's influence, he developed a phenomenology of Desire; Desire played a mediating role between need and demand. In 1947 the dialectical scope of Desire concerned Lacan. In 1953–54 he stressed its libidinal function. In 1958 Lacan continued to develop a Hegelian thesis/antithesis/synthesis model, but in the realm of the Real. Desire was not to be reduced to need as neo-Freudians had done. Between the need recorded as primal repression and the Desire whose residue is joined to this need, demand appears, calling for satisfactions that do not really satisfy. In "The Meaning of the Phallus" Lacan said: "Demand constitutes this Other as already possessing the 'privilege' of satisfying needs, that is, the power to deprive them of the one thing by which they are satisifed. . . . Hence it is that demand cancels out (aufhebt) the particularity of anything which might be granted by transmuting it into a proof of love. . . . There is, then, a necessity for the particularity thus abolished to re-appear *beyond* demand. Where it does indeed reappear, but preserv-ing (aufhebt) the structure harbouring within the unconditional character of the demand for love. . . . Thus desire is neither the ap-petite for satisfaction, nor the demand for love, but the difference re-sulting from the subtraction of the first from the second, the very phenomenon of their splitting (Spaltung)."[12] By 1973 Lacan would call the *Aufhebung* one of those pretty dreams of philosophy (Sémi-naire XX, p. 79).

In 1964 Lacan talked about the four causes of Desire: the void, the voice, the gaze, the Phallus (as well as the four "drives" and images or related fantasies which support Desire). And in 1972 and 1973 the influences of structuralism are evident in his correlation of the im-agistic part-objects of Desire (the breast, excrement, the gaze, the voice) with human, as well as inhuman, objects. The part-objects are meaningful, are signifiers, all subsumed under the formula *objet a*. In 1973 Lacan described secondary energy (or libido or Desire) as the *dérive de la jouissance* (Séminaire XX, p. 102). *Dérive* means the hollowed-out drift or wake—thus, an aftermath or effect—left by a boat in water or an aircraft in the sky. I interpret this metaphor to mean that Desire (as a motivating energy throughout life) comes from the effects or traces left in human beings by key images. Lacan also described the human subject as afloat (à la dérive). *A la dérive* refers to a boat cut loose from its moorings. Detached from any di-rect access to its own unconscious knowledge, the human subject is also adrift.

Jouissance refers to the ecstatic sense of unity which preceded an infant's knowledge of separation from the mother, a metaphorical Garden of Eden before the dividing third term—the serpent—brings knowledge of sin. We remember from the discussion of the superego in Chapter 1 that the phallic injunction to separation or differentia-tion creates repression by pushing an infant into the world of lan-guage. Just as the child has been manipulating objects for many months, it now learns to manipulate words in the same manner: both to situate self in the world and as an aid to mastering the expe-rience of division from the mother. But, since an infant cannot even begin to translate Desire into communicative words before at least eighteen months, Desire will not become humanized until then (Séminaire I, pp. 196–97). In later life the "drive" or energy that pushes individuals in all their pursuits and that animates the inert, neutral phonemes of language comes from the early effects of division and the concomitant Desire to recreate a psychic feeling of wholeness. "Wholeness" can be equated with certainty, or with lack of anxiety. In 1960 Lacan said that if he had not been able to find the necessary forcefulness in the word *pulsion* to translate the idea of the powerful force of "drive," he would have resorted to the term *dérive* (effect) (Sheridan, *Ecrits*, p. 301).

Later we shall discuss Lacan's interpretation of the Oedipus complex as the child's wish to *be* the cause of the Other's Desire (Chapter 5). This wish remains at the heart of adult sexual relations. In 1960 Lacan talked about *le désir de l'Autre*, purposely playing on the preposition *de* to make the phrase mean variously: desire is the Desire of/for/by the Other(A). Mirror-stage infants act in such a way as to attract the attention of the Real other, whose *parole* they "introject" and subsequently desire *qua* Other(A). This drama is reenacted throughout life via substitute others whose recognition is sought. Lacan borrowed Hegel's master/slave struggle for pure prestige as a structural model of the dialectical dynamic being played out in relationships around the issue of recognition. By transforming Hegel's power-based dialectic of the consciousness of self into one of unconscious Desire—*moi* versus Other(A) reified via others—Lacan aimed to criticize the nondialectical degradation of contemporary psychoanalysis, as well as the philosophers' narrow view of consciousness. When the mirror stage ends, the mother is repressed as a record of primordial, corporal, identificatory, and experiential meaning. In his essay "Lacan and the Discourse of the Other," Anthony Wilden wrote that Lacan's theory of signifying inscriptions in the Other(A) was meant to rebut the notion of the unconscious as an individual, intrapsychic entity to restore it as a function to the collectivity which created and sustains it.[13] Wilden's interpretation, however, risks reducing Lacan's multileveled concept of the Other(A) to its social order aspect. It incurs an erroneous comparison of Lacan's unconscious with the Jungian collective unconscious or with a transparent sociological imprinting. It also avoids the individual, intrapsychic, conflictual, and maternal aspect of the Lacanian (m)Other.

In Chapter 1 we referred to Stuart Schneiderman's description of Desire as the leftover or residue of the fact that something—the Other—has been repressed. In Lacan's dialectical context Desire emanates first from the *moi*'s thrust toward recognition of/from/about/ to the Other(A): Who am I? What am I of you? The space between the *moi* and the Other(A) is, therefore, Desire, a space that widens throughout life. Human conflict and anxiety are bound, then, to arise both intrapsychically and intersubjectively. An alien Desire resides at the center of one's being, a Desire whose text is repressed. Aggression need not be an innate force of impersonal, biological nature (as Freud would have it). Lacan views aggression more logically as a dialectical response to the quest to know the Other(A) via others, at whom aggression is aimed in a displaced manner when narcissistic recognition is witheld.

Lacanian Desire is both representational—a referential content of images and meanings inscribed in the place of the Other(A)—and an indestructible force that shows up in the order of chronological time as an insatiable mechanism of yearning. In this latter sense, Desire-as-libido seeks compensation for the severed *jouissance* of symbiotic union in replacements for the lost—i.e., repressed—objects of Desire (*Séminaire* XI, p. 33). Here Desire functions as a post–mirror-stage libido, which refers back to the prespecular pleasure ego constituted by the part-objects of Desire. When Félix Guattari and Gilles Deleuze portray psychoanalysis as destructive of Desire, they fail to comprehend Lacan. Lacanian psychoanalysis *can* enable a person to name a Desire, but not to destroy it. Desire exists at every point in the psychic structure: from the prespecular *moi* to the principles of drive, libido, and lack. Desire is not satiated by *moi*/other relations, since it always refers to a repressed text. Because Desiring has no final resolution, it is more than an *Aufhebung* (sublation or new synthesis) of the *moi* in search of the Other(A) through a series of syntheses with others and with various objects. Lacan's subject of Desire cannot be reduced to a Hegelian dialectic in which a fully realized, conscious "self" purportedly evolves through successive syntheses. Nor is Lacanian Desire merely an allegory of dialectical materialism (the science of internal contradictions of matter). Lacan's teachings have, indeed, explained that the "material" and the Real are not identical relations of realism.[14] In his efforts to give "body" to the reality of the unconscious, Lacan looked to phenomenology and mathematics. The invisible and abstract—i.e., formalized by topology—have Real attributes in terms of their impact on being. But any philosophy which equates seeing, thinking, and consciousness with "realism" or "objectivity" will miss the subtlety of Lacan's triadic conception of perception. Real objects and events as well as Symbolic language and cultural codes are transformed and made personal by Imaginary, mirror-stage processes, and then returned to the world in the universalizing—but not objective—Symbolic system of language that named the Real in the first place.

Throughout a lifetime the *moi* is a narcissistic function whose Desire is dialectical and paradoxical: to find and to escape knowledge of the Other(A). This is what Lacan means by his statement that the *moi* is the enemy of Desire.[15] Being limited to a few identity fixations, the *moi* is a stumbling block to the absolute and infinite push of Desire. Not only do narcissistic grandiosity, sublimated aggressiveness, and "self"-*unawareness* (miscognition) stand between the conscious reality of the *moi* and its unconscious Desires; the ego ideals (others) who are supposed to "realize" *moi* Desires also always fall short of the *moi*'s ideal ego aspirations. Lacan offers the majestic insight that wanting transcends being and makes the human condition a truly tragic one. In wanting to *be* the other, an infant is subjugated by the Other's Desire, from which it must later find distance through displacements, if individuation is to be achieved. In adult life psychic "freedom" lies in pinpointing this alien Desire in order to realize, to reject, or to modify it. The "truth" of the Other's Desire is rarely attained, however, since this requires recognition of the *moi* in the Other(A) and the Other(A) in oneself. At best Desire can be partially recognized within psychoanalysis. The Other(A), indeed, is "beyond" and outside "self"-awareness. Thus, Lacanian Desire is not equatable to Hegel's "absolute knowledge," whose whole truth the philosopher can supposedly attain. The psychic choice confronting any adult, then, is in what measure to remain under the yoke of the Other's Desire and eschew the freedom (*jouissance*) to be gained from "self"-realization, or how far to throw off the oppression of an alien Desire and thereby challenge the limitations of the *moi*. This theory displays the obverse face of the existential project, as well as the reasons for its failure. Freedom of choice—"self"-creation—cannot reside in consciousness, unless the conscious subject has gained this freedom by peering into its unconscious netherworld.

In the 1950s Lacan began to shift the focus of his drive theory from the Other/other to the *objet a*. Henceforth, he depicted the genesis of the structure of Desire by showing how *objet a*: (1) functions as invading images or representations; (2) symbolizes the mimetic transition which marks the mirror stage; and (3) stands in the final stage for post—mirror-stage substitutions.[16] The formula:

$$\text{Es} = \underline{moi} \text{ (fantasms)}$$
$$\text{(a)} = \text{the primordial objects of Desire}$$

illustrates the link between prespecular, primordial part-object representations and mirror-stage *moi* fantasies. Although the primordial signifying chain is never represented as a *perceptum*, it none-

theless conditions the fantasies which make up the unity of presubjective *moi* perception. In "On a question preliminary to any possible treatment of psychosis" (1957–58), Lacan broke the equation
down even further in relation to the pre-mirror stage. He focused on
objet a in its connection to need (primary energy):

$$\frac{\text{breast/sucking}}{\text{image } (objet\ a)} \cdot \frac{\text{food}}{pulsion \text{ (energy)}}$$

Sucking is to need (food) as the image or representation is to energy.
In essence this elemental formula says that energy derives from corporal need (dependency), in turn equated with imagistic representations. These images are linked to the mother as a whole form or
body in the mirror stage and are repressed in the post-mirror phase of
individuation. Thus primary libido (secondary energy) or Desire is
essentially composed of unconscious traces (fantasies), which later
refer to a lost sense of union. It is logical, then, that Lacan describes
the *objet a* in the post-mirror stage as the signifier of Desire deprived
of its symbolic reference to its unconscious signifieds. These signifieds turn out on analysis to be an endless chain of related fantasies
and specific meanings. Schneiderman has written that the *objet a*
can be disengaged in a psychoanalytic practice, beyond narcissism
and beyond the Oedipal nexus, as the "place of the lack [*manque-à-
être*] and its irreducibility. The *objet a* is a trace, a leftover, a remainder. We can summarize its concept by saying that it leaves something
to be desired."[17]

   In the 1950s Lacan hypothesized two libidos or two sources of Desire. The primary libido was correlated with secondary energy from
the mirror stage. The secondary libido dates from the post-mirror
stage, when it begins to mature in relation to others and language,
but not because of evolutionary and impersonal stages (such as
Freud's sexual stages or Jean Piaget's developmental ones). We know
that during the mirror stage, the object of need and the cause of Desire—the mother—were welded to form a contiguous representation
of libidinal pleasure (*Séminaire* XI, p. 220). In the post-mirror stage
Desire must be displaced away from the mother, who then, paradoxically, becomes identified with the mysterious force of repression.
This, in turn, gives rise to Desire as a libidinal lack seeking to overcome itself by sending love along the path of replacing spontaneous
fusions (nature) with cultural substitutions.

   In his Seminar Eleven (1964) Lacan sketched out this convergence
of narcissisms and Desire in the formula: i(a). Here, "i" stands for the
ideal of the ego. The (a) points to the crucial difference between the

object defined as narcissistic—the ideal ego (*moi*) or the ego ideal (others)—and the function of the *objet a*, which is intended to realize an ideal (*Séminaire* XI, pp. 244–45). The narcissistic ideal is a coefficient of mirror-stage Desire—a primary libido—while the *objet a* operates the mirror structure at a secondary libido level of substitution and displacement. In 1954 Lacan had already prefigured the i(a) formula by describing the libido as an organ, both a *part* of the human organism—the narcissistic *moi*—and an *instrument* of Desiring. Looked at in this way, the libido (unlike Freudian energy) is not fluid and does not accumulate (*Séminaire* XI, p. 171). In yet another attempt to illustrate the convergence of narcissism and Desire, Lacan described it in 1964 as a *lamelle*, a *lamelle* being something extremely flat, like a blade, which can be displaced and go anywhere. In this image, Desire/libido insinuates itself as an ubiquitous, seemingly nonexistent organ that actually animates life (*Séminaire* XI, p. 180).

In his essay "Desire and the Interpretation of Desire in *Hamlet*" (1959), Lacan elaborated the four causes of Desire—the void, the voice, the gaze, the Phallus—in their relation to human dependency on the outside world.[18] At a prespecular level, both the voice and gaze of the primordial Other were introjected as part-objects or fragments that served to paper over a void in being. These "objects" serve as the basic threads in the weave of the mirror-stage *moi*, now become aware of it-"self" as an object of the voice and the gaze of an other. In the post-mirror stage the *moi* becomes an object of the Phallic injunction to separation. The void, the voice, the gaze, and the Phallus are simply different manifestations of *objet a*, functioning alternatively as mnemic traces which first filled in a void; as structuring principles of human identity; and also as the lost object(s) of Desire that are later replaced by substitute objects, activities, and goals (*Séminaire* XI, pp. 168, 233; *Séminaire* XX, p. 87).

Serge Leclaire has called the primary objects of Desire elements of pure singularity, believing they predate the "impurity" of taking on "self" as a unity conferred by an other in the mirror stage. At that time, the elements are bound together into coherent sets by Desire. Similarly, the Desire for recognition is wed to corporal fixations, inasmuch as these elementary, prespecular signifiers fixed and delimited the erotogenic zones, although no logical connection will ever unveil them.[19] This is what Lacan meant when he described the motives of the unconscious as limited to corporal Desire. Lacan quipped that the subject of the unconscious puts the body into gear (*embrayer*).[20] At the point where psyche and soma become intertwined at the level of primary Desire (in relation to the mother), Lacan aptly spoke of a *jouissance*. The term describes what the infant loses on leaving the mirror stage and what must be sought ever after through displacements. *Jouissance* has both sexual and abstract meanings: pleasure or ecstasy, and orgasm. In a lifetime individuals continually change objects and goals in their Desiring quest. One major arena where Desire is meant to be satiated is sex. Many neo-Freudian analysts naturally view sexual behavior as the key to understanding personality. In Lacanian terms sex is important as a co-efficient of primary (corporal) narcissism and as a means of obtaining recognition from an other (secondary narcissism). Any person's "erotomania" will, moreover, offer a clue to their Desire vis-à-vis the Other(A). But no object—be it person, thing, sexual activity, or belief—will finally and permanently quell Desire. It is sorrowful, Lacan has said, that the loved person onto whom one projects Desire and narcissism serves to give proof of the image and pathos of existence. The other reveals the gap of human Desire, but cannot permanently close it ("Desire and *Hamlet*," p. 15). In love relations this imbalance prevents a perfect coincidence between Desire and the object supposed to provide sexual and psychic closure. The idealized harmony of Romantic love belongs to the myth of the androgyn.[21]

In Seminar Eleven Lacan paid tribute to Freud's genius by allowing that though Freud did not understand the causes of Desire in terms of language or transference relations, he nonetheless learned of the mechanisms of the unconscious through language and transference by listening to hysterics talk (*Séminaire* XI, p. 16). But Freud viewed unconscious Desire as complete in itself, as the Desire for nothing. In his Second Seminar Lacan showed that there was not a single passage in *The Interpretation of Dreams* (1900) that concluded the subject desires this (p. 246). Lacan finds even less logic in Freud's idea that the realization of Desire lies in the dream's elaboration per se in terms of wish fulfillment. Lacan taught the opposite: that Desire aims toward Real satisfaction, toward reality. But since Freud opposed fantasy to reality—and located the dream on the slope of fantasy—he could not see its connection to temporal reality. Lacan's redefinition of "reality" as an individual's own subjective perceptions—revealed or denied by language and catalyzed by transference—undermines the fantasy/reality opposition. And so, although the dream is hallucinatory and metaphorical, it does offer (behind the alienating, distorting "wall of language" and the mirror illusions of transference) a pristine glimpse into the workings of Desire.

While Freud's dream Desire was its own satisfaction, Lacan has hypothesized that Desire is the Desire for "something else," even if the Desired object is unnameable. So viewed, Desire testifies to a fundamental human lack, an anxiety or metonymy (*Séminaire* XI, p. 161). Desire does not point to self-induced satisfactions, therefore, but to the inherent incompleteness which drives people to seek Real objects in an effort to appease a psychic uneasiness. The Desiring subject genuinely supposes that a Real object (*objet a*) is its only goal, one capable of affording ultimate satisfaction if attained. But Real objects can never literally replace the lost objects of pre-Castration Desire. According to Lacan, the scope of Desire is infinite; it conceals itself behind the choices that people make in their efforts to be happy, as well as in dreams and common discourse. In all these situations Desire is a "message" both to and from the Other(A). The very purpose of dreams and discourse is dialectical: not to satisfy Desire, but to make oneself "seen" or to pass on a "message" (*Télévision*, p. 154). Lacan has redefined the semiotically charged term "message" (taken from Information theory) to mean a "sign in movement." When dreaming, the subject *is* already a message—a sign—situated in the succession of messages that make up her or his Other(A) discourse. The dream is not the unconscious, then, but a message which points the way to a dialectical relationship between the *moi* and the Other(A). Fittingly, Lacanian psychoanalysts have translated Freud's *Wunscherfüllung* (wish fulfillment) as the "realization of desire" which, as Schneiderman points out, is realized in the dream. Lacan added that the Desire in the dream is always the Other's Desire. "That desire must find expression in dreams," Schneiderman goes on, "suggests that it is a desire that the subject cannot accept as his own or cannot act upon" (*Returning*, p. 3). Dream Desire, thus, points to a continuity between dream thoughts and conscious lacks.

In "Desire and the Interpretation of Desire in *Hamlet*" (p. 14), Lacan "quantified" the Desire in common discourse as "the sum and module of the meanings acquired by the subject in human discourse: 'Your thing is performed by the Other in speech'" (see Chapter 3). By the time a child can verbalize the implicit question of identity, the answer has already been planted in a fictional substratum that is constituted, articulated, and built up throughout childhood in the place of an Other(A), active in time and situated in space ("Desire and *Hamlet*," p. 13). Desire, being unconscious, drives and controls individuals, not the reverse. But individuals can only truly articulate the Desire that drives them by coming to see themselves analytically as an object (*moi*) of an Other's Desire. In this manner, it becomes possible to emerge from the signifiers that cover and subjugate one in the Other(A) (Wilden, *LS*, p. 106).

In Seminar Twenty (1972–73) Lacan reemphasized his view of *la dite maternelle (lalangue)* as the source of Desire, linked to being and to need. Behind all quests and meaningful choices, as well as behind the motivation to speak and relate to others, is the question "Who am I?" The answer lies in ascertaining the Desire of the Other(A) which, in turn, always takes the form of a posture toward Law and one's own narcissism. The Desire to know or possess the Other(A) has been displaced into the Desire to be, to know, or to have. Logically speaking, these substitutive modes can be analyzed, that is, broken down, unraveled, or decoded in light of *objet a*—an object of "scientific" study. The Lacanian analyst or critic aims to uncover and recover the Other's Desire by reestablishing the archaic "chains of primary meaning," which are still actively determinant in adult intention and discourse and yet remain opaque to consciousness.[22] Various techniques are employed to surprise these "second" meanings into view. Schneiderman has written: "Lacan listens for key words, the words that the patient uses to summarize his neurosis. . . . Another of Lacan's verbal techniques is to find unconscious sense in the phonic resonance of a patient's words. . . . He accepts playing the role in the transference, and does everything he can to encourage his patient to enact his unconscious within the analytic setting. The technique relies less on interpretation, be it surface or deep, than on interruption. The flow of the patient's words is like an unpunctuated and unreadable text. The analyst interrupts to punctuate the discourse and to introduce a sense that eventually can be grasped by the analysand."[23]

We understand the difficult task challenging a Lacanian analyst when we accept that both the system of language and the system of the unconscious are closed systems; but, while complete within themselves, the two condition each other and thereby blur any final category of system or closure. The way in, so to speak, is through the speaking subject who is, in reality, a *porte-parole* for the Other's discourse. Coextensive with language, yet Desiring from within, the *je* mistakenly thinks it can represent its own totality by designating itself in a statement (Sheridan, *Ecrits*, p. 315). Theoretically speaking, the Lacanian analyst decodes *je* discourse in light of metaphorical linguistic logic. The linguist Roman Jakobson subsumed referentiality, condensation, displacement, and substitution under the categories of metaphor and metonymy. Lacan adds that the logic of these processes can be applied to unconscious meaning, even down to certain letters and phonemes.[24] This same logic characterizes dreams, parapraxes (*Fehlleistungen*), free association, and symptoms (see Chapter 4). Such a theory only makes sense, however, insofar as Lacan's theory of perception eradicates Freud's hierarchical differentiation between words and things. Whereas Freud distinguished between unconscious thing and preconscious word presentations, Lacan's new ideas on perception and cognition suggest that phonemic sounds engrave mnemic traces alongside visual images from the start of life. Gradually any signifier—from the phoneme to a sentence—can be a "personal" message (*Télévision*, p. 22). These unconscious verbal signifiers—*l'écriture*—are, nonetheless, distortions or transformations of everyday language; they belong to the identificatory logic that structures unconscious meaning.

The Lacanian analyst knows the difficulties implicit in trying to winnow out the Other's Desire through the *moi*/other transference relationship. Any specular relation, even that between analyst and analysand, is an intersubjective one of narcissistic exclusion where two *mois* try to objectify each other. Aware of this aspect of the transference, a Lacanian analyst would act in a way altogether contrary to a Kohutian analyst. Heinz Kohut's "empathic" listening assumes the possibility of the analyst's being "plugged into" a patient's unconscious. From a Lacanian viewpoint, such an approach would at worst entail listening to oneself and at best listening to the analysand's *je* distortions of Other(A) truth. The Lacanian analyst proceeds otherwise, staying alert for the truths hidden at the juncture between *moi* and *je*, which reveal an intrasubjective dialogue with the Other(A), expressed to an-other. Schneiderman has written: "Lacan himself has consistently denounced the idea of making any alliances with the patient's ego [*moi*] as purely counterproductive. If the transference is to be analyzed, this will only come about when the patient talks about others rather than himself: the first of these others is the analyst" ("Most Controversial Freudian," p. 55). The Lacanian clinician James Glogowski has written that after the literal (*je*) meaning of a statement has been completed, a second (*moi*) meaning or intentional pressure—the question of the speaker's Desire—remains in the listener's mind. "Perhaps," continues Glogowski, "this is why one speaks of recognition as *re*cognition. What was desired was known, 'cognized,' but needed to be re-cognized before it could be realized" ("Essay on Psychopathology," pp. 15, 17).

In concluding this discussion of Desire, we may assert more confidently than we did in Chapter 1 that the *Desidero* circumscribes the *Cogito*. All efforts to give meaning to one's life manifest Desire. Desire first arose in response to human prematuration and the consequent plight of the human infant. This elemental, structural (i.e., requiring an ordering) aspect to Desire determines that belief systems, love objects, material goods, and other such "substantive fillers" have essence or truth value only incidentally to their primary function—to provide the infant with a sense of continuity and, subsequently, compensate for the loss of the same. The early traumas of prematuration, separation, and repression mark humans for life as the creatures of contingency that they really are, as opposed to the creatures of knowledge and certainty they imagine themselves to be. Any sweep of human history shows subjectivity, arbitrariness, uncertainty, and interpretative fluidity—rather than objectivity, resolution, certainty, and final truth—as the characteristics of human thought. Man's history of political unrest, misunderstanding, and imperfect love are only a few examples of the reality of the human condition.

We have looked at the roles played by need and Desire in Lacan's reinterpretation of drive (*Trieb*). His third term—*demande*—is usually rendered into English as "demand," although the French verb meaning "to demand" is *exiger*. Paradoxically, Lacan's conception of need includes a sense of exigency or demand. And his account of Desire certainly entails a sense of urgency. But the word *demande* would be correctly translated from the French as "appeal" or "request," *demande* being that which implicitly asks a question and is, thus, a separate grammatical mode from the imperative. Even though the English word "demand" is stronger than the French *demande*, I have, nonetheless, chosen to retain that translation to stress the invisible bond among Desire, language, and the absolute power of the Other(A). In 1936, under the influence of Hegel's *Phenomenology of the Spirit*, Lacan described Desire as an irreducible residue between need and *demande* that also transcends them both (*Ecrits*, 1966, p. 181). In 1969 Lacan would say that *The Phenomenology of the Spirit* is incorrect in postulating a fully realized consciousness of self (*Selbstbewusstein*) that could culminate in some pinnacle of absolute knowledge. Designating himself as the sole recipient of such knowledge (as truth), Hegel missed the obvious truth. Any knowledge acquired is always already within each person.[25] Moreover, Lacanian Desire is not equatable with Hegel's absolute consciousness of self. Unconscious Desire cannot become totally realized, when at best it can only be half-said.

After 1936 Lacan pursued the relationship between Desire and *de-*

mande from other viewpoints. Demand is another of Lacan's terms for the purpose of formalizing the seemingly invisible—the Other(A) topology—by alluding to it. Seen in this light, demand would not be interpreted as a literal question. Instead, *demande* addresses the Other(A) seeking to convey the pressure of Desire; demand is the conscious link to repressed or unconscious Desire ($\mathcal{S} \Diamond D$). Desire, as a mechanism of longing, is absolute and infinite, but demand aims toward something specific, some substitute object, and is therefore finite. Yet, the unconditional nature of the demand for love shows the subject in subjection to the Other(A). In yet another turn of phrase, Lacan named *demande* "the metonymy of Desire." All demand is an appeal for love and recognition from the Other(A). But demand is doomed to repeat itself in a circuitous manner because the Other's Desire is alien, solitary, and insatiable, a condition of absoluteness and detachment (Sheridan, *Ecrits*, p. 311).

The developmental transition from mirror-stage primary desire to post–mirror-stage secondary Desire—or *demande*—coincides with a child's beginning to use language coherently. More specifically, demand will show up in sentences which start with "I want" and complete themselves by an *objet a*, referring all the way back to an inferred obscure "join" between the *moi* and primordial Desire. In this context motivation or "drive" comes from the treasure trove of signifiers found in the link between demand and repression or Law (Sheridan, *Ecrits*, p. 314). In Seminar Twenty Lacan said that demand emanates from the *je* and resides in the substitution of finite and concrete objects for the denied and obscure, infinite object of Desire (p. 114); these substitutions are just so many metonymous ways to compensate for the split between being and wanting that marked the end of the mirror stage. Thus, demand begins with the ideal ego's formation and answers finally to the superego, or the limits intrinsic to a specific *moi*. Substitute objects include language itself in the sense that it serves the same mastery function as objects (Lacan's interpretation of the *Fort! Da!* for example): Lacan has said that speaking is in and of itself a *jouissance*.

Another substitute object is sexual interaction. In Seminar Eleven Lacan described Desire as "the place of junction of the field of the *demande*—where the syncopes of the unconscious present themselves—with sexual reality" (pp. 142–43). By sexualizing reality, being, and language in relation to an Ur-libidinization of perception, Lacan attenuated the distinction between the pleasure and reality principles, which had forced Freud to define reality as desexualized

(*Séminaire* XI, p. 142). Lacan maintained that sexual stages do not form the basis of personality; Desire does. Consequently, there is no natural evolution or maturation of instinctual sexual stages (oral, anal, genital). Nor did Lacan believe in a biological foundation to personality which observation might reveal (*Séminaire* XI, pp. 61–62). Pointing out that the passage from the oral to anal stage takes place because of verbal injunctions and behavioral punishment and reward, Lacan stressed once more that language and culture have always preceded developmental stages—even before birth—and that *they* give meaning to biological being. With such arguments Lacan rendered Freud's evolutionary, "realist" maturational stages subjective, symbolic, and substitutive.[26]

Finally, it may be helpful to refer to a recent article by Allen S. Weiss entitled "Merleau-Ponty's Concept of the 'Flesh' as Libido Theory."[27] Since Lacan equates Desire with libido as the source of "drive," the concept of libido may be called a cornerstone of his epistemology. Weiss accepts Paul Ricoeur's idea that one branch of libido theory can, indeed, be traced to Lacan: Freud's interpretative hermeneutic model plus Saussurean linguistics. Deleuze, Guattari, Jean Lyotard, and others purportedly adopted Freud's other interpretative model, a hydraulic or energetic one.[28] Having made this cautionary provision, Weiss then dismisses Lacan's libido theory and places him in a category with Claude Lévi-Strauss and Roland Barthes as a structuralist thinker. According to Weiss, the libido theorists (Deleuze, Guattari, Lyotard) provide a critique of structuralism "by showing how the origins of meaning are not solely dependent upon textual interplay. For the libido theorists, meaning originates through the operation of energetic (libidinal) activity upon sign systems, such that the significative difference within each sign system is not originarily [*sic*] to be found within the system as a metaphoric/metonymic rupture of the system. The difference, the otherness, internal to every sign system is introduced into the system by a directed, pulsional activity, that is, by a libidinal determinant" (Weiss, "Merleau-Ponty's Concept," pp. 85–86).

Weiss's dismissal of Lacan's libido theory is no different from misunderstandings of his thought perpetrated by authors such as Guattari (who was analyzed by Lacan). Lacan's relocation of "drive" in Desire operates a reconfiguration on the aspects of Freudian theory that would distinguish between interpretative and hydraulic models in the first place. Desire (secondary energy) partakes of energy—*pulsion*—at the same time that it conditions concrete or linguistic meaning in reference to a primary representational chain, inseparable from the prespecular infant's corporal experiencing of the world. Weiss's error is also typical of those who do not really grasp the scope of Lacan's undertaking. Weiss, for example, discusses Maurice Merleau-Ponty's theory that the world is symbolized by the body; and the body, as lived experience, is in turn the source of the productive, generative, and creative activity of the subject. He concludes his article with the proposition that while neo-Freudians (like Lacan) see the world as founded upon repression of the libido, poststructuralists like Deleuze et al. stand in the line of Merleau-Ponty and have replaced this Freudian idea with a new theory: "new" because libido has become an active source of meaning, a creative determinant of existence (Weiss, "Merleau-Ponty's Concept," pp. 86, 94).

Weiss is unaware that the libido theorists whom he names have essentially taken their "new" theory from Lacan, but distorted Lacan's theory in the process. As we have shown, Lacan's theory demands a rethinking of the neo-Freudian concepts of repression, drive, and Desire. Like repression, Desire exists at all points of the psychic apparatus. Both play on and in language. The energetic component of Lacan's theory comes first from the dynamic fixation of Desire to key signifiers (in the pre-mirror and mirror stages) which are, nonetheless, repressed from consciousness (*Urverdrängung*). It comes secondly from the substitutive nature of post–mirror-stage Desire. Drive depends upon the active character of repression: the reverse side of Desire. *Pace* Weiss, differences are *not* found within sign systems as metaphoric/metonymic ruptures; they arise from the analogous energetic functioning of metaphor (in making meaning) and metonymy (in repressing meaning). The Lacanian libido is both of the body (primary libido) and *more* than the body. Unlike Merleau-Ponty, Lacan sees body and world as separable through analysis up to a point.[29] They are not, however, separable at a primordial level. Consequently, though Lacan hypothesizes a libidinization of perception, he does not leave us (as does Merleau-Ponty) with only the "lived body" (flesh) in relation to Mother Earth. Nor does he leave us with Desiring (sexual) energy to infinity (as do Deleuze and Guattari). Lacan has argued that the body experiences the psychic pain of division and alienation (which the impact of separation first caused) as Castration or primordial anxiety. This drama gives rise to the use of language as substitutive energy (secondary libido), in compensation for repressing a primordial Desire for constancy or Oneness (primary libido). That the components of Desire may then be analytically decoded in the conscious realm—i.e., hermeneutics—does not make them any less the energetic source and reference point of human meaning. For Lacan, Desire retains elements of the neo-Freudian view—the origins of meaning arising out of repression—while his concept of secondary libido gives rise to the "new" libido theory that Deleuze et al. have split off from Lacan's comprehensive epistemology and clumsily reinterpreted as their own. They make the error of supposing a world in which meaning as Desire can exist apart from Law (i.e., the superego or phallic division), which first created Desire as the basis of meaning.

The Lacanian Unconscious and Subversion of the Conscious Mind

In the mid- to late 1950s Lacan gave seminars on the formation of the unconscious. He used the graph of Desire reproduced in the article "The subversion of the subject and the dialectic of desire in the Freudian unconscious" (1960), in which he shows how Desire is situated in relation to a subject defined in his articulation by the signifier (Sheridan, *Ecrits*, p. 303). Verbal behavior points to "invisible" primary "texts" that must be decoded in light of unconscious Desire and its meanings. With his subversion of Descartes's *Cogito* by Desire, Lacan rejects the philosopher's picture of the mind that is, by definition, to be correlated with conscious thought. For Lacan, the mind has become an infinite network of combinatory, symbolic (figural), and linguistic associations, themselves rooted in a few identificatory fixations.

Lacan first designed the project later taken up by Piaget: to study knowledge as a process instead of as a state or as essences.[30] Where Piaget opted for a Darwinian theory in terms of sensorimotor sequences and genetic, developmental structures behind an adaptive evolution of mind, Lacan has offered a cultural one. Indeed, Lacan created a new epistemology of the human subject—by analyzing mind as a dialectical quadrature; by studying the role of effect (the mathematical fifth dimension) on persons; by combining the experiences of neonate perception with sensorimotor activity and linking both to mimesis, identificatory processes, and language. Piaget believed that "process" aimed at an evolutionary adaptation to reality. Lacan, however, has blurred the kind of distinction that separates man from reality. He paints man as a biological creature of contingency, who is subjectivized and representationalized in his genesis by the imposition of culture (symbols and language) on his corporal nature. Knowledge is, indeed, a process, but one which divides itself into unconscious, repressed knowledge as "truth," and conscious knowledge which flees from "truth" in the name of rationality, wisdom, and convention. In this theory Lacan is close to Nietzsche, who also claimed that the subject of consciousness was a "liar" and did not "know." Nietzsche, in consequence, saw "interpretation" as a false activity, a pretense at "knowing." Lacan parts company with Nietzsche—and with Derrida—by postulating a true text which "knows"—the unconscious—and in the elaboration of which all conscious use of knowledge and language is already interpretation. Concrete language is played upon by Desire, which commands its paths, rendering meaning indeterminate and often turning "communication" into miscommunication.

Before looking at Lacan's ideas on the conscious mind in greater detail, we must emphasize that his epistemology is not intended to be an ideology. Although some deconstructionists regard his thought as a system like any other—and thus one to be deconstructed—they miss Lacan's critique of those systems that implicitly aim at the closure which Lacan abhorred (Séminaire XX, p. 66). He maintained that our unitary tendencies toward the creation of systems and ideologies derive from the dictates of the identificatory process itself. Nature abhors a vacuum, physicists have taught, and Lacan demonstrated the same propensity in psychic "nature" by going outside language and thought to study the effects of the Real—prematuration, relationship to the mother and father, images, corporality—on perception. He concluded that because of the fashion in which identity is formed, human beings do not perceive by contemplating objects—that is, objectively—but through a subjective filter of representations through an emptying out of representations onto the world. Plato's world of static essences—Ideal forms—has disappeared, to be replaced by an inner world of representations from which conscious perception proceeds as if floating upward to the surface of language. These unconscious networks of fantasmatic meaning are not, however, the solipsistic representations of Idealist philosophy, any more than they are the "false" hallucinations which Freud equated with fantasy. They were first created by Real events and processes and reappear in the realm of Real experience. Although Lacan has been accused of being an Idealist—that is, of portraying a subject akin to Bishop Berkeley's self to whom nothing in the world appears except in one's own representations—he maintains that psychoanalysis is oriented toward the kernel of the Real in the heart of experience (Séminaire XI, p. 53). Here, the Real refers to the trauma and impact that first created the human subject in terms of division and Desire, an impact which never ceases to command the paths of behavior and language.

In the Lacanian context language is not a static or passive tool waiting to be manipulated by knowledge or thought. It finds its principal *raison d'être* in serving as a tool for exploring and elaborating unconscious experience within the conscious realm. By consciousness, then, Lacan does not mean consciousness of *something*. Instead, consciousness has become a mode of perception which negotiates Desire via substitutions. Given this de-ontologized picture of thought, it follows that Lacan will reject philosophical hermeneutics: the science of interpretation. Hermeneutics enjoins phenomenological thinkers to find the essence of a text by a minutely detailed description of it. Hermeneuticians are misguided, according to Lacan, in believing that meaning inheres in an object and is therefore accessible to perception through objective methods. By refusing the Freudian *Cogito*—actually the *Desidero*—at the basis of any person's experience, *they* are the philosophical Idealists (*Séminaire* XI, p. 141). Furthermore, Lacan finds the accusation of intellectualization that has been leveled at him truly paradoxical: "If one knew what I think of the Intelligence, assuredly one would be able to take back this reproach" (*Séminaire* XI, p. 148). The Desire that governs consciousness is not that of substance, Lacan has pointed out, but is there at the level of primary process (*Séminaire* XI, p. 140).

Referring to the contemporary theologian and philosopher Paul Ricoeur, Lacan stresses that the hardest thing for a philosopher is "to know the realism of the unconscious—that the unconscious is not ambiguity of behavior, nor future knowledge which knows itself already by not knowing itself, but lacuna, *coupure*, rupture, which inscribes itself in certain lack. M. Ricoeur agrees that there is something of this dimension to be reserved. Simply as the philosopher that he is, he hoards it to himself. He calls that hermeneutics" (*Séminaire* XI, pp. 140–41). Philosophers generally believe that a text holds something, some meaning that can be brought to light through the science of interpretation. It is hard for them to accept that the surface (text) does not *contain* meaning (as bottles contain wine), but takes on meaning only to conceal a deeper gap: standing behind the text is an unconscious system of repressed meanings whose roots lie in Desire.

In the 1930s Lacan studied philosophy at the École des Hautes Études. He was greatly influenced by phenomenology, and especially by its innovative interpretations of subject and object. Briefly, phenomenology is the theory of appearance fundamental to all empirical knowledge. The phenomenal world is the world of appearance, as opposed to the noumenal world-as-it-is-in-itself (das Ding an sich).[31] By showing the presence of the unconscious in the world of philosophical subject/object relations, Lacan revealed the inadequacy of phenomenological concepts in their exclusion of Desire. The phenomenological subject—Descartes's Cogito—is at the center of that mirage which makes modern man so sure of being himself, even in his uncertainties about himself. Like the phenomenologists, Lacan has also problematized "meaning." But by postulating Desire and intersubjectivity at its origin, he has taken it out of the realm of the empirically objectifiable (Séminaire I, p. 242). Insofar as perception emanates from unconscious, repressed Desire, it cannot be directly on an external object (person, text, or so on). Phenomenologists are mistaken, Lacan has said, in their articulate but deluded claims that perception occurs outside the subject, that it is an event not in the self, but around the object apprehended (Séminaire XI, p. 76). The impossibility at which phenomenology aims is a hypothetical unity in meaning between the perceived world (perceptum) and the conscious perceiving subject (percipiens). But any totalizing or unitary system—philosophical, theological, psychological—merely sends back to contingency what Lacan has designated as an inherent and permanent manque-à-être, whose proof is Desire.

Lacan has relocated the perceptum in a primary representational system, to which all secondary meaning systems refer in a "logic" of identification and substitution. By ascribing the drive toward unity (or meaning) to the gap in being which he names the Other(A), Lacan says that a person's Desire to "know" is essentially the Desire to know the Other(A): that is, truth (Sheridan, Ecrits, p. 301). Instead of the unified, conscious subject who "knows," Lacan gives us the split subject—supposing both itself and its knowledge (le sujet supposé savoir). Hegel thought the fully realized conscious subject (Selbstbewusstsein) knew what it wanted. Lacan's conscious subject thinks it knows as well but is wrong about who it is, and about what knowledge is as well. "It" is the unconscious which Hegel left out: the domain in which knowledge becomes truth. Some conceptual difficulties arise here: namely, the idea that even though the conscious subject's knowledge is presupposed elsewhere, its truthful impact on conscious life and language is both Real and present. This concept becomes tenable, however, when one grasps the difference of meaning between the French words savoir (to know factually) and connaître (to know at the level of recognition or familiarity). Jacques-

Alain Miller has tried to conflate these two meanings in English by writing the word "know" as "k(now)."[32]

Ultimately, both Hegel and Martin Heidegger were finally trapped in consciousness. Heidegger supposed that the human subject produces a set of symbolic data by its own existence (*Dasein*): Man exists as a project (*Entwurf*).[33] Lacan has criticized this phenomenological conception of a conscious subjectivity by his own anti-ontological move into language and identification; Lacan's primary unconscious subject—the opposite of Heidegger's Being as becoming—is formed as a set of Real symbolic data produced by the impact of culture and language.

While philosophy goes in the direction of substantivizing concepts into systems, Lacan talks about the structures that lie behind the drive to formulate systems. Meaning, belief, ideology, and system are only so many ever-evolving elaborations of language and identity, made up of myth, cliche, historical realities, and so on. Any final insight into the Real of the human condition will realize that all meaning-systems serve a humble purpose: to give a sense of unity and continuity to a structurally divided subject. The French psychoanalyst has said that he mistrusts the certainty and arrogance of conscious thought, which assumes unto itself a commensurability with reality when, in fact, consciousness is only a *reflection* of reality (*Séminaire* II, p. 136). "Man starts from nothing at all," Lacan urges, "and he learns by a mechanism of neutral recording which constitutes a reflection of the world that we call, like Freud, conscious or not. Man becomes aware of this reflection from the point of view of the other; he is an other for himself" (*Séminaire* II, p. 138). The only homogeneous function that Lacan assigns to consciousness is the Imaginary capture of the ego (o¹) by its mirror reflection (other) and the function of misrecognition which remains attached to it (Lacan, *Ecrits*, p. 832). Denial, objectification of others, and illusory ideals of the ego all play their part in making consciousness an irremediably limited principle of "self"-idealization and misrecognition (*méconnaissance*).

By *méconnaissance* Lacan means the original mirror-stage putting on of another's image and Desire as our own, which we repress as knowledge and repeat as a process. Thereafter, the dialectic of consciousness is made up of a polar tension between the Other's Desire in us and the tenuous relationship to objects or persons (ideals) who are supposed to satiate Desire (*Séminaire* II, p. 210). The path toward seeing one's Desire in relation to the Other(A) is not to be sought in auto-observation or through the eyes of others, therefore, but in the observation of observation (*Séminaire* II, p. 312). Authentic analytic consciousness—as opposed to the robotlike refractions which we *call* consciousness—resides in seeing oneself being seen (*se voir se voir*) in the Other(A). In privileged moments such as these, the gaze functions as the reverse side of consciousness and elides itself. The subject that sees itself as the correlative of the world of objectivity (the *je*) is not the same as the subject that feels itself surprised by *un regard vu* (the *moi*); the latter is the narcissistic subject of being which maintains itself in a function of Desire (*Séminaire* XI, pp. 79–80). Lacan means that the field of conscious perception can be disorganized by another's gaze, when the alien gaze connects with Desire, the prior and more profound perception of self, which the *je* takes great pains to hide from itself (*Séminaire* XI, pp. 83–84).

In the second part of *Being and Nothingness* (1943), Jean-Paul Sartre described the phenomenology of apprehension of others, pitching his arguments around the fundamental phenomenon he called the gaze or *regard*. In his own application of Sartre's insight, Lacan stresses that the analyst should not confuse the gaze with the fact that people see with their eyes. A person may feel scrutinized by someone whose eyes and physical being are invisible. A mere suspicion of the presence of others can trigger an inner resonance: a window, darkness, a feeling—and suddenly the window itself becomes a *regard*. In human relations the sensation of another's gaze upon one is sufficient to cause individuals to make themselves an object for that gaze (*Séminaire* I, p. 240). In moments like these the limitations of consciousness may be witnessed in what Lacan has described as a *scotoma* (Greek, obscuration of part of the field of vision).[34] The meaning of Sartre's brilliant aphorism—*Le regard de l'autre, c'est l'enfer* (Hell is the other's gaze)—becomes even clearer as we understand Lacan. The *regard* is not simply a glance cast from the eye, nor a glance from reflective consciousness, because the *regard* has the power to activate within consciousness an awareness of unconscious motivation and intentionality.

The meaning Lacan gives to the phenomenon of "seeing onself seen" is linked to his theory that the gaze is one of the first structuring mechanisms of the human subject. It was introjected as a part-object in the pre-mirror stage before the eye acquired its function of seeing and representing the subject and, consequently, before there was any sense of alterity. In the mirror stage the gaze is the dialectical bridge to self-recognition; perceptually speaking, the prespecular objects of Desire become permanently enmeshed in a network of inner vision. In consciousness the intersubjective element involved in "seeing oneself seen" has to do with knowing that the other knows that one is being looked at (*Séminaire* I, p. 244). The intrasubjective element appears mysteriously to consciousness when a person experiences "self" as an object of an-other's gaze—whether present or absent—and the gaze catalyzes a phenomenology of judgment in the form of shame, modesty, blushing, fear, prestige, rage, or so on. The other's look or words have connected with the repressed discourse linked to the Other's gaze. So essential is the gaze to Lacan's syntax of the unconscious that he has defined consciousness as the distinctive dialectical mark of the subject both oppressed by the inner gaze of the Other(A), and resentful of it. The Other's gaze triumphs over the eye, subjectivizing the relationship between gaze and eye, or seeing and knowing. Such a radical subversion of consciousness by the unconscious is the antithesis of the transparency and continuity between self and world that phenomenology assumes. The Lacanian quadrature of the human subject locates perception in the *moi* and the Other(A), but filtered up into the *je* and catalyzed by others. In daily discourse the expression "I see" usually means "I understand." In reality people often "misunderstand." This state of affairs derives partly from the incongruous and asymmetrical relationship among gaze, eye, and knowledge: a relationship that is really one of specular lure, opacity, illusion, and trap.

Unlike the gaze which is *in* us, the eye is outside, and functions like the other as a reflective promise of unification and fusion. But since the other (ego ideal) is always *outside*—that is, different—the inner eye which projects ideals is a prey to shattered illusions. Seeing and idealizing are functions tied to the power of the gaze. The eye therefore works as a principle of law or judgment like the phallic signifier and, as such, is a principle of separation and division (*Séminaire* XI, p. 96). If "seeing" basically involves projecting one's own inner reality outward to be refracted through an-other's eyes, then "knowing" is complicated at the primordial level of "self"-image and representation, long before "knowing" culminates in conscious thought. By linking the gaze to the earliest moments of the formation of the subject, Lacan has made it a part of the primordial unconscious system of representations, which are later reflected in consciousness. Because of its Ur-character, the specular gaze is separable from its unifying role in the *moi* composite and, as such, reappears as a fragment in hallucinations, dreams, or memories (*objet a*). In this capacity the eyes has been transformed in art as the staring eye of Expressionist paintings, or the eye of Big Brother in George Orwell's novel *1984* (1949).

It becomes clear that Lacan has complicated the standard subject/object dualism of philosophy by making the *moi* an organized object, which functions as a subject. It always verifies or recomposes itself in relation to objects "out there" (who also think they are subjects). Lacan accuses the phenomenological or existential subject of behaving as if it were independent of the structures imposed by language, Desire, myth, and kinship—as if all conditions derived from conscious choice. In opposition to all reifications and systematizations of conscious thought, Lacan offers the realism of the unconscious, which is above all pre-ontological, the presence of Desire itself, as well as the part-objects of Desire (*Séminaire* XI, pp. 31, 140).

Lacan's critique of the limits of consciousness casts new light on neurosis, psychosis, freedom, love, and truth. At all points of his discourse he teaches that the differences between certain normal and pathological tendencies are a matter of degree. Narcissism, Desire, aggressiveness, and alienation, for example, are the norms of ego structure. But even though a normative psyche differs from the a-normal, the differences can be explained rationally in reference to the original structuration and subsequent functioning of the subject. Thus, the specificities of the a-normal are clearly delineated in psychic structures where there is no passage from one to the other: the neurotic, the perverse, the psychotic (Jacques-Alain Miller, "Lacan the Clinician," May 14, 1984). A psychotic is, indeed, a different kind of being from a normal one, but only insofar as psychosis—a state of extreme fragmentation in language, body image, and identity concept—melodramatizes the composition of the human psyche itself. For psychosis is the limit of freedom and truth, the point at which a person is utterly object-ified and swallowed up by the lures and Desires of the Other(A).[35]

Individual freedom is also appropriated in love. In the extreme case the lover wishes to become an object for the loved one who has the same value for the other as his or her own body. The abdication of liberty which love invites situates love in its concrete form: genital love (*Séminaire* I, p. 242). "Possessing" the other is, from a Lacanian viewpoint, a revelation of the drive toward refinding the psychic fusion or seeming wholeness that predated Castration. Lacan says that existentialists understood very well the connections between the narcissistic libido, love, and aggressiveness. They also understood the negativity of human estrangement and alienation from its own roots and from others (being and nothingness). Although existentialism borrowed from psychoanalysis, its conclusions remained incomplete, however. Existentialists understood negativity only within the limits of a self-sufficiency of consciousness. Lacan, on the other hand, takes negativity (denial or *Verneinung*) as the mark of the subject against the unconscious. Imprisoned within a subject/object dualism and a semantics of consciousness, existentialism ended up in a variety of subjective impasses which Lacan lists: a freedom that found its greatest authenticity within prison walls; a demand for commitment that expressed the impotence of a pure consciousness to master any situation; a personality that realized itself only in suicide; a consciousness of the other that could only be satisfied by Hegelian murder (Sheridan *Ecrits*, p. 6).

Lacan's picture of consciousness redefines not only subject/object relations, but also the relationship of mind and body. Western philosophy long believed that man's goal was to become as contemplative and introspective as possible. Thought was viewed as nonmaterial (spirit) and body as matter. Karl Marx reacted against this attitude in favor of a materiality of experience. Freud, too, opposed the idea of man as a reflective animal and located human essence in unconscious drives and wishes.[36] Marx, Freud, Piaget, and many twentieth-century thinkers have challenged the age-old idea that thought is substance or essence in the mind (the contained), while the body is the container. In Freud's effort to erase the mind/body opposition, he reversed the situation, making body (sex) the condition of mind.[37] It is worth suggesting that, in its own way, Freud's biologism is as materialist as Marx's dialectical materialism. Freud's biological conclusions have consequently lent indirect support to a variety of twentieth-century materialisms: Piaget's developmental, genetic, and adaptive sequences of mind evolution; sociobiology's theory of the "selfish" gene; psychoneurological postulations of right-brain, left-brain mind control. Lacan transcends these dichotomies by uncovering a paradox that erases the materialist oppositions between mind and body without requiring that he grant priority to either philosophy or biology. By making thought a derivative of the effects of language and associational networks of representation, by placing Desire at the heart of meaning, by making the primary ego a sensory structure inseparable from real corporal experience, by showing the secondary or narcissistic ego as commensurate with other-oriented relationships, Lacan has libidinized philosophy and theology and ontologized biology.

One paradox revealed by Lacan is the sensual dimension of language, and the abstract, representational side of corporality. Here consciousness appears as the reflection of external reality as it is filtered through a sensorial system (*Séminaire* II, pp. 132–33). By adding body to language, Lacan is immediately plunged into a problematics of the Real. Unlike the post-structuralist deconstructionists, however, Lacan does not dispense with notions of the Real or the true. Instead, he separates truth from consciousness and knowledge and places it on the side of the Real, in structure and unconscious discourse, and linked to intentionality and Desire. He shows "truth" peeking out in language through syncopations, contradictions, repetitions, implied questions or doubt, and other such verbal or textual *aporia*.

Having briefly surveyed Lacan's relationship to some positions and impasses in philosophy, we can now talk about his view of the unconscious in greater detail. Anika Lemaire has called Lacan completely Freudian in his conception of the unconscious. As proof, she cites his acceptance of the following principles: the unconscious knows neither contradiction, negation, doubt, nor uncertainty; its processes belong to the past and to spatial concepts; primary processes are inhibited by secondary ones; there is a greater mobility of cathectic intensities in the unconscious than in consciousness (Lemaire, *Lacan*, pp. 154–55). We shall see, however, that Lacan's rethinking of the Freudian unconscious gives an entirely different picture from the standard neo-Freudian one, even though Lacan adheres to Freudian principles. As Robert Georgin has aptly observed, Lacan's theories have established that the unconscious does not leave any of our actions outside its domain. So conceived, any "rational" discourse is already "symptomatic": the *moi* is itself structured like a symptom.[38]

Freud initially portrayed the unconscious as a mechanistic place where repressed memories and attitudes were relegated to a memory bank of ideational thing-representations attached to instinctual drives. Having discovered the unconscious, Freud had to solve the problem that still plagues all of psychoanalytic enterprise: how to go from consciousness to an unconscious, which is by definition closed to conscious perusal. The answer, then as now, is through its effects and manifestations in conscious life. Freud first solved the problem of crossing the bar between consciousness and the unconscious by showing that the unconscious comes into view in dreams, jokes, "the psychopathology of everyday life," and in the symptoms of neurosis or psychosis, that is, whenever the censor is off guard. By 1920

Freud had abandoned his early interest in pinpointing the unconscious in dreams and jokes and, instead, had made the unconscious the seat of the id. Since Freud's death, most neo-Freudians have derived the standard metaphor of the unconscious from this second topology: the unconscious is a container of visual thought (fantasies) attached to id energy or drive. This neo-Freudian unconscious lacks any organization or unified will and strives blindly to gratify both its instincts and fantasies (the pleasure principle). From a theoretical viewpoint, the Freudian instinctual unconscious is a principle of explanation for disconnected and unintelligible conscious acts (Wilden, LS, p. 112). It serves as a force of continuity-in-being by breaking through the denials of consciousness and the repressions of civilization, and paradoxically protects the biological individual against social obliteration (Rieff, Freud, p. 29). But seen from a moralist's point of view, the unconscious of the second topology is a chained monster, a chaotic, insatiable, and impersonal id, pleasure-bent at any cost to individuals or society.

In "The Agency of the Letter" (1957) Lacan says that there is no original or instinctual unconscious. Everything in the unconscious gets there from the outside world via symbolization and its effects. Thus it is neither mysterious nor impersonal. Moreover, it can be described theoretically. The possible combinations of meeting between the infant and the Other(A) can be formally studied, Lacan has said, like any order that subsists in its rigor and is independent of any subjectivity (Séminaire II, p. 350). While this view of the unconscious might appear to be non-Freudian, Lacan claims to have developed Freud's early symbolic, representational model in conjunction with Freud's dynamic and economic systems. In the dynamic model Freud equated the unconscious with the repressed. In the economic model the principle of constancy delineated the unconscious by the opposition of pleasure and displeasure (Wilden, LS, p. 262). Lacan envisions the unconscious as a repressed but organized and "intelligent" discourse of the Other(A). The subject of consciousness aims toward constancy, although its goals are thwarted by the complex quadrature of the subject. Repressed signifiers in the Other(A) erect an obstacle between the moi and Desire, with the result that the unconscious "overdetermines" and destabilizes not only dreams, jokes, and symptoms, but also object relations and the unity of je discourse itself. The unconscious forces us to examine the "law" according to which no utterance can ever be simply reduced to its own statement [39] (see Chapter 4). For Lacan, perception becomes a link between conscious and unconscious realms in its dual relation to primary

(*Vorstellungsrepräsentation*) and secondary meaning. As discussed in Chapter 1, an infant perceives and, in that degree, "thinks" insofar as its perceptions are judgments made long before it enters Descartes's realm of certainty or doubt.

The Lacanian unconscious exists as a place or topology somewhere between consciousness and perception, between Desire and language. And it may be discussed theoretically in terms of its formation, its laws, its "knowledge," and its effects as decoded or "read backward" in relation to language and relationships. The French "new philosopher" Jean-Marie Benoist has written that the Lacanian unconscious is that "great combiner of signs, comprised of the restless textures of a syntax and a semantics, of a poetics and a rhetoric over which the conscious subject no longer assumed command, but in which it [the unconscious subject] was only a place, a precarious territory, and even a lacuna, a hole from whose edges the *ça* set it [the conscious subject] going to signify."[40] Benoist's prose here is not unlike Lacan's, and it demonstrates one of the difficulties of trying to understand Lacan through secondary texts. Pared down, Benoist's description says that the Lacanian unconscious is the source of a poetics of meaning. One of its agents is the *moi*. (See ch. 1, p. 12).

The *moi* provides the beginnings of a formal structure of the unconscious (*Séminaire* XI, pp. 23–24). Later it speaks the truth of recognition needs, separation, anxiety, grandiosity, jealousy, love, power aspirations, and so on—a kind of "speech" that cannot be isolated through memory. Fittingly, the very act of remembering takes on a new meaning in Lacan's epistemology. It is not a Platonic activity— the return of a form or imprint—but something which comes to humans from the necessities of structure, from where the subject was born of the lowest encounters of spoken language, that is, in terms of division and alienation (*Séminaire* XI, p. 47). Lacan therefore talks of "rememoration," not of memory. Whereas Freud saw impressions as elemental in forming the unconscious, Lacan gives this role to perception (*Séminaire* II, p. 172). The memories of perception are those of effect built up into a *moi*, which speaks to him who hath ears to hear (Sheridan, *Ecrits*, p. 141). In the first place, *moi* speech is that of primary effect. But gradually the *moi* will misrecognize the Other(A) *because* it contains the repressed history of childhood.

Freud was certain that "something" was there in the navel of the dream. That "something" is what Lacan calls the unconscious discourse, and it shows up sporadically in dreams and daily discourse, but does not involve luck, arbitrariness, instincts, or archaic images (as in Carl Jung's romantic unconscious) (*Séminaire* XI, pp. 45–46).

Freud's unconscious representations were only visual, and therefore silent. But Lacan's wide-ranging use of theories from different areas of study have enabled him to theorize links between unconscious representations and speech, which, visible in conscious life as well as in dreams, are attached to the materiality of sounds, letters, words, and the larger units of verbal messages. The issue of *how* the unconscious can be approached from consciousness has ignited many of the quarrels, defections, and schisms that surround the Lacanian School. Jean Laplanche, for example, reversed one of Lacan's central theories by insisting that the primary-process, unconscious laws of condensation, displacement, and symbolism are the regulators of conscious language.[41]

I feel sure that Lacan did not mean that the laws of language— metaphor and metonymy—directly create condensation and displacement. Language is a system of signs that is complete in itself, as is the unconscious Other(A) system. Another of Lacan's metaphors for the unconscious is that of a double sack with an opening at the center, like the *besace* carried by beggars. The unconscious is a thing set apart and closed at the interior. It can only be penetrated from outside itself—by language (*Séminaire* XI, p. 130). Lacan has not specified what the exact elemental links between conscious and unconscious language are, but he has made it clear that language regulates the unconscious, and not the reverse. Secondary process controls the frantic sliding of primary-process identifications by establishing a distance from them through labels and names. Lacan's insights of genius are: (1) that the two systems overlap, intermingle, and continually condition each other; (2) that the unconscious makes its presence felt in conscious discourse by the direction of intention (for example, "I am . . ." or "I want . . ." statements or choices which point to objects of Desire as substitutes for an inherent incompleteness in being); and (3) that the laws of these two systems work analogously and the unconscious flow of meaning can, therefore, be decoded by studying their common functions of substitution, condensation, displacement, and referentiality.

In the 1950s Lacan followed Lévi-Strauss in defining "structure" as those specific transformations which follow certain laws.[42] Lacan's unconscious is a closed meaning system of structures whose laws and functions are as logical as any inferred in the conscious order of meaning. Looked at in itself (as opposed to its effects in conscious life), Lacan's unconscious exhibits an interplay of signifiers (differentiations), tropes, and representations or memory traces that were first introjected during the first eighteen months of life as a network of visual and verbal relations, even before language gave them any stable meaning. Lacan compares the unconscious to a fishnet (*nasse*), a metaphor which contrasts directly with Freud's image of the cave of buried memories (*Séminaire* XI, p. 172). Elsewhere he says that the primordial unconscious splices itself together in a spider's web of images, "letters" (abstract signifiers), and messages. The spider's web and the fishnet suggest a material that has been woven. Functionally, it catches some bits (memory) and lets other bits slip through (what is forgotten, primordially repressed). It becomes knotted in places (neuroses, junctures of overlapping effects); it can be torn (trauma), but rewoven (through analysis). From an adult perspective, the unconscious infuses discontinuities into conscious functioning in the form of *lapsus memoriae*, errors, obsessions, and so on. Lacan has conveyed this idea by his metaphor of the bladder (*vessie*) whose intermittent, valvular movement produces discontinuity (*Séminaire* XI, p. 28). When surprised into view, the unconscious closes back on itself just as quickly as it opened.

A Lacanian analyst must, therefore, confront the problem of how to bring the unconscious into view. Lacan rejects the idea of it as a buried substance and explains that because the unconscious can only be catalyzed in Real situations, it is the nonborn, the unrealized, the evasive, the something waiting in the air, the unwritten portion of a text (*Séminaire* XI, p. 25). Mathematically speaking, the unconscious is an algorithm: a *losange* ($\Diamond$) which lies at the heart of any relationship between the perceiving subject and the realities to be negotiated (the *perceptum*). Efforts to trap the unconscious through introspection, remembering the past, talking about feelings, and so forth will only elicit the *moi* fixations and myths which conceal the Other(A) by denial and rejection. When the unconscious is caught entirely off guard and the unity of the *je* discourse is subverted, unconscious "meaning" stumbles into view and circumvents the *je* (*Séminaire* XI, p. 27). The Lacanian unconscious can only, therefore, be exposed transsubjectively. It does not inhere statically within a subject, but floats suspended in a "third" position waiting to be articulated by some interaction (Wilden, *LS*, p. 264). But even then it will remain enigmatic unless decoded analytically. In the essay "The function and field of speech and language in psychoanalysis" (1953), Lacan described the unconscious as "that part of the concrete discourse, insofar as it is transindividual, that is not at the disposal of the subject in re-establishing the continuity of his conscious discourse" (Sheridan, *Ecrits*, p. 49).

Only people freed of the illusion that others literally are as their own *moi* imagines them to be can interpret unconscious manifestations by reading backward through language. But how? Lacan replies: "It is not in a grammatical conception of the functions in which they appear that one should analyse if and how the I (*je*) and the ego (*moi*) may be distinguished or overlap in each particular subject" (Sheridan, *Ecrits*, p. 129). In other words, subject/object distinctions of grammar will not transparently reveal *je* or *moi*. A partial answer lies in Lacan's theory that the use of language is an end in itself. Although language may be used to transmit neutral information—a phenomenon Lacan calls *langue*—it is more frequently "overdetermined" by an intentionality which drives the *moi* to seek recognition from others through the medium of language—a phenomenon Lacan calls *parole*. *Parole* generates that indeterminacy of meaning which plagues philosophers, linguists, semioticians, and communication theoreticians and dispatches them on a variety of metaquests for the "meaning of meaning." Of greater interest to Lacan is the quest itself: the compelling Desire to communicate becomes a more telling feature about meaning than the content of what is communicated.

Another challenge facing the Lacanian analyst, apart from the ease with which unconscious meaning escapes detection, is that unconscious discourse is already abstract and reconstructed language (Bär, "Understanding Lacan," p. 477). "Other" language consists of diachronic symbols and signifying associations of image, sound, and body. This "abstract," intransitive language is denoted by Lacan as the "enunciated" (*l'énoncé*), the "said" (*le dit*), or the "written" (*l'écrit*). Elsewhere he puns that the Symbolic order is the *dit-mension* of unconscious truth (*Séminaire* XX, p. 97). Concrete discourse, on the other hand, evolves synchronically and uses recognizable words, social codes, rhetorical devices, and conventional thought patterns. Lacan describes this language of common discourse as the "enunciator" (*l'énonciateur*), the "saying" (*le dire*), and "scripting" (*l'écriture*). With these transitive terms, Lacan maintains the linear, present-tense sense of the speaking subject.

The person who would penetrate the unconscious domain must first renounce the assumptions of consciousness whose major mode is denial (Fages, *Comprendre Lacan*, p. 96) and also the sequentially linear, cause-and-effect logic of conscious systems. Although unconscious laws function *like* those of language, their logic is quite different. By reverse example, Lacan's own discourse shows that systematic language conventions aim to contain and corral the suspensions of meaning which the unconscious reveals. From a Lacanian perspective, the *savoir* of conscious thought appears as a fallacious substitute for unconscious "truth," which dupes man by *escaping* the circle of certainties in which people recognize themselves (*Séminaire* II, p. 16). According to Benoist, Lacan's equation of "truth" with unconscious meaning heralds not only the death of essences, of a humanism based on the myth of a substantialist subject, but also the death of consciousness as the source of meaning and the standard comparison of the human microcosm and the macrocosm of nature.

Leclaire has drawn up three categories to designate the principal dimensions of the Lacanian unconscious: (1) identificatory and substitutive (i.e., condensation and displacement), (2) objects or the dialectic between *moi* and others/Other(A), and (3) literal or the signifying elements which appear in *je* discourse.[43] We have already commented on the mechanism of substitution in our discussion of Desire. But certain important ramifications emerge from this. Not only does the substitutive function of Desire theoretically eradicate any final division between the conscious and unconscious realms, but it also implies a clarification of certain problematic deadends in philosophy, linguistics, and psychoanalysis. Among other poststructuralist philosophers, Jacques Derrida has theorized that philosophy went astray early in its existence by disconnecting Aristotle's *Poetics* from models of the mind, thus limiting rhetoric to mere stylistics, and philosophy to thought or essences. Structuralist thinkers postulated a binary metaphorics at the base of mental functioning. But neither the structuralists, who first described the laws of language, nor the post-structuralists or semioticians, who have linked language to mind, have explained *why* the mind works metaphorically or *how* the symbol system resides in the brain. In my estimation Lacan has pointed out the direction in which answers may be found to these problems. His understanding of the combined effects of prematuration, mimesis, and the impact of the outside world in shaping perception has broadened not only the scope of those who study language per se (and ignore the role of the human subject!), but also of those who leave language out of their theories of mind or self entirely.

Leclaire's second category is that of objects. We already know that any subject/object discussion of Lacanian thought requires a sense of the complexity and prismatic variability of the Other(A). We have also seen that Lacan often uses the same term in different ways to describe the various planes on which one variable in experience functions. In this way, he "constitutes a polyphony of meaning"

(Georgin, *Le Temps*, p. 89). Early in Lacan's career, the Other(A) referred to the mirror-stage relationship of identification between infant and the Real other or mother. Here Other(A) means fusion with Otherness or the alien. His key concerns at that moment were specularity, recognition, and Desire. In 1957 Lacan said that he had used a capital "O" ("A" in French for *Autre* or *Autre Scène*) in describing the unconscious as the discourse of the Other(A) in order to indicate the "beyond" in which recognition of Desire and the Desire for recognition were joined (Sheridan, *Ecrits*, p. 172). Lacan later stressed the link between specular identification and language by calling the father the Symbolic other, representative of the cultural character of the Other(A), the one who breaks up the mother/infant dyad by an implicit "no" and so symbolizes the social order in language. In another turn of the kaleidoscope, the whole social order of structuring effects and symbolic fullness—with language, codes, laws, and conventions—becomes the Other(A). In his last texts Lacan returned to the primordial nature of the (m)Other as the source of unconscious discourse that goes beyond utterance: a place where signifying material was recorded as the original memory bank of meaning. Although Other(A) effects appear at the surface of language, they can only be analyzed or decoded by a reading backward into the place of origin: the Other(A).

When Lacan talks about the *moi* as an effect of the Other(A)—a signified to the Other—he shows the *moi* being constituted there by *Wahrnehmungszeichen* (perception or signifying marks) (*Séminaire* XI, pp. 46, 138). Manifesting itself as the presence of unconscious effect in both *moi* relations and *je* discourse, the Other(A) is neither hidden nor beyond the closure of the unconscious (*Séminaire* XI, p. 119). The *moi* makes its way toward consciousness, proliferating through the masks it dons and the reflections it receives back from others in its paradoxical attempts to know the Other(A) (Desire) as well as to adapt to the social order (Law). As an agent of the unconscious, the *moi* objectifies others in the realm of Real event and specular interaction. But when the *moi* is analytically unveiled as an *object* of the Other(A), it can become an object of consciousness. The *moi* is, then, both subject and object. Lacan has portrayed the inner gaze of the Other(A) as triumphing over the eye (as seeing), and beyond the indeterminacy of the vocal register. Lacan's *moi*, which is alternatively subject and object and alternatively true and false, illuminates many of the logical impasses reached by analysts such as Alice Miller and R. D. Laing. Following Kohut, for example, Miller has described a narcissistic personality as one whose "true" and good self has been repressed.[44] Lacan removes the necessity of ferreting out a metapersonality. Individuality is both one's "true" self and someone else's fiction, thus inherently alien or other.

We come, finally, to Leclaire's third category of the Lacanian unconscious: the literal dimension. Freud was obsessed by the idea of proving the unconscious materially. As *his* proof, Lacan has offered the insistence (insertion) of the signifier or "letter," which determines the unconscious support of concrete discourse. Freud made of the unconscious and preconscious a substantive place where fantasy, memory, and representational content were statically recorded to give meaning to everything a person says (Lemaire, *Lacan*, p. 135). Having revealed the primacy of structure over substance and of effect over the literal, Lacan has dispersed Freud's unconscious fantasies into conscious discourse and made them the source of reality perception. This is the sense of Lacan's portrayal of the unconscious, in his famous "Discours de Rome" (1953), as "the sum of the effects of the *parole* on a subject, at the level where the subject constitutes itself from the effects of the signifier" (*Séminaire* XI, p. 116), that is, from the effects of difference, or otherness.

In passage after passage, Lacan has tried to forestall readers who misinterpret this theory by drawing a straight line between the unconscious and the signifiers of daily discourse. Language distances the "natural" subject from its own immediacy, causing a lack of "self"-awareness, and this effect creates the unconscious as a place of loss and disappearance. All the same, the signifier leaves acoustic traces attached to visual matter. Lacan finds support for this theory in Freud's texts. In his second topology Freud talked about a perception/consciousness system in which "perception" (*Wahrnehmung*) resided in the unconscious designated by "perception marks" (*Wahrnehmungszeichen*). These were absolutely separated from the place of consciousness (*Bewusstsein*). But Freud did not know how to join these *Wahrnehmungszeichen* to the conscious realm and so ultimately dropped this concept in favor of placing perception in the conscious system.

By recasting the *Es* linguistically as a set of signifying networks, Lacan claims to have followed Freud's original proposition that the *Es* could not become memory without being simultaneously erased both in unconscious perception and in consciousness. Such a process would be a linguistic phenomenon—an act of signifying synchrony— in which a perception would be reciprocally erased in both systems and then substituted elsewhere. In Lacan's opinion, Freud's postulation of these *Wahrnehmungszeichen* was a linguistic discovery fifty years before the advent of modern linguistics (*Séminaire* XI, p. 46). Lacan has capitalized on this moment of mutual erasure (and the problems of logic it poses) to postulate a third place linking Freud's *Wahrnehmung* and his *Bewusstsein:* the *Wahrnehmungszeichen* themselves. This concept gives Lacan an answer to Freud's problem of how to get from a silent, unconscious world of visual representations to a conscious world of verbal utterance, without having to resort to a preconscious hypothesis. In discussing the Freudian concept of *Vorstellungsrepräsentanz*—usually translated as "representation"—Lacan points out that "representation" generally means a completed rendering of a thing already represented (*représenté*) when it should include the active idea of representing (*représentant*) (*Séminaire* XI, p. 198).[45] This occurs through the agency of *Wahrnehmungszeichen* or signifiers.

The literary critic Jim Swan has shed light on this by his contention that object-relations theorists tend to overlook the Freudian hypothesis of representability. This theory belonged to Freud's economic model of quantifiable bodily and psychic energies such as libido, cathexis, charge, and discharge.[46] In his metapsychological essay "The Unconscious" (1915) Freud hypothesized that ideas which are made unconscious by repression or defense are per se unaccompanied by emotion: they are cathexes (investments or *Besetzungen*) of memory traces. But he attached affects to consciousness and discharge (*Abfuhrvorgängen*) whose ultimate manifestations were perceived as feelings (*Empfindungen*).[47] In short, ideas are repressed, but feelings are not. Swan, however, points to a logical impasse in Freud's theory. Freud places experience of the body on the side of ideas: the "represented." This would mean that knowledge about the body was repressed, but without affect, that the body was experienced in silence. Swan concludes that psychoanalysts have abandoned the economic model because they realize that "quantified and objective scientific concepts" are incapable of describing the experience of a person's body (Swan, "*Mater* and Nannie," p. 56).

Philosophers, on the other hand, have taken Freud's theory of representability seriously. Paul Ricoeur has designated this hypothesis as the one which qualifies psychoanalysis as a study of the mind. Lacan's theory of active representation via signifying perception builds a bridge between the mind and the body and also offers a way out of Freud's logical impasse. It is neither ideas nor affects which are repressed, but signifying or meaningful perceptions. In Lacan's words, it is the signifier which is repressed; no other meaning can be given to the word *Vorstellungsrepräsentanz* (*Séminaire* XI, p. 198).

As we saw in Chapter 1, the primordial *moi* is formed as a coefficient of corporal experience. But the *je* is a correlative of spoken language. Before a child speaks, however, the effects of language, corporal experience, and identifications (the affectivity of narcissism and aggressiveness) converge in the *Wahrnehmungszeichen*, and these link *moi* to *je*, mind to body, ideas to emotions, and consciousness to the unconscious. These "signifying marks" point to the place of repression in the Other(A) where the earliest experience of the body was not a silent one. The tones, phonemes, and acoustic impressions attached to images all make up part of the effect of language, which represents itself long before coherent speech in "signifying marks"; and they, in turn, are built up throughout childhood layer upon layer. When a child first begins to speak, the outside world of sound, image, and relationship activates the inner world of representations (*représenté*) in a continual, dynamic interchange of "signifying data." Man is a representational animal at every level: language, symbols, and identifications form him (*représenté*) and then represent him (*représentant*).

The body first sensualized language, and language in turn symbolizes the body. This theory has been well expressed by the Lacanian H.-T. Piron: "All our intentions find their symbolic matrix in the body and no concept expresses cultural, ethical or religious values without slipping into metaphors of the lived body. . . . The lived body affectively bathes in language, and in return language has the power to model the body, to deploy or to repress its virtualities" (Lemaire, *Lacan*, p. 150). "Signifying marks" are, therefore, inscribed in the Lacanian unconscious as a network of symbolic matrices of perception, organized initially around the elemental objects of Desire. Freud could not fathom *how* the unconscious could think and so tried to prove the existence of an unconscious out of what could be dredged up from the subliminal by consciousness (*Séminaire* XI, p. 44). Lacan's answer—that the discourse of the Other(A) "thinks"— transforms Freud's *eine andere Lokalität* from its conceptualization as the "primal sexual scene" (said to cause sexual trauma and subsequent repression) to the place of the Other(A) (where the "signifying marks" of perception are actively representational). These signifiers are ultimately those of concrete language. But, although they are transformed in the unconscious, they also provide one link for recuperating unconscious discourse in speech (*Séminaire* XI, p. 27).

Lacan's postulation of a literal connection between conscious and unconscious systems makes sense of the linguistic nature of those behavioral mechanisms that Freud attributed to the unconscious:

slips of the tongue and pen, speech disturbances, stuttering, omissions, charged silences, incoherent sounds, strange words, laughter, jokes, and so on (Bär, "Understanding Lacan," p. 486). At this level of "search," Lacanians are especially attentive to the individual signifiers of a discourse, not to the specific *memory content* which neo-Freudians try to document. By deliberately creating irruptions and breaks in an analysand's unified story; by listening for specific clusters around sounds, words, or concepts; by following displacements, similarities, and substitutions (be they of sound, word, or concept), Lacanian analysts are able to "guess" at associative elements of unconscious meaning. Lacan has referred to such unconscious signifying effects in language as crossroad words or "knots" of meaning—not unlike the *Knotenpunkte* Freud attributed to dreams—or symbolic "anchoring points" (*points de capiton*) (*Ecrits*, 1966, p. 503). Although Lacan's method of "guessing" resembles Freud's early dream analyses (in which assonance, verbal ambiguities, and synchronic coincidences were linked to unconscious meaning), Lacan has brought these effects into the here and now, into the Real, where the unconscious continually reconstitutes itself in a Hegelianlike movement of syntheses triggered by the dialectical search of the *moi* for the Other(A).

Since the combination potential of sounds and images is infinite, however, the detection of nodes of unconscious meaning in the complex meaning system of everyday language requires that an analyst be schooled in the disciplines related to language and myth such as religion, mythology, comparative literature, and the history of ideas (Bär, "Understanding Lacan," p. 534). One word—even a phoneme—may trigger a myriad of symbolic associations (*Séminaire* I, p. 294).[48] In 1953 Lacan first urged psychoanalysts to formalize the essential dimensions of their experience as follows: the historical theory of the symbol; intersubjective logic; and the temporality of the human subject (Sheridan, *Ecrits*, p. 76). Since then, Lacan has charted the territory himself with mathemes, knots, circles, and graphs. But even then, unconscious meaning can only be known indirectly. The subjective nature of perception and the evocative potential of language ensure that there can never be a full linguistic congruence between conscious and unconscious codes.

In the "Discours de Rome" (1953) Lacan described the unconscious poetically as "that chapter of my history that is marked by a blank or occupied by a falsehood: it is the censored chapter. But the truth can be rediscovered; usually it has already been written down elsewhere. Namely:—in monuments: this is my body . . .

—in archival documents: these are my childhood memories . . .—in semantic evolution: this corresponds to the stock of words and acceptations of my own particular vocabulary, as it does to my style of life and to my character;—in traditions, too, and even in the legends which, in a heroicized form, bear my history;—and, lastly, in the traces that are inevitably preserved by the distortions necessitated by the linking of the adulterated chapter to the chapters surrounding it, and whose meaning will be re-established by my exegesis" (Sheridan, *Ecrits*, p. 50).

In concluding this section, we can sum up the Lacanian unconscious as a structural (ordered), signifying (meaningful) delimitation of conscious thought and behavior, made up of all that one is, as well as of the potential for what one may become. While Freud showed the primacy of being over thought, Lacan has gone further and postulated an unconscious which is more than either being or non-being: it is a place of the nonrealized (*Séminaire* XI, p. 32). In its primary aspect the unconscious is unknowable and ungraspable as the prespecular and specular representational subject of fading. But in its secondary aspect, it is both synchronic and transindividual. And it is always an enigma to be decoded in light of repetition, substitution, transference, repression, and referentiality. What any analysis of an unconscious will reveal is a nonsubstantial, dialectical "language" of becoming, which insinuates proleptic narcissism/aggressiveness and Desire/Law modalities into all human events and interactions, thus explaining *what* motivates a dialectical movement. Therefore, even though the unconscious is the "never here," it is far from being "nothing."

Repetition, Repression, and Regression

There is no transparent "royal road" to the unconscious. But Lacan's various methods of valorizing the abstract and invisible do infer mythical joins between the unconscious and consciousness. In his essay "Remembering, Repeating and Working Through" (1914) Freud first articulated the concept of repetition (*Séminaire* XI, p. 49). He surmised that what cannot be consciously remembered—what is repressed—repeats itself in behavior. But whereas Freud thought that repetition compulsion (*Wiederholungszwang*) pointed to an effort to master a neurotic symptom, Lacan has hypothesized that the symptom is a metaphor for the human dimension and hence not neurotic per se (see Chapter 4). Clinically speaking, the symptom is a metaphor for an untranslated unconscious message. Freud viewed the symptom as neurotic but also "correctable" through a remembering which would open a door and release repressed material. Lacan, on the other hand, taught that an individual will not reach any unconscious truth along the path of reminiscence (delving into the past), but along the path of repetition in the here and now (*Séminaire* II, p. 110; *Séminaire* XI, p. 131). Lacan distinguishes, therefore, between *reminiscence*, which partakes of memory (and thus of consciousness), and *remémoration*, which belongs to the *moi* and drives human beings to relive unconsciously each instant of their history in the present (*Séminaire* II, p. 218). Lacan here echoes Søren Kierkegaard's idea that the principle of identity is precisely that of repetition. But Lacan equates the *moi* and repetition so that the phenomenon is located somewhere between the unconscious and consciousness—in the same territory as the "signifying marks" of perception.

In *Beyond the Pleasure Principle* (1920) Freud viewed repetition compulsion as a manifestation of the death instinct, the pleasure principle being their common corollary. By linking prematuration, perception, and elemental fragmentation to a metaphorical death or Real chasm in being, Lacan justifies his theory that identity is taken on in a triumph over death cum fragmentation. The mirror-stage "drive" toward constancy becomes the principle of repetition. Lacan has placed both repetition and the death drive beyond pleasure seeking, then, and moved repetition toward the reality principle. Shoshana Felman terms Lacanian repetition compulsion an interpretation of difference, in opposition to the traditional idea of identity repetition as various interpretations of the *same* unconscious fantasy replayed (Marie Bonaparte).[49] Repetition is not of independent terms or analogous themes, therefore, but is repetition of a structure of differential interrelationships in which the Other(A) always returns (Felman, "On Reading Poetry," p. 139).

When the phallic signifier splits the subject into the "I am" of cultural and linguistic meaning and the "I am" of repressed being, the repressed "I" seeks itself in social discourse by identity repetitions. Identity repeats itself in a tension between an inner ideal and outer realities, therefore, at the dialectical crossroads between finite *moi* fixations (being) and the infinite substitutions of the chain of Desire (wanting) (*Séminaire* XI, p. 131). Repetition, in consequence, vacillates beyond any pleasure principle of constancy, beyond any means of stabilization or harmony on a biological plane (*Séminaire* II, pp. 112–13). In psychotic persons identity repetition stops because the *moi* ceases to reconstitute itself in the Real; it simply desires no longer, for the *moi* has been swallowed up by the Other(A) and so has become equal to itself.

Under Lacan's molding hands, repetition has become the insistence of the unconscious in the daily present, be it through *moi* narcissism or Other(A) signifiers. Unconscious messages and fictions turn around continually as if in a machine, ready to break out of the Other's isolated memory circuit and return intermittently but repetitiously into the general game of life (*Séminaire* II, pp. 111–12). Repetition is a behavior begun in the past, but reproduced in the present. Lacanian repetition has no connection with vital adaptation as in Freud's instinctual, sexual stages; nor do people "repeat" behavior merely to recreate states of id pleasure or to master neurosis. Their repetitions march to a much deadlier beat: the effort to place "something" unified and familiar between a Real void in being and intimations of their own Imaginary nature. Repetition, therefore, is a normal mode of the subject, unaware that its curious structure makes it live the dialectical unconscious at the level of conscious life. But, as stated above, although repetition is one clue leading analysts to a glimpse of the specific structure of a patient's psyche, repetition is not per se neurotic.

Although many readers must readily associate repression with the neo-Freudian unconscious, the active and synchronic quality that Lacan attributes to repression marks it as one more join between conscious and unconscious systems. Freud initially thought that an original repression of sexual desires—caused by castration anxiety—was the cause of neurosis and it would show up as a conscious refusal of sexual "drive" representations (Leclaire, *Psychanalyser*, p. 159). Symptoms were defined as compromise formations that attempted to master repressed desires and fixations through neurotic repetition. Though repression has received sundry interpretations since Freud's death, the critic Samuel Weber has summed up the opinion of many students of psychoanalysis: without the concept of repression, human behavior would not be comprehensible.[50]

Norman O. Brown has emphasized that Freud's writings on primary repression are limited. But Freud's later ideas on secondary repression served Brown as the basis of a *Weltanschauung*: Brown interprets Freud to mean that man represses himself and then creates a society which represses him in return. Partisan theoreticians (such as Herbert Marcuse) have politicized the Freudian idea that repression causes neurosis that may be "cured" by the undoing of sexual repression. In *Civilization and its Discontents* (1930) Freud related

repression to sublimation: the pleasure principle (constancy) is sacri-
ficed to the reality principle (compromise) in the interest of civilization and economic survival. Both Brown and Marcuse hypothesized
that social ills could be "cured" by a freeing up of individual sexual
energies.

The Lacanian Leclaire believes that despite the vast body of commentary on repression since Freud's death, Freud himself never really
discovered why repression occurs (*Psychanalyser*, p. 159). But Lacan's
epistemology does include such a hypothesis. By taking Freud's
scanty sketch of primary repression seriously, Lacan upholds Freud's
statement that repression (*Verdrängung*) requires the possibility of
some prior repression as a foundation. Lacan makes *Urverdrängung*
the equivalent of the fixing of a primary, signifying chain in the prespecular and mirror-stage periods, a phenomenon he renders into
French as *refoulement*, or that which makes secondary repression or
suppression (*Unterdrückung*) possible (*Télévision*, pp. 48–49). What
is repressed in the primary instance, then, is neither sexuality nor
affect, but the earliest *representations* of Desire in their link to the
(m)Other (*Séminaire* XI, p. 198). In Seminar Two Lacan taught that
repressed material which has not surfaced in the present moment is
suspended—which is what *refoulement* means (p. 354).

Lacan equates secondary repression with his concept of secondary
libido: the Desire which coincides with the end of the mirror stage.
This second repression hides the first and thereby creates the unconscious barrier between consciousness and perception that obliges
those cognitive modes of perception to "misrecognize" the true
nature of the "self." The *moi* is an Imaginary, alien form—a symptom in which a subject believes literally without reference to its origins in repression. This misrecognition leads to denial (*Verneinung*,
dénégation), which is a form of resistance to the return of the repressed. So viewed, the *moi* is a principle of negation. Primary repression, furthermore, is a coefficient of elemental Other(A) perception,
while secondary repression operates consciousness through the substitutive mechanism of Desire. Secondary repression also entails
a surfacing of the symbolic and signifying effects in the Other(A)
through *Wahrnehmungszeichen* as points of substitutive fracture in
conscious life and discourse.

Lacan views secondary repression (*Unterdrückung*) as a participant
force in consciousness. His description of *Unterdrückung* keeps
close to Freud's idea that it is not affect which is repressed, but something more in the order of an idea: the representation of a representation (*Vorstellungsrepräsentanz*) (*Séminaire* XI, p. 198). In other

words, affect is displaced in the representation (*Télévision*, p. 38). Where *Vorstellungsrepräsentanz* is actively *représentant*, Lacan equates *Wahrnehmungszeichen* with a synchronic infiltration of unconscious data into conscious life. The signifying chain (or *représenté*) of primary repression (*refoulement*) conditions secondary repression as the latter translates itself into Desire and displays itself in speech. Secondary repression arose from the division of the psyche by language into a subject of speech and a subject of identifications. That repression functions in two different directions illuminates Freud's theory of a double inscription (*Niederschrift*) that allows conscious and unconscious ideas to coexist on different planes (*Séminaire* II, p. 112). By secondary repression, Lacan does not mean an unbinding of repressed material that can pass from the unconscious system to the conscious one.

But when did the secondary system grow up alongside the primary one? According to Lacan, secondary repression engendered the unconscious as a place of subjective "intelligence" at the moment of Castration—the primal division—and so set up the barrier of literal articulation on the other side of which is the "impossible *jouissance*" (Leclaire, *Psychanalyser*, p. 154). But by no means all secondary repressions occur at eighteen months of age. Lemaire has stressed, for example, that repressed material can play on and in consciousness as long as it goes unrecognized or denied (*Lacan*, p. 75). To cite a probable case, an overmeticulous scholar goes about scrutinizing texts and critical literature by the yardstick of inauthentic versus authentic, false versus true, and fake versus real. The full meaning of the Desire underlying his quest becomes clear only when the repressed Other(A) messages are seen at work. The scholar's mother had told him he was "illegitimate" when he was eleven. Although the memory of this disclosure was conscious, the traumatic impact of the revelation and of related fantasies had been suppressed. *Moi* narcissism had been wounded. The mature scholar had no inkling of any connection between the network of unconscious material surrounding the Real pain of learning he was "illegitimate" and his academic obsession with winnowing out the "true" and aggressively exposing the "false." From a Lacanian stance, the repressed material was clearly active and showed up in the synchronic realm as overreaction and obsession in an otherwise reasonable, professional scrupulousness. Repression, here as always, is a function of displaced, suppressed, or misrecognized material, that which resurfaces in repetitions, heavily charged word nodes, or irruptions in speech—the "play" on ordinary signifiers—if catalyzed within identification dialectics (*Séminaire* II, p. 301).

There are additional reasons why a Lacanian analyst does not try to recover lost memories or events that have supposedly been repressed. Such memories and events are all too easy for the conscious mind to invent or distort. Lacan sends analysts instead in the direction of giving mythic or epic form to that which operates itself from structure: the Real effects of a person's relationship to the Other (Desire) and to Law (*Télévision*, p. 51). The analyst knows that the signifying chain of primary repression is homogeneous: it has only one dimension and cannot thus be assimilated on a functional plane. In his essay "The Unconscious" (1915) Freud claimed that the repressed or the unconscious is the unverbalized (*SE*, 4: 135). Unconscious representations are allegedly thing-presentations, while words belong to the preconscious and conscious realms. Because of this, repression could never be "translated" into words in a transference situation. Lacan has refuted Freud here. By placing acoustic traces and *Wahrnehmungszeichen* in the unconscious and by linking primary and secondary repression to Desire-through-substitution, Lacan has placed both Desire and perception in a locus between conscious and unconscious systems. Lacan has explained that "truth"—signifying data in the Other(A)—reenters the field of knowledge, but dynamically repressed. Put another way, a signifier is reduplicated in two places—in conscious and unconscious systems—but is functionally and topographically different in each register, somewhat like an Egyptian obelisk whose hieroglyphs change meaning from one side to the other (Lemaire, *Lacan*, p. 250). Nonetheless, the primary terms which compose the truth (through narcissism, aggressiveness, and Desire) can carry their energy to the heterogeneous terms of conscious language by metaphor and metonymy. These, as previously stated, work according to the same "laws": condensation, displacement, substitution, and contiguous referentiality.

Freud's picture of repression as dramatized in *Totem and Taboo* (1912) takes on renewed meaning when viewed symbolically, instead of as a Real, albeit reconstructed event. In this book Freud imagined a primal horde which collectively murdered its leader (substitute father) and so learned repression in terms of guilt and retribution. If language has the same symbolic effect as the Oedipal structure—to distance the infant from the (m)Other-related, natural unconscious—then secondary repression can be linked to guilt over a dead father. But primary repression precedes both guilt and consciousness. Insofar as the Real father becomes confused with "no" during the period of Castration, this effect is embedded in a network of Imaginary associations to establish taboo and Law. The repressed (m)Other functions as a bridge between primary and secondary repression and emits the "message" that the Name-of-the-Father must be subverted were *jouissance* ever to be recreated. Desire may be seen as the wish to reunite with the (m)Other beyond the father's name. The father's "death" is a *symbolic* desideratum, therefore, acted out or fantasized in separate acts of social subversion.

For Lacan, secondary repression is essential to psychic health, individuation, and social functioning. Failure to differentiate from the (m)Other over the father's "dead" body is a foreclosure of the signifier for Castration—an implicit "no" to reality, society, and compromise. But even this might be a viable personal or political choice (as Deleuze, Guattari, and others have proposed), if the result were not intolerable psychic pain. In Lacan's account of repression, the most dire consequence of a refusal of Castration is psychosis. In place of the libidinally free, schizo-hero of Desire whom Deleuze and Guattari have placed beyond repression (in a curious reminiscence of the theories of Norman O. Brown and Marcuse), Lacan points to an individual who is the total psychic slave of an Other's Desire and thus incapable of his own Desire. The psychotic, paradoxically, is without libido (i.e., without "drive" or a lack-in-being).

At the psychotic limit of psychic freedom, the individual does not have enough Desire to form adequate identity boundaries and unities. The psychotic literally dreams awake and identifies "self" with the fragments and images forming that inner-world, patchwork quilt, which most people experience as a unified *moi*. But secondary repression is not just salvific; its obverse is the pain associated with closure of the *jouissance* which characterized the mirror stage. Lacan's concept of repression involves the whole of the "lived" experience of the mother, in part forgotten, in part integrated into conscious memories, and repressed in relation to Real trauma (the universal trauma being the necessity of verifying one's place in a widening sphere). It is because of repression that we are faced with a closure or scotomization of the ideology of consciousness, if we assume consciousness to be a maintenance or lucid presence of self or a transparency in our discourse (Benoist, *La Révolution*, p. 59).

The Lacanian repressed Other(A) carries no index of regression or immaturity in itself. Its effects are the same as those of daily experience in response to the Symbolic, that is, substitutive sense of an act. Repression cannot, therefore, be made synonymous with immaturity, neurosis, or infantilization (as many neo-Freudians would have it). Repression reasserts itself in the metaphorical form of Real symptoms conveying Desire's messages with their traces of unconscious truth, but in an undeciphered or undecoded "text." For the

Lacanian James Glogowski, everything in speech is represented "as for" the Other(A). Elsewhere Glogowski has written: "Desire cannot be measured. It cannot even be described through some phenomenological study, as Lacan points out in Séminaire I. Desire is the 'pensée' at the base of the dream—what remains after the analysis; the analysis, that is, of the dream itself. This is a very important technical limit. That something remains after analysis does not necessarily mean that the analysis is unfinished. It seems that there may be psychic dimensions of desire which 'ought not' be analyzed."[51] Put another way, to ascertain elements of what is repressed—*moi* fixations, signifying "letters," the effects of Castration—is to give cognitive comprehensibility to the Desire which operates individuals. But Desire cannot be chased beyond the navel of the dream into the Real nor beyond the primordial signifying chain of repressed representations. Certain things can never be known.

A third Lacanian join between conscious and unconscious systems is regression. Freud first spoke of regression to account for the figurative character of dream productions. According to Lacan, Freud had to invent such a concept to explain an intentional return to the imaged unconscious, since the dream state did not permit primary processes to move normally to motor "discharge." Because dreams appear to go backward, Freud spoke of dreaming as "regression." He then linked this concept to the visual perception system located somewhere between consciousness and perception (*Séminaire* II, pp. 177–78). In Lacan's estimation, had Freud possessed a theoretical means for linking perception with the unconscious system, an intermediary concept such as regression would not have been needed. Lacan's epistemology contains the missing concept: the signifier is repressed, but still active. This dramatic insight enabled Lacan to reject the Freudian theory of regression as a sliding into past instinctual stages of earlier history. Lacan, nonetheless, credited Freud with making intuitive distinctions between regression in structure, history, and development by such comparable concepts as the topographical, the temporal, and the genetic (Sheridan, *Ecrits*, p. 189).

But once encumbered with his concept of regression, Freud explained it by the now famous triad: ego frustration leads to aggression and then to regression. This he then correlated with his innate and instinctual evolution of sexual maturation: the oral, the anal, and the genital stages. Lacan conceded that the effects of oral, anal, and genital experience do leave permanent, representational traces in all human beings as part of the symbolic substratum (*Wahrnehmung-*

szeichen) which conditions reality perception. But the traces are part of an asynchronic, symphonic whole, either a harmonious symbolization or a disconcerted one; they are not realistic stages that later condition maturation through some biological evolution from inferior or infantile character traits (oral and anal) to superior ones (genital). Psychic maturation occurs, rather, by a liberation of one's "self"-image from the Other's Desire which, although established in the past, is always active in the present. With this theory, Lacan is able to show regression as a thing that occurs at the level of meaning rather than as an actual mechanism triggered into action by reality (*Séminaire* II, p. 128). Regression is not, then, an *instinctual* response to frustration, but an emotive immediacy adumbrated by the meaning data underlying any given discourse being set in motion (*Séminaire* II, p. 128). Earlier we pointed out that Lacan recast Freud's instincts as the imagistic, energetic equivalents of sucking, excrement, the gaze, and the voice—the primordial objects of Desire for which all later meaningful choices and experiences will be substitutes. Regression must of necessity refer to the primordial (m)Other in relation to whom oral and anal experiences, as well as visual and vocal effects, were first given meaning. So viewed, regression is always a reaction to an internalized Other(A) relation set in motion by others (Sheridan, *Ecrits*, p. 44). Lacan therefore interprets regression as a symptom of unconscious truth—a metaphor of the *moi*/Other dialectic—seeking to enunciate itself in consciousness (*Séminaire* II, p. 128). Frustration arose originally from an object's (the *moi*) being trapped in the Desire of the Other(A); but the diachronic conflict dramatizes itself in the synchronic realm of recognition dynamics.

In concluding this section we may sum up the principal characteristics of Lacanian repetition, repression, and regression as being personal, here-and-now, normative aspects of behavior. Regression reappears in relation to the most elemental structuring of being and therefore often bears the character of the aggressive obverse of narcissism. When the *moi* is threatened, its fictions and intentions thrown into doubt, the subject attempts to restore a sense of unity to its shadow illusions by aggressive defense or attack (Lemaire, *Lacan*, p. 42). Repetition, on the other hand, binds the various fragments of the subject together by constantly reaffirming the *moi* as a principle of unity in Real situations. Repetition—which is introduced by language, the *moi* in its function as symbol, and the problematic of existence itself—keeps division ("death") at bay by denying repressed material (*Séminaire* II, p. 112). And since what is repressed cannot consciously be remembered, it repeats itself in behavior and language. Finally, as the correlate of Desire, repression is a motive force in human drive. It attests to the Lacanian theory that the unconscious can never be completely repressed, because the Other(A) is perpetually active—the "ideal worker."

Transference and Resistance

Lacan's campaign against ego psychology manifests itself throughout his thought. He naturally opposed the idea that there is a *whole* self that serves as an agent of strength, synthesis, mastery, integration, and adaptation to realistic norms. Lacan perceived partisan analysts pushing analysands toward an ideal of health which merely defined group norms. In his early essays, indeed, he accused the psychoanalytic establishment of having rendered Freud's revolutionary discoveries banal. By prizing technique above the meaning of the unconscious, such analysts believed that Freud's rules themselves provided direct access to truth. But since these rules had evolved into a ceremonial formalism, any questioning of the neo-Freudian canon amounted to heresy. Lacan alleges that Freud's miraculous structures have, therefore, been reduced to the nonconceptual, nonintellectual conformism of social suggestion and psychological superstition (Sheridan, *Ecrits*, p. 39).

Lacan's particular aversion to psychoanalytic practice in the United States can be partly attributed to cultural differences in intellectual formation. Whereas pragmatism and empiricism have long reigned supreme in Anglo-American investigation, the French academy has given primacy to theoretical conceptualization from at least the time of Descartes. It is not Lacan's concern to thrash out the relative merits of induction or deduction. Nor can Lacan's epistemology be reduced to a deductive methodology. But while his "empirical" data are not those of quanitifiable studies, they are certainly "scientific": those of Jacques Monod's biological theories on perception; mathematical symbolism; ethnological realities; animal behavior; the Real of psychic pain. In a sense, the criticism that Lacan has aimed at the American establishment should be more correctly aimed at nineteenth-century Austria, where psychoanalysis was born, or at England whither it fled during World War II. Freud himself contributed to the image of the analyst as an objective, scientific observer, who regarded the patient's behavior as an object of study outside the analyst. One might even call Freud's "scientism" an Anglo-Austrian neopositivism in the wake of Darwinian evolutionary materialism. Freud, like his daughter Anna after him, increasingly stressed the defensive, synthesizing, and adaptive functions of the ego. Lacan has not, however, attacked Freud's implicit Darwinianism so much as the general Anglo-American belief in the possibility of an objectifiable reality ego.

Lacan has unflaggingly insisted that the human subject is neither unified nor unifiable. But because Lacan delimits consciousness and makes consciousness and language themselves defenses against unconscious meaning, he is not generally understood by ego psychologists who place defenses in the ego itself. The Lacanian subject (*je/moi*) is not unified in consciousness. The *moi*, however, *is* intrinsically unified—except in dreams, psychosis, and other unraveling manifestations—and projects itself into consciousness as the principle of individuality. But because it emanates from the unconscious and yet must continually verify itself through the very means of its occultation—consciousness and language—the *moi* cannot "see" itself as it really is. This is quite a different theory from the popular misconception that the Lacanian "subject" is in a state of permanent fragmentation.

The idea that the ego is whole has led psychoanalysts to analyze what they call "unconscious defenses" in terms of the conscious ego's typical patterns. Partisan analysts then apply their own conceptions of health in an attempt to remodel the patient's defenses. Lacan calls this a surface approach, which muddles psychic truth and reality and allows the unwary analyst to take her or his own unquestioned postulates to be objective viewpoints. The analysand becomes a victim of the *analyst's* illusions and is unaware that Freud's discovery did not situate truth or reality in the analyst or in technique, but placed "truth" itself in question. Lacan described a typical neo-Freudian concept of cure as the analyst's imposition of her or his own Desires and symptoms on the analysand, thereby infusing him with "reality" and making him more capable of tolerating frustration. Such a procedure is meant to "strengthen" a weak ego. What really occurs, from a Lacanian standpoint, is a deepening of the patient's alienation from the truth of his or her being. The *moi* has already been alienated in the Other(A) and in language. Subjugating an analysand to the analyst's ideals merely pushes the *moi* farther in the direction that has already led to the subjugation to the Other(A).

Current Anglo-American psychoanalytic theory has focused much attention on the analysis of a patient's resistance (*Widerstand*) as well as on transference. Resistance has a negative connotation in standard analytic speech, while transference offers the positive affective means by which to overcome resistance through the "false" love that the patient feels for the doctor. The failure of an analysand to attain a new level of behavior or understanding is labeled resistance. The analyst then aims to liquidate the defenses that cause resistance. But Lacan's elevation of the subject of the unconscious over consciousness sheds new light on the phenomenon of resistance. It is the insistence of an unconscious discourse, which prefers to repeat itself in language and behavior (rather than to know itself), that must be called resistance. So seen, resistance becomes an Imaginary function of the *moi*. Resistance is not a function of conscious ego defenses, therefore, but a revelation of the fact that *moi* (being) is different from *je* (speaking) (*Séminaire* II, pp. 148, 246, 373).

Resistance, like transference, is "invisible" proof of an unconscious topology in being. Resistance is not simple passivity or a matter of grandiosity or a dogmatic adhesion to the known. Rather, it takes on a cosmic meaning: that of maintaining a sense of "self"-unity over and above the fragmentary and alien nature of the *moi*. In other words, resistance is not just a pathological clinging to neurosis (inertia), but the human incapacity to recognize the gaps between being, wanting, and speaking (*je*), and with it the primary Other(A) meanings which condition secondary meaning in a syncopated logic from the past. *Je* speech provides a mechanism for either rendering or avoiding the *moi* discourse of identificatory truth.[52] The basis of any Lacanian transference is the analysand's imputing a "subject" to unconscious or repressed knowledge, and mistaking the source or meaning of such knowledge.

Surprisingly, Lacan declares elsewhere that resistance comes from the analyst, not from the analysand. The patient's symptoms—metaphors of unconscious truth—speak loud and clear and insist at the surface of life in language, but also above and beyond consciousness and discourse. Analysts are resisting when they do not understand the symptom or when they believe "interpretation" means pointing out to the analysand that he or she *really* desires some sexual object. For Lacan, the efficacious action of an analysis occurs when the analysand is brought to the point of naming the Desire which insists beyond his or her awareness. The difficulty confronting the analyst is that the "something" to be recognized does not already exist somewhere, as an entity just waiting to be coopted. By naming Desire, the subject creates it—gives it conscious form—as a new presence in the world (*Séminaire* II, p. 267). Once named, the Desire can be analyzed. Structurally speaking, it always reveals the "lack" in the Other(A) as it relates to Castration and the Law of the Name-of-the-Father.

Lacan claims that contemporary psychoanalysts fail to understand resistance because they view the patient as a kind of object under observation.[53] This two-body, object-relations analysis takes its model from bastard forms of phenomenology and basks in that mirage of consciousness that believes an ego can be a simple object for the other as subject. Such an assumption also leads to the claim that one ego can substitute itself for another through transference (*Séminaire XI*, p. 119). The healthy part of the patient's ego is supposed to identify with—or conform to—the analyst's ego in order to achieve "cure" by adapting to reality (Sheridan, *Ecrits*, pp. 9, 135). The endpoint of the analysis—its positive resolution—requires that the patient's ego be identified with the analyst's. In reality, the patient is encouraged to bid masochistically for approval from a master (Sheridan, *Ecrits*, p. 135). Lacan wonders humorously if a desk might not be an ideal patient? For never having had an ego, it would not resist the substitution of someone else's ego for its own (Sheridan, *Ecrits*, pp. 135–36). The only object *genuinely* accessible to the analyst is not a hidden "self" which can be archeologically unearthed, but the link between doctor and patient *qua ego* in its automatic intersubjectivity (Sheridan, *Ecrits*, p. 45). Instead of using this link to "understand" the patient, Lacanian analysts must resist their own subjective interpretations of the analysand. The analyst's Desire, indeed, should be to obtain absolute difference: the very opposite of Imaginary identification (*Séminaire* XI, p. 248). The role of the analyst is not to "understand" the patient, then, but to surprise the liberty which resides in nonsense; to see how the analysand debates with his or her *jouissance*; to ascertain to what primitive discourse effects the analysand is subjected. The analyst should restitute what is signified or implied in a discourse and, finally, decide not to decide if the "case" should so dictate.

One goal of the neo-Freudian school is to try and frustrate the analysand in order to expose the emotions that hide behind the intellect. For Lacan, frustration forms but the tip of the analytic iceberg, and he is intrigued by the metaphysical plight that makes frustration such a telling response. Analysts know how to induce it, he says, and how to link it to anxiety, aggression, and regression, but they cannot explain its source except as an empirical description of a function. Lacan's explanation of frustration has placed psychoanalysis in the category of the Ur-human science and undermined the illusion that the world is divided into normal and pathological people. Frustration initially arises from the dialectical presence of the *moi* versus the Other(A) and the *je*'s efforts to deny or convey such "knowledge," although the conflict is always replayed via others. For this reason, Lacan does not see how analysis can proceed toward truth unless aggressiveness is first aimed at the analyst (*qua* other), so that it can be returned to its source in the Other(A). Aggressiveness, therefore, is the first knot in the analytic drama. The Lacanian analyst uses the transference phenomenon as a way to get the patient to talk about the analyst, so that the *moi* can be seen in projection and eventually relocated within the Other's Desire.

Lacan never disagreed with Freud's basic discoveries regarding the unconscious. For example, he fully concurred that without transference there could be no psychoanalysis. Certain psychoanalysts have misconstrued Lacan's innovations here. For example, François Roustang misinterprets Lacan's statements regarding the liquidation of a transference in analysis (*Séminaire* XI, p. 240). Roustang's interpretation confuses the idea of liquidating transference with Lacan's play on the concept of the *sujet supposé savoir*. Lacan argued that the analyst should aim to maintain a rather continuous transference with the goal of liquidating the analysand's Imaginary projections— the narcissistic bond—that elevate *moi* fantasies over any knowledge of the Real of unconscious truth. By enabling the analysand to see that the transference with the analyst was based on fiction and illusion, Lacan hoped to teach that the Real transference was the intrasubjective exchange between the analysand's own *moi* and Other(A) and the *je* and the Other(A). What is to be liquidated or vaporized, then, is not transference as a phenomenon, nor the unconscious, but the presupposition of a unified relationship between analyst and analysand. By clinging to an Imaginary identification with the analyst, the analysand remains blocked by the other from hearing the knowledge contained in the Other(A). When the analyst's actual personhood begins to be grasped because *moi* fantasies are broken up, a paradox occurs. The subject is no longer subject to illusion, but for that moment has assumed knowledge of his or her unconscious, has assumed subjectivity.[54] By revealing various pitfalls in transference, not the least of which is the analyst's satisfaction at being recognized, Lacan demonstrated how transference could be used to lead both analyst and analysand beyond narcissistic fixations, aiming the analysand toward knowledge of his or her Desire, and away from the personhood of the analyst. Identification *with* the analyst can never be a final goal, then, since any life is an ever-moving, endlessly unfolding Desire and Law epic (*Séminaire* XI, p. 133). The analysis forms one fixed moment in the dialectical writing of the analysand's potential life story. In this way psychoanalysis is an apprenticeship in freedom won through locating the roots of the *moi* and *je* in an-Other's Desire (*Séminaire* II, pp. 108–9). The end of analysis has been described as death's death, which is paid for with a de-being but offers the freedom to live (Schneiderman, *Returning*, pp. 166–67).

But the standard neo-Freudian transference (*Übertragung*) goes in the opposite direction and works by the law of misrecognition (*méconnaissance*). In such a situation analysands think they are talking directly to the analyst about them- "selves" and solving problems once and for all. In fact, they are merely rephrasing the identity question to yet one more substitute other. Insofar as people take their perceptions to be objective and true, most analysands miss the circular subjectivity of their seemingly linear quest. In reality, both patient and doctor constitute each other subjectively—objectify each other—according to the permanent narcissistic (*moi*) modes that make up their individuality (Sheridan, *Ecrits*, p. 225ff.). In Seminar Eleven Lacan taught that—through transference—the analysand "acts" out of the reality of the unconscious (p. 158). In the countertransference, the analyst returns the sum of the prejudices, passions, embarrassments, even insufficient information which characterize the analyst at a given moment in the dialectical process (Wilden, *LS*, pp. xi–xii).

The analyst, then, is above all a human being, Lacan has said, in constant flux. However much a patient may not wish to recognize that flux, and however much the analyst may succeed by his steadfastness in creating the illusion of fixity, the facts are otherwise. The analyst is not a fixed point more than any other person. In standard neo-Freudian practice the patient's transference is considered a neurosis or distortion, yet also a path along which to reeducate the patient. The analyst, on the other hand, is not supposed to experience countertransference (unless his or her own neuroses remain unresolved). Lacan condemns this static picture of the analyst/analysand interaction as much as he condemns the illusion of an objective therapist and a fantasy-logged patient. Partisan analysts take their own perceptions as the measure of the real and true, even to the point of confusing conscious intuition with an unconscious empathy or "listening" (e.g., Heinz Kohut).

An analysand generally enters analysis with the idea that the analyst is realistic and objective and "knows" the key to her or his problems (Sheridan, *Ecrits*, p. 94). Lacan iconoclastically subverts the image of the analyst as the one who "knows," but he does not mean thereby that the analyst lacks knowledge or analytic tools. He draws attention instead to the subject who *thinks* it "knows": the speaking *je* whose *moi* fictions and certainties come from the Other(A). A Lacanian analyst proceeds by separating this Other(A) "knowledge" from the conscious attributions of blame and certainty that dwell at the surface of an analysand's discourse. Such an approach is personal and humble compared with the neopositivistic theoretical derivations, which pigeonhole and categorize neurotic symptoms to the point that a given analyst assumes he "knows" a patient's unconscious from an analysis's inception. For Lacan, the analyst is only a detective who can aid the analysand in finding out about the Other's discourse and Desire.

Standard neo-Freudian practice seeks a patient's truth in fantasy and memory and in events that lie "beyond" the language barrier. Lacan parries this theoretical thrust with the contention that psychoanalysis is not a *Wissen* (substantive knowledge), but a dialectic—a space in which the analyst shows the analysands that they talk badly or ignorantly (*Séminaire* I, p. 306). "Symptom relief" entails the momentary correction and completion of a discontinuous epic—not unlike the restoration of a defaced painting—into an identity trajectory with its own internal logic. The analysand wishes to know: Who am I? What should I do? The Lacanian analyst sits in the privileged position of representing the other (i.e., all the interlocutors of the patient's past) without being functionally involved.

Lacan's view of transference is pregnant with meaning for philosophical and literary discourse. *Any* use of language is an other/Other correlation. Like Freud, Lacan sees the transfer mechanism as a universal feature of human relating. But he has given it even greater specificity as a clinical tool and as revelatory of the human condition as well. Transference is based on the recognition strivings of the mirror-stage structure. Desire may be termed the fuel behind transference, and *jouissance* its goal (*Séminaire* XI, pp. 114, 119). Repetition points to the *moi* and intrasubjectivity; transference is the intersubjective means for bringing narcissistic truth and unconscious intentionality into view. But generally it is a function which is misunderstood and incomplete outside psychoanalysis (*Séminaire* II, p. 222).

In subjectivizing and dialecticizing perception and discourse, Lacan has dealt neo-Freudianism a double blow: (1) to the idea of a reality principle (as if one such static, lucid principle could be found!), and (2) to the idea of an autonomous, impersonal, rational, objective, healthy analyst who can be disconnected from a patient's discourse. Since any human subject is inherently split off from itself

and socially interdependent in consequence, no impersonal interaction between autonomous egos can occur. In the standard neo-
Freudian idea of transference the patient relives past traumas through
the analyst, who serves as a substitute parent or one capable of symbolizing a "better" parent. Lacan disputes a view that grants reality
to the analyst's own personhood, although he never denies that the
analyst possesses an analytic *savoir-faire*. The analyst should use
his analytic "know-how" to help an analysand find psychic freedom
by emerging from an empty dialogue of misrecognition, denial,
rationalization, and illusions which shut out the childhood that
shapes and controls his adult life.

A Lacanian analysis aims to make the analysand *aware* of the
other voices and Other(A) Desire that go unrecognized in the discourse of opinion on which the conscious subject rests its faith
(Sheridan, *Ecrits*, p. 228). The ideal analytic goal would be to eradicate the *moi*, an ideal which must remain "virtual" since a "fully
realized" subject (Hegelian or otherwise) cannot exist. At the same
time, recognition of the *moi*'s fictional and alienated roots in the
Other(A) offers the possibility of disengaging beyond the Other(A).
Analysis can only proceed in a truthful direction if the analyst implicitly recasts his question "What do you want?" as "What does the
Other(A) want of you?" The analysis is finished when the patient
can speak to the analyst about her or his own intrasubjective discourse. This approach differs radically from the Anglo-American
method of bringing an analysand to the point of separating his or her
view of the analyst as parental substitute from the analyst *qua* real
person. Lacan's quadrature (i.e., Schéma L) shows the subject engaged
in an internal dialectic, whose movement is not linear, but progressively and cumulatively spiral (Wilden, *LS*, pp. xi–xii).

A key issue in Lacan's teachings concerns the analyst *qua* analyst.
In 1962 the International Psychoanalytic Association excommuni-
cated the French Psychoanalytic Society, claiming that Lacan had insufficient facilities for training future analysts (*Séminaire* XI, p. 11).
The French analyst incessantly thereafter addressed the problem of
what "didactic" psychoanalysis is and the role of the analyst therein.
Some of the precepts that he passed on to training analysts are the following: An analyst should not talk to the analysand about the surface ego, which the former sees, since the speaking subject of meaning and memory (*je*) is not identical with the presence speaking
(*moi*) (Sheridan, *Ecrits*, p. 90). One way to help analysands sort *moi*
from *je* is by the analyst's remaining silent, acting as dummy, death,

neutral, *ignorantia docta*, in order to allow the frustration implicit in the topology of the subject's quadrature to find its own path toward truth. While an ego psychologist would respond meaningfully to a patient's demand (*demande*), a Lacanian intends to brings that "appeal" (for love) back to the identifications which conditioned it (*Séminaire* XI, p. 246). The silent analyst acts as a mock Other(A), evoking the presence of lack or loss, just waiting for the moment when the analysand's discourse will go beyond itself or trip itself up.

When unconscious irruptions appear within a seemingly unified discourse, the analyst acts as "translator" and gathers up the stumblings and repetitions to feed them back to the patient. Psychic clusters around certain sounds, words, or concepts point to an endless chain of displacements and condensations that go all the way back to a nonascertainable, primordial signifying chain of repressed associations. Lacan also uses silence's opposite by actively interrupting the patient's *je* discourse (such as reconstituted memories, day events, opinions); by sudden gestures, unexpected events, surprises, pregnant silences; or any other provocation which helps the analysand to address the Other(A). By catalyzing the disintegration of the Imaginary unity which constitutes the *moi* (and which the *je* misrecognizes); by disturbing the *je* discourse in its consistency, the Other's Desire stumbles into view (Sheridan, *Ecrits*, p. 299).

In answering his question "What is a didactic psychoanalysis?" Lacan posed an even more basic question: "What is psychoanalysis?" Invoking Pablo Picasso's "I do not seek, I discover," Lacan emphasizes that psychoanalysis is not (re)search (*Séminaire* XI, p. 12). In this spirit he offers his *own* theories as the "true" implication of Freud's discovery of psychoanalysis. These pose two further basic questions: (1) Is psychoanalysis a science? (2) What is the Desire of the psychoanalyst? Psychoanalysis was a science for Freud, Lacan insists, based on four fundamental concepts that Freud slavishly maintained at the center of all his theoretical discussions; his insistence on these concepts constitutes an "exhausting, tedious, tiresome chain" (*Séminaire* XI, p. 15). But the contemporary claim that psychoanalysis can be studied as a science, based on clinical data and experience, is in Lacan's view false. Since a science must by definition have a constant object of study, clinical data—only one period in a changing story—are an insufficient and unreliable criterion. Analysands continually change and cannot be objects of study per se (*Séminaire* XI, p. 13). This attitude partly explains why Lacan advanced his own epistemology by theory and not by case studies.

Lacan also rejects any unitary claims to a scientific basis for psychoanalysis (such as the theories developed by Reich, Laing, *Gestalt* therapists, and others). The very need to define things in unitary terms is an Idealist tendency—an Imaginary thrust—which can only lead to a philosophical cul de sac. At the other extreme, psychiatrists, behaviorists, and experimental psychologists—who reduce psychoanalysis to a positive science based on empirical observation and induction—end up in a certain theoretical obscurity. Lacan has always claimed that empiricism cannot constitute the foundations of a science because its criterion is the unity of the perceiving subject (Sheridan, *Ecrits*, pp. 293–94). Truth (arising from the Other) reenters the field of empirical science, albeit unconsciously, because the *Cogito* of the researcher is firmly rooted in her or his *Desidero* (Sheridan, *Ecrits*, p. 297).

Moving beyond the empirical into language, Lacan claims that Freud's concepts only take on their full meaning in a field of language (Sheridan, *Ecrits*, p. 39). "First principles" require a dialectical grasp of the meaning of psychoanalytic actions through words that resonate at every psychic level. The Lacanian analyst Stuart Schneiderman hesitates even to use a locution like "pre-linguistic," as something which designates a child's *experience*—there being no way to describe "experience" outside of or before language. But the infant's experience of the world is indeed rich long before it speaks coherently.

Words enable the analysand to present himself as one who makes meaning and can be understood (Sheridan, *Ecrits*, p. 9). An analyst has "ears" to hear the linguistic components to the analysand's unconscious truth only through knowledge of the myths and conventions of the field of language that initially formed the signifying data in the analysand's Other(A). Lacan's training program for future analysts has lived on and includes philosophy, logic, linguistics, history, mathematics, and anthropology, subverting the empirical direction of the human sciences and developing what Lacan has called the conjectural sciences (Sheridan, *Ecrits*, p. 145). The contemporary "scientific" direction of Anglo-American psychology, psychiatry, and psychoanalysis, however, finds Lacan's rationalist speculation and projective intuition to be contaminations of principle and, as such, insuperable.

Lacan unceasingly stressed that language is always already out there, conditioning every phase of human development even before birth. By this, Lacan does not mean that a subject is to be understood in terms of signs or codes or codified meanings, but literally—as an effect of the materiality of the signifier and the structure of metaphor. In clinical practice talking provides the basis of a "cure," not because it allows the cathartic relief of unburdening—a theory based on mechanistic charge/discharge energy models—but because the subject learns to place itself, to recuperate the gaps in its story, and to "say" its unconscious Desires. Put another way, talking allows analysands to complete their imperfectly realized accession to language in early childhood ("Who am I in my parents' discourse?") and so helps them make sense of the structures and effects that condition Desire.

With his second question—What is the Desire of the analyst?—Lacan implicitly reinforced his attack on traditional neo-Freudian practitioners. For not only does "faith" in empirical objectivity and medical authority make this question itself seem heretical, Lacan sees the focus on resistance and countertransference in contemporary training programs as its own "resistance." Desire has been the nodal phenomenon of humanness since Plato's day, hence—because the doctor is also animated by Desire—analyst and analysand are not dissimilar (*Séminaire* XI, p. 210). But a belief in established neo-Freudian canons keeps training analysts from considering their own Desire as playing any role in psychoanalysis. By clinging to the rigidified Freud, furthermore, future neo-Freudian analysts do not study the foundations of speech in childhood. Nor do they study the effects of symbolization on perception, though cognition psychologists and some medical persons are now using "image therapy" most successfully.[55] From a narcissistic viewpoint, Desire—both for the analyst and analysand—is the Desire to be recognized and verified as one fantasizes oneself to be: the ideal ego is reflected from the ego ideals of transference relations. The Lacanian analyst's Desire should be, instead, the Desire to seek truth instead of love. Only by reaching behind the substitutive myths and objects that seem to fulfill Desire can any person recognize the truth of his alien Desire in the Other(A).

In an article on Lacan in the *Encyclopedia Universalis* Jacques-Alain Miller writes: "Generally speaking, there is no theory of the unconscious as such for Lacan. There is a theory of analytic practice. The structure that one recognizes in this practice is attributed [*supposée*] to the unconscious. This necessity has always imposed itself on serious theoreticians. What shows this well is that they have always assigned a place in the structure of the unconscious to the analyst."[56] In this chapter we have tried to sketch out Lacan's theory of analytic practice based on his interpretation of Freud's four fundamental concepts and related theories, giving great scope to a discussion of Desire. The all-pervasiveness of Desire, both in analysand and analyst, led Lacan to warn that psychoanalysis could only be treated as a science with the greatest care for its theory and practice.

3

A LACANIAN
THEORY OF COGNITION

BY EXPLAINING how mind is constituted and how the symbol system comes to reside in the brain, Lacan has offered the world a new theory of cognition. This vision was elaborated slowly. In his doctoral thesis (1932) Lacan theorized that the phenomena of personality could only become truly comprehensible if studied in terms of a socially and humanly meaningful dialectic.[1] By 1936 he had introduced the mirror-stage concept, which underlies all his subsequent efforts to analyze the human subject as a relational construct: the direct product of the structuring forces of images, mimetic identification, language, and the Oedipal, triadic structure. From 1946 onward Lacan developed distinctions among categories that he named the Imaginary, the Symbolic, and the Real, dating the beginning of his "teachings" as 1953. In 1975 he added a fourth order: the Symptom (see Chapter 4). On the one hand, Lacan's categories are what he derived from his own clinical materials and experience.[2] On the other hand, by describing the multileveled dimensions that constitute consciousness through the Imaginary, the Symbolic, and the Real, Lacan created the first epistemology since Descartes to locate the source of knowledge in a different place.

Lacan's Three Orders

Among the many disconcerting effects of Lacan's discourse are his innovative uses of standard terms. It is wrong, for example, to equate his Imaginary order with imagination; his Symbolic order with symbolism; or the order of the Real with reality, objectivity, or empiricism. In a narrow and technical sense the Imaginary order is the domain of the *imago* and relationship interaction. The Symbolic is the sphere of culture and language; and the Real is that which is concrete and already "full"—the world of objects and experiences. During his career Lacan increasingly stressed that the Real order stands behind and outside the Imaginary and the Symbolic. The latter exist, in part, as efforts to account for the Real that shapes them, and on which they, in turn, put their stamp: the Imaginary by identificatory, fusional logic; the Symbolic by a differential logic which names, codifies, and legalizes. In an attempt to give even greater precision to his three orders, Lacan introduced the example of the Borromean knot in 1953. If one ring of the Borromean knot is broken, the other two are loosened as well. Any shift of equilibrium among Lacan's three orders has the same effect on the psychic system.

Lacan's three categories were intended to help psychoanalysts interpret the various levels of unconscious dimension in an analysand's discourse by pointing to joins or knots that cannot be seen in any literal sense (*Séminaire* XX, p. 112). In his effort to explain the metaphysics behind the subject's functioning, Lacan stressed basic structures and dynamic process rather than substantive elements.[3] Although all his categories wield the substantive material of symbol, concrete thing, and language, their Realness takes on its dynamic meaning because these are conflated in reference to an infant prematuration and subsequent helplessness. Thought evolves as a secondary product, then, a complex of relations rather than static consciousness of *something*.[4] By making Desire omnipresent—as the source of libido, the shadow reflection of human identificatory resonance, the essence of reality, and reflected in "objects" which give body to the insistence of repetitive patterns—Lacan replaced the mechanistic concept of energy with the dynamic process of wanting. In this way he pushed further the wager by which existentialists had subverted classical reason—showing the link between anxiety and being. The elemental dramas of separation, alienation, and Desire link knowledge, language, and love. Secondary knowledge, that is, conscious thought, aims at resolution and unity through meaning systems (opinion, belief, ideology, or theory) in an ongoing effort to interpret a primordial lack and a subsequent loss.

In adult life the three Lacanian categories seem inseparable. They work together to coordinate acts of consciousness, a coordination emanating from the Imaginary order of representations that exists as the interpretive record of the outside world's Symbolic data and of Real effects and events. In reviewing these categories, we see how extensively Lacan has made use of philosophy. James Glogowski has pointed out, for example, the connection between Lacan's idea of an unconscious space in being and Maurice Merleau-Ponty's phenomenological valorization of the mathematical concept of topology in order to impute spatial and diachronic—i.e., invisible—aspects to being. But instead of splitting topology between the visible and the invisible, Lacan reformulated the concept to mean the invisible effects of childhood, whose results are "materially" palpable in adulthood and diachronically operative on consciousness. I would equate Lacan's topological space with his Imaginary order, which operates perception in reference to the pre-mirror, mirror-stage, and Oedipal structures of the unconscious. This order makes self-reflection impossible: an impossible symmetrical unity.[5] In Seminar Twenty Lacan taught that there are three dimensions of unconscious space, but that they are mathematical instead of intuitive as Immanuel Kant believed; moreover, these dimensions are created in reaction to effects from the outer world, not, as Kant supposed, innate. In his subversion of philosophical discourse Lacan rejected the generally unquestioned assumption that mind structure is itself a unity. At the same time he argued that the structural transformations that anchor mind in mirror-stage Desire and Oedipal Law are themselves based on countable psychic unities.[6] The unconscious can count to six, he argued, because it cannot find the number two again, except via the three (Oedipal or phallic structure) of revelation (*Séminaire* XX, p. 122).

According to Lacan, Jean-Paul Sartre found no limit on the plurality of Imaginary interrelations, because Sartre by definition made each subject the unique center of his own references. By contrast, Lacan found a numerical structuration in the intersubjective field of the Other(A), which opens itself up onto the plane of language as a kind of primitive symbolism (*Séminaire* I, pp. 249–50). The conscious subject is, therefore, limited in its potential relationship choices by an Imaginary—i.e., one-dimensional—set of processes and resulting "self" myths or fables. Unconscious counting, then, is "absolute" in the sense that it refers to the identificatory processes that underlie the deployment of so-called rational processes. In Seminar One Lacan described the intersubjective relation as an Imaginary one, based on the processes commanded by the underlying invisible structure. I interpret this to mean that the projective/introjective logic of the mirror-stage experience with its dual interplay of gazes follows certain rules (as in a game). The paradox here, Lacan pointed out, was that game theory, mathematically speaking, is not an Imaginary phenomenon. It exists, rather, on a Symbolic plane (*Séminaire* I, p. 249).

In his book *Jacques Lacan: The Death of an Intellectual Hero* (Harvard University Press, 1983), Stuart Schneiderman discusses Lacan's theory of unconscious counting in relation to the sets of ordinal numbers studied in number theory. He describes o as the empty grave. One (1) is simultaneously the signifying mark of countability—the Phallus—and the number of unification between infant and mother. Two (2) refers to all the dualisms spawned by the intersubjective relation. Three (3) refers to the Oedipus structure that extends a childhood into adult life in terms of one's early relationship to mother and father. Four (4) is the number of the quadrature of the subject as well as that of the symptom. It also refers to the "telling" of one's story, i.e., the unfolding of one's life epic. The symptom shows up here when the first three numbers do not hold together. Lacan himself did not discuss 5 and 6. Schneiderman has said that an analysis of these two numbers, in light of number theory, would be so complex as to require the use of mathematical symbols.[7]

Schneiderman succeeds in explaining Lacan's difficult concept that the combinatory power of number association orders the ambiguities of the unconscious.[8] I have, however, suggested another level other than that of number theory on which unconscious counting might have a logical meaning: that of Imaginary process. While number theory refers to the differentially calculable aspects of unconscious effects on the subject that represents itself in the Symbolic, the spatial and diachronic impact of mirror-stage and Oedipal structures organize cultural and linguistic meanings around identificatory relations. At this level one might speak of unconscious numbers as pure or absolute. Insofar as the unconscious is operated by Imaginary processes of homogeneity (by the laws of condensation and displacement), the unconscious itself can only count or "think" Imaginarily.[9] In conscious life the only homogeneous function of the unconscious is in the Imaginary (perceptual) capture of the *moi* by others and the function of *méconnaissance* that remains attached to it. We might say that identificatory/narcissistic material transforms "energy" (Desire/libido) in relation to unconscious numbers, each number serving as a bridge between the associational clusters both preceding and following it (Frege's paraphrastic relation). In the "Discours de Rome" Lacan spoke about the law of marriage ties and kinship names, pointing out that statistics have shown that the freedom of choice "apparent" in establishing marriage ties is not random, because a subjective logic orients this freedom in its effects, a logic predicated on mirror-stage and Oedipal structures. "This is precisely where the Oedipus complex—in so far as we continue to recognize it as covering the whole field of our experience in its signification—may be said . . . to mark the limits that our discipline assigns to subjectivity: namely, what the subject can know of his unconscious participation in the movement of the complex structures of marriage ties" (Sheridan, *Ecrits*, p. 66). These identificatory structures are, nonetheless, susceptible of an infinitude of meanings determined by language, even interpretations which appeal mythically to numbers in an effort to clarify human mysteries.

From an Imaginary perspective, I interpret Lacan's 0 as the number of primary identification or of elemental representationalism. Although the infant is unaware that its primordial unities come from identificatory fusion with body parts and imagistic fragments, the first six months of life ensure that human beings will never perceive their bodies in a complete fashion later on (*Séminaire* I, p. 200). Zero refers, then, to the pre–mirror-stage infant whose experience of the world occurs in bits and pieces. One, by contrast, is the number marking the infant's attainment of a sense of body unity by mentally identifying with a *Gestalt* exterior to it. Therefore, it is the number of symbiosis, denoting both mirror-stage psychic fusion and corporal identification with the human form. This dual fusion gives rise to the countable unity of the "self" that is taken on in the other's mirror and substituted for a preceding disunity. One is paradoxically the number of joy (*jouissance*), as well as that of sorrow, because the unity implied is alien, borrowed, and false. The mirror-stage structure delineates the final impossibility of wholeness, even though, globally speaking, it circumscribes the drive toward unity that pushes individuals to seek resolution and certainty in all things. Number 2 would, Imaginarily viewed, refer to the Phallus. As the post–mirror-stage number of separation, 2 denotes the split (*Ichspaltung*) internalized by an infant when language and the Name-of-the-Father reveal the necessity of psychic differentiation from the mother. Beyond the corporal sense of a unity of self (1), 2 points to an awareness of self as a nameable unity. Lacan has said that 2 is important in Freud's Eros, Eros being a unifying power ("Of Structure as an Inmixing," p. 200). One, therefore, implies Imaginary identification, while 2 involves the unifying power of language. Three would connote the Oedipal gender myth that situates the mother and father in cultural identity concepts of masculine and feminine. These myths seek to interpret the drama of mirror-stage Desire and Oedipal separation. Both language and myth seek to replace what has been lost: the repressed (m)Other.

I view Lacan's unconscious 4 as the number of exogamy, that number permitting the adult reshaping of the Oedipal structuration of childhood through a process of marital-type bonding with others. This idea would not be incompatible with Schneiderman's description of 4 as denoting a person's "story" or symptom (the structure of personality). Five, then, would be the number of maternity or paternity in which the Oedipal triangle can be studied in inverted form in adult life. A child—viewed as the Phallus (*objet a*)—becomes the mirror of parental narcissism and the object of parental Desire. Six would be the generational number of perpetuity or lineage, referring to an immortality gained by the perpetuation of identity within family lines. Lacan has said that "without kinship nominations, no power is capable of instituting the order of preferences and taboos that bind and weave the yarn of lineage through succeeding generations. And it is indeed the confusion of generations which, in the Bible as in all traditional laws, is accused as being the abomination of the Word (*verbe*) and the desolation of the sinner" (Sheridan, *Ecrits*, p. 66).

Unconscious or one-dimensional numbers are formed at the join between Real event and Symbolic signifier and culminate in an Imaginary "self" text, which represents itself to consciousness as personality. At the level of Real event the dramas of birth, prematuration, identification, and separation are inherently meaningless except as dramas of effect and trauma. But insofar as the mother gives birth and (usually) early nurture, she quickly becomes confused by gender with the structural impact of numbers 0, 1, and 2. Woman comes to represent in the gender myths of a given culture (3) the primordial ineffability of Frege's 0, as well as the principle of sameness (1) and loss (2). Since the apparent opposite principle to woman is man, men are unconsciously associated with the principle of difference insofar as the rupture of symbiotic unity teaches separation through the Law of the Name-of-the-Father. Men, therefore, come to represent the laws of the social realm.

Lacan's "pure" numbers point to a preconscious syntax of Symbolic myths and Real effects, which represent the imposition of limits on "self"-development and on the human capacity for processing identificatory information. Pre−mirror- and mirror-stage mergers, as well as Oedipal separation, work by substitution, condensation, and displacement to situate cognitive development both anticipatorily and retroactively within an affective logic of identificatory fusions and substitutive Desire. Such fetters circumscribe every person's being within a set of probable choices, mocking the existentialist project of infinite "self" possibilities. These limits also mock those materialist or mechanistic theories that do not even problematize the roles of repression, repetition, and Desire in human behavior.

Nonetheless, these boundaries are obscured by the fact that substitutions, displacements, and symbolizations make it appear that human beings can choose and change, both freely and infinitely. Variability and infinite differential scope characterize the two-dimensional world of language and consciousness. But individuals do not continually reinvent themselves, because a one-dimensional concrete logic—the mirror-stage Desire for union; the reality of difference; the Oedipal injunction to substitution—conditions the abstract components that we equate with the evolution of mind. Seen from an Imaginary perspective, Lacan uses his six numbers to demonstrate that the unconscious is restricted to a few individual themes—key signifiers—which are correlated in relation to Desire and Law. These representational underpinnings permit us to speak of consciousness as a two-dimensional system built upon a one-dimensional, out-of-sight reference bank. Lacanian psychoanalysis therefore looks for explanatory models in mathematical sets of functions and models that operate by analogous laws: the structural transformations, for example, that operate identity work by a homogeneous, relational, and fusionary logic in the Imaginary and by a differential, referential use of language in the Symbolic.[10]

The introjective/projective interplay of Real events, Imaginary representations, and Symbolic meanings to produce an act of consciousness precludes any possibility of a finally totalized system of mind. This interplay also installs "overdetermination" and substitution at all levels of conscious functioning. Underlying conscious meaning is a repressed chain of signifiers, which contains psychic "truth." Substantive material such as ideas, therefore, will never reveal first causes; they lie, instead, in the Desire to "know" that plays in language along the path of the search for sameness across a map of differences. We can already say without ambiguity that Lacan's three orders do not divide between symmetrical oppositions of concepts or along binary lines of conscious versus unconscious; objective versus subjective; and so on. They describe instead the transcendence of the unconscious on consciousness in reference to six numbers, structural laws, and signifiers.

In support of Lacan's theory that the unconscious can count to six, the Harvard psychologist George A. Miller's classic article, written in 1956, may prove helpful. Miller listed the limits on "absolute judgment" (the moment before confusion or "channel capacity" takes over in the human capacity for processing information) as all being connected to the numbers 5, 6, or 7. Seven appears as the limit on human capacities in relation to one-dimensional judgments. We can hear hundreds of musical notes, but only remember six or seven tones. We use thousands of words, but only identify binary and tertiary distinctions in phonemes. We can identify scores of faces, but only remember six or seven dots at a time when they are flashed on a screen. Although Miller refuses to reach a final conclusion, he speculates that "perhaps there is something deep and profound behind all these sevens, something just calling out for us to discover it."[11] It is impossible not to infer a connection between Miller's experiments and Lacan's theory that the unconscious—the place of one-dimensional, identificatory logic—can only count to six. Lacan himself adduced two examples to point to the significance of 6 and 7 in daily life. Jehovah distinguished himself from his sway over the six days of the week by adding a seventh. Second, the Babylonian counting system, which based itself on the number 10 (the number of human fingers), remained confused until they "arbitrarily" made the system sexigesimal: 6 x 10 (*Séminaire* XX, p. 122).

The physicist Gerald Holton has written in *Thematic Origins of Scientific Thought* (1973) that certain symbolic structures (models or themata) are at the base of diverse and apparently disconnected theories, some in space and others in history. These symbolic structures point to a homogeneous manner of functioning behind heterogeneous facets. He states: "The dimension of fundamental presuppositions, notions, terms, methodological judgments and decisions . . . which are themselves neither directly evolved from, nor resolvable into, objective observation on the one hand, or logical mathematical and other formal analytical ratiocination on the other hand . . . is a three-dimensional 'space'—using the terms always in full awareness of the limits of analogy—which may be called proposition space."[12] What Holton called "proposition space" Lacan called logico-mathematical. One of Lacan's models was Fregean philosophical mathematics in which a successor relation determines that every natural number be preceded by something and followed by something else. Thus, 0 gives rise to the number 1, and so on. Although every number is in itself a complete unit, it infers a grounding and a successor (n + 1).

I have used this logic to develop an Imaginary counting system that would describe the power of the Oedipal structure and language to create a space—the unconscious—which is, in turn, interpreted by the gender myths of a given culture. Numbers 0 to 3 describe the structure of the personality, then, and 4, 5, and 6 denote a mathematical recursion of the Oedipal triangle so that adult life is lived in shadow reference to childhood history. Lacan's use of mathematical theory to reveal unconscious structures resembles Claude Lévi-Strauss's use of mathematics to show universal cultural mythic structures. The philosopher Jean-Marie Benoist has written that in Lévi-Strauss's case "the mathematical tool functions like a *révélateur* of coherence in complex and apparently irrational ensembles, and shows us that there is order where there are semblances of chaos and the erratic, and it allows us to formalize some rules underlying the phenomena studied" (Benoist, *La Révolution*, p. 330). This could as well describe the function of Lacan's mathematical tools.

The Imaginary Order

The Imaginary order was the first one to preoccupy Lacan, although he later placed it close to the Real in many of its aspects. But before we discuss it, we must dispense with the standard notion of the imagination as a "mental faculty forming images of external objects not present to the senses; fancy; creative faculty of the mind."[13] In Lacan's picture the mind does not control imagination; rather, Imaginary processes are among those that structure mind through formalizable laws, such as projection and absorption, introjection and expulsion, substitution and displacement, and so on. Nor did Lacan conceive of "imaginary" as "that which has no real existence" (*Oxford English Dictionary*). By separating the Imaginary and the Real into different categories, Lacan was free to show the very Real nature of Imaginary perception.

Lacan was certainly not the first thinker to reinterpret imagination. Among others, the literary critic Herbert Marcuse brilliantly analyzed the importance of Freud's redefinition of the imagination away from the dictionary concept and to one as a process with its own laws and truth values that exists apart from the rational processes of mind or intellect, as another faculty of mind. Marcuse pointed out that Freud's original contribution was to show the genesis of this mode of thought and to connect it to the pleasure principle.[14] Freud maintained that through fantasy—a mental activity which retains a high degree of freedom from the reality principle—human beings can link the deepest layers of the unconscious with the highest products of consciousness (art), the dream with the reality (Marcuse, *Eros*, pp. 127–28). Fantasy was seen to speak the language of the Freudian pleasure principle, thus preserving the repressed and tabooed images of freedom. The imagination uses fantasy to retain its commitment to the id, or to psychic structure as it was prior to the social reality principle, which is characterized by reason and repression. Seen in this way, imagination envisions the reconciliation of reason and pleasure, reality and fantasy (Marcuse, *Eros*, pp. 127–30).

The late philosopher Ernest Becker observed that Freud's attempt to explain man as a pleasure-seeking animal has become a progressively unbelievable assertion.[15] Becker seemed to accept Marcuse's link of the pleasure principle to Eros and fantasy as a solution to the problem. But Lacan raised the problem to another level. By placing the roots of the pleasure principle in the Imaginary union between infant and (m)Other, Lacan redefined the pleasure principle as *jouissance* or a sense of Oneness, and reshaped the reality principle to refer to the separation evoked by language and Law (Castration), which ends the mirror stage. Pleasure is therefore destined to be bittersweet and deceptive ever after. It proceeds paradoxically along the Desiring path of investing passion in simultaneous efforts to recreate the bonds of an impossible unity through substitutes and displacements and, thereby, to deny the reality principle of Castration.

In the "Project for a Scientific Psychology" (1895), Freud linked primary process thought to the pleasure principle. Lacan followed Freud here but joined primary to secondary process instead of opposing them. "Beyond the Pleasure Principle" Lacan found Desire, which is not opposed to reality/Law but is, instead, inseparable from it. By recasting the reality principle as constraint (*Zwang*)—the phallic signifier—or as suffering (*Unterlegt*, *Untertragen*) that commands the detours and displacements of the quest for *jouissance*, he showed that Desire and Law—pleasure and reality—are opposed only insofar as their conflicting injunctions make up the structure of the human subject itself.[16] At the unconscious level there is reference to a unitary impossibility, and at the conscious level, substitutive displacements. Law enters the picture as Thanatos, then, the scourge of an idealizing unitary Eros. Law provokes fragmentation insofar as it is a divisory principle that repetitively teaches the human subject the impossibility of 1—a permanent or final peace. Conflict dwells within the subject and can never be "cured" by a neo-Freudian separation of fantasy from reality, pleasure from responsibility.

But having disconnected the pleasure principle from fantasy and linked it to reality, does one simply abandon it altogether? The Canadian psychiatrist Jean Lapierre says no, insisting on some join between pleasure and relaxation. From a Lacanian perspective, I would locate such a link at the interface between need and Desire, between primal repression of needs (*Urverdrängung*), inarticulable in demand, and residue that presents itself in man as Desire (*das Begehren*). In

"The Meaning of the Phallus" Lacan said that as long as man speaks, his needs bear on something other than the satisfactions called for by demand. Thus, needs return to man alienated from the place of the primordial Other (Mitchell and Rose, *Feminine Sexuality*, p. 80). Needs belong to the realm of time (anxiety), and to the primordial domain of the physical. In that needs derive from the earliest period of life, they are registered on the prespecular slope of the Real. Disconnected from any judgmental awareness of good or bad, or from any unconscious genital "drive," Lacanian need is corporal. Could we speculate that need is registered in the muscles, and perhaps even as a unifying principle of the autonomic nervous system? Desire, by antithesis, is beyond the physical. The philosopher Alain Juranville has said: "But desire is desire of change; it is the very principle of movement. From whence the idea of a subject of desire."[17] Perhaps we could say that any adult pleasure derived from relaxation—including the sex act itself—will join need to Desire, beyond demand, and will function temporarily to alleviate the anxiety that grows up between need and Desire, and is erroneously reduced to demand.

But primary-process thought appears in "pure" form only in psychosis when the domain of repressed, verbal imagistic representations comes unhooked from the Symbolic order of language and appears at the surface of consciousness as the hieroglyphics of unconscious meaning: words and objects stand at the same perceptive level, as does the human subject itself.

In "normal" relations, the name, the word, and the thing appear separate, although Lacan shows them as unconsciously linked in an Imaginary text that serves as a pivot between the past and the present. But the Imaginary is not reducible to the *moi*, the libido, or Desire, nor is it limited to the visual or the unconscious. The Imaginary dimension in being announces itself by inferring an immediacy in behavior, or a lack of individuation in identity. In daily discourse the *moi* (unique Imaginary subject) objectifies itself by disrupting the apparent autonomy of *je* discourse to impose verbal fragments, repetitions of believed "self"-myths, and other seemingly illogical material. But the *moi* is fixed and limited, while the Imaginary transcends it and puts it into play in the realm of Symbolic codes and Real events. Anika Lemaire portrayed the Imaginary as containing everything in the human mind—its reflexive life—which is in a state of flux (*Lacan*, pp. 60–61). The psychoanalyst Donald Winnicott (who refused to believe in the value of theorizing) has been characterized by F. R. Rodman as follows: "He was always aware, I think, that his formulations are mere momentary glimpses into the flux, and never do fix it in permanent view."[18] By naming the "flux" the

Imaginary order and attempting to formalize its laws at points of join
with the other orders, Lacan tried to pin down the theoretical knowledge in psychoanalysis that *can* be expressed without equivocation.

Lacan's Imaginary order places the potential for revolution in man
by making the drive toward fusion and agreement—the impossible
one (1) of mirror-stage *jouissance*—fundamental to perception and
action. The Imaginary consequently seeks to circumvent the Symbolic order, which places the shackles of laws and norms on the absolutism of narcissistic goals. By now it should be obvious that
Lacan's Imaginary order has nothing to do with the unreal, the false,
or the uninhibited. Nor did Lacan refer to the preformed metaphors
of life, which Carl Jung described as archaic forms with creative
powers. Frederic Jameson has aptly described the Imaginary as closer
to that which is commonly designated by expressions such as symbolism or symbol.[19] Lacan referred to a newborn infant's perceptive
state as that of an unsymbolized Imaginary. The infant immediately
begins to merge with images that are equated with the body (my interpretation of Frege's o). The first images are corporeal, therefore,
and are perceptually prior and resistant to conscious symbolization,
although these primordial images form the beginnings of the symbolization of unconscious Desires. When the infant takes on an
Imaginary image of its body in the mirror stage, the prespecular visual and acoustic images may well serve as the basis of a symbolized
Imaginary text, which becomes fixed in a whole image of the human
Gestalt.[20] The bedrock of Symbolic material, which is introjected
during this first eighteen months of life, constitutes a kind of substantive—that is, symbolic—Imaginary as an Ur-identity text with
infinite creative potential.

In "Aggressivity in Psychoanalysis" (1948) Lacan described images
as mental phenomena. Perception precedes impressions, he taught,
and "excites" the nervous system, not the reverse (*Séminaire* II,
p. 173). In the pre-mirror stage certain images are constituted for
what we know as Freud's "instinctual" material. The first images imposed on infant perception are totalities or primary unities with
which the infant merges in fantasy, these images setting up the originary matrices to which all other images become attached in "hallucinatory" networks of meaning. Lacan hypothesized that the later
fantasy of a fragmented body finds its prototype in these original images and in the matrices of transient images built up around them.
Individual inflexions of identity and Desire are determined by this
early symbolic material, which accumulates throughout childhood
into fantasmatic networks of relations and assonanced meanings.
These fantasies, in turn, condition adult perception, thereby ensur-

ing that perception itself is intrinsically subjective. Although Freud took hallucinations to be "false"—fantastic distortions of reality— Lacan showed them to be true insofar as they conditioned reality perception (*Séminaire* II, p. 174).

A hallucinatory meaning network stands behind the secondary meanings of language systems. Even though there is no transparency of meaning between these primary and secondary systems, Lacan maintained that both dreams and hallucinations are potentially comprehensible and decipherable in light of the meanings inscribed in the Other(A). Dream scenarios are ultimately texts about the "self" which point to messages anchored in the primordial place of knowledge and meaning: the Other(A). In hallucinations, images and language appear disassociated from any sense of a unified identity. Paradoxically they are meant to provide a kind of order for a confused person who is "dreaming awake." Lacan did not oppose halluci- nations to reality, therefore, but took them to reveal the concrete nature of elemental mental processes. The concrete language of deaf mutes, brain-damaged individuals, psychotics, children, and poets goes to prove that there is a logic to language other than that of the abstract perfectability of system. In adult life any unraveling of an Imaginary text shows the way identity was composed as a "self" text, much as the reverse side of a tapestry betrays the tangle of threads that constitute the images making up a work of art. Imagi- nary images—both visual and acoustic—reappear in dreams, fan- tasies, paintings, psychotic hallucinations, sadomasochistic crimes, and so on. But these images are "beyond the mirror" because they portray the essential dislocation of the human subject into one or more of its identificatory components. A deconstruction of the Imaginary text reveals a fundamental disorder in the "instinctual" life of humans, therefore, instead of a neat evolution of stages as Freud supposed (*Séminaire* II, pp. 209–10).

That images play a role in the evolution of the psyche has never been doubted by poets, mystics, and artists. But images and words are generally believed to exist in different parts of the mind. More recently, brain researchers have told us that images belong to the right hemisphere of the brain, while speech is controlled by the left hemisphere. The nature of long-term memory nonetheless remains an enigma for these researchers, who cannot localize such memories in a specific area. Instead, it is thought that long-term memories are spread out over the entire brain. Such researchers portray intelli- gence arising as a concatenation of thousands of unfathomable con- nections among genetic codes and neural synapses. Lacan's linking of unconscious images and language to conscious life—via repressed

memories—would perhaps explain the mystery which neurophysiologists ponder in genetic codes, neurons, and brain cells. When
Richard Wollheim wrote in "The Cabinet of Dr. Lacan" that the
Lacanian concept of the image denies the infant what language
grants it (and thereby has a negative function), he missed the point.[21]
The role which Lacan assigns the image is so central to the formation of mind that without it there would be no human identity, no
perceptual basis to which to apply language, and no experiential link
between the lifeless phonemes of language and the sensual realities
of infant (and later adult) experience. Freud equated consciousness,
perception, and the visual, but Lacan equated the unconscious, the
perceptual, and visual and verbal (*Séminaire* II, pp. 172, 177). Culture imposes itself on nature from the start of life, building up a representational base to which all other representations refer. This
is why Lacan placed the perceptual-consciousness system in the
Imaginary (*Séminaire* II, p. 147).

In a curious paradox the language that is always already there outside human beings gives the meanings of a specific culture to universal images. It determines that there can never be an archetypology of
images apart from language—no superiority of images, no inherent
meaning to them. Since the universe is replete with images, any
later inadequacy in conscious representation and communication
comes from a deficiency in the linguistic order. On the other hand, a
lack of images—an infant deprived of stimuli—would prevent certain symbols from ever appearing. Given that both images and language are required to structure perception, Lacan duly problematizes
the manner in which this structuring occurs. Rejecting the static
idea that the imagination simply records them in a transparent and
literal fashion, Lacan gives a dynamic interpretation of the mechanisms of introjection and projection.

Freud accurately described introjection in "Narcissism: An Introduction" as the relationship of a living being to the objects it desires,
linked to conditions of *Gestalt* or the global form of its body (*Séminaire* I, p. 310). Lacan claimed, however, that Freud did not really
understand the mechanism he described. Since Freud's death, animal
ethology has described the Imaginary phenomenon of identification
in detail, as well as its function in animal behavior and mating. Literally captured by form and mirage, the eye sees images which it records in the Other(A) as memory. In Seminar One Lacan reproduced
the drawing called "the experiment of the reversed bouquet," by
which he illustrated the perceptual meeting of Real and Imaginary
objects (p. 92). In fact, he describes the phenomenon of mirage: a
Real object is refracted by light rays and presents itself to the eye as if

it were Real when, indeed, it is only virtual, or, as Lacan said, Imaginary. In the drawing the vase is Real and the bouquet in it is virtual. In the same way Real objects give rise to the Imaginary creation of similar—but not identical—objects. This conjunction between Real and Imaginary forms occasions the possibility for the free play in which introjection and expulsion alternate with projection and absorption to form the *moi* by identification with objects: primary identification works by introjection and secondary identification by projection (see Chapter 1). The drawing of the reversed bouquet illustrates for Lacan the close inmixing (*intrication étroite*) of the Imaginary and Real worlds on a psychic plane.

In Martin Thom's essay "*Verneinung, Verwerfung, Ausstossung*: A Problem in the Interpretation of Freud," the author points out that in "Instincts and Their Vicissitudes" (1915) and in "Denial" (1925) Freud spoke of a pleasure ego which is built up by attribution, incorporating good qualities and expelling bad ones.[22] Expulsion (*Ausstossung*) of "bad" objects or effects leads to denial (*Verneinung, dénégation*) just as affirmation (*Bejahung*) leads to assimilation of "good" objects. *Ausstossung* and *Bejahung* therefore constitute the first acts of judgment exercised to create a "self." Melanie Klein took over these Freudian ideas to make introjection and expulsion a simple matter of reality and literal imagination. Lacan's contribution showed that there is not a "literal" introjecting of good objects and expelling of bad ones. At the most primitive level the *Ur-Ich* or *Lust-Ich* establishes itself even prior to categories of inside/outside, and certainly before objects are attributed in relation to any idea of container or contained. In other words, the question of "self" boundaries (my Imaginary rendering of Frege's o and 1) parallels the question of the material that makes up the "self." Primary introjection is linked, furthermore, to what Lacan called *l'écriture* (scripting) or the effect of language. What is introjected here is not objects in a literal sense, but objects as perceived in relation to an effect of language: the Other's *parole* (*Séminaire* I, p. 97) (Don't eat that! Isn't that yummy?). The result, as John Forrester says in an essay entitled "Philology and the Phallus," is a fatal ambiguity in the status of the word, giving the word a dual function as sign and as image (*Talking Cure*, p. 64). The first verbal and visual introjects or concrete symbols—elementary cells of Desire—constitute the lining of the "natural" subject before it is divided into "natural" and speaking parts.

Here we see an overlap between the Imaginary *moi* and the inscriptions building up the Other(A). In Seminar Three Lacan admitted that the domain of image theory and imagination is unfathomable (*insondable*); the formative value of the image is so crucial, he said, that it joins hands with the problem of origins (*Voire même de l'essence de la vie*).[23] Man's primordial fusion with images and sounds builds up layer upon layer of representations, which turn around as if in a machine, eventually ready to leave their closed circuit of unconscious recording and return into the general repetitive game of life from which they originally came (*Séminaire* II, pp. 111–12). But this preconscious imagistic world still does not have the structure of language (although sound inscribes itself there). But grammatical language can later be separated from images, since it still keeps its own paths, its particular communications (*Séminaire* III, p. 186). The interest here is twofold: (1) the idea that language is built onto an elementary symbol system in preverbal infants is supported by current Anglo-American researches in cognitive science and in infant development, and (2) while Lacan is perfectly prepared to admit the importance of the imagistic world, he stresses that personality as a *specific* and seemingly unified effect evolves from a relationship of the subject to the signifier as language. In this way he enjoins his interlocutors not to fall into the trap of Ernst Kris and others who would imagize the body on an unconscious model (at the expense of the signifier) and in keeping with the traditional idea of "self" as a substance. Such views merely deduce the past from present fantasies or reify Imaginary projections, thus missing Lacan's revolutionary insight: it is the words which culture imposes on the infant (and on images) that create the human subject as a specificity.

The "normal" subject of perception later exists somewhere between inside and outside, as an Imaginary constellation that can enunciate itself, because language has stabilized perception by offering names and labels and a "mode" of translation. Psychotic speech, on the other hand, harkens directly back to the concrete nature of the primordial introjects. These prototypes of hallucinations—both visual and verbal—mark a return into the Real of that nether side of language ordinarily lost from view: that is, the words linked to "key signifiers"—birth, procreation, love, and death—in their unique imagistic and Symbolic associations.

In its transformational essence Lacan's Imaginary can be likened to a field that acts as a gravitational force at the center of being. In Seminar One Lacan described the Imaginary as functioning like a magnet, first through introjection, and then through projection (p. 215). The primordial gap between perception and body experience—attributable to a prematuration at birth—might be compared to the black holes of the physical universe. Black holes, formed by the death of a star, are powerful, invisible stellar traps and lures composed of gravity and density, which suck up material that comes within their range.[24] Like the physical universe Lacan's mirror-stage psychic universe is the scene of constant movement and reverberations controlled by the action of the Imaginary order. The latter operates first by introjection and then by projection as alternating— not opposed—processes. While introjection involves a structuring of the ideal ego (moi) through various effects of images and language, projection points to the mirror-stage dual relation with ego ideals (others). In Seminar One Lacan equated secondary introjection or Castration with the superego or phallic signifier. The system of language permits secondary repression to occur by splitting the "natural" moi between the state of pure being (primordial repression) and the post-mirror stage for referential "saying." Introjection is on the Symbolic slope, then, and projection on the Imaginary one.

Lacan maintained that Klein lacked the requisite theories to understand her own observations and experiments. Without adequate theories of the ego (moi) and the Imaginary, she failed to grasp that at the start of the ego's genesis, introjected parts are disassociated from each other because they belong to different registers: the Real, the Symbolic, and the Imaginary. This results in a primordial disjunction between sets of objects (which can be observed in psychosis). Lacan showed that only through a particular sequential structuring of language in relation to the primordial gaze, and then in its link to Oedipal intervention, can a subject's language come to symbolize the sets of introjected Imaginary and Real objects in connection with a Symbolic order of conventions. In other words the psychotic has language, the very private distortion of language we all have in a place of repression. But psychotic language cannot succeed in connecting inner and outer objects comprehensibly because "it" has foresworn repression, and thereby lost the memory bank which gives consciousness a point of reference.

In the Ecrits Lacan described the Imaginary as the dimension of images, conscious or unconscious, actually perceived (real) or made up (imagined). The word miraginaire was coined to stress the importance of mirror-stage identification with images or forms in the process of ego building. This perceptual fusion (confusion) with another opens the way for a child to recognize its own body as a unity, rather than as a number of disassociated fragments, and at the same time conditions the cognitive step from an Imaginary application of Frege's o to 1. Although this Imaginary identificatory function is neither substantive nor ontological, its very real existence—which operates by introjection and projection of images—later submits all psychic reality to identificatory meaning (Séminaire II, p. 296). Substantively speaking, the Imaginary was a representational "self" text even before it was a libidinal (dynamic) function. As a one-dimensional text, this meaning shows up in relationships of resemblance and agreement.

Even though Lacan's theories overlapped with those of Melanie Klein, Donald Winnicott, Heinz Kohut, and others, Lacan parted company with them in many ways. By broadening the picture of introjection and projection, Lacan shows Klein's part-objects and Kohut's self-objects (of secondary narcissism) to be limited to statically introjected images of corporal experience and parental words and attitudes. Lacan's dynamic approach erased the Symbolic bar, which is assumed to separate "self" from the noumenal world by showing that humans *are* their subjective (phenomenal) perceptions. In offering a theory on how "matter" enters or creates "mind," Lacan implicitly answers Descartes and Kant. Perception and effect operate initially (in the absence of any innate unifying principle) to record a system of referents that serves as the nucleus of the ego. These referents make up disassociated sets of relations, which coalesce around an unconscious system of countable unities (0–6). These units or unities are created by the effects of Real experience linked to Symbolic data that, when combined interpretatively, form an Imaginary text of "self" fables. This Imaginary text can also decompose into its constituent Symbolic parts in dreams, poetry, paintings, jokes, or hallucination (*Séminaire* XI, p. 192). And both point toward the Real of object and effect.

Lacan cannot, therefore, be accused—as Kohut has—of using "self" and representation as synonyms.[25] There is no whole "self" in Lacan's epistemology; instead, there are sets of signifying chains and unities, which compose "self" out of relational ensembles of meaning. The elementary signifying chains are made up of representations recorded in the Other as active meaning data (*représentatifs représentants*) that overdetermine the conscious subject and make of "self" a dialectical project of becoming, a set of potential narcissistic (*moi*) and linguistic (*je*) responses to Real situations. In the accommodation of the Imaginary to the Real, the other refracts a virtual image of the *moi*, thereby providing an approximation (but only an approximation!) of the *moi*'s own narcissistic "self" myths. Any decoding of *moi* fictions within the transference dynamic points *beyond* narcissism to the Real of the Other's gaze, which first inscribed "truth" and Desire in an infant (*Séminaire* XX, p. 111).

The Imaginary itself does not refer to orderly communication, then, but to confusion, illusion, and relationships of exclusion. We wonder how this category can be formalized at all. The answer is by understanding the "laws" of introjection, projection, aggressiveness, narcissism, repetition, regression, and repression. The Imaginary functions in relationships to objectify the other, but at the same time confuses oneself and one's *moi* in a dialectic of projected identificatory ideals. In discourse the Imaginary intervenes paradoxically as an inertia that keeps a person from really perceiving either "self" or other accurately. Meanwhile, the Other(A) remains outside this trajectory, asymmetrical to it. The Lacanian analyst's work is precisely to dissipate such confusion and restore a "sense" to the analysand's discourse (*Séminaire* II, p. 353). Lacan referred to this procedure as a resubjectivization of the subject, which would extract him from the object status into which he has been frozen vis-à-vis the Other (*Séminaire* III, p. 341). Put another way, the Imaginary transference function and "self" fables confront the analyst with the problem of how to get "beyond narcissism," when narcissism appears to be the final point in an analysis.

Dynamic repression eddies forth from the Other(A) to aid Imaginary illusion, by placing a veil of obscurity between perception and consciousness. Through suppression or dynamic repression (*Unterdrückung*), that meaning which has not succeeded in making sense of a person's life has remained suspended. Its intimations are only inferred in dreams, slips of the tongue, symptoms, misunderstandings, and so on. But since Imaginary mechanisms, for example, illusion, exclusion, and confusion, automatically block the passage of truth— a *parole* from the Other(A)—it is comprehensible why Lacan advised analysts not to make a pact of understanding or empathy with the ego, because the latter merely presents conscious illusions through memories and reconstruction of family history (*Séminaire* III, p. 182). Instead, careful attention must be paid to the links between the Imaginary, the Real, and the Symbolic where the unconscious resides.

In adult life the Imaginary is set in motion within relationships. In discourse it appears as the implied (latent) meaning of a statement or as the repressed (unfinished) part of a sentence. These second meanings refer to some diachronic aspect of the childhood drama (some reenactment of my Imaginary picture of Fregean numbers 1, 2, and 3). But since the meaning is opaque, what the Imaginary text actually reveals is a dissymmetrical relationship between the subject and its own unconscious: a relationship without reciprocity. The repressed Imaginary childhood experience (of mirror-stage effects, Castration, Desire, and Oedipal intervention) becomes a substitutive Imaginary text in adult life, a function of Desire. It follows that the substitutive Imaginary (like the libido) will be object-seeking. As ideal ego, the *moi* anticipates an elusive image of "self" in others (ego ideals). People constitute each other Imaginarily as objects in an ongoing effort or "impulse" to verify their own identities retroactively in terms of samenesses and differences. The *moi* itself has, therefore, become a symbol to be exchanged in an Imaginary, cultural signifying chain, erroneously taking itself to be the measure of the Real and true.

In Seminar Two Lacan referred to the *moi* as one of the structured forms of the living Imaginary, whose Symbolic function—offering itself as a representative symbol of a given human subject in the marketplace of human affairs—lends it an eminence in relation to the Real (pp. 371–73). But this exchange does not reveal a Baudelairean world of symbolic harmony where doubles peep out to cement unity through love, music, and terrestrial beauty. Rather, the other separates the *moi* from its own Other(A) (O → S). This blockage points to a tension between the Real and the Symbolic orders, which underlies Imaginary relations of anticipated understanding and union. Because individuals do not see themselves as robots acting out an-Other's script around a series of Imaginary fixations, the Imaginary is often free to unleash disconcerting effects on Symbolic codes and in Real situations. Jane Gallop refers to this dynamic in her essay "Lacan's 'Mirror Stage.'"[26] But Gallop fails to distinguish the mirror stage proper as a limited procedure (that establishes both an image of the infant's body as unified and the kernel of a "self"-identity) from its subsequent effects on the adult "playing out" of an individual childhood drama built around an Imaginary "self" text, and dramatized by Imaginary mechanisms. Through both function and fable the Imaginary operates on others in adult life as a sliding register of intuitive anticipation and rigid retroaction. As in *Alice in Wonderland*, the *moi* continually (re-)constitutes itself in anticipation of an ideal image being refracted, in anticipation of narcissism (re-)verified and pre-Castration *jouissance* restored. Not unlike the mirror-stage infant joyfully anticipating its own unity through body mastery, the adult anticipates psychic mastery (wholeness, constancy, glory, certainty, and joy), deploring its evanescence.

The retroactive complement of anticipation stems from the narcissistic fixations (Imaginary) that introduce conflict into the Real of human interchange. The *moi* accepts itself as an object and tries to objectify others within its text of "self"-reference. Repression, repetition, resistance, and regression all function as the blocks of denial thrown up by the *moi* to avoid seeing its origin of identity in the Other and blissfully insist on a "naturalness" in individual personality. The Imaginary is itself, then, a principle of denial, which Lacan called "misrecognition" (*méconnaissance*). Retroactive (diachronic) "self"-meaning refers back as far as the inferred prespecular phase, which became fixated in anticipatory *moi* myths. "Self"-meaning will remain opaque, however, unless decoded in its dialectical relationship to the Other(A). The conviction that one exists as a personality (and as a complete body) are Imaginary perceptions which, nonetheless, keep anxiety, if not psychic fragmentation, at bay. When it is understood that Lacan located the Freudian death drive beyond biology and primordial masochism in the unsymbolized Imaginary—the gap between body experience and a perceptual sense of unity—we can see how essential the denial mechanism (*Verneinung*) is. Man must believe in his *moi* because it stands between him and metaphorical death: corporal and perceptual fragmentation. Yet to decode the Imaginary *moi*, the analyst must reach behind the "wall of language" and beyond the wall of images, myth, memory, or Symbolic order, role, or status to reveal the cause of symptoms at the level of Real event and psychic loss, as well as in the material impact of language as recorded in the Other(A). Any ultimate pursuit of the moments of join between Imaginary and Symbolic orders leads back beyond the illusions of the transference relation to a point of fading and primal repression where identifications (fusions) initially merged with the Real.

Perhaps the ambiguity surrounding this knot or join has led the French critic Julia Kristéva to identify the *moi* with the corporeal (with the mirror stage) and the *je* with language, thereby curiously perpetuating a mind/body division along binary Cartesian lines. Kristéva concludes that the Symbolic order of language eludes the rapport of language to the body. By missing the fact that the *moi* and *je* are correlative one of the other, Kristéva depicts a semiotic Lacan. From the moment Lacan linked repression (the phallic signifier or S_1 or the "law" of metaphor) to language and recognized their locus as a Real place in the Other(A)—instead of placing them in a fantasmatic place of unreality—he had gone beyond Freud. He also differentiated psychoanalysis from semiotics by joining the human subject, the unconscious, and the signifier. While semioticians find symmetrical equivalences among sign systems, Lacan found asymmetrical movements within the human subject itself. Going in the opposite direction from Kristéva, Lacan showed, on the contrary, that language has its roots in the corporal and symbolic bedrock of the Imaginary (Benoist, *La Révolution*, p. 246). That is to say, symbols mediate between effects, things, and sounds. In Seminar Two Lacan said that "the first symbols, the 'natural' symbols, have come from a certain number of prevalent images—the image of the human body, the image of a certain number of obvious objects like the sun, the moon and some others. And that is what gives its weight, its spring [*ressort*] and its emotional vibration to human language" (p. 352). But, said Lacan, these Imaginary themes cannot be reduced homogeneously to the Symbolic.

In his 1956–57 Seminar Lacan taught that, at the Imaginary level, objects and words merge into a homogeneous *moi* structure that makes daily discourse as overdetermined as dreams or symptoms in which the thing and the name are more clearly interwoven. The unconscious material which surfaces into discourse through Imaginary "laws," therefore, is not a thing or the absence of a thing; nor a word or the absence of a word; nor an organ or the absence of an organ; but a *knot* in a structure where words, things, and organs can neither be definitely separated nor compatibly combined. Although a person can never return to the radical and elemental stage of structuring— described by Jameson as an untranslatable impressionism—the repressed Imaginary text can be ascertained as a representational shadow meaning that refers back to the prespecular objects of Desire. At the level of perception and meaning, however, it is almost impossible to separate the Imaginary from the apparent (phenomenal) "objectivity" of consciousness, although artists and some psychoanalysts know how to freeze this second meaning (Lacan's *instant terminal de voir*), which usually escapes detection. In visual terms, for example, Christian Metz has described the cinema as an Imaginary signifier. Like the camera, some paintings and poems also capture that moment of unconscious "truth" that plays at the surface of life.[27]

Since the *moi* was first created by Imaginary mergers with primary and secondary unities forming that perceptual basis by which individuals later symbolize the world, the Imaginary provides a continuity within the subject's own topology as well as the basis of the symbolic and subjective logic which stands behind language. The Imaginary text thus makes language a circular system, which always suggests its own reference and portrays the functional laws behind its own logic. It is difficult to penetrate this logic, but typical "breaks" in traditional logic or conscious reason point to a "logic" of the unconscious. In his continuing effort to show the connections between "self"-misrecognition and the proximity of the Imaginary to the Symbolic and the Real, Lacan used the example of the Real of the human body whose form first appears to the infant Image-inarily, that is, as a "mirror" reflection. People can see themselves reflected in a window, for example, at the same time that they see Real objects outside the window. Although the "self"-reflection also seems real, it is only "virtual" or Imaginary. This same confusion occurs in the process of identification and later poses problems of subjectivity in human perception of body image, beauty, and so on. Insofar as the *moi*—like the body—is also an Imaginary structure, "self"-image cannot be transparently reflected or harmoniously reestablished, so that the transposition of "identical" egos would make of psychoanalytic interchange or any other "love" relationship a matter of good will and accommodation. As I interpret Lacan here, even though there is no final phenomenological or experiential separation between the image, the body, and language, analysts must seek to decode symptoms by untangling the corporal and the image from the signifier. Language, after all, gives "meaning" to the body and the image (in a differential series of oppositions), not the reverse.

Once Imaginary meaning is decoded, it becomes Symbolic meaning. Meaning, that is to say, has left the natural realm of presence and been "translated"—distorted—via interpretive language. A dream, for example, is Imaginary before it is analyzed, and Symbolic afterward. At the Imaginary level the dream has all the value of a direct declaration of the subject of the unconscious, down to the recounting of it (*Séminaire* II, p. 296). Lacan viewed this propensity for "telling" dreams to others as illustrative of the dialectical nature of the unconscious: the dream is already a message from the Other(A) which seeks to interpret itself via others. The Imaginary therefore accounts for (1) what in language makes it mean more than it says, and (2) why miscommunication is the most telling aspect of "communication."

In contradistinction to Freud, who thought that the unconscious provided the essential continuity of human experience, Lacan described the Imaginary as that which infuses the unconscious into consciousness to create discontinuities, inconsistencies, and irruptions. Continuity resides, rather, in the Symbolic verbal chain that connects, labels, and orients Imaginary incidents, so giving import, perpetuity, and reality to otherwise solipsistic perception (*Séminaire* I, pp. 233, 244; *Séminaire* II, p. 202). Continuity is also sought in the gaze of others in reference to which any *moi* reconstitutes itself. In childhood, therefore, the Symbolic and Real orders are more important than the Imaginary. Indeed, Lacan said that only the Symbolic and Real exist for the child. I understand him to mean that since the Imaginary weaves itself together as an interpretation of the Symbolic and Real, it exists only "in process" in childhood. The child is, so to speak, on the assembly line. The Imaginary becomes visible as a specific order with laws and a logic of its own only from the vantage point of adult life.

Lacan's Imaginary repressed text would give us a different meaning for Jean Piaget's observations about the development of language. Even though Lacan's use of the concepts of structure and transformational process may well influence Piaget's late work, he fundamentally disagrees with Piaget's notion of innate mental structures that mature through developmental stages. Piaget's processes go from egocentrism to decentering, to an increase in knowledge or concrete operational thought, and finally to a refocus of perspective in propositional logic. Psychologically, he spoke of the egocentric child, the adolescent reformer, and the adult achiever.[28] Children do not speak egocentrically, Lacan said. They speak "off-stage," mimicking in rehearsal for life. Acoustic images recorded in the Other(A)—phonemes to be exact—lend the "material" support that concrete discourse borrows from unconscious language (Sheridan, *Ecrits*, p. 147). These primitive linguistic effects subsequently condition common language as invisible effects around certain sounds, images, words, and themes.

I would, nevertheless, maintain that the Lacanian Imaginary can be observed in childhood thought as the cognitive mode that we later call primary process. When a four-year-old tells his sister to wear yellow pajamas to a birthday party and be a stick of butter, or when another child says a "lion" is busy on the telephone (i.e., the *line* is busy), we are not in the presence of cognitive malfunctions or developmental levels, but are privy to the building up of unconscious meaning in its identificatory fusion of images and words. Although Piaget viewed childhood egocentric discourse as a manifestation of lack of reciprocity, Lacan used the same effect to argue that there cannot be a discourse without reciprocity. In other words, the speaking self refers to the self of identifications merely by the fact of speaking. What is reciprocal, then—albeit asymmetrical—is the Imaginary interchange between the *moi* and the Other(A), and between the *je* and the Other(A), which characterize the war within every human (*Séminaire* XI, p. 189).[29]

Although some American psychoanalysts have looked at speech as a reflection of behavior and have linked ego defense mechanisms to characteristic speech patterns (syntax and style), no overall theory has been evolved.[30] Lacan, on the other hand, has made the analysand's speech itself the focus of analysis. Language is a "coping mechanism," which reflects not behavior, but another language underneath, a language that infers conflict at junctures that can be correlated with Lacanian mathematics: the numbers 0–6 (Sheridan, *Ecrits*, p. 59). There is no clear join between these two languages, however, since acoustic images enter the Imaginary text by assonance and relation of meaning, not by the associations and narrative linearity, which characterize the Symbolic text. Reconstructed memories will reveal the Imaginary, but fail to shed any light on the unconscious, while Symbolic order homophones will not so fail.

The philosopher Merleau-Ponty asked in regard to the problem of analysis (September 1959): "Do we have the right to comprehend the time, the space of the child as an undifferentiation of *our* time, our space?"[31] Should Merleau-Ponty inquire of Lacan, the answer lies in the Imaginary order. The Imaginary, in fact, accounts for the difference between a child's and an adult's concepts of time and space, as well as for the differences in their discourse. Adult time and space are structured by clocks, chronologies, contracts—Oedipal signifiers. But the child's time and space remain active within the adult as the source of Desire, individuality, repetitious patterns, and symptoms. The child's space is unconscious space, then, whose effects can only be decoded by analysis of the original dialectic. This kind of recuperation or recovery of Other(A) "language" establishes a continuity in a person's life story. Such restoration is not, however, a matter of finding a hidden or forgotten memory or event. The problem of ontology is not to identify oneself in language, so much as to learn that language has distorted experience. *Moi* identity was taken on in an-Other's mirror. If the mirror was tilted, one saw badly in it. In the same way Lacan described the difficulty man has in accommodating himself to the Imaginary (*Séminaire* I, p. 161). The alienating gaze of the Other(A) drives people to define themselves by fables, fictions, and myths, which often lead to great personal pain, but drive them nonetheless to "live" by these dead fictions. Essentially, then, "drive" is the drive to know the trove of signifiers in the Other(A).

The Imaginary in adult life valorizes the Other(A) in its links to the mirror-stage quest for sameness and the Oedipal injunction to difference. Even the illusion that a person can find "complete understanding" derives from the narcissistic drive to eradicate difference between self and other to regain the mythical paradise of *jouissance*, and in so doing to deny Castration. This "drive" implies a greater Desire to be "right" than to "know" the truth about oneself in the exchange of opinion or theory. There is no *Wissentrieb* ("truth drive"), Lacan said. Imaginary logic stands behind the human tendency of moralizing (good or bad) and ethical judgments, therefore, as well as behind all binary and oppositional thinking. In its absolutist, moralistic nature the Imaginary is the topological, diachronic function that allows individuals to connect themselves to the world through convictions and beliefs. The laws of narcissism and aggressiveness being inherent in its structure, the *moi* of Imaginary absolutism stands behind war, ideology, and religion.

Less broadly speaking, Imaginary tendencies are revealed in the passions of love, hate, and ignorance. Even before they acquired language in any coherent sense, infants made an archaic stabilization of space in terms of which "good" was associated with *me*, and "bad" with the affairs of the "mirror" rival (Jameson, "Imaginary and Symbolic in Lacan," p. 357). This structural underpinning explains why in the realm of human interdependencies there is a fundamental instability and discord (*Séminaire* II, p. 201). The "you or me" of a war, which Lacan invoked, parallels the dialectical disunity within one's own being. By making a problem of the human effort to deny or eradicate difference, Lacan has avoided issues of substance and ideology in order to study the structures behind the human drive for unity and certainty. And by iconoclastically basing the quest for any unitary meaning in an Imaginary function (whose principal goal is to deny Castration), Lacan offers a compelling explanation for human miscommunication, dogmatism, and deceptions.

We have mentioned various vantage points from which the Imaginary text can be inferred in adult life, but we have not yet indicated that any decoding of the Imaginary depends on the intermediary of the Law: that is, the phallic third term (*Séminaire* I, p. 161). The phallic signifier links the Imaginary to the Symbolic via intentionality: an unconscious stance toward Desire, taken in the Name-of-the-Father. When individuals situate their *moi* with respect to one another by exchanging identity concepts, the invisible element in the narcissistic/aggressive posturing is a preexisting attitude toward the Phallus. The intentionality behind a given discourse structure—be it that of a master, hysteric, academic, or analyst—derives from an Imaginary relationship to an Imaginary Phallus. Beyond narcissism and mirror illusions, the analyst must look for the specific manner in which Imaginary meaning shows its—albeit disjunctive—dependence on Symbolic meaning. In language every element has value as opposed to other elements, while in the Imaginary (or Real) there is always a threshold or beginning (*seuil*) (*Séminaire* III, p. 17). It is to this beginning, with its implied continuity of image and theme, that the analyst must look. But it is the analysand's speech that will bear the resonance and residue from the Imaginary (and Real) that return to blur any final distinction between fantasy and reality (*Séminaire* I, p. 303).

Certain readers of Lacan have underrated the instantaneous fashion in which the Imaginary spills childhood material into adult life.

Such critics tend to limit the Imaginary to absolutism, lawlessness, formlessness, and lack of individuation. They take this order, therefore, to be nothing other than a prelanguage stage or a phase of pathology and childish narcissism—an id state—to be transcended on the way to Symbolic-order stabilization and individuation. Other readers, such as Jean Lyotard, Gilles Deleuze, and Félix Guattari, have taken the opposite approach and extolled the fragmented, diffractive flux or lack of boundaries which mark this realm of identificatory fusions.[32] By extension, they equate the Symbolic order of laws and rules with capitalism and patriarchy and urge that it be resisted and rejected (see Chapter 5).

Certain French feminists have taken the same position as Deleuze and Guattari by identifying the Imaginary with Desire, flux, and body—i.e., feminine "truth." The Symbolic order, by this logic, becomes the enemy territory of patriarchs and pederasts. Both positions—the Imaginary as a pathology and the Imaginary as a place of freedom—err, curiously enough, by "thinking" Lacan Imaginarily: namely, in absolutist, unitary terms. By claiming that either the Imaginary or the Symbolic is superior (or even that the two can be easily separated), such commentators fail to realize that without the Imaginary there would be no sense of identity, no basis for Desire, no representational reference point for reality perception, no mechanism by which to anchor language to any coherent sense of being a "self." But without the Symbolic to stabilize, give form to, and "translate" the Imaginary, man would remain at the same perceptual level as common animals that lack speech. The Imaginary must be sought, then, not just as a separate category, but at the join between Real events and Symbolic naming.

This join leads to the origin of knowledge as well as to the source of affect. In neurosis the Symbolic is subjugated to Imaginary laws of indistinction and solipsistic perception in an imbalance between the two orders: the adult is psychically submerged in the Other's discourse and Desire as if she or he were a child. In my focus on the Imaginary aspect of Lacanian mathematics neurosis implies difficulties in learning to count to three, that is, in coping with the (gender) myths which surround the experience of Castration. The unconscious mechanism behind psychosis points to difficulties in learning to count to two. A foreclosure (*Verwerfung*), as distinct from a denial (*Verneinung*), of Castration has occurred. Although both neurosis and psychosis stem from lack of Oedipal resolution, they function at different points of structural tension. By rejecting the psychic split from the (m)Other, the psychotic personality retains a sense of self-totality: a lack of lack (Desire). But the price paid is an incapacity to function in the Symbolic realm of displacement and substitutions. In certain psychotic episodes a disintegration of the *moi* into its Imaginary components makes of consciousness a kind of dreaming awake (*Séminaire* II, p. 283). The paranoid psychotic adheres to this Imaginary material as if it were Real, placing it at the level of the *je*. This picture reverses the idea that psychosis is a loss of reality. In paranoid psychosis the Imaginary representational text recorded in the Other(A) is alluded to in its pristine, hallucinatory purity to show the "logic" of the fragmentary underside of identity, the subjective underface of "reality."

As we survey the various levels on which the Imaginary functions, its complexity and conceptual richness come into focus. It contains the representations that make up primordial and secondary identifications; it orders the plurality of lived experiences—one's relationship to the Real; it is a phase in specular development, which later furnishes the model for maturation through relationship dynamics with respect to unconscious structures; it conditions the pictorial aspect of all ideation, operating features like resemblance; it supplies the connotative material of human experience; it serves to reify narcissistic passion, Desire, and "drive"; it is the source of ideology and belief. Given its conceptual complexity, I would suggest that with the Imaginary order Lacan first confronts the problem of what the metaphor of "mind" really means. While some linguists have reduced mind to language and others to neurophysiological structures in the brain and still others to genetic dictate, Lacan has expanded the concept of mind beyond this. To language (the Symbolic) and its Real effects, as well as to the organic functions of the brain (the Real), Lacan has added the Imaginary order: identificatory fixations and an ensemble of introjected *images* which supply linguistic phonemes and organic functions with the basis on which to build meaning.

Researchers from various disciplines in the human and physical sciences are currently engaged in redefining consciousness. Consciousness is viewed as a multileveled concept, and there is some agreement that many of its functions occur without any awareness on the part of the organism.[33] The results of such investigations refute Descartes in part and show that animals *do* have feeling and consciousness, like humans. In Seminar Three Lacan said that the Imaginary is assuredly the guide of life for the whole animal field (p. 17). What animals do not have, however, is a spoken system of language so vast and plurivalent that misunderstandings and miscommunications (as well as hallucinations) can define its parameters, alongside the communication of convention.[34] Even though contemporary theories of cognition have not proposed that an Imaginary structuring of perception operates consciousness by narcissism and Desire (as has Lacan), these researchers have, at least, thrown doubt on the tendency of neurophysiologists to limit "mind" to the brain's visual cortex. Vision, as Lacan claimed, is not just "seeing," but expresses a prior relation to an object.[35] From a Lacanian point of view, mind is made up of ensembles of meaning that order relations and transform elements. The Imaginary order is like the blind person who is not sure of what he sees, while the Symbolic order gives him guidance so that he will not stumble. Both orders are "ways of knowing" that join hands in the cogno-Desiring effort to express the Real.

Lacan's thought is, therefore, in step with those twentieth-century thinkers who have questioned the twin tyrannies of nineteenth-century positivism: mechanical causality and strict determinism. In his recent book entitled *The Turning Point* (1982), the Berkeley physicist Fritjof Capra maintains that among other disciplines Anglo-American philosophy, psychology, medicine, economics, and biology continue to base their theories and practices on a simplistic cause-and-effect theory of mind that has not conceptually moved away from Descartes or Newton. Quantum mechanics, black holes theory, relativity, and other concepts in physics have long since disposed of the old picture of a unified, stable, and serene universe. The world, from Capra's perspective, is a web of dynamic relationships among inherently connected phenomena.[36] His view of the physical universe is virtually a replica of Lacan's view of the psychic world: a picture of mind closer to modern physics and applied mathematics than to any doctrine based on mechanistic causality or evolutionary adaptation.

In 1948 Lacan spoke of the failure of theory to keep step with a revelation of the Real: "But does not the conceptual area into which we thought we had reduced the real later refuse to lend its support to physicist thinking?" (Sheridan, *Ecrits*, p. 27). But while Lacan's interpretation of the Real is his major innovation in thought and his insistence on the Symbolic's structuring capacities, a radical theory with countless implications, I find his Imaginary order both rich and original. Implicitly breaking out of the impasses of Kant (whose constitutive subject of consciousness is responsible for organizing experience) and Martin Heidegger (whose unitary "understanding of Being" shapes experience), Lacan offers the Imaginary function and representational "self" text as a link among the other orders and a bridge between conscious and unconscious realms.[37] When Edith Kurzweil writes that "although Lacan himself has continually elaborated on the constantly fluctuating relationship between its three components of fundamental psychological processes, he has never quite explained how this 'imaginary' functions," she merely reveals that she has not spent enough time with Lacan's texts. The Imaginary problematizes the origins and functions of meaning, narcissism, reality, Desire, perception, and consciousness.[38]

Parole

The technical label that Lacan borrowed from Ferdinand de Saussure to describe the presence of unconscious effects and intentionality in conscious language is *parole*. Saussure had defined *parole* as "spoken language," in opposition to the written word or system of rules which make up *langue*. The Saussurean *parole* points to the creative infinity of personal enunciations that, nevertheless, obey the finite laws of *langue*. In reformulating terms already in familiar use, Lacan pushed them to the point of their own inherent contradictions. *Parole* keeps the Saussurean sense of personal enunciations, for example, but Lacan gave a contextual explanation for the source of personal language as it relates to the power of the spoken word. The *moi* speaks a *parole* which links the Imaginary realm of primary meaning to the Symbolic realm of *langue* (linguistic norms and conventions or secondary meaning) (*Séminaire* I, p. 207). By revealing the interwoven character of these two realms, Lacan cast doubt on Saussure's original division, as well as on later linguistic theories, for example, John L. Austin's concept of utterances, which follows Saussure in keeping the social separate from the personal. To characterize the levels of inmixing, Lacan developed *parole* as a concept that sustains several functions and envelops multiple meanings (*Séminaire* I, p. 267).

First, *parole* refers to the Imaginary "request" (*demande*) for satisfaction which points toward narcissism and Desire (*Séminaire* I, p. 203). *Parole* consequently belongs to the agency of the "self"— the *je*—which transmits the *moi* request for love as the pivotal aspect of transference relations (*Séminaire* I, p. 303). In this sense, *parole* also refers to the substitutive dimension in which Desire is integrated on the Symbolic plane through *objet a* (*Séminaire* I, p. 204; *Séminaire* II, p. 273). *Parole* is that element in language, therefore, which points to Imaginary dialectics in their asymmetrical relationship to the Other(A). With this concept, Lacan made sense of the fact that "something" in language transcends information exchange, polite communication, and the formal rules of grammar. In Seminar One Lacan described that "something" as the unconscious subject whose *parole* digs out the "hollow" (*creux*) of being in the texture of the Real (p. 254). In Seminar Two Lacan emphasized that his use of *parole* was not to be confused with Saussure's idea of concept or signified. For *parole* is not the concept itself, but the imagistic/linguistic roots of being which permit human beings to represent themselves at all by referring retroactively to already "introjected" representations (*Séminaire* I, p. 267). With this reminder Lacan made the point that *parole* is more than the mouthpiece for the Imaginary; it is also something which weighs as heavily as all the Real (*Séminaire* II, p. 276). Although the *paroles fondatrices* that envelop a subject are "everything that has constituted him, his parents, his neighbors, the whole structure of the community, and not only constituted him as symbol, but constituted him in his being," at the level of effect these *paroles* belong not only to language (the Symbolic) but also to the Real (*Séminaire* II, pp. 30–31). Lacan contends, therefore, that it is not kinship laws per se that structure societies so much as the laws of nomenclature that, to a certain point, channel alliances.

Lacanian *parole* is not to be confused with conscious daytime fantasies or free associations, for Lacan intended the concept to point to the displacement of unconscious meaning and effect in language itself. Although *parole* is present when individuals use words to try and force agreement—in an effort to teach each other Imaginary "truth"—it only yields the truth (which lies beyond narcissism) when analytically decoded to position it in the place in the unconscious code from which a person is speaking. A Lacanian analyst would seek to know whether the place is "from the Other's Desire or *demande*; from the primordial split in being where the symbol was originally substituted for death; from the body libido of primary narcissism or the substitutive/Desiring libido of secondary narcissism?" and so on.

One might describe *parole*, therefore, as the libidinal quality of language, as that which demonstrates that language is not a transparent, natural, mechanical, monovalent, or simply coded medium. While *parole* is not the unconscious (any more than a dream is), it points to *moi* fixations and Other(A) Desires. To pinpoint *parole* in someone's discourse is certainly not the end point of an analysis, then, but the beginning. Lacan showed that analysts of many persuasions have isolated *parole* and then left the analysand trapped there in an Imaginary, narcissistic "self" myth. The analytic goal should be, instead, to help an analysand to interpret a *parole* by ascertaining that: (1) it is woven into speech as an implicit tension or pressure which asks for love and recognition, a *demande* that has very little to do, in fact, with the real objects that are requested; (2) it infers an identity question by which a person constitutes her/himself as a subject; (3) it motivates people to speak for the purpose of being recognized as "such and such" a subject, and in this way serves to create the future (thus an act as well as a word can be seen as a *parole*) (*Séminaire* II, p. 297; *Séminaire* I, p. 270); and (4) by sending out the messages about the *moi* that one hopes to have verified by others, it puts the unconscious into circular motion, unwittingly emitting messages from the Other (*Séminaire* II, p. 276).

Early in his career, Lacan characterized *parole* as either "empty" or "full." The *moi* speaks the "empty" word of "self"-misrecognition, while the *je* speaks the "empty" word of social cliche. Both deny the unconscious and thus eschew truth. A "full" word was sought through dreams and analytic techniques by means of suspending *moi* speech with its mythical, idealizing propensities. By tripping up the *je*, a "full" word could evolve as the conscious subject came to recognize the fictional nature of the *moi*, and to name his unconscious Desires. Although (according to Stuart Schneiderman) Lacan dropped the idea of "empty" and "full" words, he did not alter his goal of decentering the *je* to allow the unconscious to appear in ever truer colors. To this end, Lacan used the techniques of surprise, interruption, and so on to subvert the unity that makes any *je* discourse seem autonomous (*Séminaire* I, p. 268). When Lacan's own words are written down, his use of ellipsis—a suspension of meaning—becomes very obvious. So, too, does his habit of ending sentences with a variety of statements that either complete an initial clause—or run counter to it and to each other—while still leaving an impression of meaning conveyed.

The *chute de sens* found in Freud's account of memory lapses or the radical face of *non-sens* present in jokes became for Lacan prototypical of the *non-sens* which underlies all meaning. Insofar as a joke is the specific irruption of *non-sens* into the apparent meaning of a discourse, Lacan called Freud's *Witz* the umbilical cord of the *parole* (*Séminaire* I, p. 309). Lacan's various techniques for exposing the unconscious require stripping language of its overlay of unified rationality in an effort to reveal the nether side of Freud's double inscription (*Niederschrift*) where language and psyche intersect. The presence of *parole* in conscious discourse makes this possible. In psychosis *parole* need not be ferreted out; "it" fairly bombards the subject, who has become an unwitting victim of his or her own unconscious language. In normal speech *parole* functions in the Symbolic order as a focal point displaying the greater or lesser degree of satisfaction people find in the interplay of their Imaginary expectations in relation to Real events (*Séminaire* I, p. 161).

The Symbolic Order

Although Lacan began his career by developing his concept of the Imaginary order and ended it by an extensive elaboration of the Real, he gave primacy to the Symbolic order. Every person is born into a predetermined linguistic network, which forms identity and mind in conjunction with the process of mimetic identification. Language enters man surreptitiously to form a primary symbolized unconscious and, later, to create the secondary unconscious. The latter dynamically resurfaces to determine who and what man "consciously" thinks he is. The unconscious is itself a Symbolic order, therefore, instead of an energetic, instinctual, causalist, or substantialist order of desire, as past commentators have claimed. Lacan's theory that the Symbolic order of language and law creates an unconscious discourse, influencing adult speech out of the remoteness of childhood, must, then, seem a baffling proposition to some.

Some contemporary researchers have accepted American linguist Noam Chomsky's solution to the problem of language genesis. Chomsky "resolved" the riddle of how the symbol system resides in the brain by rehabilitating the Cartesian *Cogito*. He postulated innate language structures—akin to Descartes's innate ideas—which he calls "deep" or profound structures. These are transformed at the surface of language into infinite syntactic combinations. Lacan's theory implicitly rejects innate cognitive or developmental components (Piaget), which are supposed to evolve directly into communicative language. Two current areas of research lend support to Lacan's ideas that the unconscious is both imagistic and linguistic and that the language is imposed from the outside world. Dr. Howard Shevrin, professor of psychology and director of the Psychotherapy Clinic at the University of Michigan, has offered what he calls "objective evidence" for an unconscious repository of memories, wishes, and conflicting motives. From recent experiments measuring the brain's potential responses to various kinds of subliminal messages, Shevrin and others have found that the brain is humming with unconscious thoughts that shape what we pay attention to and what we repress. By presenting a picture on a screen for a thousandth of a second—too brief for the picture to actually be "seen"—brain researchers have established typical affective responses to these subliminal stimuli. A picture of a bee, for example, evokes stronger emotive response than an abstract geometric shape. More important for Lacanian thought is that subsequent "free associations" yield culture-specific words related to the bee, although the viewer has no idea he or she has seen a bee. Morever, associations to sounds are as important as associations to the sense of words, suggesting that Freud's "slips of the tongue" truly do reveal a rhyming relationship between conscious and unconscious meanings. Other researches show that children learn language best by rhyming. Finally, researchers from various areas have concluded that "selective attention"—the particular stimuli chosen from the many competing ones—shows unconscious processes at work.[39]

In "Baby, You're Incredible" Maya Pines reviews the experiment of a French obstetrician who inserted a hydrophone into a mother's uterus one-half hour before the delivery of her baby. The recording revealed a muffled conversation between the mother and doctor with both male and female tones audible. The mother's heartbeat, whooshing noises, and the music playing in the room were also audible. Another recent experiment showed that babies as young as six months can recognize changes in consonants and use some kind of rules for sorting out sounds within syllables.[40] Such "evidence" merely confirms what some areas of language study have long recognized—that "receptive language" starts even before birth, in animals as well as humans. Birds, for example, recognize their parents by sound. Chomsky and his students have measured the heartbeat of newborn infants, finding that the heart rate increases when the baby is spoken to. To date, whether established by Chomsky or other researchers, this inclination toward language has been considered a biological and neurological predisposition. Lacan shows, instead, that the effect of language is the *cause* introduced into the subject that, in fact, creates the subject as the effect of unconscious signifiers (Lacan, *Ecrits*, p. 835). Although Lacan never suggests that the sounds of a given language are registered before an infant is born, if a fetus can hear sounds and tones, then the imposition of culture on nature has begun to condition biological capacities from the time the fetus has a functional hearing apparatus.

Although never precise about the exact nature of unconscious language, Lacan's applications of the ideas of Morris Halle, Roman Jakobson, and Saussure to the unconscious are not vague. John P. Muller, an American Lacanian psychologist, writes clearly about

Lacan's use of linguistic theory, pointing out that Lacan referred to Halle's and Jakobson's isolation of twelve pairs of binary phonemes peculiar to the human vocal apparatus. These are gradually shaped into all the known variations of spoken languages within the framework of imitation and identification. Every language organizes these phonemes into increasingly complex units of sound, word, and phrase. Such organizations are governed by the laws of selection (metaphor), where substitution of one element for another is based on similarity or dissimilarity, and the law of combination (metonymy), where positioning in sequence is based on contiguity and contexture.[41] When Lacan said the unconscious is precisely structured—*as a language*—it is to metaphor and metonymy that he refers.[42] A "self" is selected, for example, on the basis of identificatory mergers with images (metaphor) within a referential context of combinations of objects (metonymy).

Although some current theories propose that humans develop language because humans have a more complex vocal apparatus and a larger brain than other animals, Lacan points instead to the premature "warp" in humans. Language shapes preverbal perception which, in turn, excites the biological, neurophysiological creature in a kind of parallelism between psyche and physique (*Séminaire* II, pp. 173–74). Lacan's theory reverses Chomsky's idea that language comes out of innate structures or genetic realities, but still explains how the growth of intelligence and the development of language are the same process. Lacan meant thereby to rectify the following impasse: "The theory of abstraction, necessary in accounting for knowledge, has become fixed in an abstract theory of the faculties of the subject" (Sheridan, *Ecrits*, p. 179). Klein's concrete but static theory of fantasy offers no alternative to this philosophical impasse. She misconceived fantasy, Lacan said, because she did not even suspect "the existence of the signifier. However, once it is defined as an image set to work in the signifying structure, the notion of the unconscious phantasy no longer presents any difficulty" (Sheridan, *Ecrits*, p. 272).

Lacan usually sticks to the idea of signifier as articulated speech, whether in conscious or unconscious discourse. But speech traces do accompany the earliest images; these *percepta* (*Wahrnehmungszeichen*) and their effects operate an unconscious network of fantasy relations prior to coherent speech. Once a child can name things, these fantasies serve as a reference bank of memories. If we define intelligence as the capacity to represent or abstract, and look at this as commensurate with Lacanian linguistic mastery (which begins around eighteen months to help transcend the pain of Castration), then it is perfectly logical—as Dr. Burton White has pointed out— that intelligence will not appear until late in the second year of life.[43] Psychic interaction with and separation from the mother, intelligence, and naming form a continuous web. Language thus becomes a ticket to group membership as well as the means to measure intelligence within a group.

As proof of the Lacanian theory, I cite an experiment carried out recently by scientists from the Aberdeen Medical Research Council in Scotland. By wiring three-year-olds for sound, they discovered that an average day's conversation between the children and their mothers totaled approximately 15,000 words.[44] Similarly, Harvard psychologists have recently observed that the differences in skill and intelligence of three-year-olds appear to be connected with the way language was introduced by the mother. In the brightest group the mothers had spent more time talking face to face with the baby. In the slower groups the mothers had talked as much, but either from another room or only to issue orders (*Baby Talk*, p. 14).

In the past two decades literary theoreticians have looked to linguistics and psychology for answers to the problem of mind, language, and meaning. Their efforts to explain how texts or readers make meaning by inventing endless categories of signification, representation, focalization, and so on only point once again to the kind of proliferation William of Ockham tried to end with his razor: to cease to seek the meaning of meaning by creating new meanings or "essences" to infinity.[45] Lacan applied his own razor to problems of defining meaning, one of which demands clarifying the nature of symbolism. An immediate obstacle to any understanding of Lacan's Symbolic order arises from the fact that, in standard usage, "symbol" and "symbolic" connote quite different concepts from his. At first glance, moreover, one is usually perplexed by his choice of the word "symbolic" to denote the orders of language and culture. The *Oxford English Dictionary* defines symbol as "mark or character taken as the conventional sign of some subject or idea or process." That is, symbols are fixed signs or entities, often thought to be mythic in origin or scope, which refer to something else. Lacan's challenge to this standard definition is based on the conviction that contemporary analogies between language and other systems of signs make a new theory of symbolism necessary.[46]

In his "Discours de Rome" Lacan publicly explored his idea that psychoanalysis and its relation to language could only be rethought and adequately formalized in terms of a new theory of symbolism.[47]

He introduced the Symbolic order to this end, by attacking the notion of a fixed, symbolic code with nondialectical, analogical interpretations (such as Jung's fixed symbolism). Borrowing the word "symbolic" from Lévi-Strauss (much as he had borrowed the notion of symbolic exchange from him),[48] Lacan emphasized that anthropologists had already alerted psychoanalysts to the death of neopositivistic symbologies. These anthropologists had removed the signal/sign system from its meaning as a spatial and iconic reflection of nature. As early as 1923, Marcel Mauss showed how gifts exchanged became symbols of the act of exchange itself in his *Essai sur le don* (Wilden, *LS*, pp. 230–31). In other words, there are symbolic functions that symbolize nothing in themselves, nor do they stand for what they represent in any fixed relationship to another meaning.

In his superb book *Rethinking Symbolism* (1974) the anthropologist Dan Sperber illustrates the arbitrary meanings that are attributed to symbols from tribe to tribe.[49] While linguists tend to address the problem of how symbols work, Sperber claims that Lévi-Strauss cleared the path for anthropologists to investigate how symbols "mean." In and of themselves, Sperber concludes, symbols do not mean. They are signs, but they are not paired with their interpretations in a code structure. Not able to ascertain the origin of the signs, however, Sperber then makes a Chomsky-like explanatory leap. Symbolic knowledge, he says, is an "implicit" knowledge—as opposed to encyclopedic knowledge—and depends upon the displacement of attention and upon evocation. Sperber thus demonstrates the logical impasse in which anthropological thinking on symbols has dead-ended. But his conclusions *can* be given a consequential meaning if we bring them into line with Lacan's rethinking of symbolism. "Implicit" symbolic knowledge, which appears by evocation and displacement of attention, is little other than *parole*, which enunciates itself through the lacunae of a normative discourse. Without understanding how such "knowledge" is put in place or how early, Sperber calls it "implicit."

Throughout his own career Freud constantly reworked his theory of symbolism. From the first edition of *The Interpretation of Dreams* (1900) through the eighth edition (1930), Freud continued to add material.[50] Anthony Wilden has pointed out that by far the greatest number of additions dealt with symbolism in dreams. Although the first edition limited the discussion of symbolism to a few pages, the fourth edition contained a new section on symbolism in the fourth chapter. Paradoxically, it is Freud's added material on symbolism that Lacan found reductionist. In his first edition Freud analyzed dreams in light of personal and associative contexts linked to linguistic patterns. Lacan called this analytic approach Freud's *first* theory of the symbol. These dream sounds and words were irreducible. Lacan described such smallest possible elements as symbols. For Lacan, Freud's added material constitutes his *second* theory of the symbol: one which alludes to a fixed code of images tied to the collective experience of humanity. This, says Wilden, was Freud's "symbology," which Lacan rejected in favor of Freud's first theory, interpreting it in light of contemporary linguistic and anthropological reconsiderations of how symbols work in associations and how they work within levels of different meaning systems.[51]

Although he was fascinated by hieroglyphs, Freud never saw how words and things could be linked in the unconscious. He thus could not pursue his first theory. Words were opposed to things and inhabited a near conscious or preconscious realm. But Lacan's critique makes Freud's second theory seem atomistic and noncontextual. By giving a fixed symbolic meaning to words and objects, Freud supposed a "natural" connection between the word and the thing symbolized. In this way Freud severed the symbol from the vast network of language by a kind of analogical interpretation and so imitated the closed-system thinking of classical physics. Paradoxically, writes Wilden, this approach was only a step beyond the Oriental dreambooks against which Freud protested. Lacan also described Freud's second theory as nondialectical. By viewing individual cases in light of "universal" symbols of the human race, Freud increasingly subscribed to a literalist, realist, mechanistic causality that actually negated the contextual conjunctures (personal, social, historical) in which persons reside (Wilden, *LS*, p. 230). Lacan, on the other hand, found Freud's first theory to be dialectical because Freud looked at the enchainment of words in a discourse and at their resultant associative or retroactive values. In this theory the symbol was seen as displaced or figurative, having latent, personal meaning, but not a fixed or universal value.

Disciples like Wilhelm Fliess, Sandor Ferenczi, and Ernest Jones construed Freud's first theory as the basis of the master's later fixing of personality in biosexual first causes. They retrospectively interpreted his first theory to mean that the psychoanalytical symbol—be it in dreams or in symptoms—should be defined as the use of a nonsexual element to stand for a repressed sexual one (Wilden, *System*, p. 33). Jones also picked up on Freud's second theory to develop the idea of the primary and universal (overdetermined) character of the thousands of symbols in the world, insofar as they all referred to a limited number of relationships: the body, birth, life, death, and kinship.[52] Recently, the literary critic David Willbern has accused Jones of petrifying Freud's ideas on symbolism and weaving them into a cohesive theory when, in fact, many of Freud's "universal symbols" were merely his own associations, as documented in interpretations of his patients' dreams.[53] Unfortunately, many early practitioners of psychoanalysis tended to reduce the second theory of symbolic overdetermination to what Ludwig Binswanger terms a sexual determinism—much as Freud's pupils had done with his first theory (Wilden, *System*, p. 33). For his part Lacan found all Jones's "failures" of interpretation instructive insofar as he at least tried to situate symbols in relationship to language, and he studied the effects of symbolism in analysis.

In his effort to discredit Lacan's thought, Richard Wollheim claimed that Lacan had not filled in the Freudian lacuna that had left no account of cognitive development—of how functions like reasoning, perception, and memory mature in an individual. Nor does Wollheim believe that Freud accounted for symbolism, i.e., how an individual acquires and uses the system of internal representations with which he encodes reality ("The Cabinet," p. 36). Although Freud did not leave systematic theories in these various areas, his nascent ideas might have led to new theories of cognition and symbolism (as well as of perception and memory) had psychoanalysis not subsequently reified his second theory of the symbol. His epigones used symbolism to explain the psychology of individuals by a preestablished substantivity of words and things connected to a biological "first cause." Lacan responds both to Jones's failures and to Freud's contemporary critics, however, by connecting the symbol to language by the signifier and by metaphor and by placing the effects of symbolism in the Other(A) from which both language and Desire issue.

Lacan pointed out that even though Freud saw unconscious thing and word representations as opposed, linguistics shows that opposition is also liaison. Unconscious representations—the "perception marks" which Lacan called signifiers—are automatically associative. Substitutions and combinations of things and words are formed analogously to the laws of language (metaphor and metonymy) and not according to the laws of grammar or classical logic. Symbols, said Lacan, are not icons, but differential (opposed) elements without meaning in themselves; they acquire value in their mutual relations. With this theory, Lacan portrayed the unconscious meaning system as closed, complete within itself, as is the system of language. One common misreading of Lacan tends to link his Symbolic *je* to signifiers and speech, contrasting these with the Imaginary *moi*, images, and the visual and dividing these along conscious/unconscious lines. Lacan taught that the unconscious signifier is both image and sound but that the visual component has no meaning apart from the external language which names it. In other words, there is no symbolism deriving from a natural analogy or even from an idea of image as appropriate to "instinct" (Sheridan, *Ecrits*, pp. 159–60). Instead, the value of the image as signifier lies in the meaning language attaches to it by some sound or thought similarity (metaphor) or by some referential implication (metonymy). The linguistic structure that enables us to read dreams at all is the very principle of the dream's meaning. The dream's story is a kind of pictorial proverb. It is enigmatic to conscious life, but decipherable through the laws of the signifier (metaphor and metonymy) when taken in dialectical relationship to the Other's Desire.

American psychiatry, however, misunderstands Lacan's "linguistic" theories. In *Critical Psychiatry* (1980) David Ingleby argues that "according to Lacan, the unconscious employs literary devices of metaphor and metonymy, etc. However, as Coulter and Ricoeur have argued convincingly . . . it is dangerous to take this analogy with language too literally, for philosophical questions arise out of the notion of an 'unconscious language' more awkward than those surrounding the concepts of unconscious experience and motivation. It will not do to simply represent Freud as simply offering a 'dictionary' of symbolic meanings; in psychoanalysis, the meaning of any symbol depends crucially on the context of its occurrence—so we are certainly not dealing with a 'shared language.'"[54] Unfortunately, Ingleby seems to have adopted Norman A. Coulter's and Paul Ricoeur's interpretations of Lacanian theory without having read Lacan himself. It is precisely the idea of a universal "dictionary of symbolic meanings" that Lacan dismantled in the "Discours de Rome." Although Lacan depicts perceived images or symbols as building up an Imaginary memory bank of representations (from the start of life)—representations which mingle with language and coalesce into identity and mind at the unconscious level—these symbols are not second, mystic meanings. They are, instead, the concrete bits and pieces—the lowest common multiples—that stand behind each individual's language and identity. Ingleby is blind to the fact that Lacan has made more sense of "context" than any other contemporary thinker.

Ingleby also misrepresents Lacan by saying that "the unconscious employs literary devices of metaphor and metonymy." Instead, Lacan said that the laws of the unconscious—condensation and displacement—work like the principal laws of language (metaphor and metonymy). What the psychic and linguistic systems have in common is an analogous manner of functioning by substitutions, combinations, and references. In the unconscious system these functions are intimately linked to Lacan's theories of pre–mirror-, mirror-, and post–mirror-stage maturation. Ingleby also errs about the nature of Lacan's unconscious symbols. In his attempts to explain them, Ingleby would do better to start with Klein's idea of part-objects than with Freud's idea of universal symbols (Jameson, "Imaginary and Symbolic in Lacan," p. 351). He would then be obliged to make the transition from the role played by Klein's theories to an understanding of the place of dialectic, structure, representation, and function in Lacan's portrayal of an unconscious discourse. Ingleby has also failed to distinguish the roles of the Symbolic, Imaginary, and Real orders in creating an unconscious system of meanings. The meaning system that makes up any personal unconscious is triggered in conscious life by an Imaginary perception that sets into motion the "text" derived from an interpenetration of Real experience and the "universals" of a given (local) Symbolic, i.e., cultural and linguistic order.

Lacan did not consider symbols to be in any way innate. He was influenced by Lévi-Strauss's idea in *La Pensée Sauvage* (1962) that nature furnishes some symbols or images (such as the moon and the stars) which organize relationships, gives relationships their structure, and in this way models them (*Séminaire* XI, p. 23). In this sense Lacan found symbols initially in the outside world. Once perceived as visual and verbal objects, their impact on being is recorded as an interpretation of the world. Their transformation from outside world to inner representation includes all the complex modifications that metaphor, metonymy, and arbitrary oppositions can impose within a particular prespecular and specular context. Consequently, there is no Kleinian transparency between inside and outside, no simplicity of moral effect (such as good versus bad) or judgment. Lacan further maintained that, insofar as symbols have an originary and primary character, they must be connected with language; they must stand behind all the semantemes of a given language (Wilden, *LS*, p. 59). Using the word "symbol" in a linguistic—not a literary—sense, Lacan meant a discrete unit, both autonomous and irreducible, which speech sounds endow with meaning in reference to other units.

Saussurean linguistics taught that "elephant" and "sun" only acquire meaning when put into relation with other formalizations. Likewise, symbols attain value only when organized in a world of differential symbols. Although the *tout symbolique* only takes on a coherence within a system of language that humanizes the impersonal Real world of symbols, insofar as the symbol is primary it spreads itself over the Imaginary domain of representations or signifying perceptions prior to speech (*Séminaire* I, pp. 202, 250). It is not the "substantive" quality of symbols that Lacan emphasizes, however—the aspect he calls "clothes for things"—but the impact and effect of symbols on perception. Preexisting Real symbols have a Real relationship to language. Symbols cause upheaval, conquest, a rape of nature, which brings about a transformation of nature, a hominization of the planet. Symbols introduce a hollow into the Real, which can be called being or nothingness, according to how the symbols are viewed (*Séminaire* I, pp. 291, 297). Even the experience of a void is imagized, given meaning. We see that Lacan has little theoretical interest in the concrete, "content" aspect of symbol—that which changes from culture to culture and person to person. Instead, the elemental structure of human ontology is to be found in the impact of symbols on perception.

The Lacanian theory that the origins of Symbolic thought can be found in relationships that already exist in Nature (even before personality formation, thought, or human relations) is quite separate from the unique impact of a given symbol system on a particular neonate. The differential, referential character of language makes the network of symbols in the external world a plurivalent, polysemous meaning system—arbitrary in meaning—in sharp contrast to the fixity of the coding used, for example, by bees (Wilden, *LS*, p. 61). By underscoring symbols as the base units behind language, Lacan dispensed not only with Freud's second theory of the symbol but also with the notion that all symbols are sexually overdetermined (except in the global sense that the elemental symbols—objects of Desire—were introjected in relation to the mother's body and the infant's sensual manner of experiencing its world).

Language liberates the symbol—be it in the outer or inner world—from its here-and-now status of solipsistic presence by both sound and concept. To "think" is a substitutive process, which substitutes the word elephant for the animal and a circle for the sun (*Séminaire* I, p. 250). In his theory that the word evokes the concept, which it then gradually replaces, Lacan reversed Saussure's attribution of primacy to the concept (signified) (*Séminaire* I, p. 201). As we have seen, the *Fort! Da!* game of Freud's grandson is Lacan's paradigm for the Symbolic order. The child assigned a symbolic value (presence/absence or plus/minus) and a functional one (mastery) to a bobbin reel. As the words *Fort!* and *Da!* came to substitute for the symbol and for its function (to master separation from the mother), sign and symbol became united (*Séminaire* I, pp. 201, 290).

By becoming autonomous symbols themselves, words offer the post–mirror-stage infant a compromise between the impossibility of possessing the object of Desire—incorporation of the mother (my Imaginary picture of Frege's o and 1)—and the possibility of embracing social reality (Frege's 2). The paradox and tragedy of being human stems from the fact that, by accepting language as a substitute for an impossible union, language itself as a symbol builds absence—Castration—into the structure of the subject and ensures that the human condition will be marked by eternal wanting (*Ecrits*, 1966, p. 319). Lacan can claim, therefore, that the structure of self or ontology comes from Real gaps (wants) in being, which Desire causes (in the form of various *objets a*) and for which Desire compensates by expressing itself in language (*Séminaire* XX, p. 100). In connecting language to Desire, Lacan makes sense of the observation that both language and Desire are marked by a sense of seeking.

Lacan's subversion of the *Cogito* find its far-reaching effect in the idea that there is no distance between ontology and "self."[55] Any Symbolic network offers very specific interpretations of the biological, genetic, and neurophysiological predispositions of the "self." What does it mean to be a girl, for example? To have a limp? To be more "verbal" than "spatial"? These family- and culture-specific meanings culminate in an Imaginary text of individuality, which points to an unconscious that is "supposed" from the fact that the speaking subject him- or herself supposes that "something" somewhere knows more than he or she. That "something" furnishes the speaker with the authority for a given opinion (*Séminaire* XX, p. 81). Lacan called this locus of the deployment of speech the Other(A).

The Lacanian idea of symbol is not that of a linguistic deferral (Jacques Derrida), therefore, nor of a double sense (Ricoeur), but that of a support system holding up the mirror of identity and mind. Lacan's symbol theory confronts us with the oldest known philosophical dilemmas. How is language born? How do we get from symbols to words? Is symbolic efficacy solely attributable to human intelligence? (*Séminaire* II, p. 223). Lacan's answers to these questions constitute the burden of discussion in this book, and the first two have been treated at length. As to the third question, we would have to respond no. Some animals also introject symbols and possess intelligence. The question can be answered in reverse. Human intelligence derives, in part, from symbolic (material and functional) efficacy. In other words, concrete symbols stand behind words, which accumulate into units of abstract comprehension: intelligence. In *Le hasard et la nécessité* (1970), the biologist Jacques Monod discussed the widely developed symbolization function in *mammifères* (the ability to play, to dream, to find new solutions to unforeseen problems, to become apprentices). He noted, however, that the absence of language in these mammals corresponded to a cortical atrophy that does not occur in man.[56]

The question then arises: Which comes first here? The cortical atrophy, which precludes language in mammals, or the human premature birth, to which Lacan attributes the capacity for language and symbol development? Since the upper primates are *not* born premature, they never have to weave their own verbal sounds into a compensatory language system. It follows that neurolinguists who attempt to explain man's development of speech have obviously not yet found a speech center in the human brain (and never will). It has been demonstrated, moreover, that when the half of the human brain that controls speech is injured, the functions governing speech are partially taken over by the other half of the brain.[57] Can we not surmise with Lacan, then, that the effects of language, identification, and perception of symbols stimulate brain functioning, and not the reverse? Humans have an unconscious because they speak; animals have no unconscious because they do not speak. Since Lacan views repression and verbal symbolization as concurrent processes, which both mark the end of the mirror stage and create a secondary unconscious, we can look for answers to the self/ontology riddle in the transformational processes that mark repression.

Lacan certainly did not mean that human infants simply "introject" symbols to which they attach words and then parrot them back in a transparent Whorfian kind of inner/outer exchange of sociological subjectivism. Rather, transformational laws change the character of symbols from one meaning order to another. The Real symbol stands outside the mental apparatus, while the Imaginary symbol represents the Real one; and the Symbolic symbol—the word—represents the representation (the word is "already a presence made of absence") (Sheridan, *Ecrits*, p. 65). To become Imaginary, the Real symbol is transformed by primary-process laws, as are Symbolic data. We could describe the symbol as having gone through the same kind of manufacturing process by which a tree becomes paper; the paper, nonetheless, is still a form of wood. But the different nature of Imaginary identificatory symbolic material and Symbolic linguistic material detaches these two meaning systems, except in the curious connections between them that appear in dreams, the psychopathology of everyday life, symptoms, and psychotic episodes.

Saussure taught that linguistic meaning is polysemous and polyvalent, and Chomsky has added that meaning is infinitely transformational. Lacan has "explained" these linguistic phenomena by showing that the polyvalent or transformational potential of meaning in language comes from the fact that the world of things is not blanketed over by the world of symbols, but is enmeshed in its vast network: to each symbol 1,000 things are made to correspond linguistically; to each thing, 1,000 symbols. In other words, every "thing" does not already exist in nature with the possibility for being a symbol. The substitutive process that links symbols to "things" is condensation (*Verdichtung*), which operates in dreams and in the *parole* (*Séminaire* I, p. 294). Even though symbols are, therefore, Real and irreducible per se, there is no univocity of the symbol in the Real, no "universal dictionary of symbols," no neo-Platonic Baudelairean *monde invisible* of hidden natural correspondences. The differential nature of symbolic language and the subjectivity of Imaginary perceptions make it possible to refer to any Real symbol in countless ways. This renders language infinitely combinatory from a creative standpoint and makes any society an arbitrarily codified system. (*Séminaire* I, p. 272).

To exemplify the different meanings of symbols in the Imaginary and the Symbolic, Lacan suggested that most people would not know how to specify left from right to a transplanetary being (*Séminaire* XX, p. 120). While the Imaginary seeks comprehension by perceptual fusing of the Real of the world and the "self," the Symbolic deters topological mergers by staking out areas, signs, labels, directions, and laws. This is the scope of the Symbolic's mediation between the Real and Imaginary. Anika Lemaire has broken aspects of the Symbolic order down into categories of language: the logicomathematical and the sociocultural. Since the two interact so intensely, however, I find it misleading to discuss them separately. But if we start with Lemaire's categories of language in relation to our earlier discussion of the symbol, we see that Lacan has rejected both the structuralist attempt to consider language as reality and the Saussurean idea that a concept is superior to sound in forming meaning.

For Lacan, a sound inscribed in the Other(A) is itself a concrete symbol: the representation of a representation. If the concept were to precede the word, then the signifier would play no part in composing the concept. Its function would simply be that of naming, of sticking a label on a thing. Such a theory does not analyze how concepts are formed and also permits the multifaceted essence of language to escape (*Séminaire* XI, p. 214). Yet symbols and "things"—whether Real or Imaginary—remain inert without language to lend them meaning. So powerful is the generative capacity of language in relation to objects that Lacan has called man an animal at the mercy of language (Sheridan, *Ecrits*, p. 264). Whereas materialist theories would resolve the Saussurean impasse by fixing the locus of language in the human brain and in biogenetic codes (and so deduce logical consequences from this alleged innateness), Lacan taught that language is outside—everywhere but *in* the biological creature. In Lacan's eyes Freud's monumental discovery was to find the field of the effects of man's relation to the Symbolic order and to track the meaning right back to the most radical agencies of symbolization in being: in dreams, fantasies, and word-and-thing presentations (*Ecrits*, 1966, p. 155).

One might, therefore, suggest that the evolutionary missing link is not *Homo subsapiens*, but *Homo loquens*! At what prehistoric moment and under what conditions did man become relatively helpless for the first eighteen months of life? Did his vocal apparatus become more sophisticated than that of the apes from which he was descended because he was a "different" species of ape? Is man's "superiority" over other animals perhaps attributable to his linguistic ability and capacity for symbol manipulation rather than to his Darwinian "survival of the fittest"?

The first pure or abstract symbol of the Symbolic order is the metaphorical Phallus. Although an infant has symbolized its perceptions from the start of life, these representations—before they are linked to Castration or social language—belong to an Imaginary mother sphere of reference which is concrete and "natural." The phallic intervention, which urges the infant gradually to repress this natural language, does not, however, obliterate the Other's capacity for retaining truths concerning primordial experience. Such a theory ensures that Lacan's thought cannot be reduced to the binary trap of the sociologists or a mere opposition of cultural and natural man. Instead Lacan infuses the concept of "natural" itself with doubts and questions. And insofar as sounds inhabit man from the start of life, we can understand Schneiderman's hesitation to use a locution, such as prelinguistic, to describe the preverbal infant. What is clear is that an incipient linguistic coherency, at about eighteen months, permanently alters the natural aspects of being, however inmixed culture and nature may already have been before that (*Séminaire* I, p. 178).

By introducing an awareness of otherness into the structure of the subject, the Phallus subverts not only the illusory symmetry of the Imaginary infant/mother dyad but also the possibility of the independent unity of any one term. Identity only "means" henceforth in relation to responses to and from others.

Lacan's hypotheses concerning language and identity formation implicitly destroy the theory of the linguist Emile Benveniste that there are not three grammatical persons, but only two—*je/tu*—which find themselves in opposition to a realm of "non-person" or *il*.[58] The *moi* of the Lacanian subject normally "speaks" to another about his or her own subject S (*Es* or *je*) as if *je* were in the third person (*Séminaire* III, p. 23). In other words, "I am" is a way of using narcissism and identification to describe the "I" who speaks. Lacan shows that there are at least seven pronoun distinctions that play around the dialectics of subject and object. And the question of subject/object interaction is even more complicated in Lacan's thought by the "fact" that, although *je, tu,* and *il* exist in the Imaginary and Symbolic registers, the subject can reconstitute itself only in Real situations. *Je* is the subject of speech (in the Symbolic) and the object of *moi* (in the Imaginary). *Moi* is the object of the Other (in the Imaginary) and the subject of *je* (in the Symbolic). *Tu*—the other—is the object of *moi* (one's attempted objectification of the other), as well as a cypher for the speaker's Other(A). In the latter interaction, *tu* becomes the Imaginary subject of an interloctur's *moi*. Here *il* can be seen not as the grammatical "non-person" of history, but as the pronoun of difference, distance, otherness, health: the pronoun of escape from the sameness of *je (moi)* and *tu* (Other). Perhaps the above may clarify Lacan's linking of language to the Oedipal structure and his claims for *il* as the pronoun of the phallic signifier. What we are discussing is not a simplistic binary split between latent (unconscious) and manifest (conscious) subjects or objects, but lacunae within discourse that reveal the discontinuities of the subject itself.

It is interesting to note that the American psychiatrist Walter Weintraub, in his book *Verbal Behavior: Adaptation and Psychopathology* (1981), does develop the theory that personality is observable in the subject's speech, style, and syntax as early as three years of age.[59] He speculates that the conservative nature of language and the slow rate at which grammatical forms change both preserve personality traits in language (p. 12). Weintraub masses many impressive studies to show that American psychiatrists and psychoanalysts are busily trying to understand verbal behavior or speech as a reflection of behavior. But none of these varied studies has any inkling of

Lacan's revelation that language actually structures personality and thus is itself the dictator of behavior. Weintraub assumes instead a linguistic normalcy similar to a psychic norm; deviations from this reflect psychopathology. But he never problematizes the concept of "personality" formation, nor does he analyze the basis of the "psychic norm." It is tantalizing, nevertheless, that countless volumes of Anglo-American "empirical" studies would find their theoretical validation in Lacan. For the diachronic memories of Lacan's *moi* reside precisely in the synchronic movement of language, where repeated failures, repressed conflicts, denied frustrations, and an Other's Desire and messages shape themselves around words, style, and syntax. Personality (*moi*) is observable in speech and syntax (as Weintraub claims) and, moreover, in the layered fashion of identificatory accretion proposed by Lacan. Weintraub's study was, in fact, prompted by his discovery that anger or stress could excite forms of language use typical of an earlier period in a person's life.

North American psycholinguists (and others who already study the interface between language and psyche) do not generally know Lacan's theory concerning the active roles of signifier and metaphor in structuring identity and mind. In 1966 the psychologist Jerome Bruner described cognition in terms of three interrelated representational systems. First, there is the "enactive" mode, in which action and cognitive consciousness are essentially the same. Thinking is action, and memory is remembered action. The second system of representation might be labeled "iconic." In 1970 Mardi Jon Horowitz called this system "image thinking," emphasizing the various sensory organizing subsystems that contribute sensory components to the imagined integrations of experience. The third mode, said to come with language learning, is what Bruner called the "symbolic" mode (Horowitz called it the "lexical" code). Based on the work of Bruner and Horowitz, the psychologist Edward Stainbrook has concluded that "language and linguistic behavior can be considered as informational coding added to action and imagery."[60]

Freud's picture of mind placed hallucinatory imagery prior to action. Lacan has located perception as "action" that precedes hallucinatory impressions, this "action" being that of identificatory fusion or psychic "investment." In Lacan's view one's earliest ontology is woven of body and psyche, with blurred inside/outside boundaries. The first act of cognition, then, is a perceptual merger with image and sound. The mergers leave behind representational traces forming the foundation of a memory bank. Lacan's hypotheses therefore contradict the static concept of language as a later development added to action and images. The problem with the theory of informational coding, viewed under a Lacanian grid, is that no reasons are given for putting imagery or information into the mind in the first place. Nor is an explanation offered for their being linked to behavior in any case. As we have seen, however, Lacan's theories of the pre-mirror, mirror, and post-mirror phases make complete, logical sense of how and why identity, memory, and language are built up in a given individual.

Lacking any explanations adequate to the infinite complexity of mind, information theorists have fallen back on genetic codes as their postulate. Looking to Descartes for support ("This language is *en effet* the only certain sign of a thought latent in my body"), Chomsky, as we have said, views language structures as innate. He concludes that man's unique ability to acquire and then use language creatively is genetic, the result of superior brain mechanisms.[61]

Since all documented efforts to teach animals language have ended in the conclusion that linguistic ability is linked to general human intelligence, Chomsky has followed an evolutionary line of thinking in finding innate tendencies for a generative, transformational grammar. In addition, he has deduced support for his theory from the discovery of separate functions for the left and right hemispheres of the brain, a phenomenon called lateralization. An interesting detail, however, is that the brain seems not to be asymmetrical at birth and is only lateralized by age five—the same period when language acquisition (basic grammar) is complete. What could a Lacanian theory of language not contribute to those linguists who are seeking to explain why feral children cannot learn language (no transference relation linked to language); why mute children can learn language (through the transference relation and a sign system); why the left hemisphere of the brain controls speech and the right is pictorial; why upper primates can only be taught the rudiments of a symbol system in a highly controlled way and even then not be able to use it substitutively, that is creatively!

Chomsky sets himself apart from information theory and its claim that the purpose of language is to inform. He maintains, instead, that language desires to communicate. But by restricting language to "communication," Chomsky also fails to encompass enough of its dimensions to give a satisfactory theory of its scope. Opposed to Chomsky's objective and universal mental structures are Lacan's subjective and local representations of representations (in the Other). By linking psychoanalysis to symbol, signifier, and metaphor and demonstrating that dreams and psychotic language are both de-

cipherable when viewed as pictures of linguistic situations, Lacan
has shown the system of language itself to be a defense against unconscious knowledge. Similarly, language attests to the presence of
an unconscious order in being that leaves no human action outside
its field. When language is first acquired within a transference relationship, it conveys illusion and confusion. Gradually language becomes clear as a system of norms and rules. An area for future investigation might be based on the following hypothesis: The reason
that brain lateralization and basic language learning are both completed by age five is that the child has by then cognitively assimilated an Imaginary number 2 (Castration) and accepted number 3
(the gender myth of identity). An infant has passed from a "natural"
to a codified social state and so learned through imitation and identification "who" it is as well as the meaning of its sexual gender. Studies that attempt to link gender differences to right-brain/left-brain
lateralization should more profitably examine how a child identifies
with the Phallus—and reflects this in language—rather than scrutinize innate brain functions. Does the child identify more strongly
on the Desiring/Imaginary slope (where words compensate for an inadequacy in individuation) or on the abstract Symbolic slope of difference (Law)? (See Chapter 5.) Whatever the results, Lacanian theory enjoins that, in understanding cognitive, linguistic capabilities,
the brain alone will provide no final answers. First we must understand the infant-cum-child, who serves as the primary center of
being and meaning.

The literary critic Michel Grimaud has written: "It is paradoxical
that more even than infantile sexuality, it is the cognitive differences
between child and adult which are the least thinkable in our societies. Without that, perhaps, it is not possible to explain the development of the person."[62] In Lacanian thought the residue of a child's
development is the Imaginary as it asserts itself in adult life in relation to Symbolic order contracts, pacts, and laws. But the Imaginary
tends to subvert these laws, whether through innocuous irony or
criminal acts. The law codes change from one stratum of culture to
another, leaving doubt about appropriate behavior. This area of
doubt also reveals the artificial and arbitrary nature of Symbolic order meaning. Since Imaginary subversion of the Symbolic comes
from a narcissistic drive toward an impossible fusion (a symbiotic
Oneness), the sociocultural and logicomathematical linguistic codes
are in this sense inseparable. If we heed Lacan's contention that it is
misunderstandings and miscommunications that characterize human dealings, rather than conjunction and agreement, we can no

longer look for the right meaning or truth in the correct ideology, political system, or religious belief (i.e., the content of the contracts and laws) (*Séminaire* I, p. 29).

The fictions in an out-of-sight meaning system—the Other(A)—determine the socioconventional meaning of contracts, pacts, and laws from culture to culture. Meaning, then, cannot ultimately be identified with linguistic function only, for it is inherently relative, relational, structural, and "self"-referential. And its roots lie in childhood cognition and resultant unconscious structure. But a linguist interested in semiotic systems and cognitive processes or a political theorist interested in economic systems and historical processes, generally speaking, tends to ignore the child within and look only at the institution. By unveiling the unconscious as a discontinuity in adult language and placing language as the elementary "letter" of meaning in the unconscious, Lacan has subverted the autonomy of the conscious subject and the "truth-reality value" of the institution.

And just as most thinkers divorce the adult from the child, most contemporary medical thinking would separate the normal from the pathological. Even harder for modern doctors to accept is Lacan's idea that symptoms such as hysteria, phobia, impotence, inhibition, anxiety, and perversion have the structure of metaphor and bear traces of normal language (*Ecrits* I, pp. 160–61). Spoken language supplies the referents which create language as fantasy—or language as information—building from sound trace to idea. Instead of describing givens a priori, language sounds linked to symbols actually create the givens and, in turn, represent them. Such a theory refutes all views that could equate language with natural expression or with codes that can be confused with information (Sheridan, *Ecrits*, p. 125). But to comprehend Lacan here requires a "willing suspension of disbelief." Language is a meaning system which appears to be complete in itself and therefore usable without any direct or empirical reference. Not only this, the language system itself gives support to consciousness, culture, and Law from the end of the mirror stage until death.

Only by grasping the idea that language is dynamically, dialectically linked with Desire and identification can one even begin to comprehend the implications of Lacan's thought. On the other hand, it is obvious that language has no beginning, except in the ways it imposes itself on each individual subject. If, as Lacan maintained, the earliest effects of language are primordially repressed, making secondary (conscious) language referential, it follows that no use of language can be objective. Language cannot, therefore, generate a metalanguage adequate to itself. No formalized language—even a mathematical one—is epistemologically privileged in relation to that which it describes, and no language can be reduced to a superstructure, for it is an infinite web which Lacan described as impossible to scan with any model. What can be ascertained are effects of the unconscious in language. The word can be taken materially as the building cell of identity and cognition, just as a number is the elementary cell in number theory (*Télévision*, p. 49).

The age-old assumption that language exists to be manipulated by man is of a piece with the philosophical chimera of an objectifiable reality. Lacan placed reality on the *moi* slope of Imaginary (fantasmatic) perception and, consequently, did not claim fixedness or verifiability as properties of reality. He defined reality instead in terms of contradiction, as uniquely individual and inherently antagonistic to anyone else's perception of it (*Séminaire* I, pp. 293, 303). Urging analysts not to be deceived by *je* material, the Lacanian Patrick Hogan has used classical logic to show that "the analyst . . . cannot assume classical entailment and remain an analyst: psychoanalytic interpretation can function only if the subject's logic of descriptions is a relevant entailment logic. . . . It is only if all consequents [sic] are relevant to their premises that the implications of the analysand may lead to an accurate construction of the causality of that subject insofar as it is determined by his logic of believed descriptions."[63] In his Seminar Eleven Lacan accused ego psychologists of trying to adjust their patients to a preconceived idea of reality, while failing to account for the fact that the linguistic signifier is not reality. Words merely provide a way to hide the Imaginary logic of believed "self"-descriptions (p. 130).

Those philosophers or linguists who opine that language-as-sign can be converted in a direct equivalence with reality are misled. The Saussurean linguistic sign simply does not take Desire or repetition into account and does not, therefore, grasp the source of human misunderstanding or intention. But our unwitting servitude to language shows that masters are as enslaved as slaves. "It is the world of words that creates the world of things," Lacan taught in his "Discours de Rome," "by giving its concrete being to their essence, and its ubiquity to what has always been" (Sheridan, *Ecrits*, p. 65). In other words, we give shape to the Real through acquired language. Lacan derived the deep and abstract generativity of human language (which Chomsky postulates) from the word (*le mot/motus*) in its materiality, its effects, and its plurivalence. The word, moreover, offers humans a way to develop psychically, neurophysiologically, and socially. "Through the obliquity of narcissism, Man is subjugated by the opaque signifier, passes through its defiles, and is thereby transformed into a subject" (Ecrits, 1966, p. 307).

When the word (mot) is considered in its subjectivity, it is rendered as parole at both conscious and unconscious levels. Lacan linked parole to the Symbolic order on its three planes: (1) the signifier of the Imaginary, (2) meaning, and (3) the Real (Séminaire III, p. 75–76). The Real dimension in a discourse is the diachronic one, which derives its authority from the Other(A). On this plane of "certainty," words seem Real or fixed. Paradoxically, the Other(A) also impugns the subject's certainty because its own reality is fictional instead of "honest." Our words, therefore, are appearances in their diachronic dimension—personalized realities—to be deciphered. With this idea, Lacan proposes that the age-old "appearance" versus "reality" split is false (Séminaire XI, p. 45). Similarly, it is not possible to verify the truth value of a parole by classical logic. Parole is governed by the logic of Desire and narcissism, which find their truth value not in distinctions between logical or contradictory hypotheses, but in the logic of loss, substitution, and power.

Turning away from classical entailment logic, Lacan used Freud and Gottlob Frege to develop a psychoanalytic-mathematical logic of his own. Colin MacCabe succinctly summarizes the value of Frege for Lacan: "For Frege the subject is the bearer of representations which it neither creates nor unifies" (Talking Cure, p. 210). To explain the metaphorical/metonymical character of the mirror-stage assumption of identity, Lacan used Frege's system where numbers are primary unities, each of which implies another number in an ongoing chain. But Lacan adds what Frege failed to see: that the human subject is produced and unified by language. The combined impact of a logicomathematical—i.e., structural—drama with the materiality of language means that every individual's history has both a universal structure (Desire and Law) and a unique story. Normal language unifies that history within the transference of interhuman relations (Séminaire I, pp. 221–22). Individuals realize themselves in the measure that their subjective structures are integrated into a social myth with an extended human value (Séminaire I, p. 215). Clinically speaking, the psychoanalyst will look for the formal structure of mirror-stage and Oedipal effects and scrutinize the meanings given to those effects. Philosophically speaking, however, Lacan's logicomathematical emphasis desubstantifies the unconscious, showing the essentialist or substantive traps that cornered Aristotle into hypothesizing a soul that could think and led Descartes to equate thought with the mind, which he in turn defined in language (*Séminaire* XX, p. 100).

To conclude this discussion of the Lacanian Symbolic, we may say that the suborder called the sociocultural by Lemaire manifests itself in the vast diversities between conventional symbols of social systems: the phenomenon that makes butter a gift of the gods in one society and a curse in another. The systematic interaction of symbols, when assimilated within a given linguistic structure, makes the symbols themselves a plurivalent network of transmuted signs. This is the importance of Lacan's reintepretation of symbols as basic realities or smallest representational units for philosophers, anthropologists, and literary critics.

Psychoanalytically, however, the importance of this suborder is in its elaboration of the Imaginary number 3, the gender myth number around which cultures organize themselves in relation to Desire and Law. In my estimation, all sociocultural orders derive from difference and abstraction (the first abstract symbol being the Phallus) and define themselves by identification with the Symbolic father. They stand in opposition to the Real other or mother, who is psychically linked to the effects of separation and loss, and—linguistically—to the concrete. This idea brings us to the heart of some of the difficulties inherent in Lacan's epistemology. If we pursue the conceptual twists in his linguistic unconscious, the Other(A) is both the unconscious and the Symbolic order, generally described by Lacan as the place of consciousness, language, and culture. If the unconscious is simultaneously loss and contains the myths that play around loss, then culture (as well as men and women themselves) merely constitutes symbols of this drama. Any infant is, therefore, a symbol in a subjective cultural chain of meaning, even before it comes to believe that it is what the Symbolic order has decreed long before birth. The formula *Il y a de l'Un* (There is Oneness—the subject of Lacan's 1971–72 Seminar) crystallizes the final inseparability of the sociocultural order from the psychic and linguistic one (see p. 223).

The Real

Lacan's order of the Real seems at a superficial glance both philosophically and empirically naive, insofar as he called it that which is concrete and already full. As we follow his multileveled mutations of the concept, however, and grasp the degree to which it problematizes standard concepts of reality, this category takes on an astounding complexity. We may well appreciate why Lacan gave it increasing attention until his death. Not the least of the implications of this category lies in its tacit deconstruction of the neo-Freudian notion of a reality principle. Freud's historic subversion of Cartesian philosophy lay in his discovery that reference to perceptual exteriority was no longer sufficient to define the reality of an object; at the same time, every real object was still an object of perception.[64] In Lacan's opaque rendering, this idea reads: "Freud's discovery is confirmed first by regarding as certain that the real is rational . . . and thereby affirming that the rational is real" (Sheridan, *Ecrits*, p. 272). But even though Freud took his patients' fantasies and symptoms seriously, thus showing that he was persuaded of the real of an effect, he was not convinced of the reality of the fantasy itself.

In Freud's construction of the psychic apparatus, impressions came first, followed by perception, attention, and then memory. The infant's attention was directed at an opposition, whether "something" was pleasant or unpleasant. It required an act of judgment (usually involving corporal experience), therefore, for memory to be constituted. But it was not necessarily obvious, as Freud believed, that pleasurable objects or experiences, or displeasurable ones, were quickly repressed to make up an unconscious memory system of the irrational, the fantastic, and, later, the sexual. To solve this problem, he placed the reality principle on the side of consciousness, truth, and displeasure. This seems perverse reasoning unless we accept the connections Freud made between neurosis and the pleasure principle, as well as between thought and sexuality. The major Freudian taboo was sexual desire for the mother. But since early pleasurable experience was intimately attached to the pre-Oedipal relation with the mother, it followed that from the moment of the apprehension of the incest taboo as the reality principle, the pleasurable sensations associated with the mother (which Freud inevitably confused with genital sexuality) had to be denied and repressed. These repressions became attached to other sexual memories of a traumatic nature and lingered on in later life as the source of neurosis, defined as dammed up libidinal (sexual) energy. To cure a neurosis, the repressed memory must be undone—brought into consciousness—and then forgotten. This was not Freud's final position, however, as Moustapha Safouan reminds us. In "Formulations on the Two Principles of Mental Functioning" (*SE*, 12:213–26), Freud defined thought in terms of sexual fantasies that more or less continuously controlled perception thereafter (*Talking Cure*, p. 77). This contention blurs Freud's early contrast of the reality and pleasure principles (with their attendant attributes of acceptable and unacceptable), as well as his final position that perception resides solidly on the side of consciousness (reality) instead of unconsciousness (fantasy).

Freud ultimately resolved his philosophical dilemma by connecting pleasure to displeasure. He hypothesized that the ego was a mediator between reality and fantasy, thought and sexuality, as well as id and superego. He also elaborated the idea of an evolution of sexual stages that matched mental development from the oral (the immaturity of fantasy and pleasure) to the anal (transition between maturity and immaturity) and the genital (maturity and reality). Logically speaking, the genital stage should then be unpleasurable. But Freud solved this problem with an ingenious twist: adult (sexual) pleasure is based on transcending infant pleasure, that is, fantasy and orality. Lacan thought that Freud's strained concepts of reality and maturity were strongly influenced by Sandor Ferenczi's 1913 article celebrating the instinctual, evolutionary sexual stages as a means of explaining reality by a trajectory from infantile (oral, anal) to mature (genital) character traits. Not surprisingly, many neo-Freudian analysts still cling to these biological and reductionist concepts of personality: oral and anal behavior implies infantilism, while genitality is the achievement of empathy, reciprocity, and harmony. Neopositivist thought such as this has not kept pace with developments in philosophy, linguistics, anthropology, or even biology itself.

But Freud lived in an era when the idea of Darwinian evolutionary stages still held philosophical sway. According to Lacan, Freud's concept of reality was probably also influenced by Jung's mythic ideas on the evolution of the human spirit. Although an evolutionary view of sexual behavior may be sustained with regard to so-called primitives (or even to the mentally ill), Lacan claimed it was more difficult to hold such views when considering children (*Séminaire* I, pp. 146–47). As we have stressed, Lacan insists that the biological development of children is always organized in relation to already existing symbols and language. By his ideas, Lacan bypassed the literalist world of the neo-Darwinians, although they can still currently be found not only among orthodox neo-Freudian analysts, but also among Chomskian linguists, neurophysiological researchers, and, most particularly, among sociobiologists.[65] Neo-Darwinianism would reduce human brain waves to chemistry and biology and interpret them as the source of behavior and adaptive drives. Such ideas have even given rise to a medical semiology, in which semioticians or students of communication theory talk about hormonal messages sent and received within an organic communication system.

Conversely, Lacan's thought is not a return to a loose mysticism or hermetic occultism, as some who stop at technical and empirical methodologies have suggested. I would place Lacan on the side of modern physics (Albert Einstein, Werner Heisenberg, Erwin Schrodinger), applied mathematics, and modern biology. In his Seminar Three Lacan tried to distinguish psychoanalysis from the "natural sciences." The natural in a field of science, he taught, occurs when language is not used to mean (something). A natural law, then, would be a formula which does not mean (substantively) (pp. 209, 211). The signifiers which compose the formulas of natural laws would be pure signifiers—i.e., symbols or mathemes—as opposed to the signifiers which make up an analysand's discourse. In the latter case, the signifier is a "correlative system of elements that take their place synchronically and diachronically, one in relation to the other" (Séminaire III, p. 213). In the former case, a true signifier signifies nothing (Séminaire III, p. 210). In analysis the discourse goes from the universal to the particular. Thus, clinical psychoanalysis, unlike physics, is characterized by the "subjectivity" of a person's discourse in the Real. Physics works in reverse: from pure signifiers to the universal (le tout), and it only "means" at the level of worldview. In the last phase of his thought Lacan tried to develop formulas that would resemble the pure signifiers of physics and so formalize (objectify) the various structures of possible psychic patterns and functions at the theoretical level.

Whether working subjectively with the clinical parole (the particulars of a discourse) or with the Real that implies an objectivity within psychoanalytic theory (the structure of the psyche), Lacan's concept of the signifier is central (Séminaire III, p. 211). Following Lacan, Safouan has emphasized Freud's error in separating desire (Wunsch) from representation (Vorstellung) (see Chapter 2). The representation takes its life from Desire. In this sense, the signifier (or representation) has both a Real and a material existence. It Real-ly does exist as dramatized by Desire. Its "material" elaboration as "an image set to work in the signifying structure" of the unconscious accounts for Freud's failure to see the inherent link between fantasy and reality (Sheridan, Ecrits, p. 272). Indeed, the unconscious fantasy is not irrational but is the site of reality perception. In contrast to a discourse whose "reality" view is easily comprehended, however, the discourse of a psychotic does not aim its meaning at the other of an Imaginary relation, whose function is to verify an uncertain image of "self"; instead, the delirious discourse stops at the signifier itself with its fundamental reference to being (Séminaire III, p. 155).

Lacan did not stress the being of consciousness (Hegel) nor of thought (Descartes) nor of meaning (linguists and philosophers), but the Real of a subject inhabited by a signifier. In so doing, he decentered the subject of being from its own consciousness, reminding us of Heisenberg's indeterminacy principle, which established that a person cannot at the same time determine where a physical particle is and how it is moving. In recent years both Heisenberg and the mathematician Kurt Gödel have demolished Einstein's hope for a unified theory of physical reality. In an analogous way Lacan has thrown grave doubt on the philosophical dream of a unified psychic reality.

Standard concepts of reality, even neo-Freudian ones, take as their general basis the neo-Platonic idea of a scrutable and preformed reality, which is readily accessible to the mind, if the correct method is used to bring forth "reality as fact." This idea could not be used to explain Lacan. He maintained that mind is not a unity; personal reality is built up by structures, effects, and the fragments of perceived fragmentations. Reality, therefore, is to be assessed in details, allusions, and wisps of meaning, instead of in unified thought systems. But in contemporary thought, the terms "reality" and the "real" are generally used synonymously, often with an ideological slant or to mean a transparent social realism. A standard dictionary definition of "reality" is: "the fact, state, or quality of being real or genuine. That which is real; an actual thing, situation or event. That which exists, as contrasted with what is fictitious. Philosophically, it is the absolute or ultimate as contrasted with phenomena or the apparent" (OED). In Lacanian thought, let it be said, the absolute is the Other(A), a principle of intersubjectivity and the cause of all subjectivity.

In Seminars Two and Three Lacan stressed that human beings have basically taken as real whatever they see as concrete, fixed, transparent, or nonproblematic—be it a tree, the stars, or a certain conception of the universe. "The meaning man has always given the real is . . . something that one finds again in the same place, whether one has been there or not. Perhaps it has moved . . . but if it has moved, one looks for it elsewhere" (Séminaire II, p. 342). The example of the stars makes Lacan's point easily. They have always been, more or less, in the same place. Man humanizes their Real fixity by naming them, thus including them in his Symbolic order. Throughout the ages, some individuals have linked this Real fixity and Symbolic familiarity to their own "self"-systems and have lent the stars an Imaginary, astrological efficacy there.

Lacan said the idea that the Real is to be found at a named point precedes even the exact sciences. His distinction here is between the confusion over naming a point and the subsequent belief that the point is then fixed (even though it may change). The Real itself is unmoveable and complete. But man's interpretations of the Real are moveable. The latter combine language with "self"-experience. The resulting interpretations compose "reality," but not the real. The "real" Real is both beyond and behind Imaginary perception and Symbolic description. It is an algebraic x, inherently foreclosed from direct apprehension or analysis. The Real, therefore, is that before which the Imaginary falters, and over which the Symbolic stumbles (*Séminaire* I, p. 298). This Lacanian idea of the Real has led to the description of it as the impossible. But Lacan clearly did not have philosophical Idealism in mind. He meant that saying or seeing the Real objectively was not possible. Perception of Real things and lived experiences are immediately filtered through a personal and interpretative grid. All the same, in the specular period before an infant can name its perceptions, there is but a small distance between the Real-ness of those perceptions and their role in creating an Imaginary system.

Reality, conversely, is perfectly knowable as a projected perception of the world, as one's subjectivity. The *moi* knows reality, conveys it even, but does not "know" the Real except in bits and pieces. Within the Lacanian psychic economy, the Real is on the inhuman or mechanical side of the Other(A). In *Télévision*, Lacan said: "Reality is only the fantasy on which a thought is sustained, 'reality' doubtlessly, but to be understood as a grimace of the Real" (p. 17). In the same interview, Lacan said that reality has little to do with the Real (*le peu que la réalité tient au réel*) which in itself is not a whole. Jameson has described this relationship between reality and the Real as asymptotic ("Imaginary and Symbolic in Lacan," p. 383). And so we arrive at a picture of the Real as that which is—minus its representation, description, or interpretation.

Although the Real of a tree cannot be impugned, Imaginary representations of treeness, and Symbolic descriptions of the same, make the Real tree a subjective one within human perception. Here, the Real is on the side of the as yet uninterpreted symbol. But the Lacanian Real is not equivalent to the visual, for it also refers to effect (what is felt). Let us take the example of time. Ordinary concepts of time belong to the Symbolic order of univocal codes, which measure time by clocks, calendars, and seasons. Imaginarily speaking, however, time is affectively measured in specular dealings as anxiety, ecstasy, or boredom. As a phenomenon of the Real, time would not ordinarily be ascertainable apart from the Symbolic and the Imaginary. But Lacan taught that the realm of psychoanalysis is, if nothing else, the realm of time: past time brought into the present. In this domain the Real is knowable in its effects: as the pain which inheres in a symptom; as the alien discourse of Otherness which informs *parole*; as the source of psychotic discourse which shuns the instability of the other ⬂ *moi* circuit to address the other in order merely to "reveal" to the other the Other's certainty.

Like the symbol, the Real both exists outside the psychic economy and witnesses to an inner conjuncture between the personal and diachronic domain and the verbal synchronic one (*Séminaire* III, p. 76). Psychically speaking, when Lacanians talk about "reality," they refer to *moi* discourse. The Real, on the other hand, points beyond *moi* fixations to the fragments or residues that reveal the Other(A) as the netherside of the subject. In paranoid psychosis the many voices, which ordinarily give the *moi* an appearance of synthetic unity, separate themselves out and speak as separate people (*Séminaire* III, p. 153). Paradoxically, these voices or verbal hallucinations are not readily familiar to the subject (as is *moi* reality), but appear as disembodied voices from the outside world, or as inner—albeit foreign—echoes. In neither case, however, does the psychotic experience these voices and verbal fragments as connected to her or his own "self"-unity (*Séminaire* III, p. 156). Typically, such psychotics disclaim responsibility for their hallucinations. If discourse opens up onto something beyond linguistic meaning, Lacan said, then it is onto the Real of the signifier in the Other (*Séminaire* III, p. 157). Here we discover the Real basis of language, that which makes speech itself interpretation.

One of the images Lacan used to convey his conception of the Real was that of a six-faceted diamond. From one angle the diamond is concrete and complete, but from another its facets seem to divide the surrounding surface (*Séminaire* I, p. 297). We could well be in the realms of chemistry and physics here with a discussion of the solid-state diamond or its refractory impact on light rays. But for Lacan, the solid-state diamond is a symbol. In its natural state—outside language—it represents absence/nothingness or presence/being, depending on one's vantage point (*Séminaire* I, p. 297). Once the diamond is named, it can no longer be "nothing," for it introduces "holes" into the Real, making all kinds of interpretations possible. Thus viewed, the Real is the umbilical cord of the Symbolic, the residue behind all articulation which cannot be eliminated.

According to Lacan, Freud tried to explain the Imaginary and the

Real between 1897 and 1914 as mechanisms of the unconscious. Jung looked for the norm of the Real in the Imaginary, while R. D. Laing would later try to make another and superior Real of the Imaginary. Lacan's categories have affinities not only in other psychoanalytic theories, however, but with various philosophies as well. Lacan's Real, for example, is not unlike Kant's *das Ding an sich*, although Kant thought "It" could be directly represented in language. For Lacan, "It" was *das Ding*, truth hiding in the unconscious Other(A). Lacan also owes a philosophical debt to Heidegger's concept of *Dasein*, seen as that which is prior to any form of investigation.[66] Unlike Heidegger's concept, however, Lacan's emphasis on human neonate prematurity and subsequent helplessness places the Real in the biological organism, as the very mechanism which makes the Imaginary and Symbolic necessary. But beyond the issue of Lacan's intellectual debts and echoes, we have the challenge of what we are going to make of his third category. Although Lacan increasingly stressed the Real, I think we would be wrong to disconnect it from its interaction with the Imaginary and Symbolic. In a recent article the literary critic Karl Racevskis described the interaction of the Imaginary with the Symbolic as two modes of consciousness representing two different ways of relating to the Real ("The Theoretical Violence," p. 36). We must not forget, however, that Imaginary perception actualizes the unconscious within consciousness. By discussing the separate functioning of the orders, one risks implying a subordination of the Imaginary and Symbolic to the Real (inferred from Lacan's later work), which borders on a reification of the Real. Indeed, the Real exists and resists, but is not a totality. We must remember what Lacan constantly repeated: in acts of consciousness, the orders are inmixed and "apparently" inseparable.

To demonstrate the importance of the Real, Lacan borrowed the Greek term *tuché* from Aristotle's search for first causes, but redefined the term to place his own view of "first causes" in the meeting of the Real with the other orders (*Séminaire* XI, p. 53). These mythical points of meeting—or impasse—we know as Lacanian knots. Between the Real and the Imaginary, Lacan hypothesized knots of signifiers (*les uns*), which belong to primary process, to *jouissance*. These later play on meaning at the level of "drive" or erotomania (*Télévision*, p. 22). The first meeting between an infant and the Real is symbolized by Lacan as the *objet a*, which refers both to the primordial gap between body experience and perception and to the images which quickly fill in this gap (*Séminaire* XI, pp. 76, 78).

From the start, *objet a* carries the dual meaning of "lack" and that which compensates for lack.

The Real meets the Imaginary at the point where food means something more than just a way to satisfy physical need (*Séminaire* XI, p. 153). While Lacanian need belongs to the order of the Real, Desire links need to images and words. Desire, therefore, is from the earliest moments a psychic coefficient of the corporal relationship with the mother, while the Real (need) resides apart from the domain of the pleasure principle (*jouissance*) (*Séminaire* XI, pp. 152–53). Desire starts out as an Imaginary signifier, aimed at recognition and constancy (Eros), while the Real of need—and the effects of prematurity—reside as coefficients of fading and fragmentation on the slope of Thanatos. Although neo-Freudian analysts who more or less equate need with desire may find it unnecessary to distinguish between the Imaginary and the Real, Lacan's emphasis on an inherent biological incompleteness (for which mirror-stage imprinting compensates) demands that a distinction be made between the Real aspects of such a plight and the interpretations that cover over the Real (objective) by the Imaginary (subjective) and Symbolic (language).

In Seminar Twenty Lacan schematized the points at which the Real accedes to the Symbolic by the following symbols or mathemes: *objet a* = concrete representations recorded in the Other(A); $\overline{\varnothing}$ = the first pure or abstract signifier (S_1), the Phallus; the Other(A) = the discourse of the mother, father, culture, and of language itself, which has been repressed and is subsequently displaced into concrete language and relationships and onto other substitute objects; $\mathcal{S}$ = the Castrated subject of speech and Desire, split off from the Imaginary *jouissance* of symbiotic unity and immediate knowledge of the Other(A) by the binary signifier (the Phallus and the divisive effect of language) (p. 86). Lacan used these four mathemes to teach that the "first cause" of an event cannot be located in any innate psychic, biological, or neurological substance or in a preformed reality of essences. We can see an existentialist idea at work here: essence does not precede existence. There is, nonetheless, a Real world of things and effects that vision and language endow with meaning and to which they then attribute essence (*Séminaire* XX, p. 34). The Real has already happened to a subject, and always returns. Lacan's "first causes" clearly differ from Aristotle's classical four causes: the material one (what things are made of); the configuration of circumstances; the trigger cause; and the final cause or goal (*télos*). Instead, the meaning that humans give to the Real evolves from the knots between it and Imaginary identificatory material and from the knots that convey its meeting with the Symbolic. Interpretations of the Real thus multiply to infinity, both within present time (the Symbolic) and while remaining anchored in the unconscious capacity for projecting the future perceptually (the Imaginary).

If the Lacanian Real can be inferred at points of join between orders, these points can also describe openings or discontinuities in the Real (Sheridan, *Ecrits*, p. 299). The Real is implied, for example, as an opening or gap between the other (ego ideal) and *moi* reality (*Séminaire* XX, pp. 122–23). When the other slips out of the *moi's* grasp—its attempts to fix others within the confines of its own narcissism—the Real instability of the human subject slips its mask. Or the Real is implied in the assumption of "self"-autonomy and lucidity, which are regularly belied by the facts of "self"-dependency and "self"-mysteries, such as dreams. Even the need for relationships and for speaking per se become symbolic indicators or pointers that something lies beyond relationship and speech. Indications of the Real show up in the suspensions of transference (not in its content), and in language, where impasses between the three orders appear as breaks or cuts in an apparently univocal signifying chain of meaning and discourse. That is, the Real is what the subject interprets, as well as the "return" of the residue of such interpretations, both in an individual's history and within the collectivities one labels historical. In both cases the Real breaks up efforts to give unity, consistency, and cohesiveness to meaning, affect, or events. But the Imaginary and the Symbolic place themselves as screens over the Real and prevent it from ever actually "thinking" itself. In this sense the Real of psychic experience lies beyond the dream (*Séminaire* XI, p. 49). It is merely inferred on the side of consciousness, as the truth of lived experience which has been representationally transformed. It is, therefore, what eludes psychoanalysis, but what psychoanalysis seeks to interpret.

When Lacan says that the "gods are of the field of the Real," mysterious, controlling forces are summoned into view (*Séminaire* XI, p. 45). These "gods" are a cipher for structure: repetitions—beyond the pleasure principle—which block paths to freedom of choice and access to joy because of mechanical rituals. The Real is not itself a symptom, then, because a symptom is a metaphor (a condensed language where Real truth can only be inferred). The Real is the kernel at the heart of psychic experience, the effect behind psychic truth, and the antithesis of philosophical Idealism. Idealist philosophers such as Kant and Johann G. Fichte thought the ego creates the world.

But they did not really solve the problem of how to get from interpretation to the world of Real objects. Lacan's solution was to separate the Real from reality (i.e., subjectivity)—be it personal or historical—and thereby create an Ur-category. Insofar as all human interpretation, whether of "self" or culture, applies to the Real of pure effects (which only attain meaning arbitrarily within language), it is the Real of the signifier that structures perception and also offers a way to individuate the objects of the world. In such a context Lacan portrays language itself as a god, an equivalent of the Other(A).

The Real is what a person drags into the psychoanalyst's office: unassimilated signifiers, obsessively or hysterically repeating themselves in an effort at "self"-comprehension and resolution (constancy), or even as testimony to the signifier foreclosed in psychosis (the Name-of-the-Father) (*Séminaire* XI, p. 54). These impasses perforate the seeming synthetic unity of a person's discourse and behavior, ripping holes in an invisible weave (*Séminaire* I, p. 222). The Lacanian analyst looks for truth, therefore, the meaning of a person's life, behind the conceptual memories of conscious reconstruction (Freud's "screen memories"); these conceal something of Real originary determination (*Séminaire* XI, pp. 49, 55). But the Real is resistant to revelation, not only because it can be symbolized (i.e., distorted), but also because it has become a part of the resistance to the primordial gap and fragmentation which Imaginary fantasies papered over with *moi* fixations and Other(A) messages (*Séminaire* XI, p. 84). Once "lack" is given meaning, it can be denied because it seems fulfilling or, at least, constant. The challenge to the analyst, then, is not to understand the analysand's Imaginary discourse, but to expose the Real hiding beyond the dream navel (*Séminaire* XI, p. 59). Such discoveries will point to substitutions for Desire which appear in *objet a* and the effects of Law discernible in discourse intention. Although each story will be unique, its formal underpinnings are predictable.

The Real will be found, if at all, in the links of a preconscious syntax to an unconscious reservoir and in the unchangeability of the numbers present in the unconscious. These countable unities make up a primitive symbolism in the Other(A). As astonishing as it may seem, the Real effects of being human create a syntax that can be deduced before the existence of concrete language (and before semantics). This preconscious syntax or Imaginary semantics is retroactively inferred, of course, not only via its effects, but also within a broad family history, for it will never appear as reconstructed memory. An analysand must be viewed generationally, then, as a *chiffre* (symptom, metaphor, victim), selected by a specific signifier and elaborated within a precise personality structure (normal, neurotic, perverse, psychotic). This will tell the story of the (m)Other's Desire and the place of the Name-of-the-Father within that Desire. While the stories that recount the effects of Real structures and signifiers are infinite, symptoms are limited, as are the resultant personality structures. Too much *jouissance* yields an obsessional personality; too little results in hysteria, and so on.

Jameson wrote that Lacan's addition of the Real to a relatively harmless opposition between Imaginary and Symbolic orders irritates contemporary philosophers and linguists ("Imaginary and Symbolic in Lacan," p. 387). We live in an intellectual climate dominated by the conviction that the realities we confront come to us preformed and preordered, not so much by the human mind (as in classical Idealism) or by the human senses (as in classical psychology) or by brain functions (as in parapsychology) as by the various modes in which human language can work. It is hardly surprising, then, that Lacan's insistence on an indestructible nucleus (an excess) behind our representations will be disturbing, if not unacceptable. For his part, MacCabe sees such objections to Lacan as already a thing of the past: "It is now so evident that for linguistics to constitute itself as a science it was necessary to drop normative concerns that one can all too hastily . . . ignore the complex play of theories and practices that were re-aligned by the Saussurean revolution" (*Talking Cure*, p. 198).

In his monumental essay on Lacan, Jameson pointed out that some critical objections to Lacan's category of the Real presuppose an epistemology in which knowledge lies in a simplistic identity with the thing. Such presuppositions are at odds with Lacan's concept of a decentered subject, which can never be directly unified with language or with the Real ("Imaginary and Symbolic in Lacan," p. 387). The Real is history, Jameson says, that which has already happened. But I would add that inasmuch as history is distorted, interpreted, and reconstructed, it is no longer the Real. Lacan showed that we humans measure the Real as fixed, as that which does not lie (*Séminaire* III, pp. 77–78). We suppose that our own views are Real, based as they are in the assumptions of our own intuition (common sense, tradition, "self"-myths). What this implies is the idea that an Other(A) knows. The Real of our propositions is disguised by conventional language. In MacCabe's phrasing: "To analyse discourse we must start from Lacan's insight that language operates on a continuous misconstruction; which misconstruction is the appearance of the subject" (*Talking Cure*, p. 199). In other words, we assert our own uncertain knowledge in an inherent effort to verify it, that is, to correct, convince, and absolve the dialectical Other(A).

Lacan attributed to Freud the revolutionary discovery that the displacement of the signifier (due to repression and denial) determines people's speech, choices, and acts—everything—and makes the human subject an effect or a representation instead of an essence or an essentially biologically determined creature (Lacan, *Ecrits*, p. 30). If Lacan had proposed only the Imaginary and Symbolic orders, we could fit him comfortably into the binary tendencies of Western philosophy. The Imaginary would be a more specific (personal) unconscious, and the Symbolic a global semiotics of language and society. But by divorcing the Real from language and placing it prior to the Imaginary, Lacan ensured the final impossibility of a congruity between these orders. At the same time Lacan's attribution of a Real functioning to symbol, structure, signifier, metaphor, and metonymy blurs any final separation between the conscious and the unconscious. Consciousness is not really distinct from the unconscious structures that operate it by the force of Desire (Law) and narcissism. Nor are intellect and affect opposed in contradiction, since affect is inverted, inhibited, and displaced in representations because it is always engaged in a specific signifying dialectic (*Séminaire* I, p. 263).

That dialectic is between the subject and the Real signifiers in the Other(A) and constitutes the human effort to objectify one's relation to the Other(A) in oneself through the ruses of consciousness, that is, through language and fantasy projections of ideals. Freud's early idea that the goal of psychoanalytic treatment was to achieve consciousness of fantasies preserved a neo-Platonic, Enlightenment optimism concerning rational or conscious insight.[67] Revisionist schools of Alfred Adler, Karen Horney, Erich Fromm, Harry S. Sullivan, and others have retained the idea that the crux of the therapeutic process is the development of insight (Rieff, *Freud*, p. 104). Lacan has taught analysts not to look for psychic freedom in conscious enlightenment, insight, behavior, "growth," ego strengthening, or adaptation, but in the truth of Desire. What must finally be stressed in any study of the Lacanian orders is that they cannot be distinguished along the lines of consciousness versus unconsciousness or fantasy versus reality. Therein lies the perversity and complexity of Lacan's thought.

4

THE

RELATIONSHIP

OF SENSE AND SIGN

In this chapter I discuss the relationship of sense and sign under four headings: (1) psychotic discourse and the origins of thought and language; (2) signifier, signified, and sign; (3) metaphor and metonymy; and (4) the symptom. The discourse which controls any subject's speech is the Other's discourse. The different aspects of this discourse are incarnated or materialized in sounds and words and therefore can be studied. In "On a question preliminary to any possible treatment of psychosis" (1958), Lacan emphasized that Other(A) discourse should interest any subject, since all are stretched over the four corners of the Schéma L, whose origin is in the Other (Sheridan, *Ecrits*, pp. 192−93). From the point of view of the Symbolic order, Other(A) discourse has a combinatory structure—symbols, sounds, or words form unconscious linguistic meaning insofar as they exist in differential opposition to each other. These oppositions work like the signs in a Saussurean signifying chain, which make meaning by referring one to the other. In Lacanian thought the Saussurean sign—language itself—bears only half the burden of making meaning and is represented as only one component in cognition. Lacan reduces language per se to the signifier and assigns to the signified the task of containing the subjective element in cognition. The latter anchors linguistic meaning (*la signification* as a recasting of Frege's *Bedeutung*) in repressed networks of visual/verbal associations (*le sens* as a recasting of Frege's *Sinn*).

The combinatory aspect of unconscious discourse is quite different from its spatial aspect. The spatial topological component (fixed signifiers in the Other) is the history of a person's life containing mirror-stage and Oedipal effects, as well as an Imaginary order myth of family prehistory. These operate a subject's life in the present with all the force of reality and immediate occurrence and attribute "x" myth or effect (signifieds) to the subject's intrinsic being. Lacan portrays the links between effect and myth as key signifiers concerning the Oedipus structure (birth, love, and procreation) and the fourth one—the most elemental—death (fragmentation, separation). These two kinds of meaning in the Other(A) show, if nothing else, that the Other(A) is a Real place of memory and that memory plays on the Imaginary, Symbolic, and Real levels. Lacan frequently criticized the philosopher Henri Bergson's influence on the development of French thought. Bergson's *élan vital* was neither biological life nor time always creating itself anew, but a signifier recorded in the past that continues to chart the course of a subject's contemporary life through the organizing principles of Desire and repetition.

By reformulating Ferdinand de Saussure's concept of the sign, as well as Lévi-Strauss's use of structure and Roman Jakobson's use of metaphor and metonymy, Lacan corrected Freud's nonproblematization of language. To this end, he worked in large verbal units—discourse, *parole*, signifieds—as opposed to the minimal and discrete units of structural linguistics. Lacan's attempts to conceptualize the mind in its shadow relation to unconscious language also situate him in opposition to Immanuel Kant. Kant placed nonsense (*Unsinn*)—the opposite of meaning—among negative values as a pure and simple absence or privation of meaning. As we shall see, Lacan's study of Daniel-Paul Schreber's delirium gives a positive value to *Unsinn* insofar as Schreber's articulations exhibit organization. Any discourse, even a delirious one, is to be judged first as a field of meaning which has organized a certain signifier (*Séminaire* III, pp. 137, 139). Lacan's discovery—that we talk to screen out the unconscious discourse—is expressed thus in Seminar Three: "the less we articulate it [the unconscious signifier], the less we talk, and the more it speaks us" (p. 157). "It" is the mechanical god who speaks all the time and understands nothing of human needs (*Séminaire* III, pp. 141, 144). The normal person talks but does not take seriously the greater part of his interior—not to be confused with introspective—discourse, whereas the psychotic has become its slave or victim (*Séminaire* III, p. 140). Just as we see the point of connection between the human subject and the Symbolic order in the navel of the dream, we see the join between the normal speaking subject and language in the decomposed discourse of a psychotic (*Séminaire* II, p. 130).

Psychotic Discourse and the Origins of Thought and Language

Lacan's most important contribution to psychoanalysis, linguistics, literary theory, and philosophy is, in my estimation, his discovery that psychotic discourse does not arise from brain dysfunction nor from the loss of reality per se. It compensates, instead, for a signifier or "letter" which has not been firmly placed—does not insist—in the unconscious. Although Lacan's explanations of how narcissism, fantasy, and the Oedipal structure occur would alone place him in the rank of innovative thinkers of genius, he is not responsible for discovering these functions. It is in his patient rereading of Freud's *Psychoanalytische Bemerkungen über einen autobiographisch beschriebenen Fall von Paranoia* (Psychoanalytic Notes on an Autobiographical Account of a Case of Paranoia) (1910), which itself interpreted Dr. jur. Daniel-Paul Schreber's *Denkwürdigkeiten eines Nervenkranken* (Memoirs of My Nervous Illness) (1903), that Lacan demonstrated what lies beyond narcissism and behind meaning.[1]

Even though the perceptual link between memory traces of objects and of words was first made in a preverbal world—and later reappears in literary discourse through what Lacan termed the "law of the universal equivalence"—there is no intrinsic or natural connection between objects and words. This necessarily implies that, in its "essence," the signifier is not present in the Other(A) in order to "mean" something (*Séminaire* III, p. 185, 188, 213). Insofar as primitive signifiers are radically unconscious and therefore inaccessible, they cannot be studied in any transparency or by empirical methods. This seemingly detached Other(A) language does reappear in its "pure" form, however, in psychotic speech. Lacan reinterpreted the phenomenon, intuited by other psychoanalysts, by linking the normal and psychotic use of language to the identificatory drama of mirror-stage and Oedipal structures. We remember that an infant is baptized into personhood by learning to oppose itself to "Mommy." In the middle territory between the symbiotic "self"-tie with the mother and the signifier of the Name-of-the-Father, a child assumes an identity (or a set of believed self-descriptions) of its own. If the psychic separation in childhood is nebulous—the father's Name not symbolized—individuals can still manage in the adult world as long as they imitate normative father/son or father/daughter Imaginary models. Psychotic episodes occur when the intrinsic lack of this key phallic signifier—the Name-of-the-Father—is challenged within the Symbolic order. The confrontation topples the mental house of cards supporting the subject's identity. Imaginary relations between *moi* and others also collapse. The ideal ego, heretofore unsymbolized, emerges as the "miraculous infant," looming forth with a new name, such as Christ, God, Napoleon, or any other name not the person's own, while the existential subject of synchronic relations (*je*) disappears. The primordial ideal ego has substituted itself for *je* and the ego ideal has taken the Other's place. A sexual link is inferred between the ideal ego, ego ideal, and the missing Phallus. According to Lacan, as the dialectic of the transference relation to others ebbs, we may contemplate the impasse concerning the role of the signifier in structuring mind.

If *moi* identity has not been solidly grounded by a symbolic identification with the Name-of-the-Father, it fails to support the grammatical language structures that we equate with interactional discourse and with cognition. If the Real father was denigrated by the mother, or if a child's experience of this father was surrounded by intolerable trauma, the unconscious signifier linking the infant to difference—the Father's Name functioning to break up identificatory fusion with the Other—is negated, or only feebly registered. Mind—mental processes—unravels into the fragmented parts which previously functioned as a unity as long as anchored by the sense of a cohesive self. In Seminar Eleven Lacan held that everything in meaning comes initially from the structure of the phallic signifier in its divisory capacity: from Castration (p. 188). Here he implies the sense (*sens*) behind psychotic discourse as well as the sense that supports normal linguistic meaning (*signification*). By not acceding to psychic Castration in childhood, the paranoid psychotic has foreclosed the signifier for death and separation and retained that psychic sense of wholeness which is on the side of immortality. In the state of delirium—without a mediating, equalizing relation to the other—the *je* speaks like a robot and reveals what lies behind and beyond narcissism and grammar. A delusional psychotic discourse implicitly alludes to the Other(A) as a mechanical god of power and destruction.

When "reality" seems to be lost (as in psychotic delusions or dreams), Lacan maintains above all that we learn how mind and identity are made by studying what takes the place of so-called reality. Psychotic discourse makes clear *inter alia* that the Imaginary "self"-text generally protects human subjects from the Real of the unconscious Other(A) and from the realization that language invades us—what Lacan termed "parasites." The psychotic is suspended, unprotected in the disorienting immediacy of a graveyard of language detached from human relationships (*Séminaire* III, p. 182). Here the Other(A) can be characterized as a haunted memory code of images and words. The psychotic makes up new compound expressions. Voices appear (as in Schreber's case) claiming to use the "basic language" (*Grundsprache*): the signifier itself has become the object of communication. Lacan convincingly argued that psychotic delusionals speak the "truth" when they boast of having gained insight into the essence of the universe (*Séminaire* III, pp. 185–86). But the truth is not that of mythical insight nor any Laingian superiority over the social order. Psychotic truth refers, instead, to the importance of language and the Oedipal Law in structuring normal discourse. *Parole* is the link between archaic messages and concrete language. Psychotic language demonstrates that reception (a key term in communications and information theory) of a message does not stop at the semiological play between the Saussurean signifier (sound) and signified (concept). Rather, it concerns the originality of the order of language itself (*Séminaire* III, p. 213). As redefined by Lacan, this code phenomenon has become the superimposition of language on a human subject. In psychosis the message communicated from the Other(A) code is the structure of the word itself—the signifier—minus its Symbolic order clarity, and its wider meaning in signifying the subject to itself and for others.

Lacan's theories of the mirror stage and Castration go far toward explaining how the symbol system comes to reside in the brain: (1) through the introjection and projection of images and sounds, and (2) through the symbolism proper of language later. But the "symbolism proper" of language has been reexamined by Lacan in terms of an inherent ambiguity and relativity. This phenomenon is inseparable from the substitutive, oppositional, or referential "laws" that operate thought (ontology) within the inmixed and internalized drama of relationship with which we are familiar. Viewed thus, mental development would arise from a symbolism in which the subject is a set of linguistic and identificatory symbols that obey structural dicta. Prior to coherent naming—circa eighteen months—a symbolism (the signifier) is registered in the Other(A) as a pure symbol and, as such, is adequate to itself. Unlike textual critics, who portray language as being dependent on grammatical, developmental, or social forms, Lacan argues that prior to any knowledge of grammar, rules, or written language, the supports of later language acquisition exist as pure symbol, as discrete elements (both visual and acoustic) that cannot be divided or reduced beyond their minimal form. But since this signifying symbolism does not appear in any mental transparency, it must be understood in relation to Lacan's concept of structure. The philosopher Jean-Marie Benoist has described Lacan's notion of structure as a bundle of transformations. But what is being transformed? In Lacanian epistemology, neither mind and identity nor language and thought are static systems. Moreover, they are perpetually transformed by the interactions of the various levels on which they simultaneously exist. Thus, the human subject itself is being transformed, ever in the act of seeking to know itself. In discussing structure, Lacan often referred to the coordinate as well as the idea of a certain number of coordinates. Such a mathematical conceptualization of structure calls for clarification, however, in order the better to understand his application of it.

As we know, Descartes invented coordinates as a way of fixing geometrical space or points by the use of algebraic values on a graph. Lacan's implication of a certain number of coordinates in his notion of structure echoes his theory that the unconscious can only count to six (see Chapter 3). Lacan fixed the manner in which unconscious space is mapped out by Fregian mathematics, in which each number specifies its own structure by implying both the structure or sequential order that preceded it as well as the one that will follow it. Prematuration gives way to mirror-stage identification, which is attenuated by Castration and, in turn, gives way to the Oedipal structuring of personality. Whether Lacan describes this succession of coordinates as metaphorical (similarity and substitution) or metonymical (contiguity and referentiality) or as simultaneously anticipatory and retroactive (the future perfect of the "self"), he alters our own contemporary ideas about "structure."

In Seminar Three Lacan maintained that structure always establishes itself by reference to something which is coherent with something else, complementary to it. Such a proposition echoes Albert Einstein's notion of relativity as always implying a fixed point, i.e., something is relative only in terms of its position vis-à-vis a point of stability (which may well in itself be arbitrary). The mirror-stage structure is, therefore, relative to human prematuration at birth. The Oedipal structure is relative to the fact of language and its Real effects, which give existence to being (être) by the act of naming, and which give autonomy to the subject by its representational deferral function. Secondary or dynamic repression permits normal speech to occur. The mirror-stage structure was formed by the division of the prespecular infant from its sense of the world-as-immediacy by the *signifier* (or pure symbol) of a unified body image. This mirror-stage image takes on its symbolic meaning in light of the fragmented body image to which it is opposed (i.e., is relative to that fixed point of experience). A similar interpretation of the Oedipal structure—itself formed as a coefficient of language—is only too obvious. A speaking, cultural self is opposed to a fusionary self built up by narcissistic identifications.

In Seminar Three Lacan also said that "structure is first a group of elements forming a covariant ensemble" (p. 207). Twenty years later, in his *Télévision* interview, he explained his idea of elements (or "letters"). Since any "letter," from a phoneme to a sentence, can be a personal message—i.e., already recorded or marked down somewhere—these elements or rudiments of knowledge (Greek, *stoicheion*) are serial parts of a subjective ensemble (*l'Un*) (*Séminaire* III, p. 22). At the level of pure symbol, Lacan depicted signifiers as algebraic numbers or figures that compose the psychic graph. He went on to say: "The word is to be taken from the same sign that it constitutes in number theories, that is, mathematically" (*Séminaire* III, p. 49). In other words, signifiers themselves—once registered within a given meaning ensemble—are fixed entities (like numbers) and harken back to the genesis of perception in signifiers (*les uns* or the first whole numbers) that lie outside the conceptual memories of consciousness.

But what did Lacan mean by "a covariant ensemble"? In my opinion he referred to the inmixing of his three orders. Cultural differences illustrate how varied the elements symbolizing a given structure can be. Interpretive variations in gender roles (3), exogamy (4), and paternity/maternity (5) constitute the corpus of ethnological and anthropological researches. Moreover, the fixed signifiers within each person's unconscious realign themselves uniquely in response to evershifting Symbolic, Imaginary, and Real stimuli (*Séminaire* III, pp. 207–8). Although a structure is a seeming unity, therefore, this unity only exists in terms of groups of signifying ensembles attached to the Real experiences of prematuration, symbiosis, separation, and the resultant myths built up around the signifiers themselves. The mirror stage, for example, can be characterized by many objects or "substantive" aspects, but the structure itself always exists in the Imaginary confusion of two beings as one (1). The Oedipal structure can branch in many directions, but without changing the process that causes language to exist at all as an interpretation of separation (the anchor of Law) and of the meaning of gender difference (2 and 3). When Lacan says, "The notion of structure is already by itself a manifestation of a signifier" (*Séminaire* III, p. 208), I interpret him to mean that order (i.e., repetition) is inherent in the idea of structure. Thus, sets of signifying symbols, formed in response to the effects of social, linguistic, and biological realities on being, compose primary meaning.

Although Lévi-Strauss's notion of structure was an obvious source for Piaget's definition of structure as a system of transformations including some laws, Lacan's innovative linking of this concept to Cartesian geometrics, Fregean mathematics, and Freudian topology gives a different consistency to the idea of structure than it was to acquire in the work of Piaget.[2] In his *La Révolution Structurale* Benoist claims—correctly in my view—that after Lacan we can no longer say structure is only form with no force or dynamism. Nor can we say that structure is opposed to history. Although Lacan's structures exclude empirical, anecdotal history, they admit history as temporality and transformation. Lacan also eradicates the image of structure as fixed and sedentary, giving instead a major role to both diachrony and simultaneity. Lacan's structural Symbolic shows, moreover, how dialectical—i.e., contradictory— thought can be a tributary of meaning.[3] Indeed, meaning is anchored in dialectical movement.

Lacan's marriage of the concepts of subject, structure, and signifier creates, as well, an entirely different meaning to that of the static Saussurean structuralism with which he is thoughtlessly associated. Lacanian theory here not only deconstructs neo-Saussurean linguistics but also throws doubt on Noam Chomsky's claim to have supplanted the usefulness of any structuralism in linguistics. More than having ramifications for the field of linguistics or cognitive psychology, however, Lacan's discourse theory straddles multiple disciplines, all advancing theories about the origins of language in relation to cognition. Acoustical experts, electrical engineers, neurolinguists, and communication and computer theorists, among others, are studying the phenomenon of language.[4] Those seeking a neurophysiological basis for language, for example, view the problems of memory and learning in an evolutionary manner: serial ordering and organizational hierarchies are seen to be typical of all cerebral activity. Behaviorists, on the other hand, tend to accept language as a simple stimulus-response exercise. Again, theoreticians of artificial intelligence see mind programming as a complex input/feedback process in language (but one that omits Desire and its effects, i.e., human motivation).

The American psycholinguists George A. Miller, Eugene Galanter, and Karl H. Pribram have recently tried to adapt a linguistic model of language to a neo-Freudian psychoanalytic model of the ego by analyzing the size and complexity of the "ego apparatus" and that of grammar and syntax as well.[5] But it is really Edward Sapir (1884–1939) who deserves the credit for demonstrating that language as a total communication system is more than speech. Sapir's pupil, Benjamin Whorf (1897–1934), revived the question of the nature and extent of the control of language systems over thought. Ernst Cassirer and his pupil, the philosopher Susanne K. Langer, added an immense amount of material on the correspondence between speech development and ego formation (Brosin, "Acculturation," p. 117). Against Whorf's behaviorist linguistic determinism, Piaget hypothesized that language development happens only within the possibilities of cognitive growth and then with a significant lag. Anticipating Piaget's approach, Lev S. Vygotsky took the Swiss psychologist's idea of cognitive limitation in childhood "egocentric" speech to be the inner voice of thought. Jerome Bruner tied cognitive and language development to a wider communicational and representational framework, in which language liberates cognition by offering a symbolic alternative to the originally static, iconic mode of child thought processes. Michael Halliday, on the other hand, stressed the creative role of language as only one aspect of ongoing development, a filter and instrument in the construction of social reality.[6] Unlike Lacan, however, all these theories focus on language in relation to a unified ego of consciousness.

But those psychoanalysts whose central preoccupation is the unconscious (and whose medium of operation is language) have not, in general, elaborated linguistic theories of their own. Over twenty years ago, the New York analyst I. P. Glauber reviewed S. Reiss's book *Language and Philosophy* (New York: Philosophical Library, 1959), and asked the question which linguists, philosophers, psychologists, and now many others have been trying to answer for decades: " 'Why is it, language being the tool of the analyst—his daily bread, so to speak—that analysts have not moved beyond a mere few building blocks of their own towards a more substantial contribution to a psychoanalytic linguistics?' " (Brosin, "Acculturation," pp. 116–17; cf. *Psychoanalytic Quarterly*, 28 [1959]: 548–53).

Chomsky, also a pupil of Sapir, departed from his early American structuralist formation to demonstrate, by a generative linguistics and transformational grammar, the inadequacy of structural linguistics as practiced today. Essentially he is responsible for the theory that the form of language is not "mechanical," imposed from the outside, but is "organic," developing from the inside; language is thus a generative system of rules and principles that offers finite means for infinite possibilities. Chomsky therefore faults the kind of structural linguistic analysis which limits itself to the surface layer of an utterance—its physical dimensions—and the categories brought to light by that dimension, while neglecting the internal mechanisms of thought.[7] He writes that language alone allows the order of the world to be instituted and provides a distance from lived experience (Lemaire, *Lacan*, p. 51). By imposing stereotypes, laws, and models, it creates our mode of perceptions of reality, which have, in their turn, been fashioned in the course of man's philogenetic, sociogenetic, and ontogenetic evolution and arise out of a static kind of genetic memory (Lemaire, *Lacan*, p. 25). With these theories combining elements of Descartes, Charles Darwin, Sapir, and Whorf, Chomsky meant to put an end to the quarrel as to whether thought was preponderant over language or vice versa. We know that Chomsky has separated competence from general cognitive processes and linked cognitive psychology to linguistic performance. The latter studies, among other devices, the implications of linguistic transformations (Williamson, "Child Discourse," p. 87). But generally speaking, generative linguists are not interested in relating their transformational models to what we know of human thought processes.[8]

Although Chomsky has been challenged by other linguists and philosophers on the issue of the source of language, I believe a theory with the scope of Lacan's is needed to answer him and other researchers who are still debating the issue of the priority of thought or language. Michael Lewis and Colin Cherry, for example, Sinclair de Zwant (Geneva School), Rodney Williamson, and others see language and cognitive development as concretely linked, and language, thought, and society as interactional and developmentally unified. But they all work along the empirical, pragmatic lines with roots in Aristotle's influence on the evolution of Western thought. Aristotle separated thought from language and rhetoric from ontology, thereby divorcing the Real world (*phýse*) from reason (*lógos*). In so doing, he set up the basis for reducing rational thought to propositional logic (syllogism) and mind to a method of using language to avoid contradictions. The problem does not lie in whether language or thought comes first, then, but in the fact that they were ever separated from each other and from identity ("self"). In the current Western intellectual climate, no matter how this age-old issue is resolved, those studying it ultimately explain "first causes" by biology (genetics or developmental stages) or by brain function.

A paradox of Lacan's teaching is that language appears as both mechanical—imposed from outside—and organic—transformationally supple—but never as genetically, biologically, or neurologically based—never innate. Psychotic discourse dramatizes the mechanical, imposed nature of language, its referential and repetitious qualities. It also reveals its intuitive, that is creative or transformational, character. Psychotic language has, nevertheless, undergone such an alteration by transformational processes of the unconscious that a linguist such as Whorf would certainly have found no connection between it and the way meaning is anchored. Lacan's analysis of psychotic language also silences those socialist critics who accuse him of founding a Romantic irrationalism on psychoanalysis and treating the unconscious as the authentic self and source of deeper wisdom.[9] He leaves us, instead, with a warped disk whose needle sticks.

In Seminar Twenty Lacan used the word *lalangue* to describe elemental language and to imply its thing- or objectlike quality. This is a language with particular ambiguities and special patterns of internal resonance and multiple meanings, where the phonemes of regular language undergo condensation and displacement to form neologisms having little to do with their phonemic usage in common discourse. Sherry Turkle gives the example of a possible confusion of sound along lines of *d'eux*, *deux*, and *dieu*.[10] Such linguistic confusions, when attached to visual images, appear regularly in dreams. In psychosis verbal hallucinations often appear alongside visual ones. When *je* convention and *moi* narcissism are suspended in dreams and psychosis, the linguistic, referential base of thought is free to float from the unconscious to the surface. The language which surfaces has already been placed there as material and sensual, concrete phonemic traces and words that describe objects. Lacan named these elements that compose Other(A) discourse "letters": "that material support that concrete discourse borrows from language" (Sheridan, *Ecrits*, p. 147). But Lacan insists that these "letters" were intuited by Freud in his early work on dreams and jokes and in the influence of philology on his thought.[11] In his unpublished Seminar Five (1957–58) Lacan spoke of the formations of the unconscious. To explain the dynamic processes of the unconscious, he constructed a Delta topology in which the elementary cell was Desire. The important point here is that the representation of a signifier ("letter") in the elementary cell (Desire) makes the unconscious dynamic. From this viewpoint, it is fitting that Serge Leclaire describes the erotogenic zones as "letters" (created by primary repression) of the alphabet of Desire.[12] Unlike concrete discourse, dream signifiers prove that there is a connection between objects, words, and Desire that exists on its own outside a system of normal linguistic or social conventions. When decoded in the light of the laws which operate unconscious language, dreams appear as uniquely personal (as opposed to any universal symbolism). They demonstrate in their connection to language that the images take on meaning only in a verbal context (not unlike a proverb) and that dream language is that concrete language spoken by a given social order and individual.

Normally repressed Other(A) language sometimes appears when a person under medication for a surgical operation speaks from the twilight zone of unconscious discourse. One such patient was obsessed before becoming unconscious with the "insight" that anesthetists and theologists (i.e., theologians) were similar, if not identical persons, because of the resemblance of the words. To explain this revelation to the hospital attendants, the patient invented the word anestheologist. Such a *portmanteau* word functions, according to Gilles Deleuze, to fuse and ramify heterogeneous series (i.e., the affinity of events and language). When language conventions disappear through loss of normal consciousness, the "mind" continues to make meaning, continues to search for Imaginary connections between objects, words, and experiences (this patient's father was a pastor and her brother a doctor).[13] Anesthetists and theologists also evoke the death signifier.

As Dr. Jean Marc Itard's study of the nineteenth-century *enfant sauvage* of Aveyron shows (although he would not have drawn that interpretation), there is nothing innate about language except the capacity of the vocal apparatus to utter a few sounds.[14] Every person who learns language starts all over from the beginning: from phonemic sounds to labeling, to combining words to form ideas. But as far as the effects of Other(A) language on normal language are concerned, one has practically no clear proof. That the unconscious cannot directly condition the relative order of spoken discourse is what Lacan called Frege's paradox: the existence of the unconscious pushes us to seek a total comprehension that cannot be achieved. The *moi* maintains the unconscious in place—by diachronic anchoring and by the *je's* synchronic respect for convention. The coherence of thought comes, therefore, from the necessity of repression.

The Harvard professor Robert Coles has recently written that what is truly compelling is the mystery of the origins of language, not the current theories on narcissism. For all Chomsky's brilliance, Coles opines, we are still left with cortical areas, inherited capacities or potentialities, and mechanisms. Given this "scientific" limitation, Coles is not surprised that both Chomsky and Piaget have avoided explaining the origins of literary accomplishment.[15] The Sapir-Whorf-Chomsky thesis that the primary regulating principle in thought and perception is the language system itself, and not the object world, conjures a picture of language as static and transparent. According to this view, human beings move the pieces of language around and control them, making it possible to derive "objective" theories of truth, meaning, and knowledge. By placing a subject at the surface of language which is an object of the Other's Desire and discourse, Lacan has blurred the distinctions between language and objects, or mind and identity. And by pointing to the psychotic as a subject who has become an object of his or her own normally repressed language, Lacan has dramatized that there are many more questions yet to be asked. These concern the origins and influence of language in relationship to transference, beyond any implicit discussion of the universal laws underlying all languages or any analysis of discourse based on the processes of cognition.[16]

In Lacan's mapping of an unconscious topography, the neopositivistic linguistic thinking of Freud is also submitted to a new scrutiny. Claude Lévi-Strauss portrayed man as the product of social structures, not the creature of "individual" essences celebrated by the philosophers of old. But Lacan relocated Lévi-Strauss's elemental structures in the unconscious as the scaffolding of the human subject instead of in kinship rules and thereby reformulated the anthropologist's static picture of man. Lacan also showed that by opposing words and things, Freud failed to see that there is always a liaison within a context of opposition. That is to say, words give meaning to things and therefore stamp them with the indelible law of naming which humanizes the world of things. The law of structure—meaning created by opposition—is more elemental than any literal or substantive character imputed to objects. The psychotic person "means" per se by being opposed to the underside of his or her own discourse; the "self" has become an object that tries to solve the mystery of a missing signifier by recourse to hallucinatory meaning. Psychotic discourse is, therefore, what Lacan (after G. De Clérambault) defined as mental automatism. He intends this in the etymological sense, where automaton is something which truly thinks by itself without a link to the *moi* to give its "subject" to thought (*Séminaire* III, p. 346). Psychotic discourse has become a use of language between disembodied *je's*, validating Lacan's claim that a subject has only one *moi* but many *je's*.

Signifier, Signified, and Sign

As we know, Ferdinand de Saussure (1857–1913) was one of the first thinkers to conceive of language as a form of communication rather than as the substance of expression. Revolutionary in its time, his "diacritical" theory of meaning pointed to the general laws that govern the operation of language.[17] Many of the original concepts spawned in his *Cours de linguistique générale* (1915) are now common, such as synchrony (timelessness), diachrony (evolution through time), and the idea that meaning evolves from values created by in terdependent terms because of their differential, oppositional character (Wilden, *LS*, p. 204). Although Saussure corrected the narrowness of neopositivistic, historical linguistics, and the empiricism of American descriptive linguistics, Jonathan Culler has argued convincingly that Saussurean linguistics was still bogged down in postulates from the Cartesian tradition.[18] According to Saussure, language is a system of signs wherein each sign is a unity made up of a signified (conceptual or psychic reality) and a signifier (phonic, acoustic image, or sound). While he based the reality of signs on the signified, he staked his ideological "certainty" on the relativization of meaning itself. Meaning evolves from the arbitrary position occupied by signifieds and signifiers in a system, and not from any "natural" relationship between signifieds and signifiers, or between signs and the world. The obvious impasse here lies in what answer one gives to the question: To what does the signified refer? Insofar as it refers to a preformed reality which precedes language, Saussure is invoking the *Cogito*.

When Saussure later distinguished between *la langue* and *le langage* (in an effort to clarify signifier and signified), he placed *langage*—as *parole*—on the side of the signifier. But this was insufficient to explain the complex physical, physiological, psychological, and social aspects of spoken language. He represented *la langue*, on the other hand, as normative, unified, total, and classifiable, as the synchronic system of differences which constitutes language. *La langue*, therefore, organized by rules and conventions within a collectivity, becomes the equivalent of grammar and gives a unity or coherence to *parole*, which is neither innate or natural. *La langue* has, in consequence, taken over the character of Saussure's signified. It follows that Saussure promoted study of the synchronic (the static and stable) over the diachronic (the dynamic and unstable). But we can see the dead end to which such reasoning leads. Meaning derives from an autonomy of language, which is only arbitrarily related to reality but, paradoxically, must also bear the brunt of being the reality which informs speech. We are left with a God-like, floating grammar, essentially attached to nothing.

It is easy to see why Chomsky's return to an explanation of language by genetic origin appears to be an advance in knowledge over Saussure's dismissal of the problem. Moreover, as Culler points out, Chomsky's attention to the creative character of language and its syntax makes Saussure's linearity and fixed forms appear archaic. But the academic activity generated by Saussure and Chomsky points as much to problems the "masters" have not resolved as to the revolutions they have caused. On the one hand, there is now a semiotic tradition that rejects the formal, static nature of Saussure's closed-system linguistics. Umberto Eco, for example, has emphasized the sign-user over the codes used (Saussure) and has differed from Chomsky in giving precedence to performance over linguistic competence. C. S. Peirce has advanced the idea of sign and explanation. Other directions include stressing cognition over Chomsky's emphasis on syntax (Ray Jackendorf). Some semioticians in France have become theoretical Lacanians, if not psychoanalysts.

Lacan used Saussure to revolutionize Freud and at the same time transcended impasses in the works of both men. I would argue that a similar philosophical impediment flaws both Freud's and Saussure's theories on language. By ignoring the social dimension of people talking together in the here and now, and opting for a universal (*langue*) versus personal (*parole*) opposition as regards meaning, Saussure was left with the speaker subordinated to the group, but with no problematization of the speaker's relation to what is spoken. In an essay entitled "Philology and the Phallus," Cambridge fellow John Forrester reveals a similar predicament in Freud's thought. As we know, Freud was greatly influenced by one of the major disciplines of his day: philology. It was not only the etymological search for hidden "key words" that had an impact on Freud's thought, however, but also the philological concept of a *Volksgeist*. Philologists believed the history of the species could be reconstructed from the *Volksgeist*. Forrester writes: "Such a recourse to the full play of recondite researches of mythologists and philologists into arcane literature and forgotten languages . . . was the working version of the theory Freud clung to to the end of his days, namely his belief in the inheritance of acquired mental characters" (*Talking Cure*, p. 49). Just as Saussure saw *la langue* as a social institution acquired by a group, Freud took the essential features of a Freudian unconscious to be acquired within a social context of "race memories." In the end, unable to explain the personal nature of language (Saussure) or of the unconscious (Freud), both thinkers became prone to use the general to characterize the particular. Nor has Chomsky's equation of "deep" universal structures of grammar with real mental structures or Jakobson's universal patterns of phonemes really resolved the problem of the uniqueness of "mind," any more than have Saussure's efforts to account for an autonomous signified present in the mind of speakers by his concept of *parole*, or Freud's belief in literalist mythology.[19]

The philosopher Ludwig Wittgenstein wrote that we do not understand language by grasping rules; human interaction is prior.[20] As we saw in Chapter 3, Lacan's coordination of the categories he calls the

Symbolic (the rules and conventions of language and society) with the Real (the world and its effects) and with human interaction (the Imaginary) forms a dual, but inmixed subject: identity (Imaginary "self"-text), on the one hand, and mind (generalized Symbolic order texts), on the other. Following Lévi-Strauss's reformulation of Saussure's concept of the sign to place the signifier in the ascendant structuring position—and the signified as the inferred outcome—Lacan referred to the signifier as language itself, which is initially spoken. With this idea, he accounted for how Saussure's *parole* is acquired from *langue* and also accounted for Freud's quandary as to how "race memories" (Symbolic order) are instilled. Lacan was, then, conceptually free to describe the signified as the unconscious identity themes or meanings derived from the synchronic impact of spoken language on a child, but diachronically retained into adult life. Although he accepted Lévi-Strauss's reversal of signifier and signified, Lacan's return to the idea that the "sign" denotes language in its concrete character marked his departure from anthropology. It also marked the remarriage of psychoanalysis to the study of language, which Lacan intended, but by a different route than either Saussure or Freud had taken.

Lévi-Strauss's reversal of Saussure's algorithm (giving primacy to the signifier) equated thought or social reality with the signifier, and the cosmos or underlying structures of mythology with the signified. Although there is a visible similarity between Lacan's Symbolic order and Lévi-Strauss's social reality, the use Lacan made of the signifier deconstructs the anthropologist's static, impersonal order. By shifting emphasis from the cultural consciousness which, for Lévi-Strauss, characterized both signifier and signified, to the idea that signifieds denote a personal unconscious with a unique text, Lacan could now move beyond the universal to the particular. Although the literary critic Jeffrey Mehlman has published an exacting study of how Lacan's use of signifier and signified actually adhere to Lévi-Strauss's interpretations of diachrony and synchrony, I believe we will more easily understand Lacan if we concentrate on the role he gives to the unconscious in its relationship to the signifier.[21]

Lacan always insisted that Freud discovered the structure of the unconscious before 1900 as well as the place of the signifier in it and recorded this discovery in *The Interpretation of Dreams*. In his own efforts to explain what Freud did not understand, Lacan's *linguisterie* followed Saussure in distinguishing between the world-as-referent and linguistic meaning, but in a more complex, elaborated theory. By placing the personal resonance of a word—which Lacan has called *parole*—between the world and the object (persons, things), and then showing how the word is made up of component signifying parts, Lacan showed that language must not only account for the world, but must also enable an infant to "individuate" or appropriate objects ontologically. Lacan's *parole*, therefore, contains three intricate parts: (1) that of signifier in the sense of spoken language, (2) that of meaning, and (3) that of discourse (*Séminaire* III, p. 86). In an essay entitled "Representation and Pleasure," the Lacanian analyst Moustapha Safouan stresses that the power of the Lacanian signifier (or spoken word) comes from its ability to create existence, to give shape to perception. In the Lacanian sense, "discourse" becomes the concrete form in which the signifier exists, linking language in the Other(A) to the social world. Whether conscious or unconscious, discourse constitutes a space of points ("letters") or places that refer to things said (*Talking Cure*, p. 83). The unconscious is composed of sounds and words which come from language; conscious language refers diachronically to these Other *paroles*, and synchronically to itself.

Students of Saussure have not resolved the problem of whether the linguistic sign as conceived by the father of linguistics constitutes a static marriage of sound to concept, or whether the differential relationship between signifier and signified—whose direct consequences cause an arbitrariness in meaning—really opens the way to a diachronic linguistics. This was not a problem for Lacan. Both synchronic time (language as a system or the Symbolic) and diachronic time (unconscious "language" plus identity) must be accounted for in any coherent logic of the signifier or of the human subject. For Lacan the relationship between signifier and signified is not arbitrary because the signifier structures the signified. Lacan's Imaginary subjectivization of language therefore links *parole* to a person's history (diachrony) rather than to synchronic time, as Saussure claimed. Maintaining his intentional reversal of Saussure, Lacan attached *langue* or grammar to present (synchronic) time rather than to history itself (diachrony) as Saussure did. Lacan's radical proposition— that the "I" who speaks rarely coincides with the "I" to whom it refers in speaking—required him to distinguish between the informational giving-and-getting function of language, which he called *langue*, and the unconscious use of language to convey Desire (by *demande*) and narcissism, which he called *parole*. Again, he looked to Saussurean terms, but reformulated their meaning. The information function of language is reduced to *la langue*—minimal in scope compared to the burden it bears in communication theory—and the evocative pervasiveness of unconscious discourse and Desire in language becomes *la parole*. Insofar as Desire is the primary organizer of human behavior—including language use—not only is Saussure's thought inadequate, but Chomsky's theory, that a universal grammar determines our use of language, is equally short-sighted.

Although Lacan's theory of the signifier and the signified has puzzled many critics, I believe his theory here is perfectly accessible, if we bear in mind that each participates in the "life" of the other. In an essay entitled "The Dream and Its Interpretation in the Direction of Psychoanalytic Treatment," Safouan tried to clarify Lacan's inmixing of signifiers and signifieds by pointing out that Lacan's "opposition between the signified and the signifier is substituted for the classical opposition between the particular and the universal. Nominalists and realists, whatever their differences, maintain the same dyadic relationship between the word and the sense" (Schneiderman, *Returning*, p. 142n6). The signifier is the word (the local universal) and the signified its sense (the particular). But one must not then make the error of equating the signifier and *je*, or the signified and *moi*. The pivotal concept that links signifier and signified is the Other(A): the unconscious itself. But theoretically and analytically there is a crucial distinction to be made between signifier and signified, and at this level Lacan retained the bar between them. While Saussure separated sound from concept to show the arbitrariness of meaning, Lacan was insistent on the radical separation to be made between concrete discourse and its character of Otherness in the unconscious.

The literary critic Paul Olson wrote recently that, although Saussure proposed an arbitrary and labile relation between signifier and signified, his "concept of the sign is essentially that of a symbol—one might even say sacrament. Once joined in the unity of the sign, the signifier becomes the outward and visible sign of an inward and spiritual meaning."[22] As we know, Saussure's microcosm of the sign offers no center of meaning other than itself. In this sense the Saussurean signifying chain of signs might be equated with the Lacanian Symbolic order. But for Lacan spoken language—the signifier—creates an-Other(A) order of reference which, in turn, becomes the (displaced) center of the Symbolic. As such, the Other(A) charts the course of conscious meaning at the level of *parole*. *Parole* is thus a global term by which Lacan refers to the presence of unconscious effects in language. Although *parole* is on the Symbolic order slope of the signifier, it conveys signifieds on the *moi* slope of the Imaginary text. A "true" or "full word" (*parole*) appears in consciousness diachronically when a signified stops the synchronic flow of linguistic signifiers by the evocation of a meaning belonging to a domain Other(A) than the semantic one of concrete discourse (*Séminaire* III, p. 92). This Other(A) meaning comes from an unconscious language, which is articulated in concrete discourse as a topological function of the border (on the fringe) (*Séminaire* XI, p. 188). Whereas Lacanian signifieds are units of meaning produced by the effects of the signifier, they represent extralinguistic themes that give coherence to inherently athematic and neutral words. Signifieds play at the surface of language, denoting unanalyzed enigmas. Since the system of language from which signifieds derive is itself a floating meaning system, it follows that signifieds will be hard to identify. Signifieds melt into the flow of language and, like the Imaginary mechanisms, conceal the Other(A). Lacan retained the Saussurean bar to insist that there has never been a clear and self-evident meeting ground between the signifier and signified. So successful is this psychic strategy, indeed, that for centuries Western thought has divorced language from mind, and mind from identity, in an effort to protect the human subject from knowing the origins of knowledge and from self-knowledge as well.

Having reversed Saussure's theory that meaning derives from a correspondence between concept and sound, Lacan argued that if sound gives meaning to concepts—be they symbol, experience, or idea—then sound comes first in creating meaning. Sounds and words proffer themselves to a post–mirror-stage infant as a way of trying to grasp the Real and "explain" the perceived. Signing or lip movements do the same for the hearing impaired. Signifiers, however, only take on their full power of expression from signifieds, which glide under the sounds of language in order to give this language personal meaning. Lacan said his signified was on the same slope as Saussure's sign. That is, both imply something standing behind them as the source of their formation. Lacan called this something "more" the signifier. Culler once misleadingly described the Lacanian "I" as a deconstructed subject, as a construct that has lost its place as a source of meaning and has become the summa of systems of linguistic conventions operating through it.[23] Culler's idea of an unconscious subject of conventions implies a Symbolic order revolving door in the unconscious that does not exist. No recuperability of conventions or signifiers will occur until signifieds are decoded in light of the transformational laws of primary-process (Imaginary) logic that ineluctably lend a unique and personal meaning to Symbolic conventions.

Saussure taught that phonemic features have no natural affinity to meaning and that they only achieve meaning in opposition to all other phonemes in a given language. But everything phonemic has not yet been isolated and studied by linguistics. Lacan alluded to the part played by an unconscious signifying chain of phonemes (Leclaire's suggestion), which enters into signified meaning clusters. As mentioned earlier, these phonemes, even when identical to the same phoneme used in concrete discourse, will mean something entirely different in the unconscious because of the structural and transformational reshaping of "material" there. Although conscious and unconscious meaning systems both work by the materiality of a given set of sounds—the representational substratum of all discourse—the radical difference of one system from the other can only be glimpsed in any pure form in dreams or psychotic delirium. The unconscious cannot, therefore, be analyzed through any obvious one-to-one conversion of sound and sound, word and word, or letter and letter.

Colin MacCabe has written that the great contribution of linguist Emile Benveniste is to have distinguished two different axes of language: the enunciation and the enunciated (*Talking Cure*, p. 195). Benveniste's intention was to use these concepts to infer an objective description of language. Lacan borrowed Benveniste's terms to show that, on the contrary, no final objectivization of language is possible. He placed his own signifiers on the side of Benveniste's enunciation—the "objective" if one will. Signifieds, however, point to the effects of what has been heard—the enunciated—as that which subjectivizes all meaning. In Lacan's recasting, the "enunciated" refers not to the history of language, then, but to the unconscious history of each individual: the *dit*-mension in being (*Séminaire* XX, p. 97). Lacan claimed, therefore, that while the signifier issues from the auditory realm and imprints its traces on the unconscious, its effects create signifieds that have nothing at all to do with the ears. That we use language at all—our motivation or libido—comes from what we try to know concerning the function of these signifieds: Who am/is "I"? (*Séminaire* XX, p. 126).

In other terms, Lacan described effect as the sense of a thing, as all the ungraspable facets of the impact of symbolization on an individual. Lacan's meaning here does not become clear until we realize that the field of effect—invisible though its operations may appear—is what mathematicians have recently called the fifth dimension (beyond the four standard dimensions of height, breadth, depth, and time discovered across the centuries). Effect, then, cannot be trapped in a test tube or empirically measured, but it can be seen "materially" in its operations. At the Imaginary and Real levels of meaning, signifieds point to narcissism and Desire: to a subject's unique interpretations of the structural effects of the Symbolic order. The truth to which the Other(A) is witness—and which concrete speech denies—is that the subject has been constituted in the Other(A), by the sum of the effects of words on him or her (*Séminaire* XI, p. 116).

In the "Agency of the Letter in the Unconscious" (1957) Lacan developed the theory that the nature of language will not *really* be questioned—even by linguists or philosophers—as long as people believe spoken language refers to some a priori essence, or even that meaning and spoken language have to be connected. Such assumptions send logical positivists looking for the "meaning of meaning" (Sheridan, *Ecrits*, p. 150). The same quest drives humanists to seek the "meaning of meaning" in metalanguages or metasystems and scientists to seek the same thing in method. The discipline of linguistics, in its theories concerning the relationship of language and meaning, indisputably led to a twentieth-century Renaissance, which has become a Copernican revolution in Lacan's hands through his splitting of language into (1) linguistic and informational meaning (*langue*), and (2) truth value meaning (*parole*). The first belongs to consciousness and the second emanates from the unconscious. In showing that dreams and psychotic language have a meaning—that of the structure of articulation—which stands outside any relationship to normal meaning and, moreover, that these phenomena problematize the normal relationship of meaning to language, Lacan brought identity and Desire into the territory staked out by linguists and cognitive theorists. Based on his clinical observations, Lacan proposed that meaning itself is a series of linguistic elaborations that seek to justify a person's unconscious relationship to the structures of Desire and Law. Lacan's critique of what Jacques Derrida called "logocentrism" deconstructs Saussure's sign to give us pure signifiers—such as the Phallus—linked to no signifieds whatsoever. The phallic signifier does not denote a meaning. It creates one by its formation of the Oedipal structure through the impact of separation on infant perception, and the concomitant linking of Castration to language as a substitutive means for individuating a "self" through Desire.

As stated at the outset of this chapter, unconscious meaning has both a combinatory aspect (interplay of oppositions or signifier) and a spatial aspect (experiences of Desire and Law or signified). Below the bar (which Lacan retained between signifier and signified), we find the representational unities of primordial repression (*Urverdrängung*), which are unfathomable. Above it, we find the words and objects which refer to them, but whose source remains enigmatic. The point is that signifieds play above the bar of repression in the guise of secondary repression (*Unterdrückung*). As themes attached to language, they give meaning and intentionality to that abundance of signifiers which only take on the shape of a person's individuality in relation to the paucity of signifieds to which they refer. We are confronted with the paradox that, insofar as they remain opaque to consciousness, signifieds exist below the bar, but, because they give value or meaning to conscious life, they play above the bar. Lacan has once more forestalled any easy, binary splitting between the conscious and unconscious along lines of signifier versus signified. Signifiers give shape to signifieds, which, in turn, resurface to lend another kind of meaning to signifiers. Signifiers, then, hold priority at both ends of the psychic scale: (1) by creating signifieds and then by offering them a medium of expression, and (2) as a means of decoding the latter. But none of this makes much sense unless we view signifieds as those clusters of "self"-meaning related to the unconscious structures of Desire and Law.

Lacan's total enterprise undertook to show that unconscious language is the language of indestructible Desire—a meaning chain of dead signifiers (Sheridan, *Ecrits*, p. 167). In this schema the structuralist conception of language as an instrument of word-transmission-message breaks down, because the peculiar quality of the Lacanian *parole* is to make heard what it does not say. *Parole* seeks the echo of a response from an-other/Other(A), rather than "communication." In other words, a person's linguistic articulations are made in relation to a lack—not the lack of existentialist philosophy or a real lack in the order of need—but the lack which Lacan described as Desire. The Lacanian picture of language reduces its informational, grammatical functions to the tip of a massive iceberg.

In Seminar Three Lacan held the function of the signifier to be threefold: (1) to fasten down or label an experience or affect, (2) to polarize or create meanings through opposition, and (3) to group meanings in bundles or create signifieds (p. 328). Desire is originally joined to the signifier as pure symbol in a kind of prethought "thought" during the mirror stage: the *moi* evolves as corporal energy joined to mental representation. In his essay "On Language and the Body," Paul Henry argues that—in Lacanian terms—thought is a proleptic mental action that precedes speech and is attached to the signifier as a trace; he claims that Lacan replaced Freud's concept of discharge (*Besetzung*) by action, making thought a proleptic, experimental action (*Talking Cure*, p. 76). (Usually translated into English as "cathexis," Freud's *Besetzung* is—in reading Lacan—better rendered by Stuart Schneiderman as "investment" [*Returning*, p. viii]). The proleptic investment of energy in a representation—the link of Desire to signifier as a trace—is a narcissistic action that aims at constancy, mastery of the body, and recognition. Henry's suggestion of proleptic thought might be better construed, then, as identificatory action or investment. This kind of thought persists throughout life in Imaginary relations, but is inseparable from Symbolic order thought proper, which can really only proceed by words.

The power of the Lacanian signifier is such that humans are the "material" of language, the impact of words resonating in them beyond anything conceived by a psychology of ideas or of consciousness. We know that Lacan gives this God-like power to spoken language because of its permanent proximity to an unconscious discourse. But Lacan's decentering of the subject bears no resemblance to Saussure's arbitrary polyvalent meaning system with its lack of center, nor to Derrida's idea of a loss of center. Derrida proposed that systems lack a true center or fixed point, although any system is itself a place of autonomy and interchangeability permitted by an "internal freeplay" (Derrida's term for a center related only to that system). For Derrida, any myth of reference is privileged only by that system, and not by any other reality.[24] By privileging unconscious *parole* over *langue*, Desire over reason, the signifier over the signified, and the Other over the *je*, Lacan attempted to demolish the common notion that any system can be complete within itself or find all points of reference therein. He used the Real of psychic pain and various material and human phenomena to argue that "signs" use people and thus have a mental—as well as linguistic—character.

One of Lacan's most convincing arguments for a functioning of the signifier beyond language and system lies in his theory that the *tu* constitutes a signifier. But unlike other theories of linguistic address, Lacan's *tu* is not spoken to for the purpose of communication per se. Although a Lacanian signifier always signifies something for someone, this idea should not be confused with the "signal" emitter of communications theory. The communication systems theoretician Gregory Bateson argued that the primary function of language as communication is to establish relationships. This is achieved by the report-command aspect of any statement. Failure to communicate derives from an overload of information and a resultant jamming of the evocative circuit between persons.[25] In this sense, punctuation within a communicational circuit is arbitrary. By contrast, the Lacanian signifier can exist as a symbol or signify nothing informative or even evocative. Any signifier can exist simply as a way of affirming one's presence to the Other (as in dreams or psychosis) and, in this sense, has no relationship to a temporal external reality. But once the signifier engages itself vis-à-vis an-other—a *tu* (you)—the Imaginary circuit is necessarily put into motion. Miscommunications and misunderstandings occur continually and cannot be reduced merely to linguistic polyvalence or information overload. Communication theory belongs to the philosophical tradition that views man as rational, unified, and "well-meaning." Lacan shows the area of human address to be Imaginary terrain, that of narcissistic "truth" displayed on a linguistic field.

The human tendency is to want to objectify the other to make sense of the prototypical *tu* within one's own "self"-myth system and thereby to stabilize the ambiguities and miscommunications which characterize human interaction. But the independent other or *tu* exists as a reminder of the difficulty of such endeavor. Lacan shows that "communication" systems work best on paper. *Tu*, said Lacan, is the fishhook (*hameçon*) of the other in the wave of meaning. *Tu* has no univocal value as a signifier, then, and keeps people from making a Real thing out of their abstract objectivizations of others. *Tu*—an undetermined signifier—serves as a point of psychic punctuation by which we try to fix the other in a point of meaning ("tu es celui qui . . ."). In the interior of our own intrasubjective discourse, the *tu* supports something comparable to our own *moi* ideal ego while not being it. Instead, the *tu* signifies our myth of the other (*Séminaire* III, pp. 337–38). Since the relationship of *moi* and *toi* is one of Imaginary exclusion or confusion (that is, we cannot readily know who the other really is or how the other truly receives us), any address to the *tu* is an invocation of our own Other(A); an effort to learn what one does not know about oneself (*Séminaire* III, pp. 342–43). The difficulty of the *moi/toi* relation (with its implicit narcissistic and aggressive fusions) forces upon Symbolic order dealings what Lacan has called the "general notion of the other"—a notion marked by "normal distance." Lacan therefore concluded that the basic reason people "communicate" is not really to secure feedback or for the effect of a message's content, but for the action itself, the goal being love and recognition. The other is supposed to take cognizance of the act of a message being sent. Put another way, *parole* is more important than *langue*; communication falls on the side of evocation and invocation of our own "self"-systems, rather than on the side of information.

Among the critics of Lacan's use of linguistics are the linguist

Georges Mounin and the semiologist Eugen Bär. Mounin concludes that Lacan's understanding of Saussure is always wrong, unspecific, and equivocal.[26] Bär maintains that, even though Lacan has evolved interesting homeomorphisms between linguistic structures and sociopsychological states and processes, he has failed to prove a strict correspondence between linguistic and psychological data.[27] Mounin does not see that Lacan has purposely subverted Saussure's sign in order to make clear the latter's epistemological cul de sac. At the same time, Lacan extended Saussure's structural concept of how meaning is made by oppositions. Neither Mounin or Bär shows any grasp of the quadrilateral structure of the Lacanian subject nor of Lacan's idea of the intersubjective and radical Otherness of the unconscious. It is hardly surprising, therefore, that Bär falls back on a priori linguistic and logical "mechanisms" as the source of meaning, thereby remaining faithful both to Piaget and Chomsky ("Understanding Lacan," p. 492). Lacan was only a mythmaker, writes Bär. There is no unconscious, he concludes, only the occasional linguistic "traffic jam" which causes verbal slips or memory lapses. Bär thus proves himself a faithful adherent of communication systems theory as well ("Understanding Lacan," p. 499). It is paradoxical that Bär should accuse Lacan of being careless and confused when, in fact, Lacan's careful attention to detail and his painstaking elaborations of a formal structuration of the unconscious make it possible to support any aspect of his thought by randomly choosing from any text and from any point in chronological time. The consistency of Lacan's epistemology has all the aesthetic beauty of a mathematical theory or the cantos of Dante.

Lacan never claimed to be a linguist. His Fregean theory of the flight (*glissement*) of the signified, furthermore, is a linguistically meaningless concept. Having discovered that the unconscious "thinks" by words and sounds and is structured by the same kinds of laws as is concrete language and that these phenomena affect normal language use, Lacan proposed that elusive signifieds—unconscious truths—give themselves up to incessant individual variations by clustering around certain words, sounds, or themes, depending on the series of signifiers under which they fall (*Séminaire* XI, p. 189). Although signifieds are a first plane on which to analyze a subject, the signifier ought, however, to remain the guide element in analysis (*Séminaire* III, p. 250). Signifiers have the virtue of being autonomous, i.e., they have their own laws which function identically whether the signifier is working synchronically in concrete language or diachronically in unconscious language. In addition to the law of articulation, signifiers are marked by the law of ambiguity (polyvalence of language); the law of meaning created by opposition of one element to another; and the law of possessing a Real dimension (no visual symbols stand behind semantemes) (*Séminaire* III, pp. 222–23). But since Saussure was not burdened with problems of "truth" or mind structure, he did not really question how meaning occurred after a concept and sound were wed in the sign.

For Lacan, the existence of the sign as a unit of linguistic meaning was only the beginning of the problematics of the mind. Insofar as Lacan's signifier can itself only "mean" in opposition to another signifier, whose existence the first signifier necessarily infers, meaning only occurs within a chain of signifers. The meaning of the chain is determined by the relation of the signifiers to each other (S-S-S-S)/S, and by their following the specific laws of metaphor and metonymy (*Ecrits*, 1966, p. 303; *Séminaire* I, p. 272). By adding metaphor and metonymy to the structure of meaning, Lacan showed that oppositions only come to "mean" in a wider context than Saussure's. A chain of opposed sounds means nothing per se (like baby gibberish). In building up the subject, opposed sounds take on meaning solely in relation to mirror-stage and Oedipal effects. Each stage joins symbol to sound, and sound symbol to the processes of substitution (metaphor and condensation) and contiguity (metonymy and displacement). The content of meaning evolved during childhood is based, therefore, on these structural underpinnings. In adult life the functional laws of Desire (metaphor and metonymy) deflect the linear, linguistic equivalences implied by Saussure and lead mind and identity in search of meaning through the substitutive detours of repression. James Glogowski has expressed these two relations of the signifier to meaning as structural (transformational) in the matrices of synchrony and diachrony, and syntactic (ordered) in its metaphorical and metonymical operations.[28] In these ways, Lacan said, even if language does not fulfill all functions, it structures everything concerning relations between human beings (Sheridan, *Ecrits*, p. 255).

But if the signifier occurs in both conscious and unconscious registers (*Niederschriften*), what need had Lacan for the signified? As previously stated, Lacan proposed the signified as unconscious meaning that does not "hear" or think itself and is, therefore, on the side of the *moi* and secondary repression as well: the unities or units formed by the signifier and its effects. An infant is subjugated to language, which imposes itself in a synchronic and vocal dimension through each successive specular identification. Language therefore "defines" symbols and gives the subject several voices, making the idea of a unified and unifying perceiver equivocal (Sheridan, *Ecrits*, pp. 180–81). These several voices make up an unconscious chain of signifiers that is repeated somewhere, and later interferes diachronically in the gaps that effective discourse offers the subject and in the thought that informs ordinary language (Sheridan, *Ecrits*, p. 297). While the signified points to the particular, the universal character of the signifier provides the analyst with a way to regulate the relationship between the subject and the world (Schneiderman, *Returning*, p. 142). If a person can come to see what has structured his mind and identity in Other(A) language, then his or her life can emerge in "truth"; otherwise "truth" is denied (Sheridan, *Ecrits*, p. 166). But "truth" can never be wholly fixed in a stable manner because of the disunity inherent in the subject and in language: a situation Lacan described as "the manifest disorder in the human organism's pseudototality" (Sheridan, *Ecrits*, pp. 126–27).

Language is an algorithm, Lacan said, an art of calculating in psychic terms. People use language to signify something for someone, thereby establishing the intrinsic intentionality of discourse. This signaling function of intentionality shows up in dreams, as well as in conversation. Freud originally viewed the dream as an enigma to be interpreted literally, and word by word. He demonstrated that dream pictures often present punning representations of verbal statements. Lacan supplied the insight that dream "thoughts" exist in chains of meaning, although not in any directly proportional relationship with a particular meaning. Instead, dream associations are often determined by sound similarities that dramatize the play of signifiers in the Other(A), making the dream an example of the psychopathology of everyday life (its meaning composed by the same laws as in the structure of jokes, symptom formation, lapses, and so on). But these "meanings" do not occur in isolation. The dream has the structure of a form of writing, Lacan said, and tells a story where all the elements are related. The latter enter the topological order of Imaginary relations and "mean" in relation to the Other's Desire, thus revealing both the diachronic function of language in the unconscious, as well as its synchronic role in structuring (*Séminaire* II, p. 199).

By subverting the by-now familiar linguistic idea of cognitive coherence between form and meaning—Saussure's *tout se tient*—Lacan might appear to have put himself in step with Chomsky's idea of a "transformational" grammar of relationships. We remember that Lacan defined "structure" as that which works by transformations via relationships. But Lacanian signifiers and signifieds, unlike

Chomsky's deep and surface structures, do not evolve in any neat hierarchy from universal (deep or unconscious) to personal and creative (surface or conscious) structures. Instead, the diachronic discourse of signifieds works proleptically upon spoken language and is not, therefore, hidden. In "The Freudian Thing" (1955) Lacan described signifieds as a concretely pronounced set of discourses that react historically on concrete language (Sheridan, *Ecrits*, pp. 126–27). Lemaire writes that, even though signifieds are generally understood by others, they are not precisely situated anywhere in the signifying chain (free flow of meaning) (Lemaire, *Lacan*, p. 38). The floating character of signifieds as well as the dynamic challenge to the *moi* posed by the *tu* (seen as a signifier) are of a piece with Lacan's claim that a subject is not simply a subject for another subject—a static two-body psychology—but represents himself as a subject for the other who is a signifier (both in his fantasy and in a social context). Since no element alone in a signifying chain conveys the full meaning of which a chain is capable, Lacan has described the human subject as nothing other than something which glides in a chain of signifiers. The subject, moreover, is the effect of one or more of the key signifiers in his or her unconscious (*Séminaire* XX, p. 48).

In adult life subjects constantly reconstitute their identities within a synchronic, cultural signifying context—a Symbolic order—to secure themselves a fixed value in terms of their Imaginary "self"-fables. A subject represents him- or herself to an-other person as signifying something cultural (a title, a profession) within a given Symbolic order, or something more basic and personal in terms of his or her own narcissism, and tries to confirm the merit of the Symbolic and Imaginary aspects of identity in light of Real events. When a subject's Imaginary ideal is confirmed by Symbolic labels and approved by Real events, the accompanying feeling is one of wholeness or *jouissance*. But the ever-jostling, power-bent signifying chain of society continually threatens the constancy and fixity of any subject's Imaginary, Symbolic, and Real constellation of joy. Compared with the Lacanian framework, cybernetics and information theory seem simplistic approaches to language. Indeed, Lacan's idea that the "messages" emitted to the other (from and to the Other) makes sense of what we all "know": that language is used daily to enforce protocol, diplomacy, assumptions, and mystification in an effort to cope with the realities of ambition, Desire, and misunderstanding—realities that encircle what we usually call "communication."

Lacan's formula *Il y a de l'Un* (see p. 183) represents the final in-

separability of the personal psychic order from the linguistic and sociocultural one. He clearly does not intend to suggest a neo-Platonic
or monistic One-ness, however, nor the gnosticism of which Bär has
accused him. Nor does he suggest by this formula that the Symbolic
order recuperates the Imaginary and the Real. Far from recuperating
the other orders, the Symbolic attests to the presence of unassimilable orders which, nonetheless, enter into being. And yet readers
who do not grasp the breadth of Lacan's thought have charged him
with an "ideological" commitment to the primacy of the signifier
and symbol. As Frederic Jameson has pointed out, Lacan problematizes the gaps and contradictions within the Symbolic order; he
does not reify them.[29] In Seminar Eleven Lacan explained the overlap
of the different orders in relation to the signifier. The first of such
occurrences takes place when a unary signifier—which I take to be
the representational material (primary and secondary unities) of the
prespecular and specular stages—surges up to form the primordial
Other(A) by representing the preverbal Desiring subject for another
signifier, the binary one (p. 199). In other words, unary signifiers are
on the side of primary repression. Castration can be equated with
the binary signifier that divides the subject between "natural" and
referential parts and makes it possible to give meaning to being by
language. While linguists, philosophers, literary critics, and others
generally bypass the structure of the signifier in their search for
meaning (either in essence or in some metasystem), Lacan derives
the human subject's signifying dependency on social meaning from
the Real effects of Castration (separation). In this sense, the binary
signifier is on the side of secondary repression. But the structure of
the signifier, whose effect causes psychic division, is linguistic (articulation, meaning made by opposition, ambiguity, and so on). The
binary signifier is, thus, causative of alienation, lack, and Desire, and
constitutes the focal point of repression.

In Seminar Twenty Lacan again took up the problem of the overlap
of the orders using the following diagram (pp. 47–49).

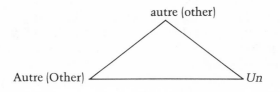

No two of these terms taken together can equal the third (or other)
term. The Symbolic One of the signifiers, the *Un* (unary or primary

symbols; binary signifiers or language), as well as the Imaginary other of transference, does not equal the Real Other(A), which is, by definition, an absence or hole. The Symbolic *Un* plus the Other(A) cannot anticipate the unpredictable reactions of the other (or *tu*) and, consequently, preclude the behaviorist reduction of being to some mechanical puppetry. Finally, the other plus the Other(A) certainly do not equal the Symbolic order, for their asymmetrical circuit lies in the Imaginary and the Real, which disrupt the Symbolic order, and falsely equates their certainties with a unity in mind and "self."

Lacan's concept of the One of the signifier denotes the Symbolic order connection between normal language and Other(A) signifiers. The *Wahrnehmungszeichen* that constitute the Other(A) make concrete language the object of a primitive linguistics (*lalangue* or *la dite maternelle*) which furnishes only the basic message (*chiffre*) of meaning. I interpret this to refer to the breast, excrement, the gaze, the voice, and the meaningful effects of pre-mirror and mirror structures. The result is a personal "sense" (*sens*), which stands behind language and relationship as well (*Télévision*, pp. 21, 24). Lacan thus defined *Un* (*les uns*) as the elementary signifiers incarnated in *lalangue* (*Séminaire* XX, p. 25). The link between the Other(A) and the *Un* is what he calls the *trait unaire* (adjective, *unien*), a *trait d'union* ("hyphen") being that which joins one thing to another. The original "links" are, of course, the primordial causes of Desire ("letters," *stoicheia*, or unary signifiers) which connect the infant to the binary Symbolic order by sound, symbol, or Real experience that form the *je* as subject of demand, not of the Other(A) (*Séminaire* XX, p. 114). Lacan shows this in the following graph:

One half of the graph represents the unary signifiers of Desire and the other half the binary signifiers (representing of representations) which join the two (*Séminaire* XX, p. 117–18). While the unary signifier acts as an Imaginary agent of mirror-stage primary meaning and binding, the binary signifier is a postspecular phenomenon, an effect of language, which splits the subject in two and, as such, is the agent of fading in the subject (*Séminaire* XI, p. 199). The unary signifier is on the side of Eros; images; *jouissance*; the pleasure principle; symbiosis; the Real; while the binary signifier is on the side of Thanatos; the *plus-de-jouir* (Desire cum lack); anxiety; words; the reality principle, unconscious truth.

The unary signifer resides on the mother or natural side of being. The binary signifier acts ("invests") on the representing-of-a-representation side of perception: the slope of the Name-of-the-Father. This *Vorstellungsrepräsentanz* is verbal/visual representation of an unconscious subject which takes primordial references as a starting point. Although the *Vorstellungsrepräsentanz* is repressed (*Urverdrängt*), it is the point of attraction (*Anziehung*) for all later secondary repression (*das Unterdrückte*) *(Séminaire* XI, p. 199). Lacan said, therefore, that the *Un* functions through unary and binary signifiers to make a connection between the Other(A), which "thinks" or operates speech, and what is thought (the Symbolic order of concrete language) (*Séminaire* XX, p. 116). The Other(A) infers knots in the Symbolic order, not by adding to it, however, but by subtracting from it: the *Un*-minus or S (Ⱥ). In reference to his theory that the unconscious can count, it should be recalled that, according to Lacan, there is an affair of life and death between numbers 1 and 2. The unary signifier conditions the illusion of "self"-unity (mirror stage) and the binary one enforces division and loss (Oedipal effect) (*Séminaire* XI, p. 199). This "affair" is subsequently played out in language and conscious life around substantive issues (mind), Imaginary fantasies, Symbolic order ideologies, and Real objects of Desire.

Lacan's concept of unary and binary signifiers provides a basis for his theory of the elaboration of *lalangue*—itself not made for communication—but which implies a source of unutterable "knowledge" in being, a tacit referent of concrete language (*Séminaire* XX, p. 25). In an article written in 1980 Jacques-Alain Miller wrote that Lacan's long theoretical construction ended up with four letters: S_1, S_2, Ⱥ, a (cf. *Séminaire* XX, p. 21). S_1 and S_2 refer to the signifying chain whose articulation is reducible to the ordered pair of an Imaginary unary and Symbolic binary signifier. The Ⱥ designates the subject who is the effect of the interplay, and *objet a* is the product. In this sense the subject is an interval or a cut in such structuring, not a being or an identity.[30] In 1975 Lacan made a distinction between the One of the signifier and the One of meaning. The One of meaning is the being specified by the unconscious inasmuch as it exists in discord to the body which is on the slope of the Real. Although the unconscious determines the subject as being by speaking, the unconscious remains discordant to being and body, which are crossed through with that metonymy by which Lacan supports desire in so far as it is endlessly impossible to speak as such. In that unary signifiers are linked to the unsayable objects that cause Desire, and while binary signifiers are joined to the creation of Desire as fading and lack—that which drives human subjects to seek substitute objects—the One of meaning or being appears to refer to the Imaginary "identity" circuit of the other (and the *moi*), to believed sets of self-descriptions. Lacan called the Other(A) a dual entry matrix, the other constituting one of its entries, and the *petit a* the other one.[31]

One way of decoding the presence of Other(A) discourse in concrete language is by ascertaining the points at which signifieds play on the signifiers of ordinary meaning. We know that signifieds denote global meaning on the slope of narcissism, sexual identity, Desire, and *jouissance* (*Séminaire* XX, p. 27). Signifieds reside also on the Imaginary slope of transference, affect, intuition, and reality perception. Although signifieds constitute the meaning a person gives the world, they obscure the neutral signifiers of ordinary language, which seeks to objectify signifieds. In his "Discours de Rome," Lacan described signifieds as the effects of symbolization which are, above all, historical scars—forgotten or undone—but recalled in acts and said elsewhere (that is, displaced in secondary repression) (Sheridan, *Ecrits*, p. 52). So viewed, signifieds are symptoms or metaphors, that is, they substitute for something else. Signifieds "mean" diachronically. They punctuate the synchronic movement of concrete language by an anticipatory/retroactive diacritics. Signifieds link being to language in a marriage of mind and "self" and are to be deciphered in light of repetitions, regressions, resistance, and repression (Desire).

Since signifieds are rarely fixed to linguistic signifiers in any direct relationship, they can only ever be rejoined to language through the mediation of a whole body of normal signifiers, which guarantee the signified "theme" an expression of coherence. This phenomenon explains why individuals only recognize meaning in global or block terms, as a "whole" or ensemble. But even though Symbolic order language gives a consistency to signifieds, it does not subsume them, for such secondary meanings never resolve themselves into pure indications of the Real; they refer to yet another meaning all the way back to the binary signifier of primordial fading and Castration (*Ecrits*, I, p. 224). Language is an open and porous system, then, which only seems to be closed. The systematic unity of secondary meaning serves as camouflage to the humble fact that individual words strung together compose mind and being as a primary meaning. This is for the purpose of conveying, seeking, protecting, and denying the "truth" that mind is anchored by unconscious knowledge, which is itself a verbal constellation. Concrete language is, therefore, always metaphorical, always standing for something else: primary objects of Desire; the split in the subject; Other(A) "messages" (*Séminaire* I, p. 262).

Although signifiers proliferate to infinity—sound and concept combinations being infinite—each individual is characterized by only a few signifieds. And these do not decompose, although they can go through innumerable variations and even be repressed in psychosis. There is an equivalence between these signifieds, viewed as markers along the path of "the ideology of personality," and the several egos or voices that constitute the *moi*. In contrast to signifiers, signifieds appear substantive in their elaborate form (a "content" or story of self). By hypothesizing the signified as a mode of insistence of the unconscious in the conscious realm, Lacan proposed that unconscious signifiers—in bundles or groups—do not remain static and dead history. "Key signifiers" around which unconscious meaning is organized into signifieds concern the six unconscious numbers: relationships of the subject toward Desire, knowledge, and power. At the level of secondary repression (*Unterdrückung*), signifieds give silent testimony to the mysterious signifiers that direct a person's future. The "return of the repressed" is the repressed itself. Signifieds thus use a diachronic route to reify personality through anticipation (Imaginary) and retroaction (Real) of "self"-meaning, playing on and in the Symbolic.

If one were to ideologize Lacan's concept of signifieds, however, and make them the basis of an analysis—psychoanalytic or literary—the result would simply be another variation of contemporary ego psychology. The signified (*énoncé, parole,* syntagma, diachrony) is psychically weak by comparison with the signifier (*énonciation, langue,* paradigm, synchrony), even though its appeal lies in its substantive character, for its mythic content lends a continuity to the subject. Not only did the signifier build up signifieds in the first place, but also concrete language has the power to transform—to rewrite—the signifieds of an unconscious text as well. New cultural signifieds can also be created. In "The agency of the letter in the unconscious or reason since Freud" (1957), Lacan used the example of Erasmus's introduction of the exegetical method (which ended the neo-Scholastic, speculative approach to knowledge) to show that "the slightest alteration in the relation between man and the signifier . . . changes the whole course of history by modifying the moorings that anchor his being" (Sheridan, *Ecrits*, p. 174). While signifieds elaborate *moi* fictions through *je* speech, their dialectical point of reference is the Other(A). The analyst faces a challenging paradox. Even though the signified is weak by comparison with the signifier, the synchronic flow of normal words, which renders concrete language a moment or rhythm, and not a duration, also makes the greater psychic agent (the signifier) more hidden than the diachronic meaning of signifieds (Sheridan, *Ecrits*, p. 304). Although signifieds impose a certain fixity or historical necessity of personality on psychic evolution, therefore, reminding us that both Georg Hegel and Freud concluded that "what is" derives from historical necessity, Lacan isolated signifiers to show that the "fate" of signifieds is variable. He thereby broadened the scope of human potential response beyond the influences of the historical Real and beyond any paradigmatic determination of personality as well.

In seeking a person's unconscious truth, the analyst must not be trapped into taking signifieds exactly as presented by the analysand. This error would be tantamount to believing that *moi* narcissism is the deepest layer of personality, rather than the fragments which hold together a sense of "self" in repeated fixations. But even these meaning ensembles are composed of *Unsinn* (isolated signifiers) when the normal, interpersonal transference relationship wanes in a psychosis. The Lacanian analyst is, in consequence, alerted to those joins or "anchoring points" (*points de capiton*, i.e., upholstery studs or sofa buttons) where signifieds hook on to the signifiers of ordinary language. The semi-orphaned scholar to whom we referred in Chapter 2 (see p. 114) used the words "fake" and "real" with a vehemence of conviction and frequency that should alert any analyst to their signifying importance. The message in his Other(A) discourse showed evident ambiguity surrounding the symbol (signifier) for father. "Anchoring points" reveal the unconscious dominance of the "letter" ("namely the essentially localized structure of the signifier") in the dramatic transformation that language can effect in a person (Sheridan, *Ecrits*, p. 153). Anchoring points are, therefore, the knots which anticipatorily tie meaning down through a diachronic function of the signified. But the analyst has no easy task in ascertaining these points of join between two different kinds of discourse.

From a psychoanalytic point of view, synchronic and diachronic meanings hook themselves together at a third point outside the sentence or discourse, where the receiver of a message gets a second meaning (the *énoncé*) after the literal meaning (the *énonciation*), and sends this second meaning back to the sender in inverted form.

This message refracts the unconscious. Benveniste thought that the grammatical sentence as such had no importance for linguists. Disagreeing with him, Lacan thought the sentence might offer a way to define "meaning" as the difference between *parole* and *langue* (*Séminaire* I, p. 272). Lacan viewed the sentence as a perfect model of the kind of anticipatory/retroactive combination which makes up the "self" as a unit of narcissistic meaning. A sentence is composed of synchronic elements which create a flow of signifying units. But the diachronic function can be found in the sentence as well. Lacan then emphasized the proleptic elements in a sentence, each term being anticipated in the construction of the others. Only with a last term, however, is the suspense resolved, the meaning of the sentence made complete. Its meaning is inversely sealed, therefore, by the retroactive effect it produces on the anticipatory terms that came first (Sheridan, *Ecrits*, p. 303). This phenomenon is familiar enough when we consider how often individuals finish the sentences of others while the other is still speaking (be it aloud or to themselves). They are sometimes surprised that the ending is not the one they had predicted. Exclamations of "Oh, *that's* what you meant" form part of the linguistic psychopathology of everyday life.

Literal, linguistic meaning contains signifiers and information or *langue*. The second or evocative meaning is the "invisible" effect of *parole*, punctuating the endless movement of words through anchoring points that reside in a recurrent spiral of unconscious meaning through conscious language. Any individual's overall discourse develops a set of unique second meanings—signifieds—which do not inhere in concrete phonemes, semantics, syntax, or any other linguistic unit. A Lacanian analyst should look beyond the associative unity of signifieds and of reconstructed *moi* memories to provoke or await an anchoring point in the appearance of seemingly disembodied thoughts. These are voices and signifiers that anchor identity in the Other(A), but that are usually hidden by the game of denial, repression, and the pretense of a univocal discourse. Indeed, being is discordant with "truth." The unconscious sends out homophonic reverberations; fragments of word or sound; brief sentences or phrases which summarize complex fixations. Minor disorientations or ticks in normal language also "signal" Other(A) messages. Although such effects seem minimal by comparison with the elegance of philosophical (and other) systems of thought, Lacan's genius was to show that these perturbations throw the concept of system itself into doubt. Symbolic systems build up into a state of near perfection and then decompose, as the Real and Imaginary continually shift Symbolic order explanations and information. The Real signifiers in the Other(A), by contrast, do not decompose. Intellectual systems are unstable and die, but the unconscious system is a conservative ecology of diachronic pieces.

As we know, the Saussurean sign constitutes meaning not by a relation between sign (the thing) and referent (reality of the world), but by a relation between the signifier and signified which is interior to language. As such, meaning is *purely* a function of the difference that distinguishes one signifier from another, the value of signifier and signified being that of a differential. In Seminar Twenty Lacan said that this Saussurean sign would be located on the slope of his own signified but disassociated from his concept of the signifier. Although some commentators have incorrectly equated the Lacanian signifier with the Saussurean sign, Lacan's relocation of the sign on the subjective slope resolves an impasse in Saussure's own thought: the notion that meaning is a static linguistic production. The Saussurean sign is not a sign of something, Lacan said, but the "sign" of an *effect* caused by the signifier (articulated speech) (*Séminaire* XX, p. 48). As such, this sign is not meaning itself, but a symbol of meaning. In like manner, the Lacanian signified is an effect of signifiers which remain unconscious. For this reason, Lacan described the signified as that continuum in a concrete discourse over which the subject (locked in the ever-moving, synchronic rhythm of words) holds no sway; he or she cannot apprehend the constant determinants underlying his or her own conscious discourse (Sheridan, *Ecrits*, p. 49).

Insofar as signifieds are elusive—their *raison d'être* beyond the bar of consciousness—Lacan's claims become comprehensible: any sound psychoanalytic theory (and practice) must base itself on the Symbolic order of signifiers, symbols, and cultural meanings, rather than on the Imaginary slope of signifieds, signs, and personal memories. The complexity of such an enterprise stems from the fact that the operations of consciousness are largely denied to itself. As a result, unearthed fantasies and observable symptoms are perhaps the most deceptive detours of all, leading away from unconscious truth, yet paradoxically pointing at it when they are seen as enigmas to be decoded. The flow of language and fusions of transference obscure the identificatory "investments" and asymmetrical Other(A) messages which point to the alien and dialectical nature of being. Illusions, confusions, and ambiguities in "communication" are caused by the inert character of the *moi* and the intrusions of an-Other's Desire in a subject's supposed autonomy.

Lacan maintained that both naive opinion and academic investigation employed all available tools to avoid seeing that the "truth" of being resides in the literal, the superficial, and the humble: in the realities of prematuration, psychic symbiosis, separation, and in the compensatory myths, substitutions, and intentionalities that cluster around Desire (Sheridan, *Ecrits*, pp. 20, 34). Lacan's conceptualization of a thinking and speaking unconscious means that dreams, neurotic symptoms, anxiety, behavior or action, relationship dynamics, the evocative nature of language, and the plurality of interpretation or of empirical findings are all interrelated. The limitations of the human subject indicate a poverty and rigidity in man's nature— reducible to structuring influences of the mirror-stage and Oedipal effects—which push individuals to keep the unconscious silent. Language itself functions as the best of all defenses against unconscious "truth."

Due to his deflection of language study away from the linguistic sign, Lacan (like Jean Baudrillard) turned many researchers against the theories generated by Saussure's "structuralism" (later resurrected as semiotics). In an essay entitled "Requiem pour les media," Baudrillard attacked the discipline of communications theory (which he thinks has arisen in Europe and the United States since World War II as an ideological support for a bourgeois political economy).[32] Baudrillard cites Jakobson as responsible for formalizing communications theory in a "model" which aims to determine the different hierarchical order of functions around which all other linguistic functions are arrayed. This is done by studying the "message" that appears as an autonomous artifact. He faults Jakobson for excluding reciprocity.[33] By focusing on the message and the sender, and by omitting the temporal and spatial parameters of communication, Jakobson typifies for Baudrillard the reductionist models required by structuralist and communications theories.

Lacan's epistemology is, in and of itself, a refutation of structuralist and communications theories. In Seminar Twenty he said repeatedly that he did not like semiotics (the science of communications systems). Semiotic models cannot account for dream work, the work of interpretation, the origins of literature, nor for the constitution of the signifying chain (which originates for Lacan in the unconscious). The reason for the inadequacies of semiotic studies, in Lacan's view, lies in the fact that meaning is not anchored (as semioticians suppose) at the level of stylistic figures or of sign and message. Meaning glides perpetually at the surface of language in a constant "translation" of the elements that constitute it in terms of

Desire. At the level of origins or causality, the anchors of meaning are always to be found in the two structural axes of unconscious Desire and Law.

Metaphor and Metonymy

Early in his career, Lacan thought that unconscious mechanisms used all kinds of tropes: periphrasis, hyperbaton, ellipsis, suspension, anticipation, retraction, negation, digression, or irony (*Ecrits*, 1966, p. 50). He noted that these are the figures of rhetorical style, just as catachresis, litotes, antonomasia, and hypotyposis are the tropes that seem to correspond to unconscious mechanisms of defense. In light of these similarities, Lacan queried in "Agency of the letter in the unconscious" whether one can really see the figures of rhetoric as simple figures of speech, when the figures themselves are the active principle of the rhetoric of discourse uttered in analysis (*Ecrits*, 1966, p. 169). By attempting a theory of the rhetoric of the unconscious and eventually a grammar of rhetoric, Lacan early strove to detach the tropes from the unconscious in order to "say" the unconscious.[34] But his dream of grammaticalizing or formalizing rhetoric became an impossibility when he realized that there is no privileged point of distance from language within language; no metalanguage; no Other of the Other.[35] Leaving behind the stylistic devices of his early interest, Lacan began to look at the laws governing the syntactic organization of the sentence surface in an effort to delineate a logic of the signifier (Lemaire, *Lacan*, p. 42). This endeavor involved him in the elaboration of only two tropes: metaphor and metonymy. These exist at the surface of the functioning of language and, in Lacan's view, control the functions of meaning in the unconscious as well.

A general dictionary definition of metaphor is: "Gk. *metaphora*—transport; the means by which one transports the correct meaning of a word to another meaning, which is only agreeable with it by virtue of an implicit comparison" (*OED*). As early as 1725, Giambattista Vico elaborated the thesis that what today are mere metaphors in our speech had, in former ages, represented the terms in which men directly apprehended the world around them and so "made sense" of their experience (e.g., the *mouth* of a river or the *head* of a pin). In recent years Derrida has emphasized the age-old view of metaphor as a trope of resemblance: not simply between the Saussurean signifier and signified, but between what are already two signs, the one designating the other.[36] Other contemporary commentators on metaphor have studied the contextual opposition of literal and new meanings or the redescription of the unfamiliar in terms of the familiar. But essentially the dialectical structure of metaphor is seen as the source of its power to restructure perception. The surrealists of the early twentieth century took this property to the point of ideological and stylistic absurdity. Lacan's critique of the surrealist position—that any conjunction of two signifiers could constitute a metaphor if the images signified were disparate—is also an argument, as we shall see, against the various theories (Paul Ricoeur, Hans-Georg Gadamer, Derrida) that propose that metaphor alone operates the symbolic properties of the mind (Sheridan, *Ecrits*, pp. 156–57).

Although metaphor does, indeed, emerge from two signifiers (in Lacan's sense), this occurs within a signifying chain. One signifier is substituted in a Saussurean chain of signs, but the word or image substituted does not merely disappear on being transformed. It remains present (repressed or signified) by its metonymic connection to the chain of meaning itself (Sheridan, *Ecrits*, p. 157). The supplanted signifier, in other words, falls from the level of consciousness to the level of unconsciousness, where it acts as a kind of latent unconscious signifier grafted onto an unconscious chain of associations.[37] Such a signifier, having become unconscious, takes on an autonomous meaning, while retaining an indirect connection by dynamic repression to the conscious chain from which it was derived. It is clear from this reasoning why the surrealist project of creating a new, everyday metaphorical language of love and imagination (psychic liberation) was doomed to fail. No verbal metaphor can be completely liberated from the unconscious chain of meaning that anchors being—and speaking—in our conservative childhood messages organized around structural effects.

By taking the fundamental opposition between signifiers and signifieds (in Saussure's sense) as the point where the powers of language begin, Lacan hypothesized that these powers only take on their full meaning in relation to metaphor and metonymy. These latter operate conscious and unconscious signifying chains by a dynamic automatism. In the signifying chain the substitution of one term for another produces the effect of metaphor, while the combination of one term with another produces the effect of metonymy (Sheridan, *Ecrits*, p. 258). The linguistic double play of substitution and combination generates the Lacanian signified as an effect of the signifier (Sheridan, *Ecrits*, p. 285). His theory only makes sense if we understand that Lacan attributed a dual function to the signifier. The first is the familiar function of Saussurean linguistics: to make meaning through oppositions and differences between irreducible elements and thereby to create the ordinary language register of heterogeneity and synchronicity. This register offers the possibility of getting back to the source of "learned" language in a child (Lemaire, *Lacan*, p. 117). Once a signifier is attached to meaning within an unconscious chain of associations, however, it changes. In our unconscious, linguistic elements are tied to visual elements, to impressions and effects, as well as to an Imaginary identificatory logic whose meaning is to be found in prespecular experience and in representations correlated with the mirror stage and the Oedipal drama. This second function of the Lacanian signifier represents one of the French thinker's original contributions to psychoanalytic theory. The signifier also functions in a diachronic, personal (i.e., spatial and topological) register to reappear as misrecognized, enigmatic, unconscious meaning or displaced affect (*Affektrepräsentanz*) imposed on conscious life and daily discourse. These meanings reappear at the surface as linguistic resonances, reverberations, repetitions, reversals, and so on and in supralinguistic elements (signifieds) that give specificity to psychic structure.

The scope and originality of Lacan's connection of metaphor and metonymy to language and self will become clearer when we grasp: (1) how he used Freud to reinterpret Jakobson, and (2) reformulated Jakobson to transcend impasses in both Freud and Jakobson. Jakobson's hypothesis that metaphor and metonymy were the two great axes of poetic language originated in Saussure's theory that the two fundamental modes of arrangement of the linguistic sign were selection and substitution of units based on similarity (Jakobson's metaphor); and combinations of units into units of higher complexity (Jakobson's metonymy).[38] In his essay "Lacan and Language: An Overview," the psychologist John P. Muller recalls that Jakobson's linguistic units refer to the basic features of the phonemes and the selection and combination of phonemes in forming words, phrases, and sentences.[39] We remember that Lacan, too, liked the idea of an unconscious phonemic chain, which differed nonetheless from the heterogeneous use of phonemes in concrete language. Before Jakobson, however, the implications of metaphor and metonymy were already present in Saussure's conception, as Martin Thom points out in his essay "The Unconscious Structured as a Language." Combination meant that each sign, made up of constituent parts—signifier and signified for Saussure and phonemes for Jakobson—could only occur with other signs. And selection meant that one must choose certain signs from a set, and this implied the possibility that another sign might be substituted for the one selected out (*Talking Cure*, p. 4).

Jakobson's merit was to recognize these laws as the rhetorical, poetic tropes of metaphor and metonymy. And despite the reductionist errors committed by Jakobson in his forcing regular patterns on language where they really do not apply, Lacan lauded Jakobson's work on metaphor and metonymy, even though Lacan claimed that before Saussure Freud had foreseen the two great axes of language in his *Interpretation of Dreams*, where he elaborated the theory that condensation and displacement maneuver unconscious material in dreams, jokes, and symptoms (Sheridan, *Ecrits*, pp. 148, 156). Moreover, Freud's idea of condensation (*Verdichtung*) also resolved itself into *Dichtung* (poetry), anticipating by fifty years Jakobson's later attribution of poetic language to metaphor (and metonymy).[40] In his Seminar Four ("La relation d'objet," 1956–57), Lacan laid conceptual groundwork to show that the primary-process work of condensation and displacement not only proceeds analagously to secondary-process metaphor and metonymy—the famous statement that the unconscious is structured *like* a language—but also that the same dynamic functions operate "self" as well. In these circumstances no final separation of mind and dream, or language and fantasy, is possible. Although spoken language works by a heterogeneous, differential Symbolic logic and the *moi* by a homogeneous, fusional Imaginary logic, the meanings of each system are formed by substitution, associational similarity, and combination. These functions enabled Lacan to see the dynamic connection between primary- and secondary-process thought, as well as the means by which primary and secondary processes could merge. In addition to the similarity of function, Lacan valorized the materiality of the signifier both in conscious and unconscious realms. In his 1953 "Discours de Rome" Lacan urged that analysts approach the Freudian corpus through its unconscious resonances that are set into motion more by sound than by meaning. Lacan then gave an example of the primacy of homophony over etymology. More concerned with the signifier than the signified, the unconscious may well take a phrase such as *feu mon père* (my late father) to mean that my father was the fire of God (*le feu de Dieu*), or even that I am ordering my father to be shot (*feu* also implying a command to shoot).[41] Muller concludes that the unconscious—structured *like* a language—consists of the interplay of phonemes, thus being neither instinctual nor primordial, and knowing nothing more about the elementary than the elements of the signifier (Muller, "Lacan and Language," pp. 4–5; Sheridan, *Ecrits*, p. 170).

We know that Freud equated the work of the unconscious with fantasy, pleasure, and primary-process thought and opposed these to the secondary-process thought of consciousness, reason, and reality. Freud, therefore, tied primary process to irrational instincts or drives. The compelling development of Lacan's thought here lies in his joining of metaphorical function to signifying representations. The functional properties of metaphor thereby move significantly closer to the dynamic roles of Desire and identificatory fusion in the structure of the human subject. For Lacan, metaphor structurally integrates disparate elements into a new meaning, but also has a dynamic representational function. The latter is a symbolic operation by which signifiers fill in the gap in being to create a repressed unconscious of associative meanings. That is, they substitute for the lack of innate representations in being. When names and labels are later placed on these primordial, "natural" representations, man is humanized metaphorically. Put another way, metaphor operates in the first eighteen months of life as a proleptic thought which derives its energy from metonymy: the infant's own incompleteness or prematuration. Piaget, it is true, defined intelligence as the use of behavior to overcome difficulties and, thus, a form of problem solving. He then equated intelligence with thought, which, in his view, emerged near the end of the second year of life.[42] I would suggest, however, that intelligence (understood as problem solving) begins at six months when the mirror-stage infant attempts to master its own corporal inadequacies and lack of motor coordination. When these efforts are finally successful (circa eighteen months), and the child begins to use language in a recognizable fashion, thought already has an anchor both in substance (symbolic metaphors) and in function (the substitutive, associational process). The dynamic referent to which language points, furthermore, is precisely the psychic material and mental energy derived from identifications and the Desire for recognition.

Freud saw no link between primary- and secondary-process functioning except in relation to the superego. Primary process was the result of censorship (forbidden sexual thoughts and impulses), the transposition or distortion (*Entstellung*) of "improper" thoughts by the condensation, displacement, and symbolization processes.[43] Primary-process effects showed up in dreams, fantasy, and jokes as efforts to repress the taboo element. Object and word presentations appeared in dreams, associated at an unknown level of similarity. The product of such complicity between words and things (images) was a compromise formation, which Freud called a condensation (*Verdichtung*). Latent or unconscious elements (with features in common) had fused together in a single manifest element—the condensation—which represented them all through overdetermination. In this way overdetermination allowed multiple interpretation, since it is built on an extensive latent or unconscious content by contrast with its laconic brevity. The other key operation which Freud found in the formation of dreams and jokes was displacement or "a veering off of meaning" (*Verschiebung*), itself a form of distortion. Freud described displacement in dreams as an "indirect representation" of both words and images that reveal the latent content. Objects or words of minor importance are selected by the censor to divert the unconscious through "substitution of a piece of symbolism, or an analogy, or something small" (Wilden, *LS*, pp. 109-10n 53). In Lacan's reconceptualization of Freudian *Verschiebung*, the substitutive elements are metaphorical. They evoke the unconscious, but do not reveal it. The significance of displacement is functional rather than substantive. The substitutive elements may, therefore, be central to the manifest content of a dream, but peripheral or even absent in regard to the unconscious (Thom, *Talking Cure*, pp. 3–4). Condensation—not displacement—is therefore the "nodal point" (*Knotenpunkt*) of a dream where, in Wilden's summary of Lacan, "the subject unbeknownst to himself seeks to 'make [the subject's life] make better sense' . . . the fundamental meaning [of the dream] being finally restored [in conscious life] by the putting into words of the images (the thing presentations)" (*LS*, p. 109).

Generally speaking, however, contemporary psychoanalysis and ego psychology have not bothered with primary-process thought nor with condensation and displacement. But some psychoanalysts have recently begun to explore and elaborate some of these concepts. David Rapaport, for instance, sees primary process as a way of enriching waking thought through a multitude of connotations. Analysts and sociologists such as Anton Ehrenzweig, Fred Weinstein, and Gerald Platt view artists as adept at a high form of primary-process thought (Marotti, "Countertransference," pp. 484, 486–87). In medical therapy the role of imagery is a growing concern for doctors, perception psychologists, and art therapists. There is also a growing body of American psychologists, actively using and theorizing about the uses of poetry in psychotherapy.[44] In a sense more radical than those who seek such connections between art and unconscious processes, Lacan has unhooked language from meaning—the Saussurean signifier from its signified—and linked it to metaphor and metonymy to demonstrate that primary-process "laws" are first created by pre-mirror, mirror, and post-mirror events. In turn, these laws not only govern behavior, as well as dreams and poetry, but also are analogous to secondary-process language functions.

Lacan's Imaginary and Symbolic orders are roughly equivalent to Freud's primary and secondary processes. The difference is, in Alan Roland's view, that Lacan removed primary process from its Freudian service as a disguise for psychosexual fantasies and gave access through metaphor to the formation of the *moi* via the phenomenon of internalization. If Imaginary images function like Symbolic order words, it is clear that words need not be separate from things, and we can begin to comprehend the functional principles behind dreams, poetry, and psychotic language. By ascribing a homogeneous—Imaginary—structure to symptoms, dreams, memory lapses, jokes, *parole*, signifieds, and the rest, Lacan surmised that the merger function between words and objects (or things and people)—based on associational similarities—ultimately refers to unknown signifiers present in the Other(A). Imaginary truth, in other words, only takes on its "sense" (*sens*) in relation to the repressed language in the Other(A), whose oppositional mode of thinking is neither rational nor grammatical but Desiring and intentional (*Séminaire* I, p. 296). One word substituted in implicit similarity for another is the very formula of metaphor; condensation, as rethought by Lacan, becomes the structure of the superimposition of signifiers which metaphor takes as its field (Sheridan, *Ecrits*, pp. 157, 160). The conscious subject is itself an object of the Other's Desire and intentionality concerning the Phallus.

Perhaps the connections between dream, metaphor, and signifier may become clearer through the analysis of a subject's dreams. A man age thirty-nine recounted a dream about traveling in a train toward his undergraduate university. In the compartment sat two young men from his student past and one modern-day colleague. On waking, the dreamer felt tremendously depressed. In the subsequent recounting of the dream, the analyst led the dreamer to uncover the one thing that all four "passengers" had in common (similarity). All were athletes as well as scholars. The metaphorical key to this condensed story was provided by the one atypical person—the passenger from the dreamer's contemporary life—whose last name was Blue. "Blue," it transpired, was also the term for the top athletic award at the undergraduate university in question. Although he coveted this prize, the dreamer had not won it. But if the signifier "blue" unravels the Symbolic order meaning of the dream, it does not reveal its signified (i.e., retroactive "self"-meaning). In Lacanian theory signifieds are those "self"-themes that recur in dream after dream and that can be equated diachronically with latent meaning (or personal context). Signifieds provide the contextual meaning to signifiers—images plus words—which manifest an infinite combinatory potential but have little meaning in their own right. In our example, the signifier "blue" is substituted for a signified, but provides a clue to the dreamer's meaning by the associations it implies in the dreamer's own "self"-text. A signified for this man was a pervasive sense of his self as physically flawed. In childhood a Real but minor congenital imperfection (*pectus excavatum*)—magnified by his mother—had convinced the dreamer that he was physically unfit. But even this Imaginary "meaning" is not the dreamer's unconscious, which yields at best a word or image that alludes to the dialectical links between *moi* and the Other(A). The unconscious contains the (m)Other's Desire—for herself, in regard to her son, as well as in her attitude toward the Name-of-the-Father. The metonymic sense of the dream just recounted refers to the man's Desire for recognition, in conjunction with a sense of wounded virility. The signifier "blue" merely signaled an unconscious chain of past associations that had remained active at the level of self-perception (*Vorstellungsrepräsentanz*). A full analysis of the dream in regard to the Other(A) would be a book: the story of this man's life as well as that of his parents and grandparents.

In Seminar Four Lacan remained faithful to Freud's intuition that the laws of the dream are the same as those of poetry. Although this idea would point to a poetics of the unconscious if pushed to the limit, dream language cannot be assimilated as conscious language on a functional plane, because it is lacking in the two-dimensional (abstract) representational material for "such logical articulations as causality, contradiction, hypothesis, etc." (Sheridan, *Ecrits*, p. 161). The dream is, instead, a one-dimensional or homogeneous, concrete language, even though its story can only be interpreted later by the heterogeneous elements of language. But one-dimensional "logic" is not static. Given Lacan's theory that various levels of perception and skill operate thought simultaneously, in conjunction with his contention that language is only one of several elements represented in the unconscious, his reminder that condensation was not a unified concept in Freud's own writings rings all the more true.[45] Homogeneous logic works by the substitutive, referential energy of Desire and identificatory "investment." The dream carries its energy from term to term by metonymic displacement of the Other(A). The dream's new associational meanings can, in turn, be decoded by the same "laws" that first formed the *moi* as a composite of similarities and substitutions, then divided it, and fashioned the human subject as a displaced set of Desires and meanings that always revert to the Other(A).

Following Freud, Lacan showed that oneiric meaning can only be decoded when broken down into constituent parts, sometimes even down to the most elemental phonemes. Such demonstrations offered him sufficient proof that the signifier has supremacy over the signified, because the former can mean something other than what it is literally saying in the dream (Lemaire, *Lacan*, p. 191). Put another way, the signifier is not equal to the sum of its parts. The dream formation is a metaphor whose associations and substitutions point backward to *moi* narcissism and beyond that to the Desire and Law that reside metonymically in the Other(A). Once decoded, the dream formation takes its place alongside *parole* and the *moi* and its signifieds as one more dialectic emanating from the Other(A). The differences between Freud and Lacan are increasingly a matter of emphasis here. While Freud's comparison of the meager dream content to the copiousness of (latent) dream thoughts convinced him of the tremendous and interminable work of condensation, Lacan looked beyond the substantive or metaphorical characteristics of the dream to its referential or metonymic functioning. The Frenchman's interest lay in the use of the dream in its relation to reality as a reciprocal source of consciousness, not as a competitor with conscious life nor as a pure manifestation of the unconscious.

The philosopher Jean-Marie Benoist has said that, by paying special attention to dream language and psychotic language, Lacan has pointed the way toward a psychoanalytical, structural poetics in Jakobson's sense, before Chomsky's metaphysical wanderings (Benoist, *La Révolution*, p. 300). Lacan opined that Freud anticipated Saussure when he implied in 1901 that the dream has the structure of a sentence in its symbolic resonances, its potential for evoking associations via sound and image, and in the substantive associations that give it an over-all meaning. Lacan made contextual sense of Freud's intuition of this phenomenon by showing that, like the sentence, a dream only "means" retrospectively. By comparing the dream to a sentence, Lacan rendered Freud's concept of overdetermination equivalent to the polysemous property of language itself and its infinite combinatory or generative capacity. For Lacan, however, the dream's ambiguous and contradictory effects (Freud's *Entstellung*) are not caused by censorship in any sense of the superego's agency. They result from the sliding of signifieds underneath autonomous signifiers that seem detached from any deeper meaning. Language (signifiers) obscures identificatory "truth" (signifieds) in the concrete discourse of conscious life, but reveals such "truth" in the dream if one can later interpret dream images through their connection to the dreamer's stockpile of language in the Other(A). The absent or latent element in a dream will always be linguistic, therefore, either somewhere actually in the dream or inferred by the images. The great importance of Lacan's thought here lies in his discovery that in dreams or *parole* the play of signifieds on signifiers makes meaning itself an enigma (Sheridan, *Ecrits*, p. 160).

Though Freud knew full well there was a link between the dreamer and his or her language, Lacan thought he failed to understand similarity's dialectical nature and could not, therefore, grasp the broadest implications of association. There is no such thing as "free" association, which is pure or static, because underlying any linguistic selection (metaphor) or combination (metonymy) lies an Imaginary dialectic (*Séminaire* II, p. 168). Where Freud found oneness—in the ego—Lacan located fragmentations, unresolvable division, intrinsic instability, permanent dialectical tension, and referential Otherness. Insofar as these make up the elemental structure of the human subject, the tendency to deny that conflict inheres in being comes from the Imaginary propensity to presume a unity and reject Castration. Benoist has summed up the difficulties which Lacan's theories pose for Western thinkers: in the name of Occidental rationality, most people participate in the same substantialist illusion which seduced Freud into bringing otherness and difference down to a concept of the Same (*La Révolution*, p. 259).

For Lacan, language is not only itself a metaphor—substituting for a sense of lack in being—but it is also a metonymy pointing to something unsaid and incomprehensible in the very act of speaking. Primary process can be seen at work on secondary process in the phenomenon of thought leaping from one linguistic phrase to another, unable to grasp all concepts and symbols at once (Lemaire, *Lacan*, p. 103). Lacan called the effect of primary process the play of signifieds on signifiers, a function that gives personal meaning to words that are neutral in the symbolic sphere but emotionally charged with narcissistic meanings in the Imaginary and by the effects of Desire and Law in the unconscious realm.

Freud hypothesized an unconscious mode of function comparable to this phenomenon of thought leaping from one linguistic phrase to another and called it psychic mobility. Dreams indicated to Freud that a free circulation of "cathectic" (sexual) energy goes from presentation to presentation by condensation and displacement, this energy seemingly not bound closely to any of its presentations (Lemaire, *Lacan*, p. 101). Jakobson demonstrated that metaphor and metonymy are agents of a similar flow and movement in conscious language. But Freud's theory of psychic energy has raised more questions than it has answered. Lacan claimed that Freud intuited the true sources of psychic energy, nonetheless, when the Viennese founder proposed *Trieb* as distinct from *Instinkt* and thereby implied the advent of an unconscious signifier (representation) (Sheridan, *Ecrits*, p. 236). Although the source of energy differs in the Freudian and Lacanian accounts of it, Lacan still shared Freud's view that there was a greater mobility of cathectic intensity—i.e., identificatory investment—in the unconscious than in consciousness. This greater mobility came not from sexual arousal, but from the Imaginary fusions that operate the *moi* through substitutions and similarities— "self"-perceptions that interpret the world—and in reference to signifiers repressed in the Other(A). Lacan's theory that psychic energy stems from the identificatory "investment" of narcissistic passion and Desire that mark the mirror-stage drama of taking on a "self" as well as from the post–mirror-stage challenge of maintaining that "self" (despite Castration and the flux of Real events) means that psychic energy must be grasped as issuing from the *moi*, posing a verbal *demande* tied to an unconscious trove of signifiers controlling Desire.

The passion of the Lacanian signified comes from the unconscious discourse of Desire that animates a subject. Because the pure action of a binary signifier first created Desire in a subject as the Other's Desire—conveyed by ordinary language and left as a linguistic residue of mythical Desires and intentions—Lacan described Desire as the furrow left in the course of the signifier, as the elemental cell of being (Sheridan, *Ecrits*, pp. 264–65). Metaphor and metonymy appropriately describe this drama, too. Substitution and combination are the mechanisms that operate Desire, both in the prespecular and mirror stages, as well as the post-mirror stage. In Chapter 3 we saw that the Lacanian Imaginary has a homogeneous way of functioning by binding disparate, prespecular elements into a corporal unity in the mirror stage, and a heterogeneous way by which Real objects are sought in the post-mirror stage in a substitutive or metaphorical chain of displacements for the lost primary object(s) of Desire (metonymy). From one point of view the *moi* is a metonymy: referring backward to sets of prespecular perceptual mergers (primary unities) and forward to a displacement of these parts by a combination, a unified body image (secondary unity). The *moi* is also a condensation or metaphor, however, since it is formed by symbol selection (*Bejahung* and *Ausstossung*), and by substituting someone else's Desire for the infant's lack of autonomy.

Lacan's theory, following Freud, of an endless Imaginary movement of meaning in the unconscious explains why we might associate emotion with "self" or personal issues and mind with language (the Symbolic). The *OED* defines emotion as "agitation of mind (Latin *emotio*: movement)." In Lacanian terms, this "movement" becomes the play of signifieds on signifiers, a relationship which shows that language and identity are no longer total or separate agencies or systems. Lacan's view of "affect" as displaced representations allows us theoretically to divorce the causes of emotion from biology itself and attach them to language and identifications. By using metaphor and metonymy to describe the laws that operate in the formation of identity as well as that of mind, Lacan undermined the substantialist, essentialist assumptions that stand behind early object-relations theory, as well as behind most linguistic, psychological, and philosophical theories of mind. He showed that similarity—not sameness—determines the linguistic axis of selection or substitution, whether one refers to the heterogeneous laws of language or to the creation of a *moi* as a homogeneous composite of objects and others.

A concrete example of how similarity functions in the creation of the *moi* may help. A one-year-old child was observed by its mother repeatedly rubbing the eyelashes of her doll. On returning from a trip of three months (her toys having been left at home), the child, now fifteen months old, discovered a doll with no eyelashes. Her response to this doll was one of great fear, accompanied by whining cries. Within a week, the mother noticed that her child fell asleep by rubbing her own eyelashes. This development could be interpreted to mean that the doll without eyelashes destroyed the dialectical illusion by which the infant was taking on a sense of her own *Gestalt*. Similarity was the functional means by which the mirror-stage child sought to reassure herself of her body form and unity. The example underlines how early a "self" is fixed by metaphorical and metonymical processes. But disturbing words or Real events will later always be able to disrupt one's fixed sense of self, since this self is really composed of bits and pieces. Lacan insists that self has an anticipatory value that it seeks to reaffirm in Real situations through the recognition of others (ego ideals meant to reify an ideal ego) and, in so doing, reaffirm its worth retroactively. But Desire prevents this drama of anticipation and retroaction from being harmonious. Since the Real objects of Desire (*objet a*) always refer to yet another Desire—both backward to primordial objects and forward in the anticipation of an impossible, final fulfillment—the objects themselves, as well as the absent signifiers in the Other(A), place the *moi* in an unstable metonymic chain of Desire.

Lacan's proposal that there is mobile energy present at both conscious and unconscious levels has set off his war against the imperialism of fixed meaning and culminated in his baroque concept: the flight of meaning. Whereas baroque painting and writing depict the breaking down of boundaries and lines, thereby imitating the changing fluidity of nature, Lacan used this phenomenon to describe the speaking subject that is split into two meaning systems which—*velis nolis*—overlap. But any effort to reduce Lacan's primary-process "logic" to that of the signified, or his concept of secondary process to the signifier, would be misleading. Signifieds are, paradoxically, created by a totality of the effect of signifiers. This paradox of separate-but-not-separate is one of Lacan's most elusive concepts. It is well known that the contradictions inherent in this problematic led Jean Laplanche to part company with Lacan. Lacan finally had to denounce publicly Laplanche's pronouncements on the intensity with which primary process affects conscious language. According to Anika Lemaire's account of their rift, Laplanche tried to define what puts a stop to primary process in conscious discourse by retaining Freud's metapsychological theory in which thing-presentations are modified by primary process in hierarchical layers: from the unconscious (thing), to the preconscious (things and words), and finally to the conscious (words). By implying that the unconscious itself causes or conditions language, Laplanche not only reversed Lacan's central contention (that the unconscious is the logical implication of language) but also reversed Lacan's anti-Platonic bias and persisted in retaining a belief in innate or a priori fixed forms of the unconscious.[46] Instead of living with the floating, sliding paradox that Lacan uncovered, i.e., separation is compensated for by language that creates the unconscious, which in turn commands ordinary language in varied and enigmatic ways, Laplanche opted for the comfort of a static, neopositivistic, and hierarchical scale with clear-cut beginning, middle, and end.

Both Desire and dreams furnished Lacan with proof of a dynamic connection between primary and secondary process. He tried, in turn, to describe these effects by the laws of metaphor and metonymy and in relation to concepts such as *lalangue, moi, parole,* signifieds, Imaginary order, and so on. Desire—as enigma—resides in the dream in pure form, although the dream formation is itself a displacement meant to satisfy Desire beyond the frustrations that conscious life elicits in response to the Other's inability to satisfy *demande*. But instead of fulfilling it, the dream merely attests to the presence of Desire as an ongoing state of longing or dissatisfaction. If the meaning of the Other's Desire were clear in the dream, a person could utilize dreams to implement the mottos "know thyself" and "to thine own self be true"; but condensation and displacement mask the meaning of Desire in the Other (Sheridan, *Ecrits*, pp. 264, 267). The dream produces metaphors by its creation of new meanings enigmatic in their unexpected substitutions and similarities. But the decoding process can only occur with respect to metonymy. The metonymic aspect of the dream signals the unconscious as the "something else" unsaid or encoded which explains why dreams resist yielding up their meaning.[47]

Lacan's proposition—that the impact of separation linked to language formed an unconscious which, by definition, throws up a resistance to understanding being—explains the limited sway of primary process over conscious language. Priority is given to secondary process by the conservative and primordially fixated nature of the narcissistic *moi* (which insists on its mythical unity), as well as by the power of convention governing the use of linguistic signs responsible for coherence of thought and the maintenance of repression by denial. But insofar as functional links exist between primary and secondary processes at all, then one is obliged to agree with Lacan that meaning is inherently ambiguous. Meaning is rarely a matter of clear, objective productions of information, intention (speech acts), simple linguistic transformations, or lucid communications. Unconscious signifiers, therefore, stand in a proleptic relationship to concrete discourse when unanalyzed, and in an extralinguistic relationship to it when decoded. Prolepsis, then, is of a piece with metonymy or displacement (*Verschiebung*), while analysis seeks to uncover the relationship of metaphor (*Verdichtung*) to the metonymic meaning of signifiers clustered around Desire and Law. Metonymy signals the resistance of meaning—the refusal of the unconscious to yield up its truths—while metaphor creates new meanings whose very existence points to a representational base beyond themselves.

In the "Agency of the Letter in the Unconscious" (1957) Lacan gave the formula for metaphor as $\left(\dfrac{S'}{S}\right)S \cong S(+)s$, in which S' denotes the signifying effect or meaning; and $\cong$ stands for congruence (Sheridan, *Ecrits*, p. 164). The S(+)s denotes a crossing of the "bar" between consciousness and unconsciousness in the creation of meaning (Sheridan, *Ecrits*, p. 158). The new formation or S is a condensed image or signifier plus a signified (personal meaning). In "La métaphore du sujet" (1961), responding to a paper presented by M. Perelman, Lacan later described metaphor as the effect of the substitution of one signifier for another in a chain, where two signifiers are reducible to a phonematic opposition (*Ecrits*, 1966, p. 890). In this brief response, Lacan rewrote his formula for metaphor to read:

$$\frac{S}{S_1'} \cdot \frac{S_2'}{x} \rightarrow S\left(\frac{I}{s''}\right).$$

This formula is intended to clarify the earlier one. It makes the point that when language (S) substitutes a word or sound for another one in the unconscious (S_1' = unconscious representational material plus concrete language), the signifier in the unconscious forms a combination that floats into consciousness as a condensation or new meaning (S_2'). The new meaning—the metaphor or S—refers metonymically to the Imaginary "self"-text or identificatory ideal ego (x), whose fables are supported by signifieds (s") that are opaque, but whose effects reflect representational elements from both conscious and unconscious realms: $\left(\frac{I}{s''}\right)$ Metaphors therefore constitute unconscious meanings, and a substitutive procedure for continually reconstituting "self" as a metaphoric constellation.

Lacan wrote in 1957 that "we accede to meaning only through the double twist of metaphor when we have the one and only key: the signified and the signifier of the Saussurean algorithm are not on the same level, and man only deludes himself when he believes his true place is at their axis—which is nowhere. *Was* nowhere, that is, until Freud discovered it" (Sheridan, *Ecrits*, p. 166). That which is signified by the metaphor—and appears in repetitions—is being and existing (Sheridan, *Ecrits*, p. 215). With this proposed difference of register, Lacan condemned the semiotic quest to find meaning at a point between the Saussurean signifier and signified, and showed the semioticians' search for a rational sign system to be just one more rehearsal of the classical tradition that has always divorced ontology from language. Lacan used metaphor, instead, to explain how language first substitutes for inchoate perceptions as a "translatable" material to reify the symbolicity of the *moi*. Not only does metaphor act as a link to the representations taken in by the infant in the pre-mirror and mirror stages, but it is also the substitutive means of coping with separation in the post-mirror phase. This metaphoric nature of the subject—the interplay of signifiers and signifieds—operates on language by returning to consciousness (in repetitions) whatever has been repressed in the Other (Sheridan, *Ecrits*, p. 200). In and of themselves, these repetitions (behavior, identity themes, switched words, or sounds) are meaningless. When decoded, however, they appear as secondary repressions—substitutes for truth—which refer to an unconscious chain of related signifiers going back to the unrepresentable, primordially repressed chain (*Urverdräng-ung*). Secondary repressed material (S_2) or signifieds of this kind will be analytically "translatable" in relation to ensembles of signifiers that make up structures as groups of meaning associations, organized around key signifiers. In a limited sense, Jakobson is right when he says that the metaphor is paradigmatic (has a general shape = the signifying Symbolic order), while metonymy is syntagmatic (the particular case of a thing that fits the paradigm = the repressed material of signifieds).

According to Lacan, the treasure trove of repressed metaphorical language was discovered by Freud in dreams. At the point where the linguistic frontier between consciousness and the unconscious exists, he argues, Freud discovered jokes (*Witz*).[48] This picture of metaphor differs markedly, however, from Jakobson's theory. Both Lacan and Jakobson derived their ideas in part from Saussure's contention that selections or substititions always maintain a connection (or combination) with the rest of a signifying chain. By connecting Saussure's theory to the unconscious process of condensation (Freud) and bringing their interrelationship into view as an Imaginary order of perception with a logic of its own (with effects on conscious life), Lacan surpassed Jakobson's narrow account of metaphor at the surface of language. A second major difference regarding metaphor theory between Jakobson and Lacan lies in Jakobson's emphasis on the concept of similarity in the structure of metaphor. Lacan sees substitution as central to the structure of metaphor. But Lacan did not minimize similarity, in my view; rather, he stressed its functional role in homogeneous Imaginary dialectics. Not only did he establish the mimetic power of similarity in the process of mirror-stage structuring (and in the subsequent functioning of an Imaginary discourse between an ideal ego and ego ideals), but he also stressed the role of similarity of sound, image, or concept in the associational play of unconscious and conscious signifiers running through dreams, jokes, or poems.

Any attempt to understand language metaphorically will, nonetheless, take on a different hue depending on whether one adopts a Lacanian or a Jakobsonian approach. Jakobsonian linguists are busy establishing the proportion between substituted and maintained elements in metaphorical similarities. Lacan, meanwhile, has compared the heterogeneous, substitutive powers of metaphor to a river basin at ebb tide, where the silt and stones of the riverbed periodically come into full view. Unconscious signifiers protrude into conscious language around sounds, identity themes, words, and effects, which will only expose their full meaning (as truth value) when retroactively decoded in reference to signifieds and the Other's Desire. Despite occasional similarities, unconscious signifiers do not, of course, offer themselves as a clear test of meaning behind conscious signifiers. Unconscious language is not only materially unstable, i.e., not anchored by normal conventions and rules of grammar, but the laws of condensation and displacement also create enigmatic associational groupings. All this underlines Lacan's second difference with Jakobson: that metaphor only takes on the fuller sense of its meanings in relation to metonymy.

Before discussing metonymy per se, we should point out the special role of metaphor in psychosis. In an analysis of Lacan's own case study of a psychotic, Jacques-Alain Miller has said that Lacanian analysts try to distinguish between (1) illnesses of mentality or psychoses (which derive from the emancipation of the Imaginary relationship), and (2) illnesses of the Other(A) or neuroses. In the first situation, ego and object are reversed, and the ego or *moi* is no longer troubled by being submitted to Symbolic scanning. Illnesses of the Other(A) function differently, however, putting the structure of enunciation itself into question (e.g., neurotics speak rhetorically in a florid effort to evade the truths in the Other). Psychosis affects speech but more importantly puts the structure of knowledge (or knowing) itself into question (Schneiderman, *Returning*, pp. 48–50). Lacan's formula for metaphor (signifying substitution) ordinarily explains dreams, repression, jokes, and signifieds in terms of condensation related to language. In psychosis the formula has been rewritten once more to read:

$$\frac{S}{\mathcal{S}'} \cdot \frac{\mathcal{S}'}{x} \rightarrow \left(\frac{I}{s} \right).$$

In his discussion of Schreber's psychosis, Lacan showed that an unconscious key signifier was missing in Schreber's personality.

The phallic or primary signifier for separation that is identified with language (S) and forms an unconscious ($\mathcal{S}$) was never adequately inscribed in Schreber's Other(A). As a result, when the missing phallic or pure signifier was thrust into doubt in Real life, the signified could no longer play above the bar of repression as secondary repres-

sion (or signifieds). The Name-of-the-Father had never been assimilated in the Other(A) and, in consequence, the idea of "self" as a set
of autonomous signifieds could be destroyed. The Fregean number of
Imaginary psychic separation (2) had reverted to the *jouissance* of
symbiosis (1) or selflessness. No signified, no principle of unity and
self-meaning, could appear in language, then, but only the grandiose
ideal ego: the unnamed, uncastrated *enfant merveilleux* who is
"spoken" by the disembodied signifiers inhabiting the Other(A). The
signifiers that now "speak" the psychotic *je* (*moi* individuality having disappeared) would normally be inaccessible to conscious life
(Sheridan, *Ecrits*, p. 200). In a graphic reversal of subject and object,
therefore, psychosis exposes the two-dimensional structure of metaphor that under normal circumstances invisibly binds subject and
meaning, being and speaking (Sheridan, *Ecrits*, pp. 164–65).

In connecting the concept of metonymy to the unconscious, Lacan
again modified Jakobson's use of a term. Jakobson attached the idea
of displacement to metaphor (similarity), whereas Lacan attributed
the Freudian concept of displacement (*Verschiebung*) to metonymy
instead. Despite this reformulation of Jakobson's view, Lacan shared
more common ground with the linguist in his conception of metonymy than in their diverging ideas on metaphor. Jakobson defined
metonymy as a substitution of signifiers having between themselves
some relationship of contiguity (e.g., *boire un verre* ["Let's drink a
glass" or share a drink], or thirty sails, meaning a fleet of boats). By
combining Freud's idea of displacement as a "veering off of meaning"
(the main method for getting around censorship) with Jakobson's
idea of contiguity, Lacan evolved the following formula for metonymy: (S . . . S') S $\cong$ S (—) s (Sheridan, *Ecrits*, p. 164). Any metonymy is always an apparent nonsense; for example, one does not
actually *drink* a glass or refer to a boat or boats as thirty sails. Lacan
meant to convey this idea by the S (—) s, where the bar (—) constitutes a resistance to meaning. Meaning actually emerges from the
combination of ideas *inferred* between the two contiguous signifiers
in play. So Lacan emphasized the displacement or referential aspect
of metonymy, while Jakobson stressed the contiguity. Lacan, in other
words, was interested in the phenomenon of indirectly represented
words or images and tried to show that contiguity is not meaningful
as an end in itself, but only in its evocation of an unstated referent.

In the sense that displacement of a word or symbol by an inferred
meaning resists unconscious meaning, metonymy is commensurate with the verbal. Psychoanalytically speaking, language represents a use of metonymy to displace the unconscious by substituting

concrete words for unconscious meaning (to which conscious meaning refers all the same). The mechanisms of defense that shut the unconscious from view, therefore—foreclosure, repression, denial—themselves have the structure of metaphor and metonymy. We should consider Schneiderman's statement in this light: that the utterances of those who have completed analysis are in some way poeticized—but are not "pure poetry"—because metaphor and metonymy are essential aspects of the unconscious structure, and not defense mechanisms (*Returning*, p. 12). We do not need a Freudian superego, or a catalogue of defenses, to regulate the "forbidden" once the degree to which language itself plays that role becomes clear. From a Lacanian perspective, then, language as a system is metonymic. Discourse is incomplete, discontinuous, lacunary; as such, it is the sure sign of something more, or of something lacking. Linguistically speaking, the "something" is an invisible body of sounds, words, and evocations. But the "something lacking" is the repressed or radical signified, which can never be stated, as in the dream's navel vanishing into the Other(A).

We see, then, that metonymic functioning occurs at various levels simultaneously. In that the question of identity is directed to the Other(A) via others, the form of discourse is itself metonymic. The signifieds, which always give meaning to language in the writing of one's story (in light of childhood effects), are also metonymic; they refer to the absent "letters" that insist in the unconscious. The dream, too, is a metonymy, thus validating Freud's insistence that the dream itself was not the unconscious, but only the royal road that led to it. Even doubts and forgotten elements are part of a dream message. Lacan depicted this idea in the formula: $\dfrac{S \ldots S'}{\Delta \ldots \mathcal{S}}$. The S . . . S' chain denotes the manifest text, while the Δ below the bar implies an unfathomable point of departure. The $\mathcal{S}$ below the bar is the latent content, or the guessed referent. For these reasons, the meaning of a dream is not apparent in its metaphoric, condensed, or compromising form as a manifest text, but lies in the lacunae or metonymies within, syntactic displacements over semantic formations.

The dream was one of the few proofs that Lacan (or Freud) used to demonstrate that there is a part of being not open to conscious understanding. The same effect ($\Delta \ldots \mathcal{S}$), however, operates on conscious life in *parole* or signifieds. But Desire is the force that connects the unconscious to all acts of consciousness in a dynamic (energetic) activism. Desire is the proof of a Real Castration which destined the human subject—as a species of metonymy—to take on its fuller meaning only within a signifying chain of narcissistic investments and repressed words. The effects of loss on an infant and the consequent lack of any permanent wholeness are the principles that drive humans to use language at all. Metonymy is for Lacan a one-dimensional structure, nonetheless, since it only alludes to meaning displaced in the Other(A). Metaphor, on the other hand, is two-dimensional and resides on the side of stability and synchrony by its creation of new and explicit meanings. It may be pertinent to note in this context that Lacan here retains Saussure's sense. Saussure portrayed combination as the diachronic function which represents *parole*, while selection was synchronic and represented *langue* (Martin Thom, *Talking Cure*, p. 4). Lacan's concept of metonymy lies on the diachronic slope of unstable meanings, of evocative *paroles* and the gaps implied by Desire. Metaphor creates synchronic meaning by infusing unconscious life into the neutral phonemes and words of the Symbolic order. But metaphor is anchored, paradoxically, in the metonymic chain of being and could itself be called the metonymy of being: the link between language, symbol, self, and process.

To use the concepts of metaphor and metonymy to argue for an unconscious language, as well as for a psychic meaning behind ordinary language which can be decoded in its links to Desire and Law, are ideas as unfamiliar to most Westerners as those of the American neurolinguist Jason W. Brown. In his essay "Brain Structure and Language Production: A Dynamic View," Brown writes: "Let us begin with the idea that language is hierarchically structured, that the words that I am now speaking have passed through a complex series of levels that form a part of the structure of the utterance, a structure that has to be traversed each moment as an utterance is realized. This process of a more or less instantaneous unfolding of language and cognition over levels is termed microgenesis. An aphasic symptom represents a destructuration within this dynamic hierarchical structure; in other words, the aphasic utterance represents or points to one of the more preliminary levels."[49] Brown's argument resonates with the same kind of logic Lacan used to prove the presence of an unconscious in consciousness. The appeal of the pathological aphasic condition, Brown says, is that the structure of a performance is revealed directly in behavior and does not have to be inferred (as in normative studies). Fragments of aphasia exist in normal utterances, moreover, and the whole inventory of aphasic errors was recovered by Arthur Arkin from the speech of normal sleep talkers (Brown,

"Brain Structure," p. 298). I view Brown's hypothesis that the ontogenesis of speech occurs at levels in cognitive structure as a support for Lacan's axiom that language does not simply appear in response to developmental maturation or phylogenetic dictate. Mind is itself an icon of perceived images and the residues of language, as they accumulate in networks of "letters" with personal and social meaning. Unlike Brown or Lacan, however, most thinkers separate man from his dream texts, or from his aphasic or psychotic language. Jakobson and Lévi-Strauss did this when they called such linguistic phenomena *idiolects*.

The generally accepted idea—that the normal and the pathological belong to separate ontological orders—can probably be attributed to well-established tendencies in Western thought from Plato and Aristotle to the present. In an essay entitled "Greek Philosophy and the Overcoming of the Word," Susan Handelman recounts how the Christian tradition followed Greek thought in separating poetics from metaphysics, rhetoric from ontology, and word from thought. Western philosophy has consequently called for transcendence of language, for elevation of the spirit of the text over its letter.[50] Both Plato and Aristotle considered the innate logic of language, for example, to be an inferior concern. They studied forms (Plato) and subject/predicate propositions (Aristotle) instead of isolated words.

Although twentieth-century linguists and philosophers have more or less eradicated the idea that thought and language are separate, their various solutions to the mind-and-language problematic have not closed the issue. Heidegger set sundry disciples off to explain meaning by a study of metaphor when he said: "'the metaphorical exists only with the metaphysical.'"[51] Other thinkers, opposed to Heidegger's joining of being and language through metaphor, have revived Aristotelian logic with a vengeance. Linguists such as John L. Austin and John Searle currently echo Aristotle's claim that "a name is spoken sound, significant by convention."[52] Culler has indicted Austin for refusing to explain meaning in terms of a state of mind, but clinging instead to a separate analysis of the conventions of discourse.[53] To this end, Austin has even used the Aristotelian criterion of true or false (the parent of propositional logic), based on his own notion of the presence of a signifying intention in the speaker's conscious mind (Culler, "On Deconstruction," p. 23). Further exposing his Aristotelian leanings, Austin has abandoned constative (i.e., declarative) and performative (i.e., speech acts) distinctions while still trying to categorize classes of the performative (Culler, "On Deconstruction," p. 28). The model Austin follows was set by Aristotle and the Greek philosopher's attention to general propositions about classes of things, which could be deductively proved from within the premises of a syllogism (Handelman, "Greek Philosophy," p. 48).

But many contemporary thinkers have abandoned classical attitudes toward language and have begun a serious study of the "livingness" of language. Following Heidegger's conception of a subject who is never in a position to shape what his experience will be like in advance, Tzvetan Todorov, Derrida, Ricoeur, Gadamer, and others have joined metaphor to mind, making metaphor itself the generative principle of logic, language, and ontology. While Ricoeur and Gadamer posit a primordial iconicity behind thought and seek a restitution of a metaphorical conjunction of thinking and images (a preconceptual metaphorical mode of ordering the world which lays the groundwork for conceptual thought), Derrida places the substitutive metaphorical process at the origin of all thought (Handelman, "Greek Philosophy," pp. 59, 61). Derrida concludes that the origin of thought is ultimately unthinkable in icons or propositions and accuses Ricoeur and Gadamer of literalizing both metaphor and metaphysics. By placing a concrete metaphorical process at the operational origin of local thought, at the juncture of word and thing, they miss the truth about metaphor. Metaphor cannot "think" itself, Derrida claims, and the idea that it can is a "white" (blank) mythology.

Aristotle's propositional and predicate laws of noncontradiction stood behind his own logic and made it impossible for him to join thought to metaphorical workings, although he correctly understood metaphor centuries before Jakobson. "Metaphor," said Aristotle, "is the application of the name of a thing to something else working either from genus to species, from species to species, or by proportion" (*Poetics*, cited in Handelman, "Greek Philosophy," p. 57). But since metaphor was contradictory because it required displacement from a fixed order "proper" sense to a "figurative" sense—thus necessitating the transgression of boundaries—metaphorical workings obliterated the law of noncontradiction and so could not reside within logic. Since Aristotle's day, metaphor's province has been restricted to poetry, dreams, and the unconscious. What sets Lacan apart from all who have worked on the problem is his insistence that metaphor's laws of functioning—not its substance—direct conscious and unconscious mind alike, as well as identity. Derrida's "white" mythology is comparable to Lacan's primordial repression or symbolization. But this Lacanian layer is Real and thus reverberates through corporal being and Desire. Moreover, secondary repressions—which can be analyzed—are built upon primary ones. In other words, although there is a primordial point of representation where metaphor cannot think itself (a level where words and things merge), its laws can, nonetheless, be used to analyze unconscious messages (signifieds) and Desires. This is achieved in terms of substitutions, both linguistic and relational, and by emanations from an unconscious reference bank, however sporadic and enigmatic. Derrida's dismantling and deconstruction of signifying language still leave untouched the problems of the human subject, truth, cause and effect, and the Real, while Ricoeur's and Gadamer's harkening back to a primordial iconicity does not explain the personal links between such icons and "self" as an energetic constellation of meanings. Lacan's connection of the conscious to the unconscious domain through signifier and metaphor brings Desire, repetition, repression, and separation into play. Lacan's use of the laws of metaphor and metonymy enabled him to study meaning on several levels—contradictory between themselves—and finally to restitute meaning at the logical level of truth value.

We may say, then, that Lacan's epistemology promotes the idea of a structural organizational metaphorics, where metaphor is first a function and only second an iconic mode of meaning. Unlike Ricoeur and Gadamer, Lacan placed the power of effect before symbol (or metaphor) in the framing of mind and ontology. In contrast to Derrida, Lacan connected effect to the Real of event and then to the Real of symbols, which operate the human subject in a metaphorical, metonymical dynamic of Desire and repetition. All knowledge and language have the structure of metaphor, in Lacan's view, in that they substitute for something else; and the something else is explained by the structure of metonymy. Derrida's "white" mythology is really another substantive denial—like the skeptics' of old—of a realm of truth and knowledge beyond consciousness, be it only the "sense" of an Other(A) meaning. Lacan's theory that cognition elaborates an unconscious *savoir* led him to a recasting of Kant's three famous questions: What can I know? What can I do? What can I be permitted to hope? These questions can only be answered, said Lacan, if one first asks: "From where do I know? Act? Hope? (*Télévision*, pp. 57–68). The answers will not appear in any ideology or philosophical discovery, nor even in the iconic nature of metaphor nor in its substitutive occultation. These questions can only be answered in relation to each person's individual Other(A) discourse. What psychoanalysis could permit a person to hope, for example, would be for some clarity about the unconscious whose subject that analysand is (*Télévision*, p. 67).

Nevertheless, many commentators on Lacan have misunderstood the fundamental role he gave to metaphor and metonymy. One critic, referring to Lacan's idea that Desire (cum lack) is a metonymy, stated: "To say that this emotional process is like the linguistic device of metonymy is to make an interesting analogy. Analogies may clarify, but they do not structurally interrelate the 'objects' of psychological and linguistic inquiry." [54] But Lacan's purpose was not to show how the psyche and linguistics are similar (he was not a psycholinguist). He demonstrated, instead, that their functional laws were analogous prior to essence or ideology, and these consequently offer a permanent means for ascertaining points of join between language and identity. Perhaps Lacan's thought here will become more accessible if we consider his suggestions on psychotic language in relation to aphasic speech (Greek *aphatos*, speechless). His discussion of the two types of aphasia make it quite clear that the causes of psychosis and aphasia are different, although there are seeming analogies in psychotic language. Let us look at some of these distinctions in greater detail.

In an essay entitled "The Unconscious Structured as a Language" Martin Thom emphasizes that metaphor and metonymy operate in conjunction in normal speech. Only in language disorders can the separate nature of the two modes of arrangement be clearly perceived. Jakobson actually distinguished metaphor from metonymy while studying the two different kinds of aphasia in 1971. He concluded that there are two poles of language, equivalent to Saussure's selection and combination. Depending on the type of aphasia (contiguity or motor disorder; simultaneity or sensory disorder), an aphasic would produce a language whose disorders centered either on metonymy (contiguity) or metaphor (substitution and selection) (*Talking Cure*, pp. 4–5). It is well known that the motor disorder aphasias are agrammatical and display a reduction of verbal stock. Relationships of contiguity, alignment, signifying articulation, and syntactic coordination are hence degraded. The speaker "names" but cannot make sentences or propositions and, thus, has difficulty with reference or metonymy (*Séminaire* III, pp. 249, 255). By contrast, sensory disorder aphasias are grammatically well developed, but occasionally paraphrase instead of naming. Linguistic relationships of similarity, substitution, or choice (as well as those of selection or concurrence) become problematic. The sensory aphasic cannot define anything, or give an equivalent, cannot use language as a meta-language. He or she speaks a discourse of synonyms that seems to mean something, but ultimately evades the specific names of things as well as adequate substitute meanings. The sensory aphasic thus has trouble with metaphor.

Lacan suggested that the "fundamental" language in the Other(A), exposed only in psychosis, resembles metonymy in its verbal structure, that is, it resists meaning or propositions. This phenomenon led Lacan to depict ordinary meaning as a metaphorical language whose referential base is an inherently "meaningless," repressed body of signifiers. In psychotic hallucinatory speech the function of making meaningful equivalences by the route of metaphor has disappeared, making of paraphrase a literal translation of the Other(A). The subject is no longer a metaphorical symbol in the social signifying chain. In place of the *moi*'s own signified position the ideal ego puts forth a delirious discourse of disconnected words. The psychotic speaks a language of pure contiguity, metonymy, evocation, allusion (*Séminaire* III, p. 249). Lacan used this theory as evidence of the power of the signifier to structure mentality. Although a psychotic enunciates the grammatical or imposed part of a word or sentence (that is, speech beyond the subject), the "sense" of those signifiers has been lost because it is disconnected from "self"-meaning contained in signifieds. Metaphor belongs to Imaginary identifications that speak an everyday language, a reality discourse. Metonymy makes clear, on the other hand, that meaning only "means" when it has a "sense" of "self"-cohesion that refers to others in such a way as to be understood. Thus, although "the signifier is the instrument with which the lost signified expresses itself," in psychotic discourse it is a signifier which has ceased to refer to any recognizable unity (*Séminaire* III, pp. 250–51). In his overall conclusions Lacan held that metaphor signals the maximum efficiency of language, saying something by saying something else (as in poetry). This is achieved by setting up oppositions between two kinds of links—the signifier and signified—themselves internal to language. But that the signified sustains it is not the most notable thing about metaphor. The partial character of psychotic speech shows that the structure of language also depends on the transfer of meaning by phonematic coordination (*Séminaire* III, pp. 256, 258).

Lacan's conclusion—that metonymy (contiguity, evocation, displacement, and lack) makes metaphor possible—has tremendous ramifications for theories of language and cognition. A baby begins to take in language by the tail—the signifier—and during its first five years assimilates a system of language more or less as a whole (a grammar). Child language does not relate primarily to concreteness (Piaget), therefore, but to metonymy or contiguity. Children only arrive at concreteness or metaphor (Ricoeur's and Gadamer's symbols; Peirce's icons) after a language ensemble is already in place (*Séminaire* III, p. 260). For Lacan, therefore, pre-mirror and mirror stages are logical instead of developmental and prerational, because they are structured by the signifier and the symbol. Functionally, this logic of language and identity is that of metaphor and metonymy, allowing contradiction, lack, repression, or effect, and opening philosophy to vaster panoramas than those of Aristotle's classical entailment syllogisms.

In his paper "Four Graphs" James Glogowski discussed the fact that the theory of topological spaces as a generalization of metric spaces was first motivated and introduced by the study of the pointwise convergence of functions.[55] Toward the end of the nineteenth century, the notion of arbitrary functions was born and, so too, the notion of studying sets of functions whose domain was no longer restricted to finite-dimensional space. Mathematical topology thus endowed "functions" with the generality of which they are capable ("Four Graphs," pp. 2–3). When Lacan refers to metaphorical and metonymical function, then, it is to mathematical efficaciousness that we should look, not to the limitations of analogy or the barriers thrown up by classical logic. When we wish to understand a meaning contextually, on the other hand, we must decipher the specific signifiers imposed in the Other(A), but which persist at the surface of language and being in an Imaginary topology of signifieds.

The Symptom

We are used to thinking of psychic symptoms, in neo-Freudian terms, as compromise formations between an impulse or conflict, and the defenses against that impulse as formations that reduce anxiety. At the same time symptoms are believed to conceal unconscious meaning. Lacan's rethinking of the relationship of the symptom to the psyche postulates that Freud confused symptom and symbol, so giving rise to the mistaken idea that the psyche is composed of a set of "rational" myths (symbol being seen here as a double for sexual material). The Lacanian symptom, on the contrary, is not a symbol, nor does it conceal meaning. It indicates, instead, an atemporal and Real order of being which persists diachronically on the slope of *parole* (as opposed to anxiety, which is a temporal phenomenon containing the dream). The symptom reveals "untranslated" unconscious meaning at the surface of the body, speech, and action. However, the analysand can learn how to translate it by the substitutive nature of metaphor and in reference to the Other (metonymy) (*Séminaire* II, p. 199). The symptom is an enigmatic meaning, then, which derives from its relation to a signifying structure—the Other(A)—which determines it (Wilden, *LS*, p. 116).

Lacan construed Freud's id-ego-superego topology of 1920 to mean that Freud intuited a radical difference (dissymmetry) between the organization of the ego and the subject of the unconscious (*Séminaire* II, p. 78). While Lacan's ego (or *moi*) is a narcissistic principle of certainty, the unconscious escapes the *moi*'s circle of convictions and reveals itself in to conscious life enigmas borne out by symptoms. The effect of the symptom thus elicits aggressive tendencies because, I would contend, any thwarting of *moi* certainty and love of self threatens the unity of the *moi*, eliciting an aggressive replay of the despair and anger of the mirror stage: the infant's dependence on the Other's *regard* (Sheridan, *Ecrits*, p. 23). Whereas Freud referred to the symptom as indicative of a psychic effort to attain equilibrium (pleasure) and the reality principle as the pleasure derived from managing symptoms, Lacan pertinently asks why the "nervous system" does not succeed in living pleasurably on any sustained basis? Why does the symptom return as suffering? Freud's observation that the symptom persists in relation to a "repetition compulsion" (*Wiederholungszwang*) was explained by Lacan as the insistence (placing) of a "letter" in the unconscious. Beyond the pleasure principle, the Lacanian symptom insists as a principle of repetition that is identity itself; and identity (i.e., *moi* certainty) resists knowledge about, or treatment of, symptoms (Sheridan, *Ecrits*, p. 23). Beyond the reality principle, the symptom persists on the slope of the "death drive," then, and points to the reality principle's Real meaning of lack: the primordial object(s) of Desire can never be refound, only substituted for (*Séminaire* III, p. 98). The symptom, therefore, is "always inserted into a global economic state of the subject. . . . The dream is only a part of the subject's activity, while the symptom stretches itself out on several fields. The methods of operation [between dream and symptom] are more analogous than identical" (*Séminaire* II, p. 150). The symptom—like the dream, Desire, and language—is a special mark (represented by E) of the human dimension.

At his Yale lectures in 1975 Lacan added the Symptom as a fourth order or category that operates consciousness. Generally speaking, his idea of the symptom is of a living metaphor of any person's un-

conscious truth, a symbolic displacement of his or her accommodation to the psychic structures of Desire and Law as the latter elaborate specific Other(A) messages. The symptom exposes repression as
a failure to translate unconscious truth and leads, therefore, beyond
narcissism (*moi* fixations) to the meaning of Desire in the Other
(Sheridan, *Ecrits*, p. 167). The symptom (which literally "cries out"
the Desire in question) has been schematized by Lacan thusly.

S ·⟺→S'←⟺→· S — Symptom (substitute
                            signifier or new meaning)
           s
(repressed signified or
unconscious signifier)

The symptom as graphed above is not an isolated meaning, but a relation to a signifying chain—the signifier of a repressed chain of
meaning. The symptom is a signifier present in conscious life as if
excluded from it. Symptoms point to personal messages of repressed
trauma, then, not to neo-Freudian, blocked sexual energy. Symptoms, like dreams, can be deciphered in a disintegration of the Imaginary unity that constitutes the *moi* (Sheridan, *Ecrits*, p. 137).
Schneiderman stresses that, if an analyst knows how to "listen," the
terms used by an analysand to describe a symptom resonate with
signifiers attached to key events in a person's history and prehistory
(*Returning*, p. 15).

In *Télévision* Lacan described the symptom as consisting of a knot
of signifiers (⊗) which are Real, i.e., not metaphors. Constituted
originally to make a chain of unconscious signifying material, these
knotted signifiers can only be untied again in the Real (p. 22). In his
book *La structure et le style* (1975) Robert Georgin proposes that
Lacan's theory of there being no predetermined meaning—only ob-
servance of the rules of syntax—must necessarily culminate in the
idea that "the word is not a sign, but a 'knot' of meaning [*signification*]. [The word] is, finally, an image of sense [*sens*] in so far as
'sense' connects to the Other(A) and must be unveiled in order to be
discovered."[56] "Sense" is also the realm of madness, Lacan says.[57]
Georgin's point is that words are not elementally as unitary as most
linguists and philosophers believe, and Lacan forces them to think
otherwise.

A Chomskian theoretician would, however, accuse Lacan of confusing competence and performance in the Frenchman's view that
the word itself can be a symptom. To forestall such miscomprehen-

sions of Lacan, Georgin points out that Chomsky's generative grammar—with its theory that syntax, made up of phonemes and semantics, makes meaning by competence (grammar) and performance (context)—evades the problem of enunciation. Psychoanalysis is the one domain of enunciation where performance (context) is not opposed to competence (grammar), but rather a particular case of competence and performance, where words are libidinally invested enigmata, designating enunciations recorded in an unconscious syntax (Georgin, *La structure*, pp. 109, 111). Lacan claimed that the exact sciences link the Real to a syntax (or order), not realizing that syntax precedes semantics and gives semantics (or meaning) its sense (*sens*). The meanings of language itself therefore interested Lacan less than the realization that any message not only has a sense beyond its meaning, but also is a series of signs (cybernetics) which must be oriented. The question is: oriented toward what? Lacan naturally replied: toward the first symbols that anchored meaning as a personal sense of things in the being of each individual (*Séminaire* II, pp. 351–52). The symptom is the substitute sign or word—a metaphor—whose "cure" (or translation) would lie in discovering which meanings are repressed in a person's language and, in consequence, are manipulating their behavior in metonymic, puppeteer style. The difficulty for analysts and human subjects comes from the *moi*'s propensity to misrecognize the meaning of a symptom. The symptom is attributed a false and literal explanation, such as "it's in the blood or genes" or "a family trait," which ignores any reference to a repressed signifier in the Other(A).

By enriching Freud's concept of condensation, Lacan proved that human beings live on several levels at the same time and satisfy contradictory tendencies. Condensation or metaphor may, therefore, constitute the identificatory law of misrecognition (*Séminaire* III, p. 97). In other words, something appears one way but is another way. The laws of miscommunication and denial (*dénégation*) are different, although connected phenomena, however. Denial is a way of resisting the return of repressed signifiers, and thereby supports *moi* misrecognition of the Other(A). Misrecognition constitutes an Imaginary Symbolic chain of "self"-myth (sI), then, while miscommunication and denial characterize the discourse of the Symbolic order itself (iS) (*Séminaire* II, pp. 170, 184). But the symptom is yet another phenomenon—that of repression (*refoulement*)—which shows what happens when meaning does not follow in a conscious Symbolic chain with internal coherence. Since repressed meaning chains do not, however, disappear, they express themselves as neurotic symptoms of undeciphered signifiers (*Séminaire* III, p. 97). Denial is the linguistic (mental) mode of repressing a symptom, while misrecognition is the narcissistic mode. In his essay "Suture (elements of the logic of the signifier)" Miller defines suture as miscognition based on repression, or the general relation of lack to the structure of which lack is an element (p. 26). Miscognition or "suture" would refer to denial and misrecognition. Indeed, a term to cover both is needed. Even if a symptom has a bodily or behavioral manifestation, since language describes narcissism, the symptom is always connected to language. Even a pun can be the filler or padding which sustains a symptom (*Séminaire* III, p. 135).

If we accept Lacan's idea that a symptom is a duplicity of meaning where at least two conflicts are in play: an actual one and a former one, we can see how secondary repression and the symptom really amount to the same thing. Virtual (former) memories "return" in an actual (Real) conflict. The symptom—as a metaphor—permits meaning to exist enigmatically in conscious life and truthfully in an unconscious discourse that, thus, doubles one's life. Although a symptom must be interpreted in conscious life by Real indices—inert scotomas, parasitical compulsions, aggressive tendencies—the duplicity of its meaning actually comes from the essential doubleness of the signifier and signified (Sheridan, *Ecrits*, pp. 15, 24; *Séminaire* III, p. 187). For "cure" to occur, then, the *moi* principle of resistance (signifieds) must overcome its own misrecognitions (Imaginary blocking)—to say nothing of *je* denial—to permit a new set of unconscious messages to be inserted. An analysand must recognize that the symptom—which is either sexual or symbolic—has merely made an object of his or her life in a "silent" effort to restore a solid grounding of "self"-truth to his or her being. At the same time, sexual or symbolic symptoms are not impersonal or categorizable, for the specificity of a symptom appears in a person's language and not in some universal psychic meaning. No analyst can know the particulars of a symptom that hide at the heart of a patient's Other discourse. A "cure," as Schneiderman points out, lies in the way things are said, as an eminently social index that excludes the indices of thought, insight, and consciousness (*Returning*, pp. 12, 14). An analyst's attention to an analysand's speech will heed the pause in the middle of the sentence—Saussure's *découpage*—which indicates both an expected meaning, and a repeated one (in the sense of *déjà entendu*). Either a diachronic signifier or another register are the domains of this second or latent (regressive) discourse, always metonymically ready to emerge under thousands of forms. Lacan thus attributes a meaning even to the suspension of sense: to not finishing a sentence. At such moments, we may "see" the split between concrete language and Other(A) messages that the speaking subject tries to counteract (*Séminaire* III, pp. 129, 138–39).

In cases of neurosis, knots are primitively recorded between one-and-a-half and four-and-a-half years of age (*Séminaire* III, p. 177). Normally *moi* signifieds block the appearance of these primordial signifiers, although some signifying effects and representations may unravel and attach themselves to language. In psychosis, by contrast, signifieds disappear, leaving no meaningful link between the concrete signifying chain of language and the primitive signifiers in the Other(A). The effects that, according to Lacan, are recorded between eighteen months and four-and-a-half years and may become the basis of neurotic structures should not, however, be regarded as the preconscious, but as its zone—the intimation of an Other(A) meaning system in being. Ernst Kris understood preconscious mental processes, said Lacan, as well as the fecundity of the Imaginary text, but Freud insisted on a radical difference between the preconscious and the unconscious. Lacan maintained Freud's division as a difference between *moi* and Other(A) by making *moi* signifieds less primordial than Other signifiers (*Séminaire* III, p. 186). But the signifier ensures that there be no final barrier between the preconscious and unconscious. "Regression" to *moi* signifieds does not lead to the Other(A) then, only the signifier does. Although the *moi* floats at the surface of conscious life (particularly in others' eyes), the signifiers in the unconscious are radically unassimilable for they consider the subject already dead (*Séminaire* III, p. 202). Symptoms, seen in this light, represent some inscription of unconscious truth from a repressed chain of signifiers.[58] It becomes increasingly clear that symptoms are not the same thing as the *moi*; narcissism does not cause the disease of the psyche. Symptoms point, rather, to Real unconscious effects clustered around Desire and Law. The symptom, therefore, is a metaphor in which either flesh (sex) or function (symbol) are taken as signifying elements (Sheridan, *Ecrits*, p. 166). One might add that the interplay of body, mind, and language in the structure of a symptom should offer sufficient proof of the relevance of biology to culture and vice versa in Lacan's thought to disconcert those critics who would dismiss his ideas as a pure culturism.

Reactions to the childhood effects of Desire and Oedipal Law generate a fairly limited number of psychic structures. These are the normative or sublimated neurotic (obsessive, hysterical, or delusional); perverted; and psychotic (paranoid, schizophrenic, or manic depressive). While each structure only "means" in terms of unique myths and particular signifiers, they can be discussed at a general level. The obsessional neurotic, for example, tries to renounce his unsatisfied Desire, and thus refuses a certain freedom of "being" by remaining a slave to the Other(A). The hysteric tries to retain her unsatisfied Desire by not defying the Father(s). Both deny Castration, the obsessive by denying that he was loved too much (his Desire saturated), and the hysteric by denying that she was not loved enough (her Desire insatiable). In the essay "Jerome, or Death in the Life of the Obsessional" by Serge Leclaire, the hysteric is described as implicitly asking: Am I a man or a woman? The obsessional asks: Am I dead or alive? Subject or object? (in Schneiderman, *Returning*, p. 108). Both imagine that the Other(A) requires their Castration and, thus, identify the Other's lack with their own *demande* (Φ with D) (Sheridan, *Ecrits*, p. 321). The Other's demand thus assumes the function of an object in the neurotic's fantasy, which is reduced to the drive (Desire) itself ($\mathcal{S} \Diamond D$). A neurotic structure logically reveals a person who does not know what she or he wants (Schneiderman, *Returning*, p. 15). If the Other(A) is absent and Desire unconscious, the neurotic is bound to be confused by her or his fidelity to a principle of ambiguity. The neurotic gives priority to *demande*, nonetheless, to the defective and unattainable being of the Other (Leclaire's essay in Schneiderman, *Returning*, p. 123). In the neurotic's myth—which avoids the Real in favor of living out fantasies or promoting symptoms—the Real father was often split in the child's psychic representation of him (Schneiderman, *Returning*, pp. 6–7). In his essay "The Neurotic's Individual Myth" Lacan wrote that the child was bequeathed the function of living out the (m)Other's Desire, the father's Symbolic function having been somehow weakened (through death, defection, alcoholism, or other cause). Lacan argues that in this type of Desire-and-Law interaction, although the nodal point of neurosis is the mother as Desiring (i.e., unsatisfied), a very special form of narcissistic splitting lies at the heart of the neurotic structure: that of a split in the psychic conception of the father so that he is idealized and denigrated at the same time, sought and fled simultaneously, and so on.[59]

But the truly radical innovation in Lacan's theory of the symptom arises from its role in psychosis. According to Lacan, the conception of the psychical process which holds the symptom to be merely an index (Jaspers) is nowhere shown to be more fallacious than in psychosis: "because nowhere is the symptom, if one can decipher it, more clearly articulated than in the structure itself" (Sheridan, *Ecrits*, p. 184). As stated at the outset of this chapter, the fundamental "message" of Other(A) language is simply that the signifier structures the subject as a symbolic entity. But without linguistic conventions or *moi* myths to stabilize them, Other(A) signifiers become detached and incoherent. In prepsychosis, an enigmatic void of confusion precedes the certainties that characterize delusional meaning (Sheridan, *Ecrits*, pp. 184–85). Delusional meaning therefore anticipates its own development—metonymical and parasitical—and is only mistakenly called intuitive. For psychotic "intuitions" quickly become inane repetitions, described by Lacan as the structure of the signifier substituting (metaphorically) for meaning anticipated, and metonymically attesting to "self"-meaning and conventional rules lost. Retroaction—a property of signifieds and of semantics—has ceased to function. In his essay "The Crane Child" François Péraldi used Lacan to compare normal and psychotic language.[60] His contrast attributes a binary structure as well as a representative function to normal language, which leads to a ternary structure in relationship to the objects which language represents. Normal language, furthermore, has a performative and conformative function in the Symbolic. Psychotic language, by contrast, resembles C. S. Peirce's icons. Psychotics make "semiotic productions," but not language (Péraldi, "Crane Child," pp. 98–100).

Péraldi clearly missed Lacan's point. Péraldi's view seems a reverse kind of Ricoeurian argumentation, in which word and symbol converge at some elemental point which is no longer really language. Psychotic language has supposedly become signs of pure representation or iconicity. Lacan showed, on the other hand, that the language spoken by psychotics dramatically demonstrates the collapse or disintegration of the Imaginary *moi* in its relationship to others, as commanded by repressed representations. Their deranged discourse elevates nonsensical language made of words and sounds over coherent representations, "self"-myths, and the rules of grammar. Instead the previously unsymbolized reverse face of the *moi* appears as ideal ego: in Schreber's case as the wife of God.

John Muller describes psychosis: "The symptom no longer signifies but is lived, a metaphor lived as real. Words do not mediate, do not refer to what is absent [the Phallus or the symbol for the father]" ("Lacan and Language," p. 27). The pain of psychosis is inseparable from Lacan's notion of the Real as the field of the death drive (fragmentation, self-dispersion). Normal language, on the slope of Castration, requires its own use as the representational deferral that allows the cultural to supplant the natural, words as substitutes for psychic insufficiency. The "gain" of psychosis lies in retaining a psychic sense of eternity and immortality, in denying the "truth" of the human condition. The structural flaw in the scaffolding of the psychotic subject, then, is the failure to deny the Other(A). Such *dénégation* ordinarily allows secondary repression to play paradoxically on language as signifieds. But delusional psychotic language no longer represses, no longer defers the search for "self" through the substitutions of Desire (the first substitution ordinarily being a coherent use of language itself), and through posing one's identity question to others. Having foreclosed the signifier for death—separation—the psychotic knows his or her place in the Other(A) and thus appears as a martyr to the unconscious in his or her fidelity to that Other (*Séminaire* III, p. 171). In laying the unconscious bare, psychosis places words, objects, and the human body at the same level. In paranoia, for example, the Imaginary is taken to be Real (*Séminaire* II, p. 315); in schizophrenia the body image itself fragments.

Unlike ordinary speaking subjects, who implicitly accept the subjectivity of the Other (which can lie and convince), psychotics must never question the Other(A). In consequence they exclude it as a principle of support for normalcy in "self"-image or language and give full rein to the fragmentary nonmeaning of its dead letters and annihilating Desires. "Mental" illness, therefore, is the illness of an unrepressed Other(A), accorded the fixed status of something Real (*Séminaire* III, pp. 77–78). In contrast to the closure of neurotic discourse (which can be decoded), psychotic speech opens directly onto pure signifiers in the unconscious; it cannot be deciphered in relation to "self" or semantics (*Séminaire* III, p. 149). In conclusion, we can say, nonetheless, that the Lacanian symptom is "meaning" from beginning to end, even if its meaning concerns only the structuration of mentality as in psychosis. The symptom is distinguished from the innate or the natural, because it is structured in terms of signifier and signified, and works by the laws of metaphor and metonymy. These laws apply to an understanding of the structure of psychosis, as well as to that of neurosis. The symptom is, therefore, the reverse side of discourse (*Séminaire* II, p. 368). In 1975 Lacan said that "what constitutes the symptom—that something which dallies with the unconscious . . . is that one believes in it" (Mitchell and Rose, *Feminine Sexuality*, p. 168). Whether the neurotic believes myth over "truth," or the psychotic believes apparent nonsense, in each case a logic of the signifier infers the structuration of mental causality in reference to the Law of the Name-of-the-Father. Therefore, the structuration of mentality has to do not only with language, but also with the learning of a gender identity.

5

"BEYOND THE PHALLUS?"

THE QUESTION OF GENDER IDENTITY

LACAN never tires of repeating that *Totem and Taboo* is wrong and that the Oedipus complex is Freud's own neurosis. He offers instead his own theories of the paternal metaphor and the Oedipal structure, which make use of his innovative concepts of the Phallus, Castration, Desire, and *jouissance*.[1] By recasting Freud's realist picture of the Oedipal complex away from both myth and biology, Lacan introduces the concept of a structure that is formed by the intervention of a third element in the original infant-mother dyad: the Law of the Name-of-the-Father. Moving from the realm of the Freudian sexual triangle per se to that of symbolic effect, Lacan leaves the scene of the incest taboo to dramatists and anthropologists. Sexual identity is not based on biology or any other innate factor, Lacan says, but is learned through the dynamics of identification and language.

In harmony with his theory that meaning does not arise from substance or essence, but from an inmixing of symbol and sound, structural effects and related associations that compose the unconscious, Lacan hypothesized that the Oedipal myth (and myth in general) is simply "the attempt to give epic form to that which operates itself from structure" (*Séminaire* II, p. 51). Lacan used the word "structure" in the early 1950s to mean that which functions like a language, that is, by order. Just as speech and lexicon are governed by the metaphoric and metonymic laws of language, so the unconscious has its own syntax and transforms images and language through analogous procedures of combination, condensation, referentiality, substitution, and displacement.[2] Consequently, any direct linking of Oedipal "structure" to biology through body configurations, gender, or genital experience or its "resolution" in genital satisfaction is a

misinterpretation of a logical, symbolic, representational, and transformational drama.

Lacan saw the effect of the Oedipal nexus as that which decides
the assignment of sex, where sex is correlated with identity rather
than gender (*Séminaire* I, p. 80). Every child is under an obligation to
submit his or her sexuality to certain restrictions or laws of organization and exchange within a sexually differentiated group and thus
find his or her place within that society.[3] The Oedipal crisis does not
occur because a child wants to possess its mother sexually, but when
the child comprehends its society's sexual rules; the crisis is resolved when the rules are acceded to and accepted. According to
Lacan, it is the Symbolic order that conveys these rules through language and the injunction to individuation. We must remember that
the Symbolic here does not mean anything representative of a second
hidden thing or essence. Rather, it refers to that order whose principal function is to mediate between the Imaginary order and the
Real. The Symbolic order interprets, symbolizes, articulates, and
universalizes both the experiential and the concrete which, paradoxically, it has already shaped contextually.

Stuart Schneiderman has written: "I have found it useful to distinguish after [Robert] Stoller between gender identity and sexual identity. . . . I call them primary and secondary sexual identification.
Thus there is a difference between being male or female and being
masculine or feminine."[4] The medically trained psychiatrist Robert
Stoller wrote in 1973: "While the newborn presents a most mal-
leable central nervous system upon which the environment writes,
we cannot say that the central nervous system is neutral or neuter.
Rather, we can say that the effects of these biological systems, organized prenatally in a masculine or feminine direction, are always
(with the exception of hypogonadal males) too gentle in humans to
withstand the more powerful forces of environment in human development, the first and most profound of which is mothering."[5] In numerous examples Stoller gives unequivocal proof of the priority of
culture over biological nature in determining sexual identity. Both
Lacan and Stoller offer evidence that sexual identity structuring begins in a pre-Oedipal period. Lacan shows additionally that, in a
given culture and family, sexual role possibilities await a neonate on
whom to impose preexisting identity functions and actually precede
an infant's biological conception.

The title of this chapter—"Beyond the Phallus?"—is a glossed quo-
tation from Lacan's Seminar Twenty. The phrase is striking because
it encapsulates the controversy surrounding his theories on the Phal-

lus and Castration in their relationship to the structuring of gender identity and sexual personality. In my view, Lacanian theory provides a particular key for understanding the socialization and symbolization processes that have shaped male and female specificity through the ages. In a meeting of this seminar (1972–73), Lacan suggested that perhaps someone should write a book entitled *Beyond the Phallus*, ironically punning on Freud's *Beyond the Pleasure Principle.* "That would be lovely," he said, "and it would give another consistency to the woman's liberation movement. A pleasure or orgasm (*jouissance*) beyond the phallus" (*Séminaire* XX, p. 69). Later on I shall follow the thread of argument in Lacan's essay and consider the reasons for the seemingly ironic tone of his joke-cum-challenge. Certain feminists do not regard Lacan's interpretation of Freud as a joke, however, and have attacked Lacan as a phallocrat.

As stated in earlier chapters, the two cornerstones in the Lacanian unconscious structure of the human subject are Desire and Law. Though the specific meanings attached to the structures of Desire and Law vary according to personal experience and historical context, the structural effects are themselves Real and shape both personal trajectory and history. The "enemy" which feminists must confront, then, is neither class structure nor patriarchy per se, but the mimetic mirror-stage processes of fusion and difference by which the human subject takes on its nuclear form between six and eighteen months of age. Insofar as the elemental illusion of sameness is concretely attached to the mother, primary Desire is enigmatically linked to the female; insofar as the secondary experience of difference is both abstract and attached to the father, law is linked to the male. Freud's error was to mistake a structural, symbolic, and representational drama for a natural one based on biology. In *Totem and Taboo* (1913) Freud argued that the tendency of younger males to subvert the law of older males arose not only out of Oedipal jealousy but also because of race memory. Lacan replaced Freud's spurious reasoning in regard to male aggressivity by explaining how memory is constituted and transmitted by language and identifications. Equally as important, he argued that a person becomes male or female by identifying (or not) as the phallic signifier, and not by any innate mechanism. Insofar as aggressivity and depression are reverse sides of the same coin, physical violence is, in my view, an Imaginary reaction practiced principally by males to validate an illusion of representing power and prestige within the public/phallic order. Depression, a principally female Imaginary reaction, attests to an identificatory loss of prestige and power.

It is essential, therefore, to insist on Lacan's (and Stoller's) distinction between gender identity and sexual identity. This distinction forestalls any literal identification of the same sex according to gender. According to Stoller, furthermore, biological and hormonal effects do not determine sexual personality, since these probably vary more from person to person than from one sex to another. Implicit support for Stoller's argument comes from Princeton medical researchers who have recently discovered that the male hormone testosterone operates identically on men and women. Since it regulates cyclical biological changes in both, their findings destroy the myth that men are free from hormonal influences while women are controlled by them.[6]

Lacan's account of the structuring of a human subject locates the source of sexual identity in the pre-Oedipal period, but dates this period earlier than Freud did. Lacan also rejects Freud's biological distinction between the sexes according to narcissism (the female on this reading being inherently narcissistic), and also divorces gender from narcissism. Narcissism arises first from mirror-stage identification and is fundamental to any identity. As demonstrated in Chapter 1, the human infant achieves a sense of continuity or well-being in the preconscious mirror stage by fusion with another.[7] Lacan called the post-mirror, disruptive third element of the father's presence the phallic signifier. Its effects gradually constitute the paternal metaphor. By making the infant aware of difference and existential aloneness, or alienation, the phallic signifier introduces the possibility of substitutive self-representation through naming.[8] In French the father's name (nom) even seems to say "no" (non) to fusion with the mother.

This Castration leaves the infant feeling incomplete, broken, an *hommelette* (*Ecrits*, 1966, p. 845). No incest wish is being punished here by fear of organ loss; instead, the fear is of loss of being or of disintegration. So potent is this drama that it inaugurates human anxiety. The phallic signifier imposes culture or order on nature, therefore, creating a permanent awareness of Otherness in the subject. Lacan's revision of Freud's Castration complex inscribes the individual in an unconscious structure of exchange: exchange of mother fusion for father "selfhood" or otherness. The devastating loss of symbiosis is repressed and displaced, but symbolically felt by its effects. This is why Lacan speaks ironically of the *faut/faux du temps*, playing on the idea that self-revelation only comes in the unfolding of a person's "epic" in time (numbers 0—6), but also on the fact that chronological time is false. The primordial separation drama creates a repressed void in being which never ceases to echo.

Experiments such as those conducted by David Kotelchuck of the University of Massachusetts must therefore be considered in a larger framework. Kotelchuck found that, in general, six- to twelve-month-old infants reacted in almost the same manner to father and mother. Twelve- to twenty-four-month-old infants preferred the mother by 55 percent; both parents by 20 percent; the father by 25 percent.[9] The problems posed by such a study tell us much about the limitations of empirical studies. For our purposes, however, Lacan does not teach about "preference," but about primordiality, its effects and structural implications for ontology. The phallic signifier does not denote any sexual gender of superiority. Nor does it place sameness above difference in any order of preference (especially in the case of two-year-olds who have not yet learned what their gender is nor what it means). The Phallus is, instead, the signifier or creator of the lack that establishes substitutive Desire as a permanent ontological state and makes adult "wanting" a shadow pantomime of the primordial drama of Desire between mother and infant.

Lacanian Desire is beyond physical need, therefore, and refers to the implicit "appeal" (demande) for knowledge of the absent Other(A) through the dynamics of identification and a person's relationship to the social order (Séminaire XI, p. 172). Its libidinal source is a lack in the Other (Sheridan, Ecrits, p. 287). The "want-in-being" of alienation is a "subversion" of the subject, which makes him or her aim not at renunciation or repression, but at the realization of Desire, the re-finding of the presocial self.[10] By "subversion," I understand Lacan to mean that adult perception is anchored in an unfathomed reality, which insists beyond any willed intentionality. The goal sought is a repetition, the replacement of the pleasure (jouissance) in the illusion of wholeness which was characteristic of the prephallic period. Jouissance means sexual pleasure, but at an abstract level it could be described as the temporary pleasure afforded by substitute objects or by others' recognition (substitutes for the original other). At this juncture jouissance and Desire meet in the concept of the plus-de-jouir.[11]

The French psychoanalyst Gilles Deleuze and the philosopher Félix Guattari have equated the Lacanian phallic metaphor—synonymous with Law, language, and the social order—with patriarchy and recommend in Anti-Oedipe (1972) that we resist patriarchy by refusing to be subjected to the Symbolic order. In this prescription, they imply that one can equate the phallic or Oedipal structure with its substantivized political attributes. Through schizoanalysis, Deleuze and Guattari claim that one can learn to recover presocial desiring individualism, circumvent the triadic Holy Family, and ally

Desire to the collectivity rather than to a power hierarchy. They extol the richness of the unconscious as production, the "free syntheses where everything is possible, the connections without end, the disjunctions without exclusivity, the conjunctions without specificity, the partial objects, the flux."[12] These authors, indeed, advocate what Lacan has shown to be an impossibility: to live in sanity in an archaic, preverbal state of psychic symbiosis. The schizophrenic hero of Desire, whom they extol, is a kind of Marcusian or Laing-like caricature of the Lacanian desiring subject. By substantivizing Desire along biological, id-state lines, they misread Lacan, although they later claimed that this book was written as a joke. For Lacan, Desire refers to sundry lacks attributable to inherent gaps in the subject's structure.

Deleuze and Guattari also misrepresent Lacan by failing to grasp that the Real effect of phallic intervention forms one part of unconscious symbolization in terms of identification with the father and, by extension, with forces of Oedipal Law. Insofar as the social order itself is internalized as difference and language, patriarchy is not simply an external order to be overthrown. All ideological readings of Lacan miss the point. In the Marxist Louis Althusser's famous misreading of Lacan, the subject and the Other(A) are equated so that the conscious subject is both master of Desire and of language![13] Even Colin MacCabe, in his critique of Althusser, succumbs to the temptation of finding fault with Lacan where there is no fault to be found. He says: "The actual sites of language use (the family, the school, the workplace) are merely unimportant variations with no effectivity inscribed in [Lacan's] theory. . . . To shift attention to the site of enunciation is to insist that it is not simply the formation of the unconscious that must be theorised but the formation of specific unconsciousnesses" ("On Discourse," p. 213). Indeed, the aim of Lacanian psychoanalysis is to unveil the specificity of a given Other(A) text in its relationship to its own *je* conventions and to the specificity of its *moi* (see Chapter 1).

Lacan attributed the very need for ideologies to the unconscious cornerstone of Desire. Whether a person defends a philosophy of capitalism or communism (or any other belief system), the totalizing drive toward building meaning systems is itself based on the structural lack in being. Since the substantive aspects of belief, which make up the *moi* passion for fixity, compensate for an inherent loss, their truth value is actually secondary. As a correlate of the original Imaginary symbiosis with the mother, Desire drives people to seek recognition at the other's expense and, if necessary, to annihilate the other to validate their own belief system. Given the absolutist nature of Desire, it is not surprising that its paths must be restricted by internal and external laws, limits, and the language of a given social order. For "fulfilled," mirror-stage Desire is both a social menace and a prison house of mental grandiosity. Suppression (*Unterdrückung*) may be seen, then, as the necessary reverse side of phallic law or taboo: a limitation on psychic omnipotence or a "good symptom." Sublimation is the overall price that human beings pay for sanity. Lacan's picture of the human subject accurately conveys the tragedy of natural being. We are faced with a choice between individuation through psychic Castration (that is, learning difference by alienation into language, social conventions, and rules) or failure to evolve an identity adequate to social functioning. Lacanian phallic Law is, therefore, a double-edged sword. On the one hand, it saves people from (m)Other domination; on the other, it tyrannizes because it is arbitrary and artificial.

One of the most prolific French feminist writers on the contemporary scene is Luce Irigaray. Like Deleuze and Guattari, she has portrayed the Lacanian Symbolic or social order as enemy territory. Ruled by phallocrats, patriarchs, and pederasts, it is an order to be resisted if women are to gain the freedom of their own specificity. In my estimation, Irigaray misrepresents Lacan in much the same way Deleuze and Guattari do, but their goals are different. She reads him substantively rather than structurally and thus sees him as prescriptive instead of descriptive and analytic. By equating Lacan's phallic signifier with patriarchy, she substantivizes the concept biologically, so that Phallus = penis = male. Her views therefore imply that males and females have natural psychic attributes in keeping with gender. By failing to accept the structural effect and symbolic nature of the Lacanian phallic signifier—neutral in its own right—Irigaray's assessment of Lacan as a phallocrat is wrong. Although Deleuze, Guattari, and Irigaray may not be mistaken in their criticisms of the patriarchal order, they err in construing Lacan's first cause explanations of human behavior as approval of it.

In *Speculum de l'Autre femme* (1974) Irigaray accuses psychoanalysis of a "masculine bias" and being arrested in the "phallic phase."[14] Little boys never discover "real female genitals," Freud said in an essay entitled "The Infantile Genital Organization of the Libido."[15] Irigaray claims that big boys, particularly male psychoanalysts, make the same error and equate female sexuality with motherhood. Jane Gallop points out that in *Speculum* Irigaray attacks Lacan without mentioning his name except in a footnote.[16] In *Ce*

Sexe qui n'en est pas un, Lacan is depicted as a profiteering cynic who gains pleasure, power, and love from being a Master.[17] Insofar as Irigaray views Lacan as merely another manipulator of women, she rejects what she calls his system of phallic values, that is, the theory of a phallic fixing of a child's destiny in terms of its perception of sexual difference.

In *Ce Sexe* Irigaray treats the Lacanian mirror stage as implicitly male and so foreign to the feminine. His mirror becomes the most recent version of a philosophical topos whose *raison d'être* is to valorize sameness and visibility.[18] In this case the unique sexual standard of sameness is the Phallus. She asks: *"And as far as the organism is concerned, what happens when the mirror reveals nothing to see?* No sex, for example, as is the case for the little girl. And to say that in the constituting effects of the image in the mirror that 'the sex (of the congener or like member of a species) matters little' and further that 'the specular image seems to be the threshold of the visible world,' does not that amount to stressing that the female sex will be excluded from it? And that it is an asexual or male sex body which will determine the feature of the *Gestalt*, that irreducible matrix of the introduction of the subject into the social order. Hence its functioning according to laws so foreign to the feminine?"[19] In *Speculum* Irigaray looked back to Freud's theories on narcissism and femininity and postulated the Lacanian mirror stage as the source of the first "narcissistic wounds" that Freud attributed to the little girl.[20] Consequently, in *Ce Sexe*, she tries to explain Freud by Lacan. She concludes that such a perception of the little girl must be reversed, and for a start she urges other feminists to follow her lead in repudiating the Master discourse. She claims that even by arguing against Freud or Lacan, we legitimize a whole system of male supremacist values and perception that view humans as essentially masculine.[21] Irigaray, paradoxically, becomes an example of her own criticism.

Although Irigaray offers no constructive formula in *Speculum*, she does advance some ideas of her own in *Ce Sexe*. She charges Lacan with excluding female bodily fluids from his list of the objects of Desire. But in "la Mécanique des fluides" she also fails to point out that Lacan omits seminal fluid from his list of objects. We know that Lacan's primordial objects of Desire—reduced in Seminar Twenty to breast/sucking; excrement; the gaze; and the voice—only refer to those paradigms prefigured in early infant life. Intent on distorting Lacan's theory for her own purposes, Irigaray calls his science infantile and claims that it bases the aim of phallic desire on an anal model.

In an intriguing comparison between Lacan and the marquis de Sade, Irigaray says that both prefer dry, anal homosexual sexuality. "Excrement, certainly, but blood from a period, no," she says, nor vaginal flow.[22] Irigaray concludes that phallic sexual theory is homosexual in its exclusion of otherness, with heterosexuality merely as a mediate homosexual form in its exchange of women between men. Lacan's discourse, in her view, perpetuates the subjugation of women perhaps more than all others ("Così fan tutti," in *New French Feminisms*, p. 101). But the only counterposition she proposes to a phallic sexual economy is woman's subtlety and pliancy, her "feeble resistance." She enjoins women to band together to create a feminine discourse that refuses Castration.[23]

What I find particularly disturbing in Irigaray's analysis is her resistance to getting Lacan "right." This is symbolized by her recent refusal to acknowledge him by name, even though her philosophical debt to him is massive. In her indirect dialogue with Lacan, his presence—like that of the Old Testament Jehovah—becomes more potent by the omission of the name. But because she misreads Lacan, she misses the chance to use his theories (1) to transcend his limitations (as other feminists have done with Freud) or (2) to make sense of suggestions that he has purposely left open. Irigaray depicts the Lacanian mirror stage as the earliest in a series of historical stages that oppress women. But her understanding of the mirror stage seems limited to its literal, visual aspect, which she reduces to the genetic or biological. The mirror stage is, of course, a metaphor for a mimetic process that occurs in intersocial relations—with or without a mirror. The mirror stage initially represents a visual, corporal unity with which the infant identifies, in contrast to the tumult felt within. This tumult arises, as we have seen, from a lack of neurological maturity and motor skills in the first few months of life. In this sense, the mirror stage presents a state of anticipatory unity.[24] The human infant's helplessness makes it dependent on the outside world in a way that other animal species are not. The mirror stage is, therefore, a metaphor for the alienation that first forms the ego from the outside world through identification with others.

In Seminar Three (1955–56) Lacan described the first eighteen months of life thus: "the human *moi* is the other and at the beginning the subject is closer to the form of the other than to the surging forth of its own tendency. At the origin, it is a collection of incoherent Desires—that is the true meaning of the expression *corps morcelé* [fragmented body]—and the first synthesis of the *ego* is essentially *alter ego*; it is alienated" (p. 50). Since the infant identifies with the human form as a center of unity outside itself, human awareness of "self" starts out based on a lie. The subsequent effects of this original disjunction or assymetry range from the psychotic production of a double (as in the *Doppelgänger* phenomenon) to the kind of bodily disintegration depicted by Hieronymus Bosch.[25] Throughout adult life, the mirror-stage effect will function dynamically to diffract the supposed unity of discourse and prevent people from feeling "one" with themselves.

Irigaray fails to deal with Lacan's idea that both females and males are "victimized" by the imposition of an-Other's image, discourse, and Desire. Men, like women, are pursued by an identity dilemma: "Who am/is 'I' in the eyes of others/the Other(A)?" Nor does she consider the problem of how soon sexual difference is really learned. The period between six and eighteen months is certainly far too early for girls and boys to have interpreted their gender difference in terms of the cultural significance assigned to it. Although the Lacanian infant introjects the surrounding world from the start, the little girl does not attribute a penis to her mother at this stage any more than she sees herself deprived of one. Juliet Mitchell also supposes that female infants do not perceive themselves as different from male infants. Both sexes are satisfied with a bisexual disposition. She states: "Everything that Freud writes confirms that there is no important psychological differentiation in this pre-Oedipal situation."[26]

With the onset of the Oedipal stage, Freud saw the little girl become "phallic" until puberty, when she is supposed to undertake the difficult transition from "virility" to "femininity." Mitchell's comments on Freud's thought take a different tack, however: "But this [pre-Oedipal] situation is not a stage, not an amount of time, but a level. At another level the culturally determined implication of sexual difference is then always already in waiting" (Mitchell, *Psychoanalysis and Feminism*, p. 52). Mitchell's first level is, of course, the Imaginary "self"-text made up of the Symbolic and the Real. The Other(A) level is that order of Symbolic myths that unremittingly impose themselves on the newborns in their realm and attribute public prestige to maleness despite inherent attributes of either sex. As so often, the claims of Anglo-American empirical studies unwittingly support Lacan's theory. A recent British study, for example, shows that fathers cuddle girl babies more, but talk more to boy babies. An American researcher found that fathers feed and diaper more if the baby is male.[27]

Irigaray has confused the fixing of a species-specific *Gestalt* during the mirror stage with the phallic fixing of sexual identity that occurs *after* the mirror stage. This leads her to believe that Lacan prescribes a phallocracy. The blind spot causes her to distort what I find most important for feminist theory: Lacan's epistemology comes the closest of any modern thinker's to demystifying the basic causes and differences of sexual personality. It is true that he has never advocated his theories be used to change woman's history. This distinction is essential: Lacan's description of the primary structures underlying the patriarchal order is far from any philosophical support for maintaining such an order.

The initial fixing of a sexual personality, then, occurs between eighteen months and five years of age. It involves a secondary identification with the stereotyped characteristics of one parent or the other, as defined by a given culture and within a specific family. Generally speaking, both sexes identify with the mother first: her body, her activities, her clothes, and her gestures. While societies encourage such behavior in little girls, it is discouraged in little boys who are informed from the earliest months that "boys do not do that" (wear mother's jewelry, wash dishes, wear a fluffy pink dress, and so on). Freud's early bisexual and phallic phases—common to both sexes—give way to a common mimetic identification with the female on the Imaginary plane. Language's imposition of the Symbolic on the Imaginary is consequently crucial to any maintenance of patriarchy. By five years of age children have acquired grammar and learned whether to call themselves "he" or "she." To discuss the third-person pronoun merely in terms of the historical (as does Emile Benveniste, for example) is an error.[28] The third-person pronoun— even in those languages which find some other grammatical device for denoting gender—is always taught ambivalently, amid jokes and the utmost gravity. In other words, we assimilate society's gender myths within our own psychic structure, and each individual learns the version applied to him or her. It makes sense, to take another example, that psychotics are transsexual, because they have never learned adequately to count to an Imaginary 3. By remaining Imaginarily confused between 1 and 2—symbiosis and Castration—they are fused with the mother and so not subject to the father's Name, which she contains; both woman and man; or neither. Normal children do count to 3, however, in learning and interpreting an Imaginary relation to loss.

The confusion of sexual organs with gender identity is a secondary occurrence, which is synonymous with Oedipalization between eighteen months and five years of age. It is conditioned by identification, interpreted by language, enshrined in myth, and passed on as "natural" truth. The critic Frederic Jameson has pointed out that "many attacks on the Lacanian doctrine of the phallic signifier seem to be inspired by their confusion of the penis as organ with the phallus which is signifier, function or metaphor" (Jameson, "Imaginary and Symbolic in Lacan," p. 352). Anthony Wilden, John Brenkman, Irigaray, and others have fueled the misunderstanding by talking of Lacan's phallocracy.[29] But Michèle Montrelay, a practicing psychoanalyst in Paris, has used Lacanian theory to connect language to body organs: "Confusion and coincidences: hearing is very close to the eye, which is seen by the child as an eye-ear, an open hole. . . . The confusion of organs gives us not only the image of the confusion of names but also their collusion with *jouissance*" (Schneiderman, *Returning*, p. 83).

Perhaps the early confusion of organs and language (which persists in myth) have led various commentators to group the mirror stage with the paternal metaphor. It bears repeating that the Lacanian phallic signifier and its divisive effect begin to terminate the mirror stage when the infant has reached approximately eighteen months of age. The learning of language is inseparable from this process. Any given linguistic order will then gradually teach a child about his or her physiology as well as about the "roles" (masquerades) which children are to assume as adults because of anatomy. Although the most obvious distinction is between male and female, value judgments will be inculcated with regard to race, height, weight, aesthetic preferences, and so on. Desire will aim toward the "desirable" and only be thwarted by what Law demarcates as unattainable.

Freud defined the Oedipus complex as the organized ensemble of loving and hostile desires felt by the child toward her or his parents. This has been recast by Lacan to account for the evolution that, little by little, substitutes the father for the mother. Serge Leclaire sums up this new interpretation as follows: the mother is taken as the central and primordial character in the complex, and the father as the principal and ultimate reference. Between six and eighteen months of age, the infant identifies with a unified, corporal image of "self," which corresponds more or less to identification with the mother's body. Gradually, the child identifies with the object of the mother's Desire as well. Wishing to be all for her, he or she wants to be the signifier of her Desire—the Phallus in the symbolic and signifying sense of that which replaces lack (Sheridan, *Ecrits*, pp. 288–89). At this post-mirror juncture, the first signified for the infant is the Phallus or paternal metaphor. But since the child does not know what the mother's Desire really is, the first and only real and concrete signified for the child is its Desire for pleasing and fusing with the mother. Both boys and girls detach themselves rather quickly, therefore, from identification with being the object that mother desires since they see that, despite their efforts at being what she wants, she remains dissatisfied.

This fact points the child toward otherness, i.e., to the referentiality of the father. The first metaphorical signifier here is the Name-of-the-Father spelling prohibition, separation, difference, and individuation by Castration (my Imaginary view of Frege's 2). Since the child cannot fill her lack, the mother is now the mediator permitting the birth of substitutive Desire through Castration. She also ushers in the acceptance of prohibition and Law. In this post-mirror stage the child learns the relation of the mother to the father's word and tries to gain access to the Symbolic: that is, to the father's Law (roughly Freud's periodization of one-and-a-half to four years of age). In this second phase the father is revealed *as refusal and as reference* (Leclaire's italics). In the third phase the father's real penis is equated with having the Phallus or not. The psychic evolution of the Oedipus complex, then, is an identificatory reshaping of the subject, complete when a child renounces identification with the object that pleases Mama—(to be or not to be the "Phallus") (*Séminaire* III, p. 189)—and is concerned now with having or not having the penis (Schneiderman, *Returning*, pp. 121–22). In Seminar Three Lacan maintained that the elemental identity question (which returns as a symptom in psychosis) is the *to be or not to be* a man or woman. But this question is posed for the subject on the plane of the signifier, that is, in the Real of the words in the Other instead of on the plane of specular identification (p. 189). The mirror is splintered by the word.

Perhaps Irigaray's conviction that Lacan is a phallocrat—one who sees the Phallus as the archetype of sexual value—arises from her listening only to selected portions of Lacan's discourse on sexual identity. The residue of the *malentendu* may lie in Lacan's wish to remain faithful to Freudian theory. In Seminar Three, for example, Lacan followed Freud's idea that the female slowly gains her heterosexual, feminine identity through the paternal object and not through the mother (p. 193). Freud had said that girls must gain their own femininity by renouncing their first love object (the mother) and becoming, instead, the feminine love object (the mother!) that the man has always desired (Irigaray, *Speculum*, p. 33). But Lacan stated with increasing conviction over the years that the Imaginary identification with the mother is the bedrock text of "self," the site of the primordial discourse of the unconscious—*la dite maternelle*—which organizes all human behavior for both sexes around Desire. The psychotic, moreover, testifies to this by confusion of sex and gender: Am I a woman, or am I a man? Even though a female gradually identifies herself as a sexual object for a male, therefore, and takes his identity to reflect her own in the Symbolic order, she still does not relinquish her *moi*. Nor does she relinquish the intrasubjective dialogue with the Other that has dictated to her what a woman is. And, finally, she does not lose the mirror-stage yearning for *jouissance* beyond the Father's name.

What Irigaray does not account for, then, are those things which Lacan himself leaves obscure in his various scriptings of the development of feminine sexuality: the primordial, maternal effects of the pre-mirror and mirror structures on both sexes. Irigaray, like other feminists who blame the male sex per se for woman's oppression, perpetuates the idea of a natural battle between the sexes and so fails to evolve the theoretical understanding necessary to herald change. For as long as feminists deny or simplify the facts surrounding woman's history by appeals to innate difference, mythology, and ideological utopias, or by a refusal to analyze, we cannot confront cause and effect in any way that would eliminate some of the prejudice and anger blocking deeper investigation. The crux of the matter, in my view, lies in a confusion of the terms "feminism" and "femininity." Schneiderman has expressed the opinion that feminism and femininity stand in direct contradiction.[30] I agree with this insofar as I see sundry feminism(s) as a reaction against any inferiorization of woman on the basis of gender. Femininity, on the other hand, seems to me an ideological acceptance of woman's position as adjunct to the male, be it in role behavior, dress, discourse, or the rest. Since woman's place has historically differed from man's place and has generally been subsidiary, femininity and feminism(s) are bound to come into conflict. They need not be mutually eradicating, however, since the one has to do with sexual identity and the other with gender distinctions. If a social realism made up the whole of the problem, then equal work, equal pay, and so on would eliminate the misunderstanding between the two genders. This has not happened because the problem of gender identity is far more complicated and deadly than its surface manifestations in divisions of domestic labor or the varied, seesaw sublimations of power politics.

The issues are as large as mind structure and social organization itself. The problem—as I interpret Lacan—has to do with a maternal linkage, at the level of effect, of mother and female with infant experiences of loss and Castration during the first two years of life. Any implication by feminists, therefore, that patriarchy inheres in the substantive realm of consciousness and "will" dooms the sexes to that repetition of history which derives from the primordial and culminates in the formation of the unconscious. If one thinks in terms of unconscious structures, however, the phallic signifier's power derives from its function of privileging culture (represented by father merely as the opposite principle to mother) over nature (represented by mother), and by its symbolic link to conscious awareness, individuation, and language. Sexual identity is therefore learned through identificatory experiences with the mirror-stage and phallic structures, and through linguistic interpretations of these ineffable experiences.

The phallic signifier is the first pure signifier of difference. It is, therefore, the reference point for an infant's development of the capacity to use symbols as signifiers. Lacan used Freud's grandson's *Fort! Da!* game with the bobbin reel as a paradigm of the connection between language, separation, and symbolization. The infant cries Gone! Here! both to represent and to master the presence/absence dilemma of the mirror stage. When they eventually lose their direct link to symbols, words seem autonomous, and people lose sight of their representative (*représentant*) function. The capacity to label and name bridges the gap between a structural defect in being and the demands of society by compensating for the loss of spontaneous fusion with the mother.

Words at this stage are themselves transitional objects, floating between the hazy inside/outside boundaries of infant perception. Preconscious links to sexual identity have certainly been discussed by many analysts—not to mention the poetry which has celebrated this "*Gestalt intramondaine*" throughout the ages. Lacan labels this early Imaginary material as pathemes and describes it as "le chatoiement innombrable de la grande signification affective" (the innumerable shimmering hues of affect's vast meaning). It is the child's world, with universal equivalence as its law (*Séminaire* III, p. 185). But the richness of images, resonances, and the hauntings of the Imaginary are not Lacan's point. His originality lies in the roles he accords to "lack" and to the signifier.

As the first signifier of the social or Symbolic order, the Phallus commands exchange and communication. But it also symbolizes the nonclosure and disunity that it introduces permanently into the human subject by replacing the simultaneity of perception with the deferred nature of language and consciousness. This structural drama is given myriad interpretations from one culture to another. Embodied in language and myth, these interpretations dictate to an infant the sexual role that it is to play, one decided before its birth. The only constant among the varying interpretations, writes Edmond Ortigues in *L'oedipe africain* (1966), is the Oedipal structure itself, and even that is not limited to the nuclear family.[31] A second constant would be the link between mirror-stage identification and female caretakers. The success of culture over nature is not, therefore, as Lévi-Strauss has said, in marriage exchange, but in the initiation into compromise and submission to the Law of the Name-of-the-Father at around eighteen months of age. While the mirror-stage identification with the mother provided a sense of triumph over an original experience of fragmentation, secondary identification with the father divides this already tenuous sense of unity. For Lacan, this split forms the ontological foundation of human knowledge and identity in terms of a cultural self-alienation and allusive Desire, which are both born of Law. Underlying all "meaning," then, is a drama of fusion and separation, which has created the unconscious as a system whose knowledge is elementally structural and transformational.

What the French psychoanalyst offers to feminist theory, therefore, is a picture of the place of man and woman within a history of symbolization and meaning (*Séminaire* XX, p. 69). The two major experiences of identificatory fusion and subsequent separation mark the subject for life. An implicit intentionality thereby sets individuals off on a paradoxical quest for Imaginary sameness and Symbolic difference. Although there is no intrinsic gender meaning to this structural drama, it first becomes confused at a secondary, substantive level with gender and later with sexual organs. In defense of the idea that there is no natural causality to sexual identity, Lacan has said that man and woman exist as pure signifiers, the nature of things being the nature of words (*Séminaire* XX, p. 68). In the "Agency of the Letter in the Unconscious" (1957) Lacan said that the whole structure of language is to be found in the unconscious, the elemental unit of meaning being the letter: "By 'letter' I designate that material support that concrete discourse borrows from language. This simple definition assumes that language is not to be confused with the various psychical and somatic functions that serve it in the speaking subject—primarily because language and its structure exist prior to the moment at which each subject at a certain point in his mental development makes his entry into it" (Sheridan, *Ecrits*, pp. 147–48).

Lacan does not, in my view, mean that physiological realities are shaped by an Idealist universe of words; he means merely that language offers to the psychosomatic—the Real—a way to give itself meaning. Sociology and anthropology, indeed, have established that the Real of gender difference is less important in forming identity or mentality than the environment and culture. To these Lacan has added structure and language. Even though the Phallus does not refer to the real father, then, nor to the sexual organ, Lacan used this term to underline the idea that the biological father, the penian part-object, and the phallic differential function are confused in language. The historical plight of women has been the linguistic and representational misunderstanding that translates "be" as "have," and Phallus as penis.[32]

We can see that by using linguistics and cultural anthropology, Lacan is not constricted—as was Freud—by a biological and spatio-temporal scenario. Freud failed to recognize the relative nature of the Oedipus complex (Lemaire, *Lacan*, p. 58). By focusing on the implications of Castration and its Oedipal ramifications for the organization of a person's psychic structure, Lacan has offered a viable theory of the elementary information processes of the human symbol system construed as an identificatory counting system. His thought on the effects of the pre-mirror, mirror, and post-mirror stages culminates in a theory of how the human mind comes to reside in the brain.[33] And the answer to how language enters the brain lies in the Real of human prematuration, transference relations, and a phonemic chain in the vocal apparatus, not in some Chomskian innate dictionary within our cranium.

The Oedipal structure is a problematic phenomenon for Lacan, not a natural one. There are no logical, genital, or genetic developmental sequences of maturation in his epistemology, therefore, only a vision of life-long efforts to position oneself toward the radical effects of a superficial physical difference. But there is an obscurity in Lacan's thought that probably explains the divided opinions over whether he was a phallocrat or not. As stated, Lacan's stance is clear regarding the duplicity between the signifier and the signified that constitutes men and women as effects of the symbolization process, but in a dissymmetry that generally privileges one sex over the other. This dissymmetry is problematic, and not solved simply by observing that the primary love bond for both sexes is forged with the mother. As Freud intuited, the difficulty arose in an Imaginary interpretation of a Real phenomenon—the opposition of penis $(+)$ and female genitalia $(-)$. The interpretation of this anatomical difference belongs to the Symbolic order of signifiers; identification with one parent or the other is an Imaginary process.

Ernest Jones, Karen Horney, and others tried to correct Freud's ex-

planation of the "one down" status to which Freud consigned women because of penis envy. They called for a "different but equal"
standing, in which "my vagina" would equal "your penis." Jones and
Horney were mistaken, however, about how the normative psyche is
structured and the dissymmetry has remained in place. As throughout history, women largely occupy an adjunct status. Further proof of
this is furnished by data showing women more depressed than men
by a ratio of approximately 4 to 1. In *Unfinished Business* (1981)
Maggie Scarf explains this disparity by suggesting that women are
more "attachment oriented" and thus more easily wounded by the
vagaries of relationships.[34] But why are women more attachment oriented? Even if this were so, why should it be wounding? Modern
women cringe at Freud's claims that they are castrated, without a
penis, narcissistically wounded and that they must, therefore, gain
ego compensation by attaching themselves to males who have a
penis. According to this view, women are narcissistically vulnerable
and consequently prone to melancholia from the moment they comprehend their defect.

It is logically difficult to fault Lacan for stating the obvious: the
Phallus is a privileged signifier. This fact implies—in the subject's
own retrospect—that the phallic signifier has been determinant in
structuring sexual personality. Psychic normalcy, neurosis, and psychosis, moreover, are structures that organize themselves around attitudes to the subject's own gender. Normalcy or sublimation consists in an ultimate identification with the phallic principle, for the
male by the fact of embodying it and for the female by association. In
other words, public prestige and patriarchy are synonyms, whether
we refer to a military operation or to a street gang. Why is this so?
Why were Jones and Horney mistaken? In a letter to me dated No-
vember 19, 1981, Stuart Schneiderman commented: "The paradox of
Lacan's formulas for masculinity and femininity [is] that he retains
the primacy of the phallic function for femininity and attempts to
extract the element of envy from the position of not having the phallus: thus not having and not wanting to have." Lacan's writings demonstrate that he found all this a puzzle. If sexual identity and culture
organize themselves around the equation: penis = Phallus = male =
privilege, and women purportedly do not object, then (1) how is such
privilege established? and (2) why are women not envious? Schneiderman continued: "We know that sometimes there is simply indifference. Indifference is an interesting word here: is it related to equality?" Schneiderman is doubtless right in part. Many women are in-
different (the defeat of the American Equal Rights Amendment, for

example), or they would not have accepted their "place" across the centuries and across vastly differing cultures. Female depression and passive aggression, on the other hand, speak loudly as a sign that women do care. The dilemma—and Lacan has made this clear—is how to reprogram the *moi* once it has been essentially formed by age five. How are "new" messages to be inserted in an Other(A) that is older and stronger than any individual's own narcissism? How can one get beyond narcissism (identity) to even know the Other's Desire?

Lacan's thought does provide a clue to these mysterious questions. If all sexual and gender identities conformed to set molds, then the matter would be simple: Reality principle, evolutionary sexual stages, norms. . . . But we everywhere discover variations, not only within highly formalized cultures, but even within families. Freud injected biological norms into the heart of cultural experience and has been taken to task for this ever since. In Lacan's teachings the three basic variations—normalcy, neurosis, and psychosis—are psychic structures that show a very precise organization. Although each variation manifests recognizable patterns of erotomania, the fundamental causality lies in the original intersections of the Imaginary, Symbolic, and Real, and the particular organization of those few key signifiers that simultaneously underlie sexual identity and culture.

Normalcy means accepting messages already in the Other(A) and repressing well (as in being a "good citizen"). Such normalcy does not confer happiness or freedom from conflict but demands blind submission to the social order and eschewal of unconscious truth. The hysteric, on the other hand, poses questions regarding psychic truth. Am I a man or a woman? *Why* should this happen to me? What do I want anyway? In Seminar Three Lacan said that the neurotic talks on and on, trying to solve the riddle: "The neurotic asks his neurotic question, his secret and stifled question, with his *moi*" (p. 196). Signified takes precedence over signifiers. Repression, then, works less well in a neurotic structure than in a normal one. But the psychotic personality has not repressed the effect of Castration at all nor symbolized the idea of the "self" as incomplete. In Real situations the psychotic can reconstitute the *moi* by Imaginary allusions or models, but does so without the signifying knowledge of Castration (*Séminaire* III, p. 183). When Freud depicted psychotics as latent homosexuals, he accounted for their plight by a fear of literal emasculation. But Lacan showed that the sexual difficulty in psychosis hinged on a primordial foreclosure (*Verwerfung*) of the idea of gender difference itself. While neurosis and homosexuality are caused by a denial (*dénégation* or *Verneinung*) of the equivalence between gender and sexual personality, heterosexual normalcy grows out of an acceptance of social interpretations of the Castration drama. This is how I would explain Freud's conclusion that women's "normalcy" and femininity consisted in an acceptance of their phallic atrophy (Irigaray, *Speculum*, p. 21). Lacan never made this literalist error.

I do believe, however, that Lacan erred in one early theory of how phallic privilege comes about. Arguing from the Real of symbols (irreducible in themselves) as the referents of language, as well as his Saussurean view of language working only by differential oppositions, Lacan says that the "symbols" of gender difference—the sex organs per se—may well explain phallic privilege. Symbols rule everything, Lacan said in Seminar Three: "Where there is no symbolic material, there is an obstacle or defect to the realization of the identification essential to the realization of the subject's sexuality. This defect comes from the fact that, in one specific, the Symbolic lacks material—because it must have some. The feminine genitals have a character of absence, of emptiness, or of hole which causes them to be found less desirable than the masculine genitals in the latter's provocative aspect, and causes an essential dissymmetry to appear" (p. 199).

Lacan transcends this symbolic literalism regarding the penis, as we shall see. But he never reversed his symbolic depiction of female genitalia as a *vide* or *trou*. It is hardly surprising, then, that women who do not conceive of their genitals in those terms should have attacked Lacan. In *Télévision* Lacan once more suggested a symbolic realism vis-à-vis the genders by saying: "The sexual impasse conceals the fictions which rationalize the impossibility out of which [the impasse] arises. I do not call [the fictions] imagined; I read in them, like Freud, the invitation to the real which is their counterpart. The family order merely translates that the father is not the genitor, and that the mother remains to contaminate the woman for *le petit d'homme*; the rest follows" (p. 51).

But Lacan himself never saw the Oedipal drama as a literal one. In his essay "The Signification of the Phallus" (1958) he wrote that while the penis "is the most tangible element in the Real of sexual copulation, and also the most symbolic in the literal (typographical) sense of the term, since it is equivalent there to the (logical) copula. It might also be said that by virtue of its turgidity, it is the image of the vital flow as it is transmitted in generation" (Sheridan, *Ecrits*, p. 287). "All these propositions merely conceal the fact," Lacan continues, "that it can play its role only when veiled, that is to say, as itself a sign of the latency with which any signifiable is struck, when it is raised (*aufgehoben*) to the function of signifier" (p. 288).

The difference between the genders is not really based on organs, but on a game of "as if. . . ." In the same essay Lacan claims to have found his innovative definition of the Phallus in Freud: "For Freud, the phallus is not a phantasy in the sense of imaginary effect; nor an object (part-, internal, good, bad, etc.) in the sense that this term tends to accentuate the reality pertaining in a relation. It is even less the organ . . . that it symbolizes (penis or clitoris). And it is not without reason that Freud used the reference to the simulacrum that it represented for the Ancients. For the phallus is a signifier . . . the one which conditions the signified" (Sheridan, *Ecrits*, p. 285). But since, for Lacan, one signifier only signifies by being in opposition to another, the phallic signifier becomes the symbol for man himself. Woman becomes the opposite symbol, necessary for any meaning to exist: "The fact that the phallus is a signifier means that it is in the place of the Other that the subject has access to it. But since this signifier is only veiled, as ratio of the Other's desire, it is the Desire of the Other as such that the subject must recognize, that is to say, the Other insofar as he is himself a subject divided by the signifying *Spaltung*" (Sheridan, *Ecrits*, p. 288).

By combining linguistic and psychoanalytic theory with his own mirror-stage theory, Lacan suggested early on that the historical privilege given to the Phallus lay mainly in its double nature as penian part-object and as differential trait in the father's ushering in of the post-mirror stage. The separation trauma is linked to the Name-of-the-Father at an abstract level, and the meaning evoked in the Imaginary becomes a paternal metaphor. The phallic signifier is therefore inscribed at the origin of the unconscious meaning system where Law, Desire, language, separation, and gender merge in a drama subsequently repressed. It is this merger that Lacan terms the Oedipal structure or, in Melanie Klein's words, a preliminary Superego.[35] And societies organize gender roles, functions, and rituals around this difference, whether we refer to male social prestige or tribal rites affirming manhood in terms of anatomical difference. An abstract signifier gradually becomes concretized around a biological image. So viewed, the relations between the sexes turn on whether "to be" castrated or "to have" a penis, although both refer to an illusion. The shaping of societies—the Symbolic order—around sex stereotypes could, therefore, be said to arise from the treatment of an Imaginary perception as a Real one.

Personally, however, I do not think the penian part-object plays an initial role in its own later valuation. It is of interest that in Seminar Twenty (1972–73) Lacan struck it from his list of the primordial objects of Desire. In 1956 Lacan said: "It is insofar as the function of man and woman is symbolized, it is insofar as [the function] is literally torn from the Imaginary domain to be situated in the Symbolic domain, that any normal, finished sexual position is realized" (*Séminaire* III, p. 200). In 1968 a member of Lacan's school published the essay "The Subjective Import of the Castration Complex" in the first issue of *Scilicet*. Following Lacan's arguments the author writes that it is not known why woman is associated with Castration. Indeed, the unconscious does not know any opposition between masculine and feminine in an innate sense.[36] In 1975 Lacan argued in his "Seminar of 21 January" that insofar as there is no genital drive inscribed in the unconscious, there is no genital force per se that pushes men and women together. Woman, then, is a symptom of man's belief in a mythic, universal Woman (*La Femme*) who will be the source of his pleasure and his truth (Mitchell and Rose, *Feminine Sexuality*, p. 168).

To explain the association between women and Castration I would give greater scope to the link between mother and infant prior to Castration and hypothesize that the painful effect of individuating is the reason that women are identified with loss. The *vide* is not the female genitals (in opposition to a turgid penis), but the fact that the mother symbolizes the loss that becomes the unconscious. The void, as part-object that causes Desire, would take on meaning in terms of early nurture (food). The father is privileged over the mother because his gender difference symbolizes the opposite of need or loss. Paradoxically, repression, alienation, and dialectical otherness are brought about by the father's intervention. This line of argument would valorize Lacan's contention that the integration and introjection of the Oedipal image occurs in an aggressive relationship, since it occurs in Imaginary conflict (*Séminaire* III, p. 240). If the Oedipal drama were really caused by an interpretation of differences in sex organs, Symbolic privilege might as easily be conferred on the woman for her large, pregnant belly or her full breasts—both conceived in opposition to male "lack." Instead, the issue is decided by the power of primary effect. Only later on are symbols used as an explanation of this "mystery."

Another reason for privileging the phallic signifier can be traced to the father's functioning on one more representational plane than the mother. In addition to standing for the Symbolic order of difference, the Imaginary father enters an infant's perception as a rival for the mother's recognition and *regard*. And the actual biological father serves as a presence—or absence—who signifies Real effects. It seems likely to me that the barred article in *la* (*l̶a̶*) *femme* means that the mother enters unconscious perception only on the Imagi-

nary and Real planes; she does not attain the differentiated or separate status characteristic of the Symbolic order until late in the
child's development, and even then only in part. Not only is the
mother the first real Other and never completely separate from her
child, but she is also its primordial unconscious voice. Even if the
mother were not the primary caretaker, her Real being requires a
natural signifier: that of giving birth. So the father's connection to
the Symbolic order may well provide this extra dimension of phallic
prestige. To quote Lacan: "The Symbolic order in its initial functioning is androcentric. That is a fact" (*Séminaire* II, p. 303).

Claude Lévi-Strauss said that women defined the cultural order by
opposition to the natural, animal world as the object of exchange in
marriage. But Lacan disagreed. Woman is not the initiator of culture,
since culture is androcentric. She is, instead, the symbol of a "word"
exchanged between men (*Séminaire* II, p. 303). Pessimistic about
woman's chances of complete liberation, Lacan says (in 1955): "Woman is introduced into the symbolic pact of marriage as an object of
exchange along fundamentally androcentric and patriarchal lines.
The woman is thus engaged in an order of exchange where she is an
object; indeed is what causes the fundamentally conflictual character of her position—I would say without exit. The Symbolic order
literally submerges her, transcends her" (*Séminaire* II, p. 304).

In 1958 in his "Guiding Remarks for a Congress on Feminine Sexuality" Lacan asked why marriage holds out even in the decline of
paternalism.[37] One might amplify Lacan's speculation that woman as
lack is transcendent to the order of the contract propagated by work.
If woman stands for lack only insofar as she is not inscribed in the
unconscious in any totalized sense, it follows that Lacan viewed
analysands as people in search of woman (Miller, "Another Lacan,"
p. 2). Let us suggest here that exogamous relations seek to recreate
the mirror-stage illusion of wholeness—the One of meaning—when
in reality they repeat the disharmony and dissymmetry caused by
Castration.

Inasmuch as psychic health requires differentiation from the natural and parasitic Other(A), the Other's opposite represents personhood within the group. Groups are thought of as male—therefore
the androcentric social body—though all-female groups do exist, curiously enough, often secretly or in dispersed networks. Woman is
alien and dangerous, then, not because patriarchy wills it so, but because she reminds all of us of our own psychic Otherness. At times
Lacan seems to set the Symbolic or patriarchal order on a footing
with the Real because it has stood so long in place. This is counter-
balanced by Lacan's doctrine that the unconscious text can be re-

written; that the relationship between signifiers and signifieds can be altered; and that the Real has nothing to do with fixity.

With Lacan, therefore, we are in a universe that completely reverses the familiar notion of biology as the prime mover of culture. Realist theories, such as penis envy, give a false account of what actually exists only at the Imaginary level of unconscious representation and effect. The conservative and persistent nature of the Symbolic order tends toward objective interpretations of these subjective realities and thereby fixes social norms and the trappings of gender identity. In the essay entitled "God and the *jouissance* of Woman" Lacan described man and woman as pure signifiers (*Séminaire* XX, p. 68). Man has historically been portrayed as complete—a *tout*—and woman as incomplete—a *pas-toute*. The conception of woman as a *toute* through motherhood is a contradiction in terms, since her value stems from the relationship to an-other and not from her own being. Since the phallic signifier heralds difference and the advent of language, the male represents the societal prototype, and it follows—within a verbal signifying chain where the male is the standard—that the female comes off as derivative and secondary.[38] But Lacan has added that neither woman nor man can signify the difference of the sexes.[39] Difference, in other words, is not an intrinsic attribute of either sex. The penis, as a separate or third entity, signifies the difference. As we have seen, Lacan treats the penis as privileged because of a confusion of the virile member with a phallic signifying function. The Phallus introduces the alienating effect of difference into the pleasurable and natural mother-infant dyad, and this Oedipalizing, dividing effect gradually becomes substantivized around the Name-of-the-Father. Lacan points out, however, that the purely signifying and thus arbitrary nature of the Name-of-the-Father is nowhere more obvious than in the fact that paternity is not provable; in some cultures, indeed, is not necessarily associated with copulation and birth (Sheridan, *Ecrits*, p. 199).

The penis makes sexual rapport possible, then, not in its physical reality, but in an interpretation of it as a principle of difference. It is stating the obvious to say that humans seek difference from self to join with an-other sexually, whether heterosexually or homosexually. Only in psychosis is no sexual other sought. Strictly speaking, then, sexual object choice depends more on psychic illusion and confusion than it does on hormonal drive. In erotic relations, Lacan has said, a fragment reminiscent of clothing, perfume, voice, and so on, causes Desire and not the Imaginary wholeness of a beloved's being. In fetishism an object itself—detached from the body—becomes the object of perverse Desire. Erotic Desire is for an organ, then; love is for a name. Even though they are different phenomena, however, love and Desire coalesce by love's being a supplement for what one lacks in the Other (Sheridan, *Ecrits*, p. 263). Insofar as the penis has been confused with the phallic function of inscribing difference, Lacan says that every person enrolls in the phallic function (Bouazis, *Essais*, p. 12). Every person, in other words, takes a position toward gender difference. But this difference has not yet been fathomed and interpreted during the eighteen-month prespecular and specular stages, and only begins to have meaning as language is acquired along with a sense of identity.

We might perhaps be forgiven a moment's speculation at this point. Modern research has established that (1) the left brain in human beings governs concrete and verbal functions, while (2) the right brain governs abstract and spatial ones. But the brain is not lateralized—i.e., specialized—until the age of five, the same age by which grammar is acquired and a primary sexual identity fixed.[40] This strongly suggests to me that identification with the female principle, that is with the natural, is responsible for structuring the left hemisphere: the sense of the concrete arises from the natural and the verbal out of a compensation for "loss." But identification with the male principle tends precisely away from "loss" and requires assimilation of an abstract phallic signifier. This identification would develop the right hemisphere's capacities for abstract and spatial thought. On this reading, brain functions would not determine a person as abstract and male or concrete and female per se, but would furnish eloquent proof of the effects of language and transference on structuring—in this case lateralizing—the brain. Such a theory would account for the more concrete and verbal tendencies of lower-class men who do not identify with their (often absent) father, but rather with the maternal principle of loss. Similarly, it would illuminate those empirical studies showing that highly successful professional women share only one thing in common: an identification with their fathers away from the mother. The nongender specific distinction I would insist on, then, is between: a *moi* identification with (1) the effects of loss and attendant dependency and (2) with those of gain and independence.

We said earlier that Lacan does not consider the penis to be the catalyst of sexual rapport in itself. It is the *objet a* of Desire, which really supplements—or in this sense makes possible—sexual rapport (Bouazis, *Essais*, p. 17). In their secondary form the primary objects of Desire (the breast, excrement, the gaze, the voice) refer to fantasies, sex organs, or fetishistic objects. Linked to the four supports that are later considered the cause of Desire—the gaze, the voice, the void, the Phallus—the primordial *objets a* play their role in the ear-eye drama, where what is seen is inseparable from what is heard. For, although these partial objects of Desire may not always be visible, the discourse itself is visible in the sense of material. In linguistic terms the Oedipal drama has been translated to mean that the male—mistaken for the Phallus because he has a penis—is *tout*. The corollary is that women, who do not have a penis, become *pas-toute*.[41] The mistranslations of the Real (male = *tout*; female = *pas-toute*) are not only false perceptions, then, but also misrepresentations of the phallic function itself. Automatically, the phallic signifier refers to incompletion, to the presence of other signifiers. In other words, difference can only signify itself in relation to something else. And, indeed, the phallic signifier belongs to the *pas-tout* of language or discourse, since language is a differential, referential, open, and essentially incomplete system.

Lacan talks of the impossible aspect of sexual rapport—just as he refers to the body as a symbol of impossible unity—and we realize that sexual desire is a part of the larger drama of Desire (*Séminaire XX*, p. 14). Desire aims at "knowledge" of the Other (who am I?), and hence at an unconscious satisfaction. But the Lacanian unconscious is incomplete and experienced in conscious life as a lack, so no object (or recognition) is adequate to the task of joining the conscious and unconscious subjects in a state of final satisfaction, transparency, or knowledge. Freud offered Thanatos as an explanation of the failure of a universal Eros; Lacan points to the phallic signifier as the scourge of unity. Division and dialectical difference inscribed in the Other(A) foreclose the possibility of totalizing, harmonious unity of the kind the infant imagines when in the symbiotic state. Out of this inadequacy arises every kind of compensatory attachment to objects, people, ideologies, and so on.

Lacan claims, given the substitutive nature of human relations, that what man approaches in the sexual act is not so much the woman's body (or the Essence of Woman) as the cause of his Desire (lack). As the *objet a* of Desire—both in terms of part- and whole objects—he puts her in the place of the dark face of his own unconscious being. And he identifies her with the unconscious, the unknown, and truth—what Lacan tellingly terms the face of God. In this sense, man finds fulfillment through woman precisely because of a lack that he consciously denies. Sexually speaking, women serve as objects of exchange on a symbolic parity with the phallic signifier.

That is to say, the man's unconscious dependence on his mother's Desire leads him to identify with the Imaginary object of her Desire, as she visualizes it vis-à-vis the Phallus (Sheridan, *Ecrits*, p. 198). The male, on this reckoning, takes a woman as an Imaginary supplement to his Imaginary lack in a substitution where, according to Otto Fenichel's theory, girl = Phallus.[42] We would then be obliged to say that the man makes love to complete himself; the woman's role is as catalyst in his psychic drama. Her specificity, therefore, is subordinated to the man's quest for his own denied psychic truth, in compensation for his own identification with the Phallus. Lacan concludes that there is no "eternal feminine" (Goethe), no *la* in *la femme*. This also means, insofar as the phallic signifier stands at the origin of language and connotes male, that the signifier denoting female is always referential. So word usage mistakes *a* man for *the* man (colloquial Latin: *ipse* = himself, the Master) and a specific woman for any woman. This generic Woman only exists as an Imaginary fantasy.

Although Lacan finds all love essentially narcissistic, the woman's lovemaking is not a counterpart of the man's (*Séminaire* XX, p. 12). She does not aim directly at embracing her unconscious being, but takes pleasure in the man's *savoir* and his *parole*. Lacan sees woman here striving to attain an associational value: to enjoy the status which he (as *tout*) gives her (as *pas-toute*) within the social discourse (*Séminaire* XX, p. 75). In the sex act her goal is to acquire vicariously the status conferred by the phallic signifier.[43] In either case the physical or Real aspects of the sex act are secondary to its psychic value. I understand Lacan to mean that man takes his sexual pleasure in woman principally on the Imaginary slope, while she finds hers in him on the Symbolic plane.[44]

Identification with the Phallus, then, conveys the feeling that one is *tout*. But the long-established structure of patriarchy perversely blames woman for the loss that occurred at the father's behest. Because birth and the early care network are identified with the female gender, the painful dissolution of the nurturing bond by Castration leads to permanent ambivalence and profundity around the idea of the (m)Other. In consequence, feelings toward the mother are more unfathomable and ambiguous than those toward the father. The Symbolic order is synonymous with difference and the escape from loss and identified with order (over chaos and confusion) and law (in the Father's name). The Imaginary order of sameness is linked to the primal bond with the mother. And human beings flee from the sameness of self into the difference of others. This perhaps explains why Lacan and the later Freud emphasized the effects of gender difference over those of birth. In his "Philology and the Phallus" John Forrester reminds us that between 1907 and 1914 Freud argued the first and most important question for a child was: "Where do babies come from?" After 1920 Freud thought the child's main question concerned the difference between the sexes (*Talking Cure*, p. 58). In Seminar Three Lacan observed that everything in the Symbolic order obfuscates the animal fact of procreation and its implicit foreshadowing of death (p. 202). The question of birth is usually solved rapidly by some mythic reference to storks, cabbages, or—for a child—equally mythical semen and ovum. The burning question for a three- to five-year-old is what it really means to be a boy or a girl.

In his essay "On the Signification of the Phallus" Lacan also asks why, as psychoanalysts such as Klein have shown, the primordial mother should be imagined as possessing the Phallus? He states: "The Kleinian fact that the child apprehends that the mother 'contains' the phallus may be formulated more correctly" (Sheridan, *Ecrits*, p. 289). In Lacan's "more correct formulation" there is no penian part-object inside the mother's body, but there is a signifier or, albeit unconscious, an attitude toward the Phallus. Woman's first discourse (lodged in the child's unconscious) transmits an image of the Symbolic order and of the place of the Phallus within it. The first linking of males to power is conveyed, therefore, by the mother. John Berger has aptly said that "the surveyor of woman in herself is male."[45] Insofar as the Symbolic order is androcentric, he is right. It assigns values to signifiers and determines the relative merits of males and females on a hierarchical scale. But more elemental than the male eye within—the one which Irigaray locates in the mirror—is the female eye (*regard*) within all of us. For, as conveyor of an androcentric view, the primordial eye that upholds the Symbolic order is the mother's and therefore female.[46] The sexual identity of both boys and girls, then, is established in relation to the mother's attitudes toward the Phallus (*Séminaire* XX, p. 75).

The clichés describing woman as inferior or superior are, in my view, symptoms required by the Real effects of the birth and separation network. Lacan has exposed the puppet strings that operate the myth of an "eternal feminine." Woman is not the source of psychic "truth" due to any inherent gender trait, but is often mythologized thus because language must interpret the effects of the primordial and of loss on being. Since the ideas of (m)Other and woman are so hard to disentangle, I believe that femininity and masculinity are Oedipal interpretations of Castration. Ideologically speaking, femininity identifies itself with Castration-as-loss and prepares the way for normative womanhood or homosexuality; masculinity first experiences Castration-as-loss, but later denies this loss and incompleteness, as in lesbianism or normative manhood. Feminism(s) seem to me to lie uncomfortably between the two, but perhaps the more truthfully for that.

It is not possible to reduce self-perception simplistically to male or female, then, in a Lacanian framework. Nor does it help matters to fabricate new myths, such as the Electra complex, to explain old myths surrounding sexual differences. But Lacan situated the Oedipal structure in the unconscious and revealed that it is based on Real experiences. His contention that psychosexual identity is culturally learned is not, of course, new. Donald Winnicott, Wilfred Bion, and others have advanced this theory. Lacan's great originality lies in his description of the unconscious dialectic between *moi* and Other(A) in relation to Desire and the Phallus. Any Lacanian analysand must discover the mother's attitudes toward the phallic metaphor; toward the real father; toward her own sex; toward the baby's gender. Does a man identify with phallic power, for example, thus fleeing the (m)Other within? Does a woman refuse the patriarchal stereotypes of the Symbolic order and thereby incur the accusation of being "phallic"? Does a woman identify with the traditional mother/wife role, shunning direct public power in favor of maternal dominance or sexual power? Does a man identify as a seeker of the Phallus, rather than possessor of it, and thus as a homosexual? To what inner gazes and voices is one's *moi* subjugated?

In "The Signification of the Phallus" Lacan treated as a philosophical problem the fact that some girls represent themselves to psychoanalysts as castrated in the traditional sense of being deprived of a penis. Similarly, he found it theoretically challenging to consider why Castration would assume its full clinical weight, as far as the formation of symptoms is concerned, only after the male or female subject's discovery that the mother is castrated (Sheridan, *Ecrits*, p. 282). Irigaray has taken Lacan's depiction of this symbolic drama literally and castigated him for identifying Castration with women. Moustafa Safouan has, in turn, defended Lacan against Irigaray in his book *La Sexualité féminine dans la doctrine freudienne*.[47] Irigaray would not moralize about Lacan's linking of Castration to the mother, Safouan maintains, if she really understood his thought. The iconoclastic French psychoanalyst showed Castration to be an Imaginary perception—made at the level of identification—which is treated as Real, even though it derives from the arbitrary and inherently neutral Symbolic order of language and conventions. Earlier I have argued that Lacan erred in his excessive stress on the phallic symbol's definition by its opposite and his consequent portrayal of the female *sexe* as a hole and an emptiness. The Imaginary supplies this absence, he said (*Séminaire* III, p. 198). But most women do not care about not having a penis biologically speaking because they do not in this sense feel lacking. This "fact" belongs to the order of the Real. But they do care about male incomprehension of their Real sexuality and the linking of phallic myths to their human potential. But insofar as males fixate sexually on the organ that represents their gender, and females identify their being and bodies as first and foremost sexual, the misunderstanding is apt to remain. Lacan taught that things do not work harmoniously between man and woman. The differences in normative sexual identification are not the least of the reasons. Since myths describing the sexes are enshrined in language, they help to create identity structure around symbol and signifier, both within culture and family structure. The Symbolic imposes itself on the female Imaginary to teach her about an absence that is not one, except insofar as no being is complete.

This is an opportune moment to answer Naomi Schor's question posed in her paper "*Eugénie Grandet*: Mirrors and Melancholia." She asks: "Why does the daughter pay a higher price? Or rather: Why does the son successfully perform the work of mourning, while the daughter remains mired in melancholia?" (p. 20). The answer follows logically within the Lacanian cycle: the daughter, linked to the mother by gender, is more closely bound Imaginarily to (1) the primary experience of the unconscious as loss (as an effect of separation) and (2) the secondary (and erroneous) Symbolic order interpretation of woman as lacking. Insofar as the primary unconscious Desire is the (m)Other's, the daughter is closer to the personal and the narcissistic (the *moi*), while the son is urged by the Oedipal structure and by language to "transcend" the Other's influence to "find" himself within the social (public) group.

Again, since the unconscious is a gap, a hole, a negation, it resembles metaphorical death. While the son can flee the unconscious discourse by gender identification away from it (yet still embrace it through the displacement of object relations), the daughter is trapped both by gender identification and by the social injunction to be the other/Other for a man. The work of mourning is to "kill the dead," that is, to detach oneself from the introjected power of an "object" who is lost or dead. The (m)Other within is associated with loss and in this sense is half-dead. In this way it can be shown that daughters, who live closer to the primordial unconscious by the "law" of identification, also live closer than do sons to the task of mourning: the detachment of themselves from the Other(A) as object.

What no one has yet suggested, to my knowledge, is a scrutiny of woman's "history of oppression" and male denial of this as the result of a "double Castration" (my term). At the Real structural level of primary Castration, both males and females experience loss of the symbiotic attachment to the mother as a kind of Castration. At the secondary or substantive level, Imaginary representations and social meanings are attributed to the mother and father in an effort to understand or explain the separation drama. Secondary Castration inheres in Imaginary and Symbolic efforts to explain a Real effect. The Other(A) is the place of the unconscious and thus is either a dark-faced and absent part of oneself which one must flee or a mysterious force which one renders divine and proceeds to worship. The primordial (m)Other at the mirror-stage, structural base of the ego becomes confused with woman; and women are consequently seen as secretly powerful. The mother within both sexes therefore implies an unseen dominance. This makes woman—as her displacement—someone to be feared, denied, ignored, denigrated, fought, and conquered—or conversely worshipped and enshrined. But whether woman is generically feared or extolled, the individual's attitude toward women implies a position toward their own unconscious. Either posture—woman as insufficient and inferior or woman as mysterious and superior—testifies to the division (*Ichspaltung*) in the subject that reveals the unconscious as a sense of Otherness or absence.

In "Another Lacan" Miller says: "Indeed, there is a signifier for the male [the phallic signifier] and that is all we've got. This is what Freud recognized: just one symbol for the libido, and this symbol is masculine; the symbol for the female is lost. Lacan is thus entirely Freudian in stating that *woman* as a category does not exist. . . . The absence of the signifier *woman* also accounts for the illusion of the infinite, which arises from the experience of speech, even while that experience is finite. . . . Naturally, if the Other signifier, that of *woman* existed, it could be assumed that things would come to an end. The analysand therefore appears as a kind of Diogenes with his lantern, but in search of *woman* rather than a man. . . . The passion for things symbolic has no other source. Science exists because *woman* does not exist. Knowledge as such substitutes for knowing the other sex. . . . Lacan contends that the unconscious shouts but one message, the absence of relation" (see note 4 to Introduction, p. 2).

The compensatory myths which describe woman are what I mean by secondary Castration. They create and then perpetuate a substitute set of beliefs, which are propounded as "natural" truths and then find their validity in theology, mythology, biology, science, politics, or economics. In this way a structural, symbolic, and inherently value-free drama is substantivized. For when men or women see *woman* as inferior to man, they tacitly admit that self-identification with phallic/public power—either by supposing that you are the Phallus or by supposing that you must ally yourself with it—necessitates a clear differentiating away from the Other within. When the realization dawns on a child that penis implies Phallus, and Phallus means social authority and prestige—whether a person is male or female—the stance that a person takes toward the mother's metaphorical Castration will determine sexual identity in terms of submission, denial, revolt, and so forth.

Feminists who reject Lacan's argumentation have construed his concepts of Phallus and Castration in a literal sense and therefore view his thought erroneously as prescriptive and finalistic. In my reading of Lacan I find quite the reverse: a theoretical basis for a continued feminist rewriting of Other(A) messages that can promise some change in the light of a more profound understanding of psychoanalytic causality and through an elucidation of signifying effect. I find no a priori Lacanian support for phallocentrism—any more than for Lacanian-supported feminism. Lacan discovered the phallic signifier, its effects and the resulting structure of substitutive Desire. These intrinsically neutral elements give rise to ideologies of the masculine and feminine that cluster around the male-female difference and dramatize themselves in a parade.

Woman's history will never appreciably change without a theoretical understanding of why there has ever been discrimination against women along gender lines. If Lacan's new epistemology is valid, however, the task placed before feminists is truly monumental, and, in part, impossible. The "catch-22" lies in the circular nature of the dilemma itself. After Castration a mother's unconscious Desire is communicated to the infant, along with her attitudes toward the Phallus and messages about the infant's place within the symbolic, structural drama. To short-circuit this system, then, one must either change the gender of the primary source of nurture and identification (and I do not merely mean equal parenting à la Dorothy Dinnerstein) or change the unconscious Desire of mothers who, by accepting their femininity at all, support a system of phallic values.

The problematic term "femininity," as it is currently mythologized, pertains largely to the physical reality of a woman's body. While the phallic refers to a secondary identification with social power, femininity stems from primary identification with the mother's palpability. As we have frequently stressed, the first human knowledge is corporal knowledge, and it comes through contact with her body. By contrast, however concrete its effect, the phallic signifier is abstract and symbolic. But the mirror-stage experience is not only concrete; it is also sensual as well. The primordial corporal-maternal effects of the mirror stage consequently haunt males and females with an evanescent female image in the internal mirror forever. This archaic structure's physical nature makes woman's sexuality problematic for both sexes, and itself an object of fetishism, the highest value being placed on woman at the body level of Lacan's primary narcissism. Whether she is feared as a seductress or sought as a sex object or idealized as a mother, woman's supreme value is supposed to reside in her physical being. And by raising a primary identification with their own sexuality to a secondary level of identity, women participate in their own oppression. Consequently, although some critics have read Lacan's *pas-toute* description of woman to mean that she is a minus sign in sexist terms, a lacking being, I see him untendentiously exposing the structure that underlies the sundry substantive meanings extrapolated out of it.

Nor do I discover the doom scenario in Lacan's epistemology, which is encountered in biologically based descriptions of the human sexual drama. His symbolic and structural concepts, indeed, take him from a conservative camp and place him in a radical one. For if sexual identity is not joined to gender in any direct proportion, then interpretations of the Oedipal structure could be endowed with new meanings through changes in myths and laws. The tragedy implicit in Lacan's teachings concerns the impasse of the Real for both sexes. No subject will ever be whole. No love or sexual relation will be perfectly harmonious. The optimistic implications for feminists in Lacan's thought lie in its potential for modifying the fixity of the Symbolic order by redefining the meaning of gender and by reshaping the relationship between signifier and signified. In his essay "The Insistence of the Letter in the Unconscious" Lacan points to the formative role of the signifier and asks: "So how do you imagine that a scholar with so little talent for the '*engagements*' which solicited him in his age . . . that a scholar such as Erasmus held such an eminent place in the revolution of a Reformation in which man has as much of a stake in each man as all men? The answer is that the slightest alteration in the relation between man and the signifier, in this case in the procedures of exegesis, changes the whole course of history by modifying the lines which anchor his being" (Sheridan, *Ecrits*, p. 174).

Such a restructuring can only be accomplished to the degree that women cease consciously to regard themselves chiefly as adjunct figures. Such a considerable responsibility for change would require women to see through the mystifications which link them to inferior or superior virtues. In "She?" the literary critic Claudia Crawford maintains that Lacan continued the Nietzschean, Derridean view of woman as symbolizing the essence of truth: woman as source of the primal unconscious (which contains psychic truth) is still the deceitful temptress who mystifies herself—promising, yet witholding that which she has and after which men continually seek.[48] Basing her essay on Lacan's "La chose freudienne" (1955), Crawford refers to Lacan's rewriting of the Actaeon myth. Actaeon discovered the goddess Diana bathing nude; she then turned her attendant nymphs into hunting dogs that tore Actaeon to pieces for his "privileged knowledge." But in Lacan's version the discovery of unconscious truth leads not to death, but to life. For only by pushing further and grasping the Other's Desire and extracting oneself from its superimposed meanings, does one find a measure of freedom. Why should the same unburdening not occur for women at large? Why must women be only "feminine" and "normal" in their incomplete Oedipal resolutions?

A reversal on any large scale would, of course, demand that the messages surrounding the phallic signifier and Castration be altered. Any Lacanian discussion of Woman as truth, therefore, should not make the error of equating essence, truth, and Woman. "Essence" in the sense of *être* (*moi*) is created by the combined elemental images, signifiers of language, and the Real of effects recorded individually in the Other as memory. When the truths constituted by those now Real signifiers are decoded, the analyst does not unveil Derridean "untruth," but the articulation of truth itself in discrete, fictional elements. Amid these "truths" are the cultural stereotypes of masculine and feminine. The more pressing logical problem that Lacan's epistemology presents is this: if the Name-of-the-Father is an organizing principle of sexual identity and of culture, which ensures societal order and psychic "health," how can such an effect be changed without dire consequences for the fabric of society itself?

Schneiderman has raised the query: Why can feminism not just live with the idea that the function of the Name-of-the-Father is its own subversion? (letter of August 13, 1981). My answer is that the cost in female depression, passive aggression, and disturbed children is simply too great a price to pay, when we know that aggressiveness—in all its forms—can be mitigated through secondary identification with a prestigious group (Sheridan, *Ecrits*, p. 22). Although a successful Oedipal resolution is culturally defined as what constitutes a given group's prestige, there is no mere sociological determinism at work here. Instead we are confronted with each person's balance between his or her ideal ego and superego.[49]

I maintain, therefore, that femininity elaborates a philosophy of gender insufficiency, in which the ideal ego itself identifies with secondary Castration and thereby supports a masculinity (superego) conceiving of itself as complete sufficiency. From this perspective, masculinity is as big a ruse as femininity, both constituting the terms of an ever-widening flight from the trauma of primary Castration. In consequence, the bulk of a given social order is peopled by players wearing sexual masks, who act out their fundamental fears and resultant antagonisms around issues of "my mammocracy" versus "your phallocracy."

Another argument for continuing to transform the meanings presently attached to man and woman—besides the possible gain in understanding, if not freedom—concerns the nature of the concept of the Name-of-the-Father. Schneiderman has pointed out that, according to Lacan, there is no Name-of-the-Father, only names. Lacan also said that the name of "the name of the name of the father is woman, who does not exist, and is not everything" (letter of August 13, 1981). I interpret this to mean that the Law of the Name-of-the-Father per se refers to the Real of structure and effect—the creation of an unconscious order—while on the Imaginary and Symbolic planes fathers have many names. In Seminar Three Lacan stressed that in some cultures even river spirits are thought to be responsible for impregnation (back cover). So I would paraphrase Lacan's complex formula as follows: the father's name, as represented by the mother in her Imaginary attitude toward him or toward fatherness (that is, her Desire vis-à-vis the Phallus), is inscribed as a Real effect on the child. The outcome of this drama is that the Symbolic Name-of-the-Father never stands on its own apart from the idea of woman. The Real impact of the difference between the sexes gives the father the illusion of power which the unconscious steals back.

Lacan's mirror-stage effect can thus be taken as an ancillary argument for the possible transformation of Other(A) messages in the Symbolic order by means of the verbal and Imaginary identifications. A systematic refusal of secondary Castration is required to change woman's history. Ideally, the mothers of the future would reject the substantive interpretations conjured out of the Oedipal drama, which distort woman's reality and potential, and pass on messages that do less to handicap their children along gender lines. The mother's Desire would change to contemplate phallic possibilities for herself as well. Revised psychoanalytic concepts of normal and neurotic have made a beginning, under the stimulus of recent feminist activity. Women are learning to find pleasure beyond the traditional role of motherhood, where the infant has been symbolically equated with the deficient penis.

The particular tragedy, however, for daughters who identify with their mothers along traditional gender and role lines is that they refuse a complete primary Castration (that is, an adequate difference or psychic separation) and thereby accept secondary Castration! By refusing an Oedipal resolution, they value themselves essentially as adjuncts, wives, and mothers. When males identify away from the mother along gender and role lines, they symbolically affirm primary Castration—the necessity of separation—and are forced to create a self outside the mother's domain. Freud noted, for example, that boys tend to love their mothers less ambiguously than do girls; the latter even seemed to hate their mothers at times because—he hypothesized—they lack penises. Such a perception makes more sense from a Lacanian standpoint. By identifying away from the (m)Other within, males not only mollify the pain of primary Castration but also avoid the narcissistic pitfalls of secondary Castration. Females, on the other hand, are doubly castrated: first, by identification with the mother's gender and, second, by deferring to the myths that link that gender with loss. It is hardly surprising, then, that sons feel less ambiguity toward their mothers than do daughters. Male difficulties with the internal (m)Other, on the other hand, are displaced onto other women.

Since Irigaray sees woman as the victim of male mediation, she misses the greater tragedy: that her gender identification with the traditional mother limits her sphere of influence to Imaginary politics and primary (body) narcissism. One can, of course, make a case for the value of body narcissism—"speaking the body"—and for the superiority of Desire over Law, but then men and women remain stuck in the same old antithetical corners, with new words to describe the dilemma.[50] If woman is to be seen as the equal of man—neither inferior or superior—and man is to question his falsely assumed place of privilege, then the understanding must spread that sexual identities are sociostructural constructs and not natural ones. Such awareness must gradually permeate the Symbolic order. A critique such as Irigaray's, therefore, which opposes male and female and talks of the "laws of the feminine," bears within the seeds of further destruction for women, since it offers no theoretical means of understanding those Other(A) structures that freeze men and women into battle lines.

Although Lacan was generally pessimistic about the possibilities of altering the Symbolic order, history itself records the slow rewriting of the meaning of gender difference. As women attain to increased public power and prestige, these new realities are being accounted for in language. Different messages, words, and myths are giving yet another significance to old dilemmas. So viewed, Lacan's wry "beyond the phallus" joke does indeed seem to characterize our historical moment. If one looks at the rest of his comment, however—an orgasm or ecstasy beyond the phallus—he probably meant to emphasize the final impossibility of psychic unification through sexual rapport for either male or female. Giovanni Bernini's *St. Theresa* graces the cover of *Séminaire* XX. Perhaps Lacan chose this illustration as a metaphorical repetition of his idea that no human subject is self-sufficient. St. Theresa—nun, mystic, virgin—is experiencing ecstasy (orgasm), while Cupid smiles nearby. Is Bernini himself implying that the basis of mystical transport is sexual? Lacan provocatively uses the word *jouissance* in different contexts to mean both orgasm and ecstasy. At an abstract level, *jouissance* refers to a narcissistic pleasure rediscovered in the other, reminiscent of mirror-stage union. But this illusionary wholeness can never be recovered. Not only was it fictional in the first place, but it can only afterward be sought through displacements and substitutions for the original objects of Desire. Sexual rapport is merely one more such displacement or substitution. When Lacan asks if there can be "pleasure or orgasm" beyond the Phallus, then, he is not really asking a sexual question. Rather, he is pointing out that one must seek pleasure—sexual or otherwise—by adopting a stance toward the Phallus. One believes one *is* the Phallus; or one submits to it; or one rejects it; and so forth. But in all these postures, Desire—as a structural lack in the subject—defines the trajectory of pleasure and freedom in their relation to power and Law. Does Bernini's sculpture suggest that St. Theresa's sexual pleasure is somehow related to God? Is Lacan saying that her pleasure comes from submission to the phallic Law?

At another level, the Lacanian Phallus is the obstacle to *jouis-*

sance for both sexes. The Phallus, paradoxically, facilitates sexual rapport by its injunction to difference, but also gives the lie to the myth of an innate and natural harmony of the sexes. The Phallus necessitates displacement and substitution in human relations and ensures that sexual unity is only achieved through psychic mediation. I detect a characteristic irony in Lacan's "beyond the phallus" statement, therefore, since he appears to have little theoretical interest in focusing on bodily sexual needs or orgasmic pleasure as ends in themselves. Rather, he seems interested in what structure and language make of our bodily natures. And it is in this sense that one must take his jest seriously. When we ask if there can be ecstasy or pleasure beyond the social order—for the Lacanian Phallus symbolizes that order—we are confronted with the age-old dilemma of submission to arbitrary dicta versus a rebellion in the name of Truth, ideals, pleasure, and so forth. The attempt to subvert the phallic order, however, inheres in its genesis. The Imaginary order, based on primal fusion, will constantly try to overthrow the Symbolic order of difference in its quest for unity (*jouissance*).

These paradoxes may explain why Lacan's critics are confused and so intent on misreading him. Lacan has taught that one cannot overthrow the phallic or social order without paying the price demanded by that order: a social rejection that ranges from mild disapproval to imprisonment or incarceration in an asylum for the mentally ill. The two-horned dilemma that any child faces, then, is how to accept the paternal Law and thus be castrated—that is, separated—or to refuse it and remain subjugated to the mother. The way in which a child resolves this dilemma will determine its place in society as normal, neurotic, homosexual, heterosexual, and so forth. Those who do not resolve the Oedipal crisis in a manner acceptable to their societies could be viewed as the knots in a cultural signifying chain. Criminals are those who refuse to attribute any genuine governing power to the artificial laws set up in the Name-of-the-Father. Revolutionaries defy the codes of the Symbolic order in the name of political ideals and ideology. Hysterics simultaneously worship and resist the phallic signifier. Psychotics are those who have initially failed to learn (i.e., have foreclosed) the Law of the Name-of-the-Father: a disproportionate lack of distance from their own Other(A) messages saddles them with tragic identity difficulties and with little "realistic" sense of boundaries. In a state of psychosis the subject actually comes unhooked from the Symbolic order of norms and is set "afloat" in a sea of unmediated images, hallucinations, grandiose fantasies, and detached signifiers.[51] To foreclose the differentiating phallic signifier—the third term—orients a person toward the incestuousness of Desire, rather than the differentiated boundaries of selfhood. Not having undergone primary Castration, the psychotic has no set sexual identity. Moreover, Desire stops because substitution is no longer functional. But even when a person's Oedipal resolution falls within the cultural parameters of normalcy, Oedipal conflicts are never totally resolvable. They arise at numerous junctures in any life, because the Oedipal nexus was put in place by other people and is recalled into play later by the fluctuations within the Real and in relationships.

We have established Lacan's claim that one of the functions of language is to compensate for the psychic division undergone through the Oedipal experience (see Chapter 1). Although there is no directly proportional link between unconscious and conscious language, a person's earliest identifications later govern the use of language with an unconscious intentionality. One who identifies with phallic forces, for example, will use language to represent her or his ego on the slope of the Master and base this authority on "knowing." The Lacanian hysteric is one who poses the very question of sexual identity by addressing her or his discourse to the Master (*Séminaire* XX, "A Jakobson," pp. 19–27). Although the unconscious intentionality underlying these discourse structures is not sexually predetermined, the patriarchal order tends to make masters of men and hysterics of women. It should be stressed here that Lacan described the master discourse as one based on ignorance and opinion that mask unconscious truth. By denying the trauma of primary Castration, the master discourse unconsciously perpetuates the suppression of the person's own division and thus enables him or her to retain an unchallenged belief in her or his autonomy. Lacan located the hysteric's discourse close to the analyst's, that is, close to the search for being in terms of unconscious truth. Lacan claimed that his own discourse was grounded in the structures both of the hysteric and the analyst.

There can be no "beyond the phallus," then, if by this one understands beyond differentiation, society, language, law, and reality. The Symbolic order keeps its subjects from plunging headlong into incestuous lures and hallucinatory desires. Nonetheless, the Symbolic order is changing all the time. As changing sex roles reflect new economic and historical realities and force shifts in the language and myths describing women and men, the secondary meanings attached to Castration are increasingly degenderized. And such changes raise several questions. Can a woman, for example, separate carrying and bearing infants from their subsequent nurture? Can early infant nurture, indeed, be separated from woman per se? Would a change in the gender of the primary caretaker simply change the signifier of Castration and imprint it on males, as it has on females? If the separation trauma were to be less gender-related, what impact would this have on the learning of sexual identity? Would a more androgynous being evolve? Would the Oedipal drama, if made less gender specific, come to center around individual—not sexual—power and prestige?

Lacan has never said, moreover, that female sexuality is the outcome of thwarted phallic strivings (as did Freud). Nor does Lacan attribute female sexuality, as did Heinz Kohut, to a natural biological development.[52] It is always to the double effects of Castration on women that he points: (1) through separation, and (2) through the arbitrary sequences of power = penis = Phallus or conversely, lack or loss = no penis = Castration. The Lacanian psychoanalyst Safouan focuses principally on what I have termed primary Castration and stresses that all human beings are castrated. Men are not the Phallus; women do not possess the organ which symbolizes it.[53] But the danger in such an equation is that it could simply leave old anomalies in place and women still "one down." And Montrelay points to even stranger confusions. She explains the male's alternately worshipful and fearful attitude toward woman as his being disarmed before the veiled fragment that is the Phallus and that she contains: "Disarmed. A father is always disarmed before his daughter, whose body without a penis provokes him where a phallus and not a penis exists. He does not have this phallus that is not a penis (so he believes) but the Mother, the place where he confuses his own and his child's, does."[54]

Insofar as both man and woman are signifiers, and insofar as the signifier is something that represents a subject for another signifier, men represent the Phallus or social prestige for women, while women represent "love" and truth for men. Men symbolize power and public involvement; women symbolize personal and sexual involvement. He can supply what she lacks in social prestige; she can make him whole again. Josette Féral has written: "Woman remains the instrument by which man attains unity, and she pays for it at the price of her own dispersion."[55] If profound social change is to occur, then, the meanings attributed to the inherently neutral phallic signifier must be altered in the Other(A), all the while remembering that woman's dispersion resides in the irrecuperable part-objects of unconscious Desire.

Primary Castration is unavoidable and universal if one is to live in sanity (Frege's 2). Secondary Castration attributes meanings to the structural differentiation drama in terms of gender difference (Frege's 3). The impact of this combined experience sets men on a quest to be the Phallus by trying to embody power and prestige. And women try to marry as high up the phallic ladder as possible. For most men, however, the climb to social power entails power by association, compromise, and submission, just as it does for a woman whose fate is linked to her ability to win phallic approval. To the degree that the meanings of the mirror-stage and Oedipal structures are degenderized, however, the eternal struggle for power remains—but is forced to seek new forms if gender identity per se does not provide them.

Oedipus at Colonus posed the question: "Is it when I am finally nothing that I become really a man?" Lacan told his Seminar in May 1955: "It is there that the next chapter begins: beyond the pleasure principle" (Schneiderman, *Returning*, p. 94). In Seminar Two Lacan emphasized that beyond the pleasure principle lies the autonomous principle of repetition, or insistence, which is discernible via a transference object who serves as a screen on which to project the unconscious text. Repetition gives the subject a sense of unity and constancy through a preestablished coherence of relationship and linguistic understanding (p. 222). In Lacan's own theoretical terms, then, woman's equality could only be achieved by disrupting the history of repetition, by sowing disunity among standard social codes, practices, and linguistic commonplaces, and by altering the structure of object relations. Irigaray's creation of a new language that pleads with women to refuse what I have termed secondary Castration would indeed be a step in that direction. But it is Lacan's thought that gives us the basis of a new theory on which to continue the rewriting of woman's and man's history. Lacan's admiration for Oedipus at Colonus focuses on the hero as taking responsibility for his fate, as taking up his place in the social order. The issue for women and men is to define that place anew.

To conclude, everything comes down to a narrowing of focus. This pressing global need to change the social, linguistic order depends, ultimately, on the need to restructure the myths attached to the humble experiences that create the human subject as a structure of Desire and Law. Although mirror-stage identification and phallic differentiation are not biologically determined, their usual effects are predictable. If Lacan is right, then, we know what must be restructured. Not by overthrowing patriarchy cum capitalism will human beings gain the freedom of Desire that tantalizes Deleuze and Guattari. Nor will feminists eradicate phallocratic, that is power-based, values, even if they live in exclusively female groups. Marxism and feminism would simply evolve their own phallocracies, because recognition and power needs inhere in the structure of the subject. With Lacan, then, there can be no tomorrow of communist egalitarianism that will abolish power structures, no utopia where women's superior values replace men's tarnished ones. But there can be a tomorrow where differentiations are made along individual lines. As that day comes closer, both sexes will anticipate their own future disillusionment by understanding the complexity of the subject's quadrilateral structure: in relationship to society and in its own paradoxical strivings.

NOTES

Lacan's published works include editions and transcriptions of an extensive oral teaching and wide lecturing activity. His teaching took place in different academic institutions, but always went under the name of the Seminars (*les Séminaires*). He began giving his seminars in 1953 and finally stopped altogether in 1980. Currently, five of his yearly seminars have been edited by Jacques-Alain Miller and published in French by Seuil (Paris): *Livre* I (1953–54), *Livre* II (1954–55), *Livre* III (1955–56), *Livre* XI (1963–64), and *Livre* XX (1973–74). Only one of these seminars—Seminar XI—has been translated into English by Alan Sheridan, and published by Norton (New York) and Hogarth (London). *Séminaire* VII (*L'éthique de la psychanalyse*) is due to appear in 1984 or 1985 (in French). When finally published, Lacan's seminars will total approximately twenty-one or twenty-two volumes.

Dr. Jacques-Alain Miller, director of the department of psychoanalysis at Paris VIII, is responsible for establishing the texts and for editing the seminars. Only those seminars prepared by Dr. Miller have Jacques Lacan's approval as official versions. This is not to say, however, that anyone who can read French does not have access to the remainder of the seminars. Indeed, *Livre* XXII (1974–75), *Livre* XXIII (1975–76), and *Livre* XXIV (1976–77) have already been published in various issues of the official Lacanian journal *Ornicar?*. Abridgments of Lacan's seminars from 1956–59 were published in the *Bulletin de Psychologie*, edited by J.-B. Pontalis. Although these renditions do not have the stamp of Lacan's final approval, they give an account of the following seminar topics: "La Relation d'objet et les structures freudiennes" (Object relations and Freudian structures); "Les Formations de l'inconscient" (Formations of the Unconscious); and "Le Désir et son interprétation" (Desire and its Interpretation).

Other seminars have been published in journals or book collections, or exist in abridged form in Lacan's *Ecrits*, published in 1966. "Desire and the Interpretation of Desire in *Hamlet*" (1959), translated into English by James Hulbert, appeared in *Yale French Studies* 55/56 (1977). The "Seminar on the

Purloined Letter" (1966), translated into English by Jeffrey Mehlman, appeared in *Yale French Studies* 48 (1972). "Seminar of 21 January 1975," translated by Jacqueline Rose, appeared in the collection *Feminine Sexuality* edited by Juliet Mitchell and Jacqueline Rose (1983). This seminar had already appeared in *Ornicar?* in 1975. Lacan's *Ecrits* (1966) contains: "Le séminaire sur 'La Lettre volée'" (1966); "Introduction au commentaire de Jean Hyppolite sur la *Verneinung* de Freud" (séminaire de technique freudienne du 10 février 1954); "D'une question préliminaire à tout traitement possible de la psychose" (the most important aspects of the 1955–56 *séminaire*); "La science et la vérité" (the opening lesson from the 1965–66 *séminaire*: "L'objet de la psychanalyse"). Of these portions or abridgments of seminars, Alan Sheridan's translation of nine essays from Lacan's *Ecrits* contains only one: "On a question preliminary to any possible treatment of psychosis" (1955–56).

Approximately half of Lacan's seminars are available in French in official texts. The other half are available in pirated editions, which are photocopied transcriptions of tapes of Lacan's seminars made by private individuals, or the tapes themselves. Thus, the person who reads or understands French has the possibility of wide access to all of Lacan's seminars. But in addition to the seminars, Lacan published many other items. His dissertation was published in 1975 by Seuil under the title *De la psychose paranoïaque dans ses rapports avec la personnalité*. This was Lacan's thesis for the doctorate in medicine (Diplôme d'état) in 1932. Numerous texts that would otherwise be scattered here and there have been placed in a bibliography by Anthony Wilden in *The Language of the Self* (Baltimore: Johns Hopkins University Press, 1968). This bibliography includes pieces both by and about Lacan.

Long before Lacan began to crystallize his thought in his teaching that started with the first seminar in 1953, he had been lecturing to various psychoanalytic groups. His *Ecrits* was published in Paris by Seuil in 1966. This book contains twenty-eight essays, plus five short essays of opening or retrospective commentary on what is to follow in the collection. The *Ecrits* is divided into seven parts, plus Appendices I and II. The volume also includes an index of the major Lacanian concepts, a table with commentary on Lacan's graphic representations, a list of Freud's terms in German, a name index, and a bibliographical guide. The *Ecrits* takes us from the beginning of Lacan's writing and lecturing activity in the 1930s up to the 1960s. Included are lectures given to psychoanalytic congresses, to hospital clinics or congresses, to institutes, and to university conferences, as well as pieces written expressly for a given journal, psychoanalytic book series, or encyclopedia. Some of the essays are remarks that Lacan made to colleagues or students, tributes *in memoriam*, or commentaries on published books. But not even half of these essays are available in English. The major source is *Ecrits: A Selection*, translated by Alan Sheridan (New York: Norton, 1977). Nine of the essays from the *Ecrits* compose Sheridan's edition. Sheridan's "The agency of the letter in the unconscious or reason since Freud" ["L'instance de la lettre dans l'inconscient ou la raison depuis Freud" (1957)] has also been translated by Jan Miel as "The Insistence of the Letter in the Unconscious" and appeared in *Yale French Studies* 36/37 (1966). Sheridan translated "La signification du phallus" (1958) as "The signification of the phallus." Jacqueline Rose has also translated this essay as "The Meaning of the Phallus." It appears in the Mitchell and Rose collection, *Feminine Sexuality*. Sheridan translated the "Fonction et champ de la parole et du langage en psychanalyse" (1953) as "The function and field of speech and language in psychoanalysis." Wilden translated this essay—the Discourse of Rome—as "The Function of Language in Psychoanalysis," and it appeared in his *The Language of the Self*.

In addition to Lacan's *Ecrits*, there is another source of the *Ecrits* available in French. In 1966 Seuil also published a book called *Ecrits I*. This edition was preceded by an unedited version of some of Lacan's essays. The *Ecrits*, which appeared in one volume in 1966, contained only edited essays. *Ecrits I* is an edited version of five essays from the *Ecrits*, plus the three short essays containing opening or retrospective commentary on parts I, II, and IV of the *Ecrits*. *Ecrits I* contains selections from the first half of the larger volume. *Ecrits II* appeared in 1971 (Seuil) and contains seven essays, all taken from the second half of the *Ecrits*. The twelve major essays included in *Ecrits I* and *Ecrits II* anthologize the *Ecrits*, but not in chronological order.

For further bibliographical information regarding works by or on Lacan, one can go to the French bibliographer Joël Dor, *Bibliographie des travaux de Jacques Lacan* (Paris: Inter Editions, 1983). Two bibliographies are in preparation in English. Michael Clark is preparing an annotated Lacan bibliography to be published by Garland (New York). This bibliography will cover work in French and English, as well as translated and selected original works in several languages. James and Mary Ruth Glogowski are preparing a bibliography entitled *Lacan in North America: A Citation Analysis*, which will track Lacan's influence in North America. The influences cited will be indexed and arranged by discipline grouping. In addition, other English language material on Lacan has appeared in three issues of *Lacan Study Notes*, *a Newsletter*, published in 1983 and 1984. The editor, Helena Schulz-Keil, reports that the format will expand to that of booklet or journal size. *The Annual of Lacanian Studies*, currently in preparation, will be the official English-language forum for material by Lacan translated into English, transted essays by French Lacanians, and essays contributed by North American Lacanians. The *Annual* will appear under the auspices of *Ornicar?* (La fondation du champ freudien). The editor-in-chief, Jacques-Alain Miller, will name various English-language editors.

In my book I have used material by Lacan from every available source, principally in French. There are, however, six major sources and one translation source. I have used these seven references so often that after the first complete citation of each in the notes, these texts will be short-cited in my book. They are as follows: *Séminaire* I, *Séminaire* II, *Séminaire* III, *Séminaire* XI, and *Séminaire* XX. In order to give the English-speaking reader the fullest possible access to the sources, I have always referred to Sheridan's translation of essays in the *Ecrits* when possible. When there was no English translation of a given *Ecrits* essay, I translated the material and gave the French reference to *Ecrits* (1966). I have not referred at all to *Ecrits I* or *Ecrits II*. Since my references to Sheridan always refer to page numbers, I will list the essays in his edition and the inclusive pages. "The mirror stage as formative of the fuction of the I" (pp. 1–7); "Aggressivity in psychoanalysis" (pp. 8–29); "The function and field of speech and language in psychoanalysis" (pp. 30–113); "The Freudian thing" (pp. 114–45); "The agency of the letter in the unconscious or reason since Freud" (pp. 146–78); "On a question preliminary to any possible treatment of psychosis" (pp. 179–225); "The direction of the treatment and the principles of its power" (pp. 226–80); "The signification of the phallus" (pp. 281–91); "The subversion of the subject and the dialectic of desire in the Freudian unconscious" (pp. 292–325). On occasion I have referred to Wilden's translation of "The Function of Language in Psychoanalysis" or to Rose's translation of "The Meaning of the Phallus." In such cases, I have noted their books.

My references to essays in the *Ecrits* also go by pages. They are as follows: "De nos antécédents" (pp. 65–72); "Propos sur la causalité psychique" (pp. 151–93); "Du sujet enfin en question" (pp. 229–36); "A la mémoire d'Ernest Jones: Sur sa théorie du symbolisme" (pp. 697–717); "Position de l'inconscient" (pp. 829–50); "Appendice II: La Métaphore du Sujet" (pp. 889–92).

Introduction

1. Jacques Lacan, "Seminar of 21 January 1975," in *Femine Sexuality: Jacques Lacan and the Ecole Freudienne*, ed. Juliet Mitchell and Jacqueline Rose and trans. J. Rose (New York: W. W. Norton, 1983), p. 163.

2. Jacques Lacan, "Propos sur la causalité psychique" (1946), in *Ecrits* (Paris: Editions du Seuil, 1966), p. 153.

3. William Kerrigan, introduction, in his *Interpreting Lacan: Psychiatry and the Humanities*, vol. 6, ed. Joseph H. Smith and William Kerrigan (New Haven, Conn.: Yale University Press, 1983), p. xxi.

4. Jacques-Alain Miller, "Another Lacan," in *Lacan Study Notes* 1, no. 3 (Feb. 1984): 3.

5. Peter McCormick, "Moral Knowledge and Fiction," *Journal of Aesthetics and Art Criticism* 41 (Summer 1983): 400.

6. Jacques-Alain Miller, "Suture (elements of the logic of the signifier)," *Screen* 18, no. 4 (Winter 1977–78): 25.

7. Cathérine Clément, *Vies et légendes de Jacques Lacan* (Paris: Bernard Grasset, 1981), p. 154.

8. Jacques-Alain Miller, "Commentary on the graphs," in *Ecrits: A Selection*, trans. Alan Sheridan (New York: W. W. Norton, 1977), p. 332.

9. *Le Séminaire de Jacques Lacan, Livre II: Le moi dans la théorie de Freud et dans la technique de la psychanalyse* (1954–55), text established by Jacques-Alain Miller (Paris: Editions du Seuil, 1978), p. 284.

Chapter 1. What is "I"?

1. Stuart Schneiderman, personal correspondence. Dr. Schneiderman stressed, in a letter to me of Aug. 13, 1981, that the Lacanian ego is intrinsically unified, but the subject split (p. 2).

2. Stuart Schneiderman, *Returning to Freud: Clinical Psychoanalysis in the School of Lacan*, trans. and ed. Stuart Schneiderman (New Haven, Conn.: Yale University Press, 1980), preface, pp. 2–3.

3. Jacques Lacan, "Propos sur la causalité psychique" (1946), in *Ecrits* (Paris: Editions du Seuil, 1966); and "Aggressivity in psychoanalysis" (1948), in *Ecrits: A Selection*, trans. Alan Sheridan (New York: W. W. Norton, 1977), p. 15.

4. See n. 9 to the Introduction for a full reference to *Séminaire* II, 1954–55, p. 284. Jacques Lacan, "Le Séminaire sur *La Lettre Volée*" (1966), in *Ecrits*, 1966, p. 53; "D'une question préliminaire à tout traitement possible de la psychose" (déc. 1957–janv. 1958), ibid., p. 548. The diagram of Schéma L in the 1957–58 essay is simplified to:

where a¹ denotes the *moi* while a denotes others or alter egos. See also "On a question preliminary to any possible treatment of psychosis" in Sheridan, *Ecrits*, p. 193. The 1955 and 1966 versions of Schéma L are more complete, containing arrows that point out the directionality of the Sa¹aA vectors.

5. *Le Séminaire de Jacques Lacan, Livre XI: Les quatre concepts fondamentaux de la psychanalyse* (1964), text established by Jacques-Alain Miller (Paris: Editions du Seuil, 1973), pp. 69–73.

6. *Le Séminaire de Jacques Lacan, Livre XX: Encore* (1972–73), text established by Jacques-Alain Miller (Paris: Editions du Seuil, 1975), p. 112.

7. Anthony Wilden, *The Language of the Self* (Baltimore, Md.: Johns Hopkins University Press, 1968); cf. Wilden's essay "Lacan and the Discourse of the Other" (ibid., pp. 159–311).

8. *Le Séminaire de Jacques Lacan, Livre I: Les écrits techniques de Freud* (1953–54), text established by Jacques-Alain Miller (Paris: Editions du Seuil, 1975), pp. 130–31.

9. J.-B. Fages, *Comprendre Jacques Lacan* (Toulouse: Edouard Privat, 1971), pp. 51–52.

10. Jean Laplanche, *Life and Death in Psychoanalysis*, trans. and with intro. Jeffrey Mehlman (Baltimore, Md.: Johns Hopkins University Press, 1976), p. 51.

11. Sherry Turkle, *Psychoanalytic Politics: The French Freudian Revolution* (New York: Basic Books, 1978). This book has a thorough discussion of Lacan's conflicts with orthodox neo-Freudianism across the years.

12. Sheridan, "The Freudian thing, or the meaning of the return to Freud in psychoanalysis" (1956), in *Ecrits*, p. 135.

13. Sheridan, "The function and field of speech and language in psychoanalysis" (1953), in *Ecrits*, pp. 37–38.

14. Sigmund Freud, "On Narcissism: An Introduction" (1914), in *The Standard Edition of the Complete Psychological Works of Sigmund Freud*, ed. James Strachey (London: Hogarth Press, 1953–66), 14:83–84. References to the *Standard Edition* will henceforth be abbreviated as *SE*. "Mourning and Melancholia" (1916), *SE*, 14: 249–51; "Group Psychology and the Analysis of the Ego" (1921), *SE*, 18: 129.

15. Jacques Lacan, *De la Psychose paranoïaque dans ses rapports avec la personalité suivi de Premiers écrits sur la paranoïa* (Paris: Editions du Seuil, 1975), p. 324.

16. In the Middle Ages the concept of immanence meant that human potentiality could only be completely fulfilled when individuals let the image of God in themselves shine through. Cf. G. D. Josipovici, "From Analogy to Scepticism," in *French Literature and Its Background: The Sixteenth Century*, ed. John Cruickshank (London: Oxford University Press, 1968), p. 3.

17. François Rabelais, *Gargantua, Oeuvres complètes*, ed. Pierre Jourda (Paris: Editions Garnier Frères, 1962), cf. chap. 57.

18. Michel de Montaigne, *Les Essais*, ed. and text established by Albert Thibaudet (Paris: Gallimard, Editions de la Pléiade, 1950); cf. "L'Apologie de Raimond Sebond" (Livre II), ibid.

19. Cf. Jacques Lacan, "Propos sur la causalité psychique" (1946), in *Ecrits* (1966), pp. 173–76. In discussing Alceste, Lacan reveals a link between love and madness, paranoia, and the narcissistic *moi*.

20. Jean-Marie Benoist, *La Révolution Structurale* (Paris: Denoël/ Gonthier, 1980), p. 38. Descartes's mechanistic thought was based on the model of a fixed point.

21. Elisabeth Roudinesco, *Un discours au réel: théorie de l'inconscient et politique de la psychanalyse* (Paris: Maison Mame, 1973), pp. 15–16.

22. Roman Jakobson, "Linguistic et poétique," in *Essais de linguistique générale* (Paris: Minuit, 1960), cf. chap. II.

23. Charles J. Stivale, "Gilles Deleuze and Félix Guattari: Schizoanalysis and Literary Discourse," *Sub-Stance* 29 (1981): 47.

24. Richard Wollheim's statement "Lacan assigns clear priority to symbolism over cognitive development" reveals that he does not understand Lacan's epistemological interpretation of the function of images and symbols in creating cognition (mind). Richard Wollheim, "The Cabinet of Dr. Lacan," *New York Review of Books*, Jan. 25, 1979, p. 36.

25. In pursuit of this insight, Lacan reaffirmed, near the end of his life, that Freud's discoveries of genius lay in the early period of his research and thought. The international center that today teaches Lacan's interpretations of Freud's texts is the Ecole de la Cause freudienne, 1 rue Huysmans, 75006 Paris, France.

26. Cf. Jean Laplanche and J.-B. Pontalis, *Vocabulaire de la psychanalyse* (Paris: Presses universitaires de France, 1967), pp. 67–70.

27. Lacan felt that the future of a scientific basis for psychoanalysis lay in

studying Freud's early works, particularly those which related the unconscious to language and symbolism. Sheridan, "The function and field," pp. 57–60.

28. Cited by Martha N. Evans, "Introduction to Jacques Lacan's Lecture: The Neutrotic's Individual Myth," *Psychoanalytic Quarterly* 48 (1979): 389. See, too, Sigmund Freud, "Papers on Metapsychology," *SE*, 14: 117–215, esp. p. 169.

29. Stuart Schneiderman, "Psychoanalysis and *Hamlet*," *DAI* 72 (1975), 23503A.

30. Sheridan, "The agency of the letter in the unconscious or reason since Freud" (1957), in *Ecrits*, pp. 164–65.

31. Didier Anzieu, for example, has said that Lacan's Freudian orthodoxy is a myth and his mirror stage more illusion than scientific observation. Fages, *Comprendre Jacques Lacan*, p. 49.

32. *Le Séminaire de Jacques Lacan, Livre II: Le moi dans la théorie de Freud et dans la technique de la psychanalyse* (1954–55), text established by Jacques-Alain Miller (Paris: Editions du Seuil, 1978), p. 290.

33. In a bibliographical note Sheridan explains that Lacan's essay delivered at the sixteenth International Congress of Psychoanalysis, Zurich (1949), and entitled "The mirror stage as formative of the function of the I as revealed in psychoanalytic experience" is a later version of an essay called "Le stade du miroir," which was supposedly delivered at the fourteenth International Psychoanalytical Congress at Marienbad in 1936. This latter paper was allegedly published in 1937 in the *International Journal of Psychoanalysis* as "The Looking-glass Phase" (*Ecrits*, p. xiii). In a letter to me, dated July 5, 1982, Stuart Schneiderman wrote that to his knowledge no copy of this early paper exists or has been published (p. 1). In an essay entitled "Lacan's 'Mirror Stage': Where to Begin?" Jane Gallop analyzes the larger implications of this bibliographical lacuna (*Sub-Stance* 37/38 [1983]: 118–28).

34. Although Richard Wollheim and other critics have argued that Lacan adduced no evidence in support of this mirror-stage concept, they obviously have not followed Lacan's advice to look at what animal studies teach about the formative effects of mimesis in species identification: "That a *Gestalt* should be capable of formative effects in the organism is attested by a piece of biological experimentation that is itself so alien to the idea of psychical causality that it cannot bring itself to formulate its results in these terms. It nevertheless recognizes that it is a necessary condition for the maturation of the gonad of the female pigeon that it should see another member of its species, of either sex; so sufficient in itself is this condition that the desired effect may be obtained merely by placing the individual within reach of the field of reflection of a mirror." See Sheridan, "The mirror stage as formative of the function of the I as revealed in psychoanalytic experience" (1949), *Ecrits*, p. 3. See also Lacan, "Aggressivity in psychoanalysis," pp. 17–18.

35. Arthur Efron, "Psychoanalytic Theory of Human Nature: The Current Dilemma," unpublished paper, part of which was presented Nov. 15,

1978, at the Center for the Psychological Study of the Arts at the State University of New York−Buffalo.

36. Robert Weiss, *Experience of Loneliness: Studies in Emotional and Social Isolation* (Cambridge, Mass.: MIT University Press, 1974). Cf. Zick Rubin, "Seeking a Cure for Loneliness," *Psychology Today*, Oct. 1979, pp. 85−86 especially.

37. Efron, "Psychoanalytic Theory," pp. 28, 29, 30. Cf. Daniel Yankelovich and William Barrett, *Ego and Instinct—The Psychoanalytic View of Human Nature—Revised* (New York: Random House, 1970), pp. 393−94; Ernest G. Schachtel, *Metamorphosis: On the Development of Affect, Perception, Attention, and Memory* (New York: Basic Books, 1959), pp. 117, 127, 159.

38. Sheridan, "The direction of the treatment and the principles of its power" (1958), in *Ecrits*, p. 246.

39. Efron, "Psychoanalytic Theory," pp. 5, 37. Cf. Friedrich Brock, *Haut-, Tiefen- und Labyrinthorgane*, vol. 1 of *Bau und Leistung unserer Sinnesorgane* (Bern: Francke, 1956).

40. In accordance with Laplanche and Pontalis, Jeffrey Mehlman has written that Lacan did not see the incipient ego as a product of evolution through oral, anal, and genital stages, but as a corporal entity, a privilege of the "edges" (*bords*). Mehlman, "The 'Floating Signifier': From Lévi-Strauss to Lacan," *Yale French Studies* 48 (1972): 18.

41. Michèle Montrelay, "The Story of Louise," in Schneiderman, *Returning*, pp. 82−83.

42. Serge Leclaire, *Psychanalyser: Un essai sur l'ordre de l'inconscient et la pratique de la lettre* (Paris: Editions du Seuil, 1968), p. 72; see chap. 3 especially.

43. Serge Leclaire, *On tue un enfant* (Paris: Editions du Seuil, 1975), p. 88.

44. Sheridan, "Subversion of the subject and dialectic of desire in the Freudian unconscious" (1960), in *Ecrits*, p. 315. See also "Commentary on the Graphs," ibid., pp. 333−34.

45. Michel Grimaud, "Psychologie et littérature," in *Théorie de la Littérature*, a collective work presented by A. Kibédi Varga (Paris: Picard, 1981), p. 258.

46. Jody Gaylin, "Don't Stick Out Your Tongue at a Newborn," *Psychology Today*, Dec. 1977, pp. 24, 26. Cf. also *The Competent Infant*, 3 vols., ed. Lois Murphy, Joseph Stone, and Henrietta Smith (New York: Basic Books, 1978); Leslie B. Cohen and Philip Salapatek, *Infant Perception*, 2 vols. (New York: Academic Press, 1975); Richard N. Aslin, Jeffrey R. Alberts, and Michael R. Petersen, *Development of Perception*, 2 vols. (New York: Academic Press, 1981); Michael E. Lamb and Lonnie R. Sherrod, *Infant Social Cognition* (London: Erlbaum Association 1981); Jay Belsky, *In the Beginning* (New York: Columbia University Press, 1982).

47. Efron, "Psychoanalytic Theory," p. 22. see Victor Smirnoff, *The Scope*

of Child Analysis (New York: International Universities Press, 1971), pp. 95–96.

48. Efron, "Psychoanalytic Theory," p. 22. See Joanna Steinberg, review of four books on childhood and infancy in *Psychology Today*, Aug. 1977, pp. 94–99. See also Aidan Macfarlane, *The Psychology of Childbirth*, Harvard University Press series, The Developing Child (Cambridge, Mass.: Harvard University Press, 1977).

49. Efron, "Psychoanalytic Theory," p. 22. See L. P. Lipsett and H. Kaye, "Conditioned Sucking in the Newborn," *Psychonomic Science* 2 (1965): 221–22; L. P. Lipsitt, H. Kaye, and T. N. Bosak, "Enhancement of Neonatal Sucking through Reinforcement," *Journal of Experimental Child Psychology* 4 (1966): 163–68.

50. Efron, "Psychoanalytic Theory," p. 22. See Tina Appleton, Rachel Clifton, and Susan Goldberg, "The Development of Behavioral Competence in Infancy," in vol. 4 of *Review of Child Development Research*, ed. Frances D. Horowitz (Chicago: University of Chicago Press, 1975), p. 156.

51. Efron, "Psychoanalytic Theory," p. 23. See Michael Lewis, *The Origins of Intelligence: Infancy and Early Childhood* (New York: Wiley & Sons, 1976), p. 54.

52. Efron, "Psychoanalytic Theory," p. 24; Lewis, *Origins of Intelligence*, p. 54.

53. Efron, "Psychoanalytic Theory," p. 25; Appleton, Clifton, and Goldberg, *Review of Child Development Research*, pp. 102–3.

54. René Spitz, "Metapsychology and Direct Infant Observation," in *Psychoanalysis—A General Psychology*, ed. R. M. Lowenstein (New York: International University Press, 1966).

55. Child development researcher Burton White has written: "We know for certain that the newborn human literally cannot survive without a relationship to a more mature, more capable human. I am talking here about simple survival. A newborn baby is helpless. Physical survival is impossible unless somebody provides for him." White, *The First Three Years of Life* (New York: Avon Books, 1978), p. 127.

56. For an important study of the case of the "wild child" (*l'enfant sauvage*) from a Lacanian viewpoint regarding the role of identification in ego formation, see Octave Mannoni, "Itard et son sauvage," in *Clefs pour l'imaginaire on l'Autre scène* (Paris: Editions du Seuil, 1969), pp. 184–201.

57. Margaret Mahler, Fred Pine, and Anni Bergman, *The Psychological Birth of the Human Infant: Symbiosis and Individuation* (New York: Basic Books, 1975), p. 44.

58. Dorthy Dinnerstein, *The Mermaid and the Minotaur: Sexual Malaise and Human Malaise* (New York: Harper & Row, 1976), p. 111.

59. One might compare Wilhelm Reich's concept of "character armor" without which there can be no self. In 1952 (in a letter included in *Reich Speaks of Freud*) Reich declared that it was dangerous to try to dissolve character: "'You see, the armor thick as it is and as bad as it is, is a protective

device, and it is good for the individual under present social and psychological circumstances to have it. He could not live otherwise.'" Quoted by Frederick Crews, "Anxious Energetics," in *Out of My System: Psychoanalysis,
Ideology, and Critical Method* (New York: Oxford University Press, 1975),
p. 159.

60. Lacan's concept of the dialectical quadrature of the human subject
would, nonetheless, invalidate object-relations claims such as the one made
by psychoanalyst Heinz Lichtenstein "that the relation between mother and
infant does . . . represent an inner state of oneness, in which there is no differentiation between the infant's I and the mother." Lichtenstein, "Identity
and Sexuality: A Study of Their Interrelationship in Man," *Journal of
American Psychoanalytic Association* 9 (1961): 194.

61. Jacques Lacan, "De nos antécédents" (1966), *Ecrits*, 1966, p. 67; see
also "Propos sur la causalité psychique" (1946), ibid., pp. 184–85.

62. Samuel Weber wonders why Lacan ignored a remark of Freud's that
would seem to anticipate his own theory of the mirror stage. In *Beyond the
Pleasure Principle* (1920) Freud told the story of a small child who learned
to make himself disappear in a mirror, accompanying this action with the
sounds "baby o-o-o-o!" My guess is that Lacan wished to forestall the one-
to-one connection between his own conception of the mirror stage and an
actual mirror, which this anecdote might suggest. Weber, "The Divaricator:
Remarks on Freud's *Witz*," *Glyph* 1 (1977): 25.

63. Anika Lemaire, *Jacques Lacan*, trans. David Macey (Boston: Routledge & Kegan Paul, 1977), p. 81.

64. Lacan's use of the *trait unaire* concept refers to the French word *le
trait d'union*, meaning "hyphen," and evokes the infant/mother symbiosis
where two beings are connected as one synthesis by such symbolic hyphens
as language, the voice, the gaze, and so on. But mother and infant are indeed
separate. This perceptual confusion has, predictably, given rise to both object-
relations theory, which stresses the sameness of mother and infant, and sociological theories, which emphasize the links between self and society. Examples of excellent sociological treatises are George H. Mead, *Mind, Self
and Society* (Chicago: University of Chicago Press, 1934), and Solomon E.
Asch, *Social Psychology* (Englewood Cliffs, N.J.: Prentice Hall, 1952). Lacan
departed from the two-way static transparency between sociological concepts of self and society (or between infant and mother, or between self and
language) by splitting the subject. His thought accounts for the introjection
of mother, society, and language, but reveals the "self" as a dialectical,
opaque, dynamic, transformational quadrature.

65. Ernest Becker, *The Denial of Death* (New York: The Free Press, 1973),
pp. 3–4. See also White, *First Three Years*, pp. 125–26, for a well-phrased
discussion of sibling aggressiveness toward an infant by a sibling of up to
three years older.

66. Jim Swan, "*Mater* and Nannie: Freud's Two Mothers and the Discovery of the Oedipus Complex," *American Imago* 31 (Spring 1974): 57.

67. In *Life and Death in Psychoanalysis* (note 3, p. 67) Laplanche writes

that Freud decided his essay "On Narcissism" (*SE*, 14:83–84) was incomplete, if not monstrous, and rapidly discarded it.

68. In *Vocabulaire* (note 12, p. 262) Laplanche and Pontalis point out that Freud owed his idea of withdrawing the libido from the object (other) back to one's self to Karl Abraham, who had advanced this theory in 1908 in a discussion of *dementia praecox*.

69. Freud, "The Ego and the Id" (1923), *SE*, 19:31.

70. Swan, "*Mater* and Nannie," p. 8. See Freud, *New Introductory Lectures*, *SE*, 22:63.

71. Erik H. Erikson, *Childhood and Society* (New York: W. W. Norton, 1963).

72. Norman N. Holland, "Human Identity," *Critical Inquiry* 4 (Spring 1978): 451–70, especially p. 467.

73. For a concise discussion of Kohut and Kernberg, see Susan Quinn, "Oedipus vs. Narcissus," *New York Times Magazine*, Nov. 9, 1980, sec. 6, pp. 120–31. See also Moustapha Safouan, "The Apprenticeship of Tilmann Moser," in Schneiderman, *Returning*. This essay discusses Moser's book *Years of Apprenticeship on the Couch* and examines the reasons for the failure of Moser's analysis, which was conducted in line with Kohut's theories by one of his students.

74. From a brochure entitled "International Imagery Association and the *Journal of Mental Imagery* present 5th American Imagery Conference," at Chicago (Oct. 8–11, 1981) and New York City (Nov. 12–15, 1981).

75. Heinz Kohut, *The Analysis of the Self*, no. 4 in the monograph series The Psychoanalytic Study of the Child (New York: International Universities Press, 1971), pp. 147–48.

76. In an incorrect interpretation of Lacan, Wollheim ("Cabinet of Dr. Lacan") writes: "He says next to nothing about . . . mechanisms like introjection, projection, projective identification, which later psychoanalysts have carefully and fruitfully distinguished" (p. 44). Lacan's mirror-stage theory and his concept of the Imaginary order are based on these very concepts. But unlike Melanie Klein and other object-relations theorists, Lacan viewed these processes as dialectical and dynamic in response to man's fetalization. See Chap. 4 herein for a detailed discussion of the transformational processes that function to create and then operate a "self."

77. See Karen E. Paige and Jeffrey M. Paige, *The Politics of Reproductive Ritual* (Berkeley: University of California Press, 1981). See also Bruno Bettelheim, *Symbolic Wounds* (New York: The Free Press, 1954). Bettelheim and the Paiges view primitive sexual rituals as male efforts either to imitate the female or to claim their power over the female reproductive capacity. Could the rituals not be literal, symbolic attempts to interpret the meaning of sexual difference by valorizing those *different* parts of the body?

78. The classic source for the Narcissus story is Ovid's account in *Metamorphoses*, Book III.

79. Sheridan, "The direction of the treatment and the principles of its power." Lacan stressed the interminable aspect of psychoanalysis, a view in

keeping with his theory that the subject is permanently involved in the real-ization and writing of its own dialectical story. Just as Freud had begun to write the solution to the "infinite" analysis, Lacan writes, he died (p. 277).

80. Anthony Wilden's excellent translator's notes to Lacan's essay, "The Function of Language in Psychoanalysis," occupy pages 91–156 of *The Language of the Self*. The notes chronicle those thinkers who influenced Lacan.

81. Henry W. Sullivan, *Tirso de Molina and the Drama of the Counter Reformation* (Amsterdam: Rodopi NV, 1981). In a discussion of the theater of the Golden Age in Spain (the *comedia*), Sullivan defines the baroque as "the artistic representation of an internal conflict caused by the irreconcilable claims of monolithic belief and irresistible doubt competing for the same metaphysical 'space'" (p. 124).

82. The philosophical reverberations surrounding the issue of topology between Lacanian thought and Merleau-Ponty's writings were suggested to me by James Glogowski in a letter of Aug. 31, 1981 (p. 1). See also Maurice Merleau-Ponty, *The Visible and the Invisible*, trans. Alphonso Lingis (Evanston, Ill.: Northwestern University Press, 1968), p. 203.

83. In the translator's preface of *Returning*, Schneiderman writes: "The French *aggressivité* has been rendered by Sheridan as 'aggressivity.' Unfortu-nately this word does not appear in any dictionary that I have been able to find, and thus I have chosen the word 'aggressiveness,' which is commonly used in the English language. The reader will have no difficulty in distin-guishing 'aggressiveness' from 'aggression,' since the former refers only to intended aggression or an aggressive attitude" (p. vii).

84. Octave Mannoni, "Je sais bien, mais quand-même," *Clefs pour l'imag-inaire ou l'Autre scène*, pp. 9–33.

85. Shoshana Felman, "La Méprise et sa Chance," *L'Arc* 58 (1974): 44–45.

86. "Le Séminaire de Jacques Lacan, Livre VII: L'éthique de la psych-analyse" (Mar. 1960), unpublished.

87. In *On tue un enfant* Leclaire describes the "miraculous infant" or *moi* as a "primordial unconscious representation where the wishes, hopes and nostalgias of everyone are knotted together more densely than in any other place. . . . There is for everyone always a child to be killed, a grief to be continually made and remade out of a representation of plenitude" (p. 12). The translation is mine.

88. John Arnold Lindon, "Melanie Klein, 1882–1960: Her View of the Unconscious," in *Psychoanalytic Pioneers*, eds. Franz Alexander et al. (New York: Basic Books, 1966), p. 370.

89. An interesting empirical study pointing to the early interiorization of the mother was reported by Bridget Romana in "Lights! Camera! Interface!," *Psychology Today*, Nov. 1981, p. 22. Romana describes a study reporting that two-year-olds left in an unfamiliar playroom played more, stayed longer, and explored more, if they had a clear photograph of their mother to hold.

90. Cf. Lacan, "Position de l'inconscient au congrès de Bonneval reprise de 1960 en 1964" (1966), in *Ecrits*, 1966, pp. 829–50.

91. Herbert Marcuse, *Eros and Civilization: A Philosophical Inquiry into Freud* (New York: Vintage Books, 1962).

92. Jonathan Culler, "Prolegomena to a Theory of Reading," in *The Reader in the Text: Essays on Audience and Interpretation* (Princeton, N.J.: Princeton University Press, 1980), p. 56.

93. James Glogowski, "Four Graphs of Jacques Lacan," p. 5, unpublished paper.

94. In a letter to me (Aug. 13, 1981), Stuart Schneiderman describes the Lacanian ego as "the most resolute enemy of desire" (p. 2).

95. In a letter to me (Aug. 31, 1981) James Glogowski raises the issue of Merleau-Ponty's revolutionary conceptualization of topology as non-Euclidean (1959) and of Lacan's use of topology to describe the structures of the unconscious. Glogowski points out Merleau-Ponty's use of the Greek words for *ego* and *nobody* and stresses the problematic posed by Lacan in which the "I" is both somebody and nobody.

96. Quoted by Norman O. Brown, *Life against Death* (New York: Vintage Books, 1959), p. 106.

97. Ronald D. Laing, *Self and Others* (New York: Random House, 1969), passim.

98. In "Lacan and the Discourse of the Other" Anthony Wilden points out that Lacan's reinterpretation of the *Fort! Da!* in Freud's *Beyond the Pleasure Principle* is a radical one. Lacan did not relate this phonemic opposition directly to the specific German words but, instead, to the binary opposition of presence and absence in the infant's world (p. 163).

99. See Gerald E. Wade, "The 'Comedia' as Play," in *Studies in Honor of Everett W. Hesse*, ed. W. C. McCrary and José A. Madrigal (Lincoln: University of Nebraska Press for the Society of Spanish & Spanish-American Studies, 1981), pp. 173–74. See also Johan Huizinga, *Homo Ludens: A Study of the Play-Element in Culture* (Boston: Beacon Press, 1950), and Donald Winnicott, *Playing and Reality* (New York: Basic Books, 1971).

Chapter 2. Lacan's Four Fundamental Concepts

1. In *Séminaire* XI Lacan taught that psychoanalysis is a science because its object of study—the unconscious—can be ascertained through observation and analysis of repetition, regression, transference, and the *objet a* of Desire.

2. Frederic Jameson, "Imaginary and Symbolic in Lacan: Marxism, Psychoanalytic Criticism, and the Problem of the Subject," *Yale French Studies* 55/56 (1977): 338–95, especially the discussion of the triadic complexities of Lacan's three orders.

3. *Modern Concepts of Psychoanalysis*, ed. Leo Salzman and Jules H. Masserman (New York: Philosophical Library, 1962), p. 174.

4. Philip Rieff, *Freud: The Mind of the Moralist* (Garden City, N.Y.: Doubleday, 1961), p. 35.

5. Cf. Jean Laplanche and J.-B. Pontalis, *Vocabulaire de la psychanalyse* (Paris: Presses universitaires de Frances, 1967), pp. 359–60; references hereafter cited in text as *Vocabulaire*.

6. Quoted by Bruno Bettelheim in "Freud and the Soul," *The New Yorker*, Mar. 1, 1982, p. 89.

7. François Péraldi, "American Psychoanalysis," in *Psychoanalysis, Creativity and Literature: A French-American Inquiry*, ed. Alan Roland (New York: Columbia University Press, 1978), p. 34. See also the discussion by Laplanche and Pontalis of Freud's distinction between *Instinkt* and *Trieb*, and Lacan's development of the concept *Trieb* by the term *pulsion*. *Vocabulaire*, p. 203.

8. Richard Wollheim, "The Cabinet of Dr. Lacan," *New York Review of Books*, Jan. 25, 1979, p. 36.

9. J.-B. Pontalis, "On Death-Work," in *Psychoanalysis, Creativity and Literature*, ed. Roland, esp. p. 92.

10. Alternative behaviorist systems of "need" theory have evolved in recent years, notably by Abraham Maslow. Maslow views needs in their hierarchical insistence on satisfaction as the determinants of human behavior. After hunger and warmth, in his scheme, the psychic needs of security, love, and recognition follow. From Maslow's list, Lacan retains only the most elemental of physical survival tendencies at the level of pure need. Cf. Abraham Maslow, *Motivation and Personality* (New York: Harper & Row, 1954).

11. J.-B. Pontalis once defined *Trieb* as "a constant demand for work imposed upon a psychical apparatus, the complex modalities of its response to whatever is a 'foreign body' for it, but compels it to function, being the very object of analysis." "On Death-Work," pp. 85–86.

12. Jacques Lacan, "The Meaning of the Phallus" (1958), in *Feminine Sexuality: Jacques Lacan and the école freudienne*, ed. Juliet Mitchell and Jacqueline Rose (New York: W. W. Norton, 1983), pp. 80–81. See also "The signification of the phallus," in Sheridan, *Ecrits*, pp. 286–87.

13. Anthony Wilden, *The Language of the Self* (Baltimore, Md.: Johns Hopkins University Press, 1968), pp. 264–65; references hereafter cited in the text as *LS*.

14. Elisabeth Roudinesco, *Un discours au réel: théorie de l'inconscient et politique de la psychanalyse* (Paris: Maison Mame, 1973), p. 37.

15. Stuart Schneiderman, personal correspondence. Dr. Schneiderman writes that the most resolute enemy of desire is the ego (letter of Aug. 13, 1981, p. 2).

16. In his essay "Lacan and the Discourse of the Other" Anthony Wilden writes that, after introducing the Other in the late 1950s, Lacan transformed the other into the shorthand *le petit a*, and finally in the Schéma R into *l'objet petit a*. After 1953 Lacan reinterpreted Melanie Klein's theories about object relations and part-objects. This evolution served as a refinement in his elaboration of differences between pre-mirror and mirror stages and enabled him to distinguish between an ideal ego, ego ideals, and objects

of Desire. (Wilden, *Language of the Self*, p. 267). See also Sheridan, "On a question preliminary to any possible treatment of psychosis," in *Ecrits*, especially p. 197.

17. Stuart Schneiderman, *Returning to Freud: Clinical Psychoanalysis in the School of Lacan*, trans. and ed. Stuart Schneiderman (New Haven, Conn.: Yale University Press, 1980), p. 7; references hereafter cited in the text as *Returning*.

18. Jacques Lacan, "Desire and the Interpretation of Desire in *Hamlet*" (1959), *Yale French Studies* 55/56 (1977): 11–52.

19. Anika Lemaire, *Jacques Lacan*, trans. David Macey (Boston: Routledge & Kegan Paul, 1977), p. 163; references hereafter cited in the text as *Lacan*.

20. Jacques Lacan, *Télévision* (Paris: Editions du Seuil, 1974), p. 60. This is a two-part television interview of Lacan, with marginal notes established by Jacques-Alain Miller.

21. J.-B. Fages, *Comprendre Jacques Lacan* (Toulouse: Edouard Privat, 1971), pp. 31–32; references hereafter cited in the text as *Comprendre Lacan*.

22. James Glogowski, "An Essay on Psychopathology," p. 4, unpublished paper. See J. Lacan, "Les formations de l'inconscient," *Bulletin de Psychologie* 12 (Nov. 1957): 293–96.

23. Stuart Schneiderman, "The Most Controversial Freudian since Freud," *Psychology Today*, Apr. 1978, pp. 52, 55.

24. In "An Essay on Psychopathology" Glogowski points out that Freud's analysis of Heinrich Heine's *familionairely* joke interprets it in terms of letters that signify the joke's meaning (p. 2). See Sigmund Freud, *Jokes and Their Relationship to the Unconscious*, ed. and trans. James Strachey (New York: W. W. Norton, 1963), pp. 17, 19. By analyzing the pieces of letters in the neologism, Freud arrived at the interpretation: " 'Rothschild treated me quite as his equal, quite familiarly—that is, in so far as a millionaire can'" (p. 17). From an entirely different perspective Barbara B. Brown provides support for the idea that unconscious messages and words control our minds and bodies without our knowing it. See her *New Mind, New Body—Biofeed-back: New Directions for the Mind* (New York: Harper & Row, 1974).

25. "Le Séminaire de Jacques Lacan, Livre XVIII: L'envers de la psych-analyse" (June 1969), unpublished.

26. In "Subversion of the subject and dialectic of desire in the Freudian unconscious" (1960) Lacan said that desire finds form in the first instance by representing need only by means of a subjective opacity that produces the substance of desire. Desire begins to take shape in the margin where demand is separated from need, the margin that opens up an appeal to the Other which introduces the impossibility of universal satisfaction (which is called anxiety). In this margin the phantom of the Other's Omnipotence instills itself in one's demand, thus installing also the need to check the phantom by Law (Sheridan, *Ecrits*, p. 311).

27. Allen S. Weiss, "Merleau-Ponty's Concept of the 'Flesh' as Libido Theory," *Sub-Stance* 30 (1981): 85–95.

28. Paul Ricoeur, *Freud and Philosophy* (New Haven, Conn.: Yale University Press, 1970); cf. Weiss, "Merleau-Ponty's Concept," p. 95n1.

29. James Glogowski, "Four Graphs of Jacques Lacan," unpublished paper. Glogowski points out that since a subject does not know that it imagines itself in a series of images (of body and things) and signifiers, to acquire such knowledge is both tragic and potentially curative. For cure to occur, "the subject must be precipitated from the world of images in order to return to that world and recognize it for what it is and not as the totality of the self" (p. 12).

30. Jean Piaget, *Psychology and Epistemology: Towards a Theory of Knowledge*, trans. Arnold Rosin (New York: Penguin Books, 1978), p. 2.

31. *Dictionary of Philosophy*, ed. D. D. Runes (Ames, Ia.: Littlefield, Adams, 1958), p. 231.

32. Jacques-Alain Miller, "Lacan the Clinician," oral presentation at the Colloquium "Love, the Drive, the Object" (May 12–14, 1984), New York University, Deutsches Haus, May 14.

33. Eugen S. Bär, "Understanding Lacan," in *Psychoanalysis and Contemporary Science 3*, ed. Leo Goldberger and Victor H. Rosen (New York: International Universities Press, 1974), p. 528.

34. James Glogowski, personal correspondence. In a letter to me (Jan. 8, 1982), Glogowski writes: "Schneiderman hesitates even to use a locution like 'pre-linguistic,' as something which designates a child's *experience*— there being no 'experience' outside of or before language. And I think about all those testing obsessions that psychologists have. Lacan is always frustrating in this regard by such definitions as locate the unconscious somewhere between perception and consciousness; where consciousness itself is a 'scotoma.' Psychic causality is entirely eclipsed by the 'scotomatization' of the testing impulse" (pp. 1–2).

35. Sheridan, "On a question preliminary to any possible treatment of psychosis" (1957–58), in *Ecrits*, p. 215. Lacan returned here to a dialogue he had had with Henri Ey ten years previously ("Propos sur la causalité psychique," 1946) to answer a question about psychosis that he had left in suspense.

36. Norman O. Brown, *Life against Death* (New York: Vintage Books), pp. 7–8.

37. Philip Rieff quotes Freud as saying that "the mental is based on the organic" (*Freud*, p. 4). See Freud, "Psychogenic Disturbance of Vision" (1910), *SE*, 11: 217; see also *SE* 4: 41–42 (*The Interpretation of Dreams*).

38. Robert Georgin, *Le Temps freudien du verbe* (Lausanne: L'Age d'Homme, 1973), p. 89.

39. Jacques Lacan, "Appendice II: La Métaphore du Sujet" (1961), *Ecrits*, p. 892.

40. Jean-Marie Benoist, *La Révolution Structurale* (Paris: Denoël/Gonthier, 1980), p. 24.

41. Jean Laplanche and Serge Leclaire, "L'inconscient, une étude psychanalytique," in *L'Inconscient* (VI Colloque de Bonneval) (Paris: Presses uni-

versitaires de France, 1981), and "The Unconscious: a psychoanalytic study," trans. P. Coleman, *Yale French Studies*, 48 (1972): 118–75.

42. Cf. Jacques Lacan, "Of Structure as an Inmixing of an Otherness Prerequisite to Any Subject Whatever," in *The Structuralist Controversy: The Languages of Criticism and the Sciences of Man*, ed. Richard Macksey and Eugenio Donato (Baltimore, Md.: Johns Hopkins University Press, 1975), pp. 187–88.

43. Serge Leclaire, *Psychanalyser: Un essai sur l'ordre de l'inconscient et la pratique de la lettre* (Paris: Editions du Seuil, 1968). On p. 133 Leclaire reduces these three categories to three corresponding terms: letter, object, and subject.

44. Alice Miller, *Prisoners of Childhood* (New York: Basic Books, 1981).

45. In "Position de l'inconscient" Lacan says that repression (the *nachträglich* or *après-coup*) has a temporal impact on the subject because of the retroaction of the signifier, which is a completely different thing from the "final cause" (*Ecrits*, p. 839). The memory, which implies the repressed unconscious, manifests itself, among other ways, through repetition, described by Lacan as repetition of the symbol which is not constituted by man, but is constitutive of man. "Le Séminaire sur *La Lettre Volée*" (1966), in *Ecrits*, 1966, p. 46.

46. Jim Swan, "*Mater* and Nannie: Freud's Two Mothers and the Discovery of the Oedipus Complex," *American Imago* 31 (Spring 1974): 57.

47. Ibid., p. 56; Freud, *SE*, 14: 178.

48. In the "Discours de Rome" (1953) Lacan attacked the behaviorism of a psychoanalyst such as Jules H. Masserman, whose "scientific method" would not allow for any complexity or polyvalence between symbols and language. Sheridan *Ecrits*, pp. 62–64.

49. Shoshana Felman, "On Reading Poetry: Reflections on the Limits and Possibilities of Psychoanalytic Approaches," in *The Literary Freud: Mechanisms of Defense and the Poetic Will*, ed. Joseph H. Smith (New Haven, Conn.: Yale University Press, 1980), p. 139.

50. Samuel Weber, "The Divaricator: Remarks on Freud's *Witz*," *Glyph* 1 (1977): 1–2.

51. James Glogowski, personal correspondence, letter of Jan. 8, 1982, p. 2.

52. In "The Freudian thing, or the meaning of the return to Freud in psychoanalysis" (1953), Lacan said: "To consider only resistance, whose use is increasingly confused with that of defence, and all that this implies in terms of reductive manoeuvres . . . it is well to remember that the first resistance with which analysis has to deal is that of the discourse itself in that it is first a discourse of opinion, and that all psychological objectification will prove to be bound up with this discourse. . . . But the principle adopted . . . [in the 1920s] of the primacy to be accorded to the analysis of resistance hardly led to a favourable development." Sheridan, *Ecrits*, pp. 129–30.

53. In "The Freudian thing" Lacan plays on the phenomenological notion of "thing" to indict psychoanalysts for their own naive "thingism." In a

humorous, extended metaphor, he compares the image of an ego under analysis (observation) to a wooden desk. The point to be stressed is that analysts who take the analysand as an object to be scrutinized miss the fact that analysands are speaking beings whose unconscious truth moves in and through language. Sheridan, *Ecrits*, pp. 132–35.

54. François Roustang, *Psychoanalysis Never Lets Go*, trans. Ned Lukacher (Baltimore, Md.: Johns Hopkins University Press, 1983), pp. 104–5.

55. Maggie Scarf, "Images That Heal: A Doubtful Idea Whose Time Has Come," *Psychology Today*, Sept. 1980, pp. 33–46. See also the *Journal of Mental Imagery*, published by the Eidetic Institute, A. Ahsen (New York: Brandon House).

56. Jacques-Alain Miller, "Lacan (Jacques)," *Encyclopaedia Universalis* 18 (1980): 118.

Chapter 3. A Lacanian Theory of Cognition

1. Jacques Lacan, *De la psychose paranoïaque dans ses rapports avec la personalité suivi de Premiers écrits sur la paranoïa* (Paris: Editions du Seuil, 1975).

2. Lacan says that his theories do not come from taking Freud's texts and then teaching them as if to expound upon the truths of the New Testament. Freud's texts are no closer to the "light" than the categories Lacan has tried to delineate based on his own analytic practice. *Séminaire* XX, p. 97.

3. In his unpublished paper "An Essay on Psychopathology" James Glogowski quotes Michael Lane's definition of a structure as "a set of any elements between which, or between certain sub-sets of which, relations are defined" (see Lane's *Introduction to Structuralism* [New York: Basic Books, 1970], p. 24). Glogowski goes on to discuss Lane's definition in light of Jean Piaget's theory of a structure as a system of transformations. If there is a link between these two definitions, it lies in the idea that for a transformation to occur, first something must exist to be transformed, i.e., a set of relations (pp. 7–8).

4. Jean-Marie Benoist, *La Révolution Structurale* (Paris: Denoël/Gonthier, 1980), p. 260.

5. Shoshana Felman, "The Originality of Jacques Lacan," *Poetics Today* 2 (Winter 1980/81): 5.

6. Jacques Lacan, "Of Structure as an Inmixing of an Otherness Prerequisite to Any Subject Whatever," in *The Structuralist Controversy: The Languages of Criticism and the Sciences of Man*, ed. Richard Macksey and Eugenio Donato (Baltimore, Md.: Johns Hopkins University Press, 1972), pp. 190–91.

7. Stuart Schneiderman, *Jacques Lacan: The Death of an Intellectual Hero* (Cambridge, Mass.: Harvard University Press, 1983), pp. 2–8.

8. In Sheridan, *Ecrits*; see Lacan's footnote no. 33, referring to *Le hasard* by Emile Borel, p. 108.

9. Ellie Ragland-Sullivan, "Counting from 0 to 6: The Lacanian Imaginary Order," *Annual of Lacanian Studies*, ed. Jacques-Alain Miller and Patrick Hogan, under the auspices of La fondation du champ freudien, in preparation. This essay is also available as *Working Paper* No. 7 from the Center for Twentieth Century Studies, University of Wisconsin–Madison.

10. On a Symbolic plane Lacanian mathematical theory deals with integers (natural numbers) and numerical progressions. On an Imaginary plane the theory of topological structures as developed by James Glogowski in his unpublished paper, "Four Graphs of Jacques Lacan" (pp. 2–3, 7), is meaningful. "The theory of topological spaces, as a generalization of metric spaces, was first introduced and motivated by the study of pointwise convergence of functions" (Seymour Lischutz, *General Topology* [New York: McGraw Hill, 1965], p. 209). Glogowski borrows the notion of studying sets of functions endowed with topological structure from Nicolas Bourbaki (the pseudonym for a group of mathematicians who work on the foundations of mathematics) in an attempt to explain how sets of functions can map elements into different spaces that are, nonetheless, simultaneous in structural relation. Lacan used linguistic functions to structure analytic functions, thus developing a theory in which the subject has a dual relationship to a signifier, both on the concrete linguistic level (*langue*) and on the unconscious level (*parole*).

11. George A. Miller, "The Magical Number Seven, Plus or Minus Two: Some Limits on Our Capacity for Processing Information," *Psychological Review* 63 (Mar. 1956), especially p. 97.

12. Gerald Holton, *Thematic Origins of Scientific Thought* (Cambridge, Mass.: Harvard University Press, 1973), pp. 57–58.

13. *Oxford English Dictionary*, 4th ed. rev. (Oxford: Clarendon Press, 1951), p. 592.

14. Herbert Marcuse, *Eros and Civilization: A Philosophical Inquiry into Freud* (New York: Vintage Books, 1962), p. 128.

15. Ernest Becker, *The Denial of Death* (New York: The Free Press, 1973), p. 98.

16. In *Jacques Lacan* (trans. David Macey [Boston: Routledge & Kegan Paul, 1977], pp. 61–62), Lemaire discusses Edmond Ortigues's *Le Discours et le Symbole* (Paris: Aubier, 1962). Ortigues adopts Claude Lévi-Strauss's analysis of the prohibition of incest to explain that what is forbidden is coincidence between kinship relationships and those of alliance (marriage) on pain of abolishing the Family, which alone allows every person to know who he or she is. In this sense the name, in so far as it is an element conveying relations of proximity, is a token of the recognition of individuals by one another. The conflicting injunctions of Desire and Law, in other words, derive from the imposition of culture on nature. In "Propos sur la causalité psychique" (*Ecrits*, pp. 182–83) Lacan describes the importance of an intervention in the infant-mother dyad as a "dose of the Oedipus." The effects of such Castration mediate, desensitize, and teach an infant to constitute the

world and reality in time and space. Bertrand Russell described such aspects of the fundaments of perception as "sentiments of distance" and a "sentiment of respect." *Analyse de l'Esprit*, trans. M. Lefebvre (Paris: Payot, 1926).

17. Alain Juranville, *Lacan et la philosophie* (Paris: Presses universitaires de France, 1984), p. 111.

18. F. R. Rodman, personal communication, Oct. 19, 1978, in Arthur Efron's unpublished paper, "Psychoanalytic Theory of Human Nature: The Current Dilemma," p. 29.

19. Frederic Jameson, "Imaginary and Symbolic in Lacan: Marxism, Psychoanalytic Criticism, and the Problem of the Subject," *Yale French Studies* 55/56 (1977): 351.

20. Jacqueline Rose, "The Imaginary," in *The Talking Cure: Essays in Psychoanalysis and Language*, ed. Colin MacCabe (London: Macmillan Press, 1981). Rose discusses Lacan's analysis in Seminar One of the case history of a six-year-old boy named Robert. By focusing on the boy's lack of initial motor and linguistic coordination, Lacan emphasized the relationship between Imaginary control and the experience of the mirror stage (pp. 136–37).

21. Richard Wollheim, "The Cabinet of Dr. Lacan," *New York Review of Books*, Jan. 25, 1979, p. 3.

22. Martin Thom, "*Verneinung, Verwerfung, Ausstossung*: A Problem in the Interpretation of Freud," in *Talking Cure*, p. 162.

23. *Le Séminaire de Jacques Lacan, Livre III: Les psychoses* (1955–56), text established by Jacques-Alain Miller (Paris: Editions du Seuil, 1975), p. 186.

24. William J. Kaufman, *Black Holes and Warped Spacetime* (San Francisco: W. H. Freeman, 1979).

25. Robert Coles, comments on the articles appearing in *New Literary History* 12 (Autumn 1980): 209–10.

26. Jane Gallop, "Lacan's 'Mirror Stage': Where to Begin?" *Sub-Stance* 37/38 (1983): 118–28.

27. Christian Metz, *Essais sur la signification au cinéma*, 2 vols. (Paris: Klincksieck, 1968; 1972). See also *Film Language*, volume 1 of *A Semiotics of the Cinema* (New York: Oxford University Press, 1974).

28. Barbara Inhelder and Jean Piaget, "An Essay on the Construction of Formal Operation Structures," in *The Growth of Logical Thinking: From Childhood to Adolescence*, trans. Anne Parsons and Stanley Milgram (New York: Basic Books, 1958), p. 345.

29. In *Lacan et la philosophie* Juranville discusses the implications for philosophy of Heidegger's and Lacan's abolishing the idea of absolute knowledge. By this Lacan means that the Other(A) remains outside consciousness. Not only is the Other(A) Real, it also imposes an excess in each human subject as that person relates to the world. Thus, the idea of a final mastery, either in knowledge or psychic health, is a myth (p. 62).

30. Cf. Walter Weintraub, *Verbal Behavior: Adaptation and Psychopathology* (New York: Springer Publishing, 1981). In the preface Weintraub

attributes his interest in speech as a reflection of behavior to Dr. Jacob Finesinger (then chairman, department of psychiatry, University of Maryland School of Medicine). Finesinger taught his students that syntax and para-language were as important as meaning in understanding an analysand and believed the future of psychotherapy research lay in the microscopic analy-sis of small samples of recorded speech (p. viii).

31. Maurice Merleau-Ponty, *The Visible and the Invisible*, trans. Al-phonso Lingis (Evanston, Ill.: Northwestern University Press, 1968), p. 203.

32. At the Colloquim on "Post-Structuralism in Francophone and Anglo-phone Canada" (May 10–13, 1984), University of Ottawa, Dr. Jacques-Alain Miller (the keynote speaker) agreed to answer a variety of questions on the evening of May 12. One of the things he told the audience was that Deleuze and Guattari had written the *Anti-Oedipe* as a kind of joke. They later abrogated responsibility for the book.

33. Ellen J. Langer, "Automated Lives," *Psychology Today*, Apr. 1982. Langer coins the term "mindlessness" to describe a condition in which people unwittingly respond to the world as if they were automatons. Mind-lessness is a state of reduced mental activity in which people respond to a situation without considering its novel elements (p. 60). Could "mindless-ness" not be equated with an Imaginary fantasmatic mode—seen as the most elemental perceptual way of knowing—always just below the surface of concentrated consciousness (i.e., the engagement of "mind" in coping with novelty)?

34. Robert C. Solomon, "Has Not an Animal Organs, Dimensions, Senses, Affections, Passions?" *Psychology Today*, Mar. 1982.

35. Glogowski, "An Essay on Psychopathology," p. 6.

36. Fritjof Capra, *The Turning Point* (New York: Simon & Schuster, 1982), reviewed by Eric Wanner in *Psychology Today*, Apr. 1982, pp. 90–92.

37. Charles Larmore, "The Concept of a Constitutive Subject," in *Talking Cure*.

38. Edith Kurzweil, *The Age of Structuralism* (New York: Columbia Uni-versity Press, 1980); see the chapter entitled "Jacques Lacan, Structuralist Psychoanalysis."

39. Howard Shevrin, "Glimpses of the Unconscious," *Psychology Today*, Apr. 1980, p. 128.

40. Maya Pines, "Baby, You're Incredible," ibid., Feb. 1982, pp. 48–50.

41. John P. Muller, "Psychosis and Mourning in Lacan's *Hamlet*," *New Literary History* 12 (Autumn 1980): 148–49.

42. Lacan, "Of Structure as an Inmixing." Lacan says that it is probable that words are the only material of the unconscious, but the unconscious is not an assemblage of words. The unconscious, nonetheless, is precisely structured (p. 187).

43. Burton L. White, *The First Three Years of Life* (New York: Avon Books, 1978), p. 22.

44. *Baby Talk* (Toronto: Gaylord Publishing Co. for the H. J. Heinz Co. of Canada, Ltd., 1981), p. 15.

45. In contrast to the tendency of thinkers to express new concepts by inventing new terms, Lacan has redefined terminology already in use.

46. Ellie Ragland-Sullivan, "The Magnetism between Reader and Text: Prolegomena to a Lacanian Poetics," *Poetics* 13 (1984): 381–406, in which I argue that prior to linguistic syntax an Imaginary semantics subjectivizes the representation of reality. It roots perception in an unconscious network of symbols that are subsequently dispersed into language through a projective/introjective symbolicity inherent in perception, and in terms of a logic of narcissism and Desire that functions by laws analogous to those of language.

47. In the conclusion to the second part ("Symbol and Language") of "Discours de Rome" Lacan claimed that psychoanalysis would never establish a scientific grounding for its theory until it adequately formalized the historical theory of the symbol, intersubjective logic, and the temporality of the subject (Anthony Wilden, *The Language of the Self* [Baltimore, Md.: Johns Hopkins University Press, 1968], p. 51).

48. Karl Racevskis, "The Theoretical Violence of a Catastrophical Strategy," *Diacritics* 9 (Fall 1979): 37.

49. Dan Sperber, *Rethinking Symbolism*, trans. Alice L. Morton (London: Cambridge University Press, 1974), pp. 84–85.

50. Sigmund Freud, *The Interpretation of Dreams*, ed. and trans. James Strachey (London, 1953, vols. IV, V of *SE*; rpt. New York: Basic Books/Avon, 1966), pp. xii–xiii.

51. Anthony Wilden, *System and Structure: Essays on Communication and Exchange* (London: Tavistock, 1972), pp. 34, 40.

52. See Ernest Jones, "Theory of Symbolism" (1916), in *Papers on Psycho-Analysis* (orig. publ. 1948; London: H. Karnac, 1977).

53. David Willbern, "Freud and the Inter-penetration of Dreams," *Diacritics* (Spring 1979), especially p. 108.

54. David Ingleby, "Understanding 'Mental Illness,'" in *Critical Psychiatry: The Politics of Mental Health*, ed. D. Ingleby (New York: Pantheon Books, 1980), p. 64.

55. Patrick Hogan, "Remarks on the Formal Analysis of Mental Causality," p. 1, unpublished paper.

56. Jacques Monod, *Le hasard et la nécessité* (Paris: Editions du Seuil, 1970).

57. Norman Geschwind, "Some Comments on the Neurology of Language," in *Biological Studies of Mental Processes*, ed. David Caplan (Cambridge, Mass.: MIT Press, 1980), see especially p. 314.

58. Colin MacCabe, "On Discourse," in *Talking Cure*, p. 191.

59. Weintraub, *Verbal Behavior*, especially chap. 3 ("Developmental Aspects of Speech and Personality").

60. Edward Stainbrook, "Poetry and Behavior in the Psychotherapeutic Experience," in *Poetry in the Therapeutic Experience*, ed. Arthur Lerner (New York: Pergamon Press, 1978), pp. 10–11.

61. *An Introduction to Language*, ed. V. Fromkin and R. Rodman (New York: Holt, Rinehart & Winston, 1974), pp. 22, 188.

62. Michel Grimaud, "Psychologie et littérature," in *Théorie de la Littérature* (Paris: Picard, 1981), p. 263.

63. Hogan, "Remarks on the Formal Analysis of Mental Causality," p. 7. I would contend that a "self"-logic of believed descriptions is an Imaginary one.

64. Moustapha Safouan, "Representation and Pleasure," in *Talking Cure*, p. 75.

65. See, for example, Georg Breuer, *Sociobiology and the Human Dimension* (Cambridge: Cambridge University Press, 1983), in which he examines the failure of sociobiology to account for human empathy.

66. Eugen S. Bär, "Understanding Lacan," in *Psychoanalysis and Contemporary Science 3*, ed. Leo Golberger and Victor H. Rosen (New York: International Universities Press, 1974), p. 518.

67. In *Freud: The Mind of the Moralist* (Garden City, N.Y.: Doubleday, 1961), Philip Rieff quotes Freud's statement from the *Introductory Lectures* (1916–17) that "the task of the psychoanalytic treatment can be summed up in this formula: 'Everything pathogenic in the unconscious must be transferred into consciousness'" (pp. 104, 404).

Chapter 4. The Relationship of Sense and Sign

1. Lacan's essay "On a question preliminary to any possible treatment of psychosis" contains the most important parts of the seminar given during the first two terms of the academic year 1955–56 at the Ecole Normale Supérieure (Sheridan, *Ecrits*). In this essay Lacan reinterprets Freud's study of the Schreber case and adds his own original ideas. The article by Freud in question here can be found in the *SE*, 12: 3. Throughout *Séminaire* III Lacan elaborated his innovative interpretation of the Schreber case.

2. Jean Piaget, *Le Structuralisme* in the series Que Sais-je? (Paris: Presses universitatires françaises, 1970), pp. 6–7.

3. Jean-Marie Benoist, *La Révolution Structurale* (Paris: Denoël/Gonthier, 1980), especially pp. 36–40.

4. Henry W. Brosin, "Acculturation, Language and Secondary Process," in *Evolving Concepts in Psychiatry*, ed. Perry C. Talkington and Charles L. Bloss (New York: Grune & Stratton, 1969), pp. 113–14.

5. G. A. Miller, E. Galanter, and K. H. Pribram, *Plans and the Structure of Behavior* (New York: Holt, Rinehart & Winston, 1965), p. 154. See Brosin, "Acculturation," pp. 114–15.

6. Rodney Williamson, "Child Discourse: Some Cognitive and Interactional Issues," *Ottawa Hispanica* 4 (1982), especially pp. 84–89, for a discussion of various positions taken by linguists and psychologists on the relative relationship of language to thought.

7. Anike Lemaire, *Jacques Lacan*, trans. David Macey (Boston: Routledge & Kegan Paul, 1977), pp. 28–29.

8. Michel Grimaud, unpublished book manuscript, "Frameworks for a Science of Texts," p. 7.

9. John Bird, "Jacques Lacan—the French Freud?" *Radical Philosophy* 30 (Spring 1982): 13. Bird, in my view, confuses Lacan with psychoanalysts such as R. D. Laing, who hypothesize the "true" self as one opposed to a false social self. Bird refers to socialists such as Collier who clearly mistake Lacan for Laing. See also A. Collier, "Lacan, Psychoanalysis and the Left," *Socialist Review* 2 (1980): 51–57.

10. Sherry Turkle, *Psychoanalytic Politics: The French Freudian Revolution* (New York: Basic Books, 1978), p. 244.

11. John Forrester, "Philology and the Phallus," in *The Talking Cure: Essays in Psychoanalysis and Language*, ed. Colin MacCabe (London: Macmillan Press, 1981), pp. 46–47.

12. Serge Leclaire, *Psychanalyser: Un essai sur l'ordre de l'inconscient et la pratique de la lettre* (Paris: Editions du Seuil, 1968), p. 160. See also Sheridan, "Subversion of the subject and the dialectic of desire in the Freudian unconscious" (1960), in *Ecrits*, p. 303.

13. Personal experience. When consciousness fades and language ceases to function by normal conventions, the mind scans for meaning in terms of an individual's own set of Imaginary myths and substitutions. Psychosis reveals varying stages of dissolution of Imaginary material, all the way back to the dissolution of an image of body unity in some forms of schizophrenia. See also Gilles Deleuze, "The Schizophrenic and Language: Surface and Depth in Lewis Carroll and Antonin Artaud," in *Textual Strategies: Perspectives in Post-Structuralist Criticism* (Ithaca, N.Y.: Cornell University Press, 1979), pp. 277–95.

14. Octave Mannoni, "Itard et son sauvage," *Les Temps modernes* 233 (Oct. 1966); rpt. in *Clefs Pour l'imaginaire ou l'Autre scène* (Paris: Editions du Seuil, 1969).

15. Robert Coles, comments on the articles in *New Literary History* 12 (Autumn 1980): 209–10.

16. Turkle recounts (*Psychoanalytic Politics*, pp. 244–45) the meeting where Lacan asked both Noam Chomsky and Roman Jakobson if linguistics could help psychoanalysts with the problems of punning and ambiguity. Are puns intrinsic to language or merely accidental features of particular languages, for instance? Chomsky responded that such matters were not problems for a scientific linguistics, for linguists were obliged to study similarities in language, and not the differences among them.

17. Anthony Wilden, "Lacan and the Discourse of the Other" in his *The Language of the Self* (Baltimore, Md.: Johns Hopkins University Press, 1968), p. 214.

18. Jonathan Culler, *Ferdinand de Saussure* (New York: Penguin Books, 1977).

19. In an unpublished paper entitled "The Child's Acquisition of Phonology from Initial State to Steady State by Way of Autosegmental Analysis," Christine Futter summarizes studies in child phonology and analyzes the state of the field. Most current research has disproved Roman Jakobson's theory that infants progress from babbling to rule-bound language by uni-

versally ascertainable patterns of language acquisition based on a system of featural oppositions (R. Jakobson, "Child language, aphasia, and phonological universals," 1941; trans. 1968). Individual variations are far greater than any universality of pattern, although salient feature patterns do seem to govern a child's phonetic production of an adult target word (pp. 3–4, 11; see the work of N. Waterson). Futter opines that the "input" from outer world language must have some impact on an infant's "output," but stresses also the strategies employed by individual children to organize linguistic "input" (p. 33). The value of Futter's paper is in her patient account of how "grammar construction" does not initially take place in a binary, linear, generative way. Autosegmental phonology shows that children perceive language in pieces—and as if along a musical score—before moving into the rule-bound system of the adult speaker (p. 34; see the work of J. Goldsmith). Futter questions Chomsky but does not move on to the role of transference in the autosegmental acquisition process, thus revealing that linguistics working at its own boundaries can still dismiss the evidence at hand, i.e., "input."

20. Cited by Hilary Putnam, "Convention: A Theme in Philosophy," *New Literary History* 13 (Autumn 1981): 4.

21. Jeffrey Mehlman, "The 'Floating Signifier': From Lévi-Strauss to Lacan," *Yale French Studies* 48 (1972).

22. Paul P. Olson, review of Jonathan Culler's *Ferdinand de Saussure, Modern Language Notes* 93 (Dec. 1978): 1044–52.

23. Culler, *Ferdinand de Saussure*, pp. 80, 82.

24. Jacques Derrida, *L'Ecriture et la Différence* (Paris: Editions du Seuil, 1967).

25. Anthony Wilden, *System and Structure: Essays on Communications and Exchange* (London: Tavistock, 1972), pp. 226–27.

26. Georges Mounin, *Clefs pour la linguistique* (Paris: Seghers, 1971).

27. Eugen Bär, "Understanding Lacan," in *Psychoanalysis and Contemporary Science 3*, ed. Leo Goldberger and Victor H. Rosen (New York: International Universities Press, 1974), p. 473.

28. James Glogowski, "Four Graphs of Jacques Lacan," p. 17, unpublished paper.

29. Frederic Jameson, "Imaginary and Symbolic in Lacan: Marxism, Psychoanalytic Criticism, and the Problem of the Subject," *Yale French Studies*, 55/56 (1977), especially p. 531.

30. Jacques-Alain Miller, "Lacan (Jacques)," *Encyclopaedia Universalis* 18 (1980): 111.

31. Jacques Lacan, "Seminar of 21 January 1975," in *Feminine Sexuality*, ed. Juliet Mitchell and Jacqueline Rose (New York: W. W. Norton, 1983), pp. 164–65.

32. Jean Baudrillard, "Requiem pour les media," in *Pour une critique de l'économie politique du signe* (Paris: Gallimard, 1972), pp. 219–20.

33. Roman Jakobson, "Linguistics and Poetics" (1958), in *The Structuralists: From Marx to Lévi-Strauss*, ed. Richard and Fernande De George

(Garden City, N.Y.: Doubleday, 1972); see p. 89 therein for his schematization of verbal communication.

34. Cf. Shoshana Felman, "La Méprise et sa Chance," *L'Arc* 58 (1974), especially pp. 41-42, 48, for a discussion of Lacan's efforts to ascertain a rhetoric of the unconscious and to establish a grammar of that rhetoric.

35. J.-B. Pontalis, *Après Freud* (Paris: Gallimard, 1968), p. 47.

36. See Jacques Derrida, "Structure, Sign, and Play in the Discourse of the Human Sciences," in *The Structuralist Controversy: The Languages of Criticism and the Sciences of Man*, ed. Richard Macksey and Eugenio Donato (Baltimore, Md.: Johns Hopkins University Press, 1975), p. 249, where he says: "The whole history of the concept of structure . . . must be thought of as a series of substitutions of center for center. . . . Successively, and in a regulated fashion, the center receives different forms or names. The history of metaphysics, like the history of the West, is the history of these metaphors and metonymies." In another essay Derrida includes all the figures called symbolical or analogical under the category of metaphor. See Derrida, "White Mythology: Metaphor in the Text of Philosophy," trans. F. C. T. Moore, in *New Literary History* 6 (Autumn 1974), especially p. 13 (orig. publ. as "La mythologie blanche," *Poetique* 5 [1970]).

37. Jacques Lacan, "A la mémoire d'Ernest Jones: Sur sa théorie du symbolisme" (1959), *Ecrits*, 1966, p. 708.

38. Roman Jakobson and Morris Halle, *Fundamentals of Language* (The Hague: Mouton, 1956), pp. 56, 76.

39. John P. Muller, "Lacan and Language: An Overview," paper presented at the State University of New York at Buffalo, Jan. 31, 1981. See "Two Aspects of Language and Two Types of Aphasic Disturbances," in Jakobson and Halle, *Fundamentals of Language*.

40. See Roman Jakobson, *Essais de linguistique générale*, 2 vols. (Paris: Minuit, 1963, 1973). See also his "Linguistics and Poetics," p. 85.

41. Muller, "Lacan and Language," p. 7. See Sheridan, *Ecrits*, p. 210.

42. Cf. Burton L. White, *The First Three Years of Life* (New York: Avon Books, 1978), pp. 174-75.

43. Arthur F. Marotti, "Countertransference, the Communication Process, and the Dimensions of Psychoanalytic Criticism," *Critical Inquiry* 4 (Spring 1978); see David Rapaport, "Cognitive Structures," in *The Collected Papers of David Rapaport*, ed. Merton Gill (New York: Basic Books, 1967), pp. 631-34. Marotti explains that Rapaport sees the classic mechanisms of the primary process (condensation, displacement, and symbolization) not as distortions of thought, but as ways of enriching waking thought with a multitude of connotations (p. 484).

44. Arthur Lerner, ed., *Poetry in the Therapeutic Experience* (New York: Pergamon Press, 1978).

45. The concept of "condensation" has different meanings in Freud's *Interpretation of Dreams, Introductory Lectures on Psychoanalysis*, and *Jokes and Their Relationship to the Unconscious*.

46. Lemaire, *Jacques Lacan*, p. xiii (preface by Jacques Lacan).

47. Lacan's linking of dreams to language shows the limitations of theories such as that of Robert Rogers in *Metaphor: A Psychoanalytic View* (Berkeley: University of California Press, 1978). Rogers studies the interaction between primary and secondary process thought—especially in poetry—but does not really account for linguistic dynamism in poetry or in dreams or for the aphasic characteristics of psychotic language.

48. Mary E. Ragland-Sullivan, "The Language of Laughter," *Sub-Stance* 13 (1976): 91–106.

49. Jason W. Brown, "Brain Structure and Language Production: A Dynamic View," in *Biological Studies of Mental Processes*, ed. David Caplan (Cambridge, Mass.: MIT Press, 1980), p. 287.

50. Susan Handelman, "Greek Philosophy and the Overcoming of the Word," *Essays in the Socio-Historical Dimensions of Literature and the Arts* 1 (Spring 1980): 47.

51. Ibid., p. 57. Cf. Paul Ricoeur, *The Rule of Metaphor* (Toronto: University of Toronto Press), pp. 12–13. Ricoeur interprets Heidegger to mean that the transgressions of metaphor and those of metaphysics are one and the same transfer.

52. Handelman, "Greek Philosophy," p. 51. See Aristotle, *De Interpretatione*.

53. Jonathan Culler, "Conventions and Meaning: Derrida and Austin," *New Literary History (On Convention I)* 13 (Autumn 1981): 19, reprinted in his *On Deconstruction: Literary Theory in the 1970s* (Ithaca, N.Y.: Cornell University Press, 1982).

54. Sam Kinser, "Logic of the Signifier: Constitution of the Subject," p. 18, unpublished paper.

55. Glogowski, "Four Graphs of Jacques Lacan," p. 2. See Seymour Lischutz, *General Topology* (New York: McGraw Hill, 1965), p. 209.

56. Robert Georgin, *La structure et le style* (Lausanne: L'Age d'Homme, 1975), pp. 106–7.

57. In his "Propos sur la causalité psychique" (1946) Lacan said that madness is lived completely in the register of meaning. As a phenomenon, madness is not separable from the problem of meaning for the human being in general, that is to say, the problem of language for man. The whole question of the ineffable is posed in madness by language. "Man's language, this instrument of his lie, is traversed from one end to the other by the problem of his truth" (*Ecrits*, 1966, p. 166).

58. Jacques Lacan, "Du sujet enfin en question" (1966), *Ecrits*, 1966, pp. 234–35.

59. Jacques Lacan, "The Neurotic's Individual Myth," trans. Martha Noel Evans, *Psychoanalytic Quarterly* 48 (1979): 417.

60. François Péraldi, "The Crane Child," in *Psychoanalysis, Creativity and Literature: A French-American Inquiry*, ed. Alan Roland (New York: Columbia University Press, 1978).

Chapter 5. Beyond the Phallus?

1. Elisabeth Roudinesco, *Un Discours au réel: théorie de l'inconscient et politique de la psychanalyse* (Paris: Maison Mame, 1973), p. 200. Roudinesco refers here to an unedited Séminaire of Lacan's, "Le Séminaire de Jacques Lacan, Livre XVIII: D'un discours qui ne serait pas un (1970–71)," unpublished.

2. Jacques Lacan, "Of Structure as an Inmixing of an Otherness Prerequisite to Any Subject Whatever," in *The Structuralist Controversy: The Languages of Criticism and the Sciences of Man* (Baltimore, Md.: Johns Hopkins University Press, 1975), pp. 187–88.

3. Anika Lemaire, *Jacques Lacan*, trans. David Macey (Boston: Routledge & Kegan Paul, 1977), p. 81. See also *Ecrits* (1966), p. 277.

4. Stuart Schneiderman, letter to me, Nov. 19, 1981, p. 1.

5. Robert Stoller, "The 'Bedrock' of Masculinity and Femininity," in *Psychoanalysis and Women*, ed. Jean B. Miller (Baltimore, Md.: Penguin Books, 1973), pp. 273, 276–77. Stoller sees family psychodynamics as shaping gender identity in infancy.

6. T.V. Interview, *Hour Magazine*, Host, Gary Collins, WHEC, Spring 1982. See also Mary B. Parlee, "Moody Men," *Psychology Today* (London) 5 (Jan. 1979): 40–43.

7. Fitzhugh Dodson, *Tout se joue avant six ans*, trans. and ed. Robert Laffont (Verviers, Belgium: Marabout Service, 1970), p. 38. Dodson recounts the well-known experiment conducted by Frederick II of Prussia. In trying to discover the "original" language of humanity—Greek or Latin?—Frederick isolated several newborns and prohibited their nurses from speaking to them. When the infants eventually spoke, he hoped to learn which of the two languages was innate. Although the infants were physically well cared for, they did not live long enough to speak. All died of unknown causes.

8. Anthony Wilden, "Lacan and the Discourse of the Other," in *The Language of the Self* (Baltimore, Md.: Johns Hopkins University Press, 1968), p. 186. Wilden refers to Lacan's unedited Seminar Four (1956).

9. David Kotelchuck, *Prognosis Negative: Crisis in the Health Care System* (New York: Random House, 1976).

10. In "Imaginary and Symbolic in Lacan: Marxism, Psychoanalytic Criticism and the Problem of the Subject," Frederic Jameson suggests that Lacan's doctrine of the decentered subject—"The Subversion of the subject and the dialectic of desire in the Freudian unconscious" (1960)—which aims at the realization of desire (rather than at renunciation or repression) might offer a model for the elaboration of a Marxist ideology of the collective alongside a Marxist "science" (*Yale French Studies* 55/56 [1977]: 394–95). In my view, Jameson's suggestion is a misinterpretation of Lacan, who shows that Desire by its very nature is individual and not easily subordinated to any collectivity, and this because Desire is the product both of renunciation and repression at the level of psychic effect.

11. In "Lacan's Early Contributions to Psychoanalysis" in *Returning to*

Freud, Stuart Schneiderman describes the Lacanian concept of *plus-de-jouir* as a surplus, something that is left over after the experience of *jouissance*. "Generally I conceive of it as something left to be desired" (p. 7).

12. Gilles Deleuze and Félix Guattari, *Capitalisme et schizophrénie: l'Anti-Oedipe* (Paris: Minuit, 1972), p. 63.

13. Colin MacCabe, "On Discourse" in *The Talking Cure: Essays in Psychoanalysis and Language*, ed. MacCabe (London: Macmillan, 1981), p. 212.

14. Luce Irigaray, *Speculum de l'Autre femme* (Paris: Minuit, 1974).

15. Jane Gallop, "Impertinent Questions: Irigaray, Sade, Lacan," *Sub-Stance* 26 (1980): 57. See Freud's essay "The Infantile Genital Organization of the Libido," *SE*, vol. 19.

16. See Gallop, "Impertinent Questions." She finds Lacan's influence in Irigaray's reading of Kant (p. 57).

17. In one of the chapters of *Ce Sexe qui n'en est pas un* (Paris: Minuit, 1977)—"Così fan tutti"—Irigaray compares Lacan to Don Alfonso from Mozart's opera with its feminine plural (i.e., *tutte*). Don Alfonso wins money by betting on a permanent *malentendu* between the sexes. Cf. Jane Gallop, "Impertinent Questions," p. 59.

18. Naomi Schor, "*Eugénie Grandet*: Mirrors and Melancolia," a paper, given in Jan. 1981 at the University of Vermont, French department, published in *The (M)other Tongue: Essays in Feminist Psychoanalytic Interpretation*, ed. M. Sprengnether, S. N. Garner, and C. Kahane (Ithaca: Cornell University Press, 1985).

19. Luce Irigaray, "La 'Mécanique' des fluides," *L'Arc: Jacques Lacan* 58 (1974): 55 (italics hers). Irigaray quotes from Lacan's essay "Le stade du miroir" in *Ecrits* (1966), pp. 94–95. "La 'Mécanique' is also in *Ce Sexe*.

20. See Schor, "*Eugénie Grandet*," n. 14. The essay by Freud to which Irigaray refers in discussing narcissism and femininity (in *Speculum*) is "Some Psychical Consequences of the Anatomical Distinction Between the Sexes," *SE*, 19: 253.

21. Luce Irigaray, "Ce Sexe qui n'en est pas un," in *New French Feminisms*, ed. and introduction, Elaine Marks and Isabelle de Courtivron (Amherst: University of Massachusetts Press, 1980). Irigaray maintains that the Freudian concept of the sexual relationship does not mention woman and her pleasure. Woman's erogenous zones cannot stand up by comparison with the valued phallic organ (p. 99).

22. See Gallop, "Impertinent Questions," pp. 60–61. In "Françaises, 'ne faites plus un effort," in *Ce Sexe*, Irigaray "responds" to the marquis de Sade whose libertine loved the blood he caused to flow by his own sadistic methods but considered menstrual blood taboo (p. 199).

23. See Gallop, "Impertinent Questions," p. 65. In "Quand nos lèvres se parlent" in *Ce Sexe*, Irigaray urges women to combat phallocracy by resisting phallic militancy. She praises woman's subtlety as one strategy of defense (p. 214).

24. In "Lacan's 'Mirror Stage': Where to Begin?," *Sub-Stance* 37/38 (1983), Jane Gallop recounts an initially enthusiastic acceptance of Cathérine

Clément's idea that all Lacan's thought is found *en germe* in the mirror stage concept: The "rootstock" (*souche*) of all later identifications (cf. Cathérine Clément, *Vies et légendes de Jacques Lacan* [Paris: Bernard Grasset, 1981]; and Sheridan, *Ecrits*, p. 2). Gallop analyzes her early attraction to Clément's statement and deduces that it is not so clear where to "begin" with Lacan. "Natural" or instinctual maturation, for example, anticipates development, but paradoxically as a moment in a *process* (p. 122). However, Gallop does not deal with Lacan's insistence that there is no developmental (Jean Piaget) or instinctual (Freud) maturation, but only the Imaginary accretion of self-images, the Symbolic build-up of language codes, conventions, and identity myths, and the interaction of these two with the Real. The mirror stage is a necessary moment in the process of "self"-unification. Gallop sees Lacan as presenting a tragedy by his separation of anticipation from retroaction (p. 123). Gallop does not point out that insofar as the mirror stage antici-pates a mental image of bodily unity and an incipient sense of identity, it thereby retroactively defends against the void and fragmentation of the pre-mirror state. Thus, there is no final separation of anticipation from retro-action. Instead, Lacan offers a theory of how the *moi* is continually consti-tuted, and Imaginarily reconstituted in the eyes of others throughout life, and represented by language (in the Real)—or conversely, unraveled in psy-chosis. Gallop concludes that Lacan's "beginning" is only description and abstraction (p. 126). On the contrary, Lacan shows that the beginning of the mirror stage lies in the concrete experiences of the pre-mirror stage (for ex-ample, birth, hunger) in terms of its impact. The anticipatory/retroactive character of the mirror stage derives from its Fregean character: standing in a dependent relationship both to the pre-mirror stage and to the post-mirror stage. The ending of the mirror stage by Castration fixes this period as a resi-due of Real experience whose effects will be interpreted and reinterpreted throughout life.

25. In "The mirror stage as formative of the function of the I as revealed in psychoanalytic experience" Lacan says that one does not need Hieronymus Bosch to "see" the fragmented body, for this form is "tangibly revealed at the organic level, in the lines of 'fragilization' that define the anatomy of phan-tasy, as exhibited in the schizoid and spasmodic symptoms of hysteria" (Sheridan, *Ecrits*, pp. 4–5).

26. Juliet Mitchell, *Psychoanalysis and Feminism* (New York: Vintage Books, 1974), p. 52.

27. Christopher T. Cory, "Male Bonding in the Nursery," *Psychology To-day*, Feb. 1979, pp. 23–24; the researcher is Ross Parke of the University of Illinois at Champaign-Urbana.

28. MacCabe, "On Discourse," pp. 189–98.

29. See Irigaray, *Ce Sexe*; John Brenkman, "The Other and the One: Psychoanalysis, Reading the *Symposium*," *Yale French Studies* 55/56 (1977); Anthon Wilden, *System and Structure: Essays on Communications and Exchange* (London: Tavistock, 1972).

30. Schneiderman, letter to me, Aug. 13, 1981, p. 1.

31. Edmond Ortigues, *L'Oedipe africain* (Paris: Plon, 1966).

32. In "The Signification of the Phallus" (1958) Lacan says that the relations between the sexes are actually governed by a "to seem," which replaces the "to have" in order to protect it on the male side and to mask its lack on the female side, and which projects the ideal or typical manifestations of each sex (Sheridan, *Ecrits*, p. 289).

33. The social scientist Herbert Simon has been quoted as saying in a summary of the status of behavior and social science: "Since the human mind resides in the brain, we cannot be satisfied with our explanations of human thinking until we can specify the neural substrates for the elementary information processes of the human symbol system. Of these connections we know next to nothing" (*Science*, July 1980). Quoted by Peter Barglow, M.D., in *Commentary*, Oct. 1980, p. 10.

34. Maggie Scarf, *Unfinished Business: Pressure Points in the Lives of Women* (New York: Ballantine Books, 1981), pp. 95–96.

35. Leo Bersani, "The Subject of Power," *Diacritics* 7 (Fall 1977): 16.

36. "The Phallic Phase and the Subjective Import of the Castration Complex" (1968), in *Feminine Sexuality*, ed. Juliet Mitchell and Jacqueline Rose (New York: W. W. Norton, 1983), pp. 119–20. This article was first published anonymously, as was the custom, by a member of Lacan's *école freudienne* in the first issue of *Scilicet* (the journal of Lacan's school, founded in 1964), in 1968. See the note by Mitchell and Rose in *Feminine Sexuality*, pp. 99–100.

37. Jacques Lacan, "Guiding Remarks for a Congress on Feminine Sexuality" (1958), in *Feminine Sexuality*, ed. Mitchell and Rose, p. 98.

38. Lacan postulated that instead of a free flow of instinctual energy, which Freud imagined, there is a free flow of meaning, an endless movement of signifying possibilities. In the signifying chain of language, each signifier is an interdependent and irreducible sign whose meaning is determined in relation to another signifier to which it is joined by the specific laws of metaphor and metonymy. Thus, the signifier "means" synchronically in terms of referential, oppositional elements, and diachronically through substitutions and combinations (Sheridan, *Ecrits*, pp. 255, 303).

39. Charles Bouazis, *Essais de la sémiotique du sujet* (Brussels: Editions Complexe, 1977), p. 15.

40. In "Some Comments on the Neurology of Language" Norman Geschwind suggests that language may not be innate, but the result of experience. As evidence of this (for him unlikely) possibility, he points to the fact that brain lesions incurred in childhood cause only mild speech impairment, while the same defects in an adult are severe. A plausible explanation is that language is laid down in both hemispheres, and a child with a brain lesion will probably have a differently developed right hemisphere than a normal adult (*Biological Studies of Mental Processes*, ed. David Caplan [Cambridge, Mass.: MIT Press, 1980], pp. 302–4).

41. Haig A. Bosmajian, "The Language of Sexism," *ETC: A Review of General Semantics* 19 (Sept. 1972), 305–13. See also Vivian Gornick, "Watch Out: Your Brain May be Used Against You," *Ms.*, Apr. 1982, pp. 14–20.

42. Cf. Lacan's discussion in "On a question preliminary to any possible treatment of psychosis" (Sheridan, *Ecrits*, p. 207).

43. Ellie Ragland-Sullivan, "Lacan, Language and Literary Criticism," *Literary Review* 24 (Summer 1981), especially her discussion of the intentional links between gender and discourse, based on Lacan's essay "A Jakobson" (*Séminaire* XX, pp. 19–27), on pp. 574–77.

44. In support of his antibiological view of ego formation, Lacan says that the main characteristic of the feminine sexual attitude does not derive from an active-passive opposition, but from the *masquerade*—that which in humans belongs to the Symbolic order (*Séminaire* XI, p. 176).

45. John Berger, *Ways of Seeing* (Harmondsworth: Penguin, 1972), p. 47.

46. "Do Boys Need Father Image," Chicago *Sun-Times*, Nov. 18, 1979, p. 86, col. 1. This article reports on empirical studies done by psychiatrist Dr. James Turnbull, who has proved that boys learn to be "masculine," not by modeling on their fathers, but in terms of their mothers' images of what "masculine" is.

47. Moustapha Safouan, *La Sexualité féminine dans la doctrine freudienne* (Paris: Editions du Seuil, 1976).

48. Claudia Crawford, "She?," *Sub-Stance* 39 (1981): 94.

49. Catherine Millot, "Le surmoi féminin," *Ornicar?* 29 (Apr.-June 1984): 114–15. In her discussion of the relationship of the ideal ego to the superego, Millot says: "Let us note that it is a demand which is at the origin of the formation of the ideal ego for everyone: a demand of the subject addressed to the Other, and which has seen opposed to itself an end point of non-receiving. It is on the basis of this refused demand, on the basis of a privation, that the subject identifies itself to this Other who has the power to answer it. . . . The question is that of the relationship between the initial demand, at the origin of the formation of the ideal ego, and the final demand, that of the superego."

50. Hélène Cixous, "The Laugh of the Medusa," *Signs* (Summer 1976), a revised version of "Le rire de la méduse," *L'Arc* (1975): 39–54, trans. Keith and Paula Cohen. Cixous urges women to "speak themselves," "write themselves." "Write your self. Your body must be heard. Only then will the immense resources of the unconscious spring forth. . . . To write. An act which will not only 'realize' the decensored relation of woman to her sexuality, to her womanly being, giving her access to her native strength; it will give her back her goods, her pleasures, her organs, her immense bodily territories which have been kept under seal; it will tear her away from the superegoized structure in which she has always occupied the place reserved for the guilty" (*New French Feminisms*, p. 250). See also "Femmes, une autre écriture?" (*dossier*), *Magazine littéraire* 180 (Jan. 1982): 16–41.

51. Stuart Schneiderman, "Afloat with Jacques Lacan," *Diacritics* 1 (Winter 1971). Schneiderman is the first to apply the term "afloat" to Lacan's subject.

52. Heinz Kohut, *The Search for the Self: Selected Writings of Heinz*

Kohut, 1950–1978, ed. Paul H. Ornstein, 2 vols. (New York: International Universities Press, 1978), p. 228.

53. Moustapha Safouan, *Structuralisme en psychanalyse* (Paris: Editions du Seuil, 1968).

54. Michèle Montrelay, "The Story of Louise," in Schneiderman, *Returning,* p. 89.

55. Josette Féral, "Antigone or the Irony of the Tribe," *Diacritics* 8 (Sept. 1978): 71.

INDEX

Abraham, Karl, 319 n

Adler, Alfred, 195

Affirmation (*Bejahung*; absorption), 138, 144, 244

Aggressiveness: and clinical practice, 37, 38, 122, 123; and the ego (*moi*), 2, 57, 118, 154, 259, 301; and the ego's paranoiac structure, 30, 37–39, 47, 63, 154, 155; and Freud's triad, 117; and the Imaginary (order), 147, 269; and the narcissistic relation with others, 1, 46–48, 77, 96; and the neonate body, 36. *See also* Narcissism

Ahsen, A., 326 n

Alberts, Jeffrey R., 316 n

Alexander, Franz, 321 n

Alienation: and constitution of the ego, 2, 25, 27, 96; and Desire, 46, 47, 271; and the ego as object, 46, 52, 60, 63; and language, 14, 38, 39, 56, 64, 224, 273; and the mirror stage, 30, 131, 275, 290; and separation trauma, 88; and "truth," 120; its source in the Other, xvii, 15, 154, 231, 271. *See also* Identification

Althusser, Louis, 272

Analysand: and Desire, 84, 193, 289; and discourse or speech, 131, 147, 153, 155, 260, 262; and Imaginary myths, 155, 181, 193, 260, 262, 295; and unconscious source, 153, 160, 297; the hysteric, 194, 264, 285, 305; Lacan and Kohut compound, 37–39, 84, 147; the obsessional, 193, 194, 264; transference and resistance, 119–29. *See also* Analyst; Lacan

Analyst: and the absent unconscious,

102; and discourse or speech, 108, 109, 115, 147, 150, 153, 155, 260, 305; and the *moi*, 50, 112, 229, 230, 285; and the Other's Desire, 83, 84, 195, 272; and the Real, 150, 193; and the *remémoration*, 109, 115, 153, 193; and the signifier, 229, 262, 299; and structure, 131, 151; Kohut, 34; Lacan and Kohut compared, 37–39, 84, 147; transference and resistance, 119–29; unconscious "logic," 160, 181. *See also* Analysand; Lacan

Animal studies, 17, 157, 163, 164, 171, 173, 175, 178

Anthropology, 5, 35, 36, 166, 167, 171, 180, 183, 185, 208, 211, 267, 283

Anticipation (prolepsis), 25, 27, 110, 135, 149, 160, 201, 217, 218, 223, 227–30, 244, 246, 265, 275. *See also* Retroaction

Anxiety, 37, 39, 55, 77, 112, 122, 131, 139, 149, 180, 226, 232, 258, 270

Anzieu, Didier, 315 n

Appleton, Tina, 317 n

Aristotle, xv, 62, 104, 182, 183, 190, 191, 205, 253, 254, 258, 335 n

Arkin, Arthur, 252, 253

Artaud, Antonin, 332 n

Asch, Solomon E., 318 n

Aslin, Richard N., 316 n

Augustine, Saint, 30

Ausstossung. See Expulsion

Austin, John L., 159, 253, 254, 335 n

Autre. See Other(A)

Bachelard, Gaston, 12

Balint, Michael, 33

343

Note on the Author

ELLIE RAGLAND-SULLIVAN is professor of French language and literature at the University of Illinois in Chicago, where she has taught since 1970. She received her Ph.D. from the University of Michigan (1972). Her critical interests include the French Renaissance, pedagogical innovation in the literature classroom, the origins of language, and psychoanalytic theory and the applications of psychoanalysis to literature. Her previous publications include *Rabelais and Panurge: A Psychological Approach to Literary Character* (1976), as well as articles in such journals as *Sub-Stance,* the *Modern Language Journal, Paunch, Hartford Studies in Literature, Nineteenth-Century French Studies,* the *French Review,* the *Literary Review,* the *Journal of Higher Education, Kentucky Romance Quarterly, Gradiva: International Contemporary Journal,* and *Poetics.* She has also published several chapters in books of essays. She has begun work on her next book developing a Lacanian poetics that concentrates particularly on genre theory and the relationship between reader, text, and representationalism.